Victorian Women Poets: A Critical Reader

Victorian Women Poets:
A Critical Reader

Edited by

Angela Leighton

BLACKWELL
Publishers

Copyright © Blackwell Publishers Ltd 1996
Introduction and arrangement of materials copyright © Angela Leighton 1996

First published 1996

2 4 6 8 10 9 7 5 3 1

Blackwell Publishers Ltd
108 Cowley Road
Oxford OX4 1JF
UK

Blackwell Publishers Inc.
238 Main Street
Cambridge, Massachusetts 02142
USA

British Library Cataloguing in Publication Data

A CIP catalogue record for this book is available from the
British Library.

Library of Congress Cataloging-in-Publication Data
Victorian women poets : a critical reader / edited by Angela Leighton.
p.   cm. -- (Blackwell critical readers in literature : 2)
Includes bibliographical references (p.   ) and index.
ISBN 0-631-19756-7. -- ISBN 0-631-19757-5 (pbk.)
1. English poetry--Women authors--History and criticism. 2. Women and literature--Great Britain--History--19th century. 3. English poetry--19th century--History and criticism. I. Leighton, Angela, 1954-   II. Series.
PR 595.W6 V52 1996
821'.8099287--dc20
95-22458
CIP

Typeset in 10.5 on 12 pt Garamond
by CentraCet Ltd, Cambridge
Printed in Great Britain by
TJ Press Ltd, Padstow, Cornwall

This book is printed on acid-free paper

Contents

Adelaide Procter

Christina Rossetti

Michael Field

Rosamund Marriott Watson

Mary E. Coleridge

General

Introduction

One of the most exciting developments in feminist criticism of the last decade or so has been the rediscovery of a tradition of Victorian women's poetry. Until recently the names of Dora Greenwell, Adelaide Procter, Amy Levy, Agnes Mary Robinson, May Probyn, Michael Field, Augusta Webster, Mary Coleridge and Rosamund Marriott Watson, for instance, were largely unknown. However, since the revival of interest in Elizabeth Barrett Browning and Christina Rossetti in the 1980s, the focus of attention has progressively widened. A host of new voices has emerged, defying the assumption that, before the twentieth century, women's poetry consisted of a few chance lyricists and invalid hymn writers.

I have therefore opted, in my choice of essays, for range rather than concentration, for a mixture of familiar and unfamiliar poets, of established critics and younger, newer voices, of published and unpublished work. In choosing to cover as wide a field as possible I have reluctantly had to omit some of the pioneering critics of women's poetry: Ellen Moers, Margaret Homans, Cora Kaplan, Gilbert and Gubar and Kathleen Hickok, for instance. The influence of these will, however, be felt everywhere in this collection. Other more recent voices, like Helen Cooper, Virginia Blain, Glennis Stephenson, Elizabeth Helsinger, Marlon Ross, Joseph Bristow, Kathy Psomiades, Stuart Curran and Kathy Burlinson, had to be omitted for simple reasons of space. None the less, I hope that this collection will open rather than close the whole area of criticism of nineteenth-century women's poetry.

One advantage in dealing with a new body of literature is that the rules of critical engagement have not set hard and fast. Old debates about interpretation – the use of biography, the tension between political and aesthetic readings, the question of poetic value and canonization, the conflict between old historical and new historical approaches, the validity of psychoanalytic, poststructuralist, postcolonial or feminist readings – are all given fresh attention and impetus in these essays. Victorian women's poetry inevitably invites analysis from across the spectrum of contemporary theory, thus also helping to reset the terms of that theory. Implicitly or explicitly, all these essays contribute to a debate on methodology, while entering into a mutual dialogue on such topics as the nature of home, the market, mothers and muses.

Tricia Lootens sets the scene with her powerful analysis of Felicia Hemans's 'internal resistance' to the imperial myth of home. Using recent theories of Englishness and empire, she argues that the connection between 'domestic happiness and military glory' is not as unquestioningly close in Hemans's verse as it might seem. Certainly, on the one hand, home carries the flag of empire and national identity in her verse; it is the motivation and justification for military enterprise. But on the other hand, and precisely as a consequence of military adventure, home is also a graveyard. Strewn with the bodies of the (male) dead, its mournful emptiness is suggestively unlocalized and cosmopolitan. Lootens's discussion of Hemans's 'Casabianca' might be compared with Isobel Armstrong's account of the same poem in '"A Music of Thine Own"': both regard this famous and infamous patriotic poem as one which visibly shows the cracks between domestic, national and gender politics. Hemans, like many of these women poets, is internally at war with the ideology she seems to sanctify. In a suggestive piece on Emily Brontë, Stevie Davies similarly presents home, not as a safe, socio-economic unit, but as a space opening up beyond the limits of the living and the dead. For Brontë, home is 'mother earth' – a place which has no allegiance to any power or creed, but in which is reserved the idea of the lost mother, whether the literal progenitor or the mythical origin of life and speech. Such an earthly home, Davies argues, creates 'a forcefield of silence' around the texts of the poems.

The connection between motherland and the making of poems, between matria and matrix, is explored by Sandra Gilbert in her classic essay 'From *Patria* to *Matria*'. Italy, she argues, is transformed by Barrett Browning, Emily Dickinson and Rossetti 'from a problematic country in Europe to the problem condition of femaleness' itself. The slip from political to personal is a recurring feature of their poetry, and one which teasingly misaligns expected associations. Italy, as 'the home, even the womb, of European art', preserves the possibility of a 'matriarchal law' at the heart of things – especially at the heart of things English. The poetic home is thus the other country, the land unconquered by patriarchal domination, a property not owned by the father. Such a home is unhomely. It is also the lost territory of the woman's body. Barrett Browning's voluptuously maternal Italy, like

Emily Brontë's mother earth or Rossetti's orchards of the south, evokes this here-and-there, familiar-strange contradiction which runs through Victorian women's poetry. Such a contradiction, Gilbert points out, bears not only on the nature of femininity, but also on the nature of poetic language – on that to-ing and fro-ing between words and silence, sense and strangeness, which is, in a sense, the very condition of poetry.

The theme of home as an ambiguous, liminal place is continued in Gill Gregory's intriguing analysis of Adelaide Procter's 'A Legend of Provence'. This foreign tale, told in a ghostly English home, works as a double narrative, the legendary past shadowing the ordinary present. In the framing English (male) narrative, the girl tells a story and finds a husband; in the French (female) tale (told by the girl), a nun loses her innocence, finds her mother and returns to herself. Like the various other thresholds discussed in my own essay, '"Because men made the laws"', Procter's threshold of the convent is at once a place of division and of reassimilation. Katharine McGowran's evocative reading of four poems by Mary Coleridge similarly defines the threshold as a place of strange meeting, where older poetic wardens threaten the very status of the new 'I'. The step in or out of the home is a risky crossing for the female imagination, and these poets confront it in full awareness of its potential displacements. In a challenging new essay on Rosamund Marriott Watson, Linda Hughes examines how the folk ballad allows for a devastating critique of home. No longer part of a dialectic of inside and out, safety and danger, home now harbours violence and horror within. As if coming full circle from Hemans, Marriott Watson's verse hints at a violence perpetrated *by* women, by wives and mothers, even.

Home thus focuses the various tricky axes of gender, politics and aesthetics – forces which it is harder to keep apart in poetry than in the novel. It provides the central pivot around which women's 'homeless' poetry circles. Jerome McGann, in an early seminal essay on Christina Rossetti, points out that her work, far from being mild and consolatory, is in fact full of a 'pitiless sense that the world is a scene of betrayal' – a betrayal that is most bitter 'in the relations between men and women'. This Foucauldian reading of the text as a scene of power then leads to a number of exhilarating close readings of individual poems. McGann shows how Rossetti's ambiguous use of the pronoun emphasizes the secretiveness both of the self and of poetic meaning in general. Her poems thus open up another scene of betrayal, between poet and reader, so that the ideological power game which underpins sexuality is reproduced as a game of the text. Isobel Armstrong takes this key idea of the secret and develops from it her own impressively large-scale theory of Victorian poetry. She claims that in women's poetry of the period there is 'a disjunction between the secret feelings of the mind and the form of the representation. The representation then becomes the barrier feeling is designed to break.' Far from being vessels of overflowing expressiveness, women poets feel most acutely and fruitfully the paradox of the 'open secret'. The incommensurability of form and feeling, reserve and spontaneity, is one which they all test out.

If Foucault's 'repressive theory' underlies McGann's and Armstrong's interpretations, Freud and Kristeva underpin Terrence Holt's challenging essay on *Goblin Market*. He too searches out the nervous points between economic, sexual and religious registers, arguing that the self-sufficient home is 'contaminated', like everything else, by the market principles of exchange. Like the poetic use of parenthesis, which seems to bracket off what it actually connects, the home cannot be protected from the traffic of power. Ultimately, however, this is a poem about poetry, specifically women's poetry, burdened by its own 'lack' of the penny of sexual power. Holt's negative and rather essentialist Freudian conclusions evidently cause him some unease, and might be compared with my own more cheerfully feminist and McGann's new historicist readings of *Goblin Market*.

If home is associated with the idea of the mother, the mother is associated with the muse. Dorothy Mermin, in an important early essay, 'The Damsel, the Knight, and the Victorian Woman Poet', argues that in order to be 'both knight and damsel, both subject and object', the woman poet must choose. Either she may resort to passive solipsism, indifferent to all knights, as does Rossetti, or else, like Barrett Browning, she may take a sexual revenge. If the muse is male – a Pan, a goblin or the beloved – he must be resisted, evaded or ignored by the poet who desires him. Only if the poet reverses the sexual roles and becomes herself the 'erotic object of male imagination', as Emily Brontë does, can the game of desire be played out. Dolores Rosenblum takes a similar line in her fine essay on Rossetti's religious sensibility, 'Watching, Looking, Keeping Vigil'. The issue of who is the model, who the poet, is complicated for Rossetti, who was, in her own life, both poet and model. Rosenblum connects the religious importance of self-denial, a state of being seen only by an unseen God, with the artistic problem of being 'a visual icon'. Either way Rossetti is 'the observer seeing herself observed'. But because this short-circuit of consciousness is set in the no-time after death, Rossetti both satisfies the demands of total narcissism – there is no one *except* herself in this place – as well as the demands of total self-consciousness – the dead woman is nothing *but* an observed object. Precisely this contradiction, she argues, is the source of Rossetti's poetic 'self-possession'.

Contemporary feminist criticism has too often avoided the religious dimension of Victorian aesthetics. Identity, for these poets, often has as much to do with self-denial as with self-assertion, with rejection rather than possession of the muse. Even George Eliot, as Kathleen Blake shows in her concise essay on *Armgart*, is susceptible to the argument from self-mortification. Brought low, not so much by Christian morality as by the egalitarian demands of her sister sex, the great opera singer accepts her artistic failure and retires into obscurity. However, Blake proposes that the work's 'double critique of the conflict of love and art' results in another resolution of the woman's hard choice. Armgart, who seems to have lost both art and love at the end, in fact finds a new version of both. Blake's optimistic interpretation of the work is corroborated and developed by Margaret Reynolds.

It seems that, denied the traditional supportive mythology of the muse, and cut off, politically and practically, from other members of her sex, the Victorian woman poet must often find herself in a homeless zone of the imagination. It is no wonder, then, that she heads for the foreign countries of Italy, heaven or death. Joyce Zonana, however, countering the traditional view that 'the muse must be external and Other to the poet', suggests that Barrett Browning inaugurates a new kind of courtly poetics. In *Aurora Leigh*, she claims, the poet discards both her male muse, Romney, and her female muse, Marian Erle, to find herself, instead, as 'both muse and poet' in one. In particular, Aurora finds her own body. Thus the platonic notion of the muse as the anima, shadowy and intangible, is supplanted by the idea of a literal, 'embodied' inspiration, which is already present in the poet, but which she only finds at the end of a long epic quest. Susan Conley, in her suggestive essay 'Poet's Right', worries at this same possibility. She proposes that Rossetti provides Michael Field with both an anti-muse (a poet in her own 'right' cannot be a muse in the old sense) and with the possibility that 'writer and muse' are the same thing, 'thrilling', like Daphne or Syrinx, to a sense of their own power. Thus the traditionally violent, possessive or erotic relationship between subject-poet and object-muse is challenged by many of these critics in their search for an alternative story of influence.

The figure which most frequently haunts the consciousness of these poets, as an emblem of poet and muse in one, is of course Sappho, or her re-embodiment in the nineteenth century: Corinne. Chris White, in her detailed discussion of Michael Field's Sapphic poems, shows how the figure of the classical poet offers later women a model of the poet as virgin, or Virgin Mother, which profoundly alters the conventions of love poetry. The 'Tiresian' poet, she argues, shifts between the various available forms of address, whether male or female, virginal or erotic, secular or religious, just as Sappho, the original woman poet of the south, remains a creature of fragmented texts and myths which elude sexual fixing. The fact that two women wrote together under the name of Michael Field allowed them to escape the voyeuristic 'networks of power' which dominate traditional love poetry. Their Sapphic fragments and other love poems thus achieve a flexibly interchanging model of authorship. Margaret Reynolds, in her witty, wide-ranging essay on the influence of Sappho on Victorian women poets, proposes that many poets' love-and-death poems are in fact invocations of the original muse-mother: Sappho. Re-reading works by Hemans, L.E.L., Barrett Browning, George Eliot, Rossetti, Michael Field, Robinson, Probyn and Coleridge, she suggests that the last song, echoing from 'long ago', is neither a piece of arcadian theatre nor a compulsively suicidal gesture of self-denial, but the beginning of a new acceptance of poetic power. Remembering Sappho becomes, for these poets, a bid to be remembered in their turn; the 'memory love-letter' to the past becomes a promise to the future. In claiming that the figure of Sappho inhabits many of the ambiguous pronouns of women's poetry, Reynolds shows how the ancestor may return as the self, the mother as her daughters and the muse as the poet. The woman poet's 'last song' is thus always still being written, as it is read, now.

If, as Isobel Armstrong declares, 'Victorian expressive theory . . . created a discourse which could accommodate a poetics of the feminine', the ways in which women negotiated that expressivity, individually and collectively, is a story which is still in the process of being written. This collection of essays will, I hope, provide some helpful, enjoyable and inspiring viewpoints on the road.

Acknowledgements

For permission to use copyright material the editor and publisher would like to thank the following: Isobel Armstrong, for '"A Music of Thine Own": Women's Poetry – an Expressive Tradition?' from *Victorian Poetry: Poetry, Poetics and Politics* (1993), 318–47, copyright © 1993 Isobel Armstrong, by permission of Routledge; Kathleen Blake, for '*Armgart* – George Eliot on the Woman Artist', *Victorian Poetry*, 18 (1980), 75–80, copyright © 1980 Kathleen Blake, by permission of *Victorian Poetry*; Susan Conley, for '"Poet's Right": Elegy and the Woman Poet', from *Victorian Poetry*, 32 (1994), 365–73, copyright © 1994 Susan Conley, by permission of *Victorian Poetry*; Stevie Davies, for 'The Mother Planet', from *Emily Brontë: Heretic* (1994), pp. 171–82, copyright © 1994 Stevie Davies, by permission of The Women's Press; Sandra M. Gilbert, for 'From *Patria* to *Matria*: Elizabeth Barrett Browning's Risorgimento', *PMLA*, 99 (1984), 194–209, copyright © 1984 *PMLA*, by permission of *PMLA*; Terrence Holt, for '"Men sell not such in any town": Exchange in *Goblin Market*', *Victorian Poetry*, 28 (1990), 51–67, copyright © 1990 Terrence Holt, by permission of *Victorian Poetry*; Linda K. Hughes, for '"Fair Hymen holdeth hid a world of woes": Myth and Marriage in Poems by "Graham R. Tomson" (Rosamund Marriott Watson', *Victorian Poetry*, 32 (1994), 97–120, copyright © 1994 Linda K. Hughes, by permission of *Victorian Poetry*; Angela Leighton, for '"Because men made the laws": The Fallen Woman and the Woman Poet', *Victorian Poetry*, 27 (1989), 109–27, copyright © 1989 Angela Leighton, by permission of *Victorian Poetry*; Tricia Lootens, for 'Hemans and Home: Victorianism, Feminine "Internal Enemies", and the Domestication of National Identity', *PMLA*, 109 (1994), 238–53, copyright © 1994 *PMLA*, by permission of *PMLA*; Jerome J. McGann, for 'Christina Rossetti's Poems', from 'Christina Rossetti's

Poems: A New Edition and a Revaluation', *Victorian Studies*, 23 (1980), 237–54, copyright © 1980 *Victorian Studies*, reprinted by permission of the Trustees of Indiana University; Dorothy Mermin, for 'The Damsel, the Knight, and the Victorian Woman Poet', *Critical Inquiry*, 13 (1986), 64–80, copyright © 1986 University of Chicago Press, by permission of the University of Chicago Press; Dolores Rosenblum, for 'Christina Rossetti's Religious Poetry: Watching, Looking, Keeping Vigil', *Victorian Poetry*, 20 (1982), 33–49, copyright © 1982 Dolores Rosenblum, by permission of *Victorian Poetry*; Joyce Zonana, for 'The Embodied Muse: Elizabeth Barrett Browning's *Aurora Leigh* and Feminist Poetics', *Tulsa Studies in Women's Literature*, 8 (1989), 241–62, copyright © 1989 *Tulsa Studies in Women's Literature*, by permission of *Tulsa Studies in Women's Literature*.

Every effort has been made to trace all the copyright holders, but if any have been overlooked the publishers will be happy to make the necessary arrangements at the first opportunity.

1

Hemans and Home: Victorianism, Feminine 'Internal Enemies', and the Domestication of National Identity

Tricia Lootens

If any phrase still evokes Victorianism as conceived early in this century, surely the first line of Felicia Hemans's 'Casabianca' does. 'The boy stood on the burning deck' conjures up a familiar vision of unconscious ironies and lost innocence. Calling to mind drawing rooms where parents comfortably weep to the recitation of earnest or sullen children, the line revives the mockery, nostalgia, and anxiety with which early twentieth-century critics approached Victorian writing. To quote 'the burning deck' raises a smile; to suggest that Hemans's verse be studied seriously raises the spectre of creeping Victorianism. Wendell V. Harris worries that unless we admit works such as 'Casabianca' to be beyond the literary pale – the 'real, if unstated, limits' of canonicity – we may be driven to 'defend the sentimental description and inspirational storytelling that delighted our grandparents' (117). More dramatically, Virgil Nemoianu warns feminists that recuperation of 'margin- alized' women's literature could 'backfire cruelly': what if the likes of Felicia Hemans were unleashed on unsuspecting classrooms (240)?[1] At points, the survival of critical literary study seems to depend on twentieth-century critics' power to relegate to the parlours of the past the complacent Victorian pleasures represented by Hemens and her patriotic verse.

That Hemans's verse should thus symbolize Victorianism, and particularly Victorian patriotic feeling, is both fitting and ironic. Perhaps no single poet's work better expresses the power of Victorian domestic patriotism, which sought to cast warriors as tender homebodies and children's playing fields as military training grounds. Enlightenment patriotism might tend to invoke liberty, whether defined by reason or constitutional monarchy, and Romantic patriotism might call on the organic unity of the folk nation.[2] But Victorian culture tells soldiers that they fight for home, and it often does so in the voice of Felicia Hemans. Hemans's verse is never simply Victorian, however; and where it is most Victorian, it is perhaps least simple.

The Burning Deck: Patriotic Passions and Instabilities

Few poetic careers can have been more thoroughly devoted to the construction of national identity than was that of Felicia Hemans. From her first mild critical success, *England and Spain; or, Valour and Patriotism*, to her dying dream of composing a great patriotic work, Hemans positioned herself as a national poet. Her fascination with patriotism and her 'engrossing' if ambivalent 'delight in military glory' (Chorley 1: 21–2) were central to her work and inseparable from her famous melancholy and her concern with defining womanhood.

Ironically, what led Hemans to anticipate (if not, indeed, partially to effect) the Victorians' assumption of an intrinsic connection between the values of domestic sanctity and of imperial domination may have been her attempts to reconcile Romantic concepts of organic national identity with earlier thought. For Hemans was deeply committed to a form of Enlightenment thinking that envisioned the glory of nationalism as international. Like William Hazlitt, she believed that 'patriotism is . . . a law of our rational and moral nature'. a 'broad and firm basis' on which 'collateral circumstances' such as 'language, literature, manners, national customs' are merely a 'superstructure' (Hazlitt 68). She thus won fame not only as a poet of English patriotism but also as the author of 'The Landing of the Pilgrim Fathers' (*Poetical Works* 431–2), and she glorified the courage both of Crusaders and of their Arab opponents. She wrote bloodthirsty British victory and battle songs, but her martial verse also celebrated (carefully chosen) armies of Greeks, Germans, Moors, Norwegians, Spaniards and Welsh, among others. However anglicized and homogenized, Hemans's protagonists are nothing if not diverse in 'collateral circumstances'.[3]

All the same, Hemans was steeped in Scott and Wordsworth; she dreamed of nations united not merely by reason but also by mythic folk identities inseparable from relations to the land. While Hazlitt envisioned patriotism that could not be 'in a strict or exclusive sense, a natural or personal affection', Hemans's patriotism attempted to unite such an affection to 'reason and reflection' (Hazlitt 67), thus creating a stable, satisfying feminine position that inextricably connected nation and family.[4] By her own account, she failed in this endeavour. Like many Romantic poets, she never produced the unified, monumental work of which she dreamed; her great regret, she said on her deathbed, was that she had never created 'some more noble and complete work . . . which might permanently take its place as the work of a British poetess' (Chorley 2: 213).

Even aside from conflicts between Enlightenment internationalism and what Marlon Ross calls 'the romance of Wordsworthian organicism' ('Romancing' 65), Hemans's national project may have faced insuperable obstacles. As the daughter of an Irish father and a part-German, part-Italian mother and as a resident of Wales for most of her life, Hemans herself might well have wondered precisely what a 'British poetess' was; and as a woman, she faced major challenges to her ambition of writing patriotic poetry altogether. By 1808, the year in which her first book, *Poems*, was published, Hemans was already aware of her quandary. 'My whole heart and soul are interested for the gallant patriots' of the Peninsular War, she wrote an aunt, 'and though females are forbidden to interfere in politics, yet as I have a dear, dear brother . . . on the scene of action, I may be allowed to feel some ardour . . .' (Chorley 1: 25).[5] Hemans's strategy seems transparent, and indeed throughout her career the poet was to 'plac[e] her political interest behind the veil of domesticity and writ[e] political poems that take as their immediate concern the trials of feminine affection' (Ross, *Contours* 285). In the end, however, the domestic veil may have been as destabilizing as the political interests it sought to feminize.

In 1812 Felicia Dorothea Browne married a soldier, Alfred Hemans, and though the marriage failed, she retained her 'ardour' for military subjects. If, as Norma Clarke asserts, Hemans's most successful work, 'Records of Woman', continually 'return[s] to and rework[s] the central event in her life as a woman artist: her husband's desertion of her . . . and her continuing literary fame' (80), it may also be true that the book returns to and reworks central issues in her life as a female patriot, including ambivalence about the connections between domestic happiness and military glory. Given the continuing critical tendency to read women's intellectual commitments as the result of their romantic experiences, it might be tempting to attribute such ambivalence to Hemans's marriage. This explanation would be a mistake, however, for the unmarried Felicia Browne was fully conversant with the patriotic positions of her time and was already grappling with (or seeking to evade or mediate) conflicts within their constructions of femininity and of domestic values. In *Poems*, published when Hemans was fifteen, the dialogue 'The Spartan Mother and Her Son' (13–14) casts war purely as a chance to win either honour or a 'glorious grave / Crown'd with the patriot-honours of the brave'. 'My noble Isadas', the Spartan mother says, 'to me what pride, / Were thou to die – as thy brave father died!' The remainder of the volume seems consistent with this position: the tear called up by the hero's death in 'Sacred to the Memory of Lord Nelson', for example (55–6), is 'sweet' and 'enthusiastic'. Nevertheless, as a note in *'The Domestic Affections', and Other Poems* points out (89), in the same year that *Poems* was published Hemans composed a work in which self-division with respect to patriotism is unmistakable: 'War and Peace: A Poem' (*'Domestic Affections'* (89–121).

The overall argument of 'War and Peace' is irreproachably conventional: although war is evil, 'if *ever* conscious right, / if *ever* justice arm'd [God] for the fight', it is in the battle between 'Albion' and France, the 'Typhon of the world' (115, 106). At points, Hemans's imagined victory song seems to usher in nothing less than the millennium:

> 'Goddess of th' unconquer'd isles,
> 'Freedom! triumph in our smiles!
> 'Blooming youth, and wisdom hoary,
> 'Bards of fame, and sons of glory;
> 'Albion! pillar of the main!
> 'Monarchs! nations! join the strain!
> 'Swell to heav'n th' exulting voice;
> 'Mortals, triumph! earth, rejoice!
>
> (119)

And yet, close to halfway through the poem, something happens. On one page, Hemans celebrates Sir John Moore's victory at Corunna, promising him 'high on [his] native shore a Cenotaph sublime' (110); on the next, she introduces figures of mortal mourners, successors to her earlier personification of Britain as a 'Queen of Isles' whose 'sorrow' over lost heroes merely 'paled the kindling cheek of pride' (97, 98). 'Near the cold urn th' imploring mother stands! / Fix'd is her eye, her anguish cannot weep! / There all her hopes with joyful virtue sleep!' The mother will die of 'soul-consuming grief' that '[m]ourns in no language, seeks for no relief' (102). So will the 'fair lovely mourner o'er a Father's tomb', deprived of the chance to offer 'filial sweetness' at the 'hour of death'. 'Ah! who can tell the thousands doom'd to moan, / Condemn'd by war, to hopeless grief unknown!' 'Thou, laureate Victor!' Hemans apostrophizes her country,

> when thy blazon'd shield,
> Wears the proud emblems of the conquer'd field;
> When trophies glitter on they radiant car,
> And thronging myriads hail thee from afar;
> . . . .
> *Then* could thine eyes each drooping mourner see,
> Behold each hopeless anguish, caus'd by thee;
> Hear, for each measure of the votive strain,

> The rending sigh that murmurs o'er the slain;
> See, for each banner fame and victory wave,
> Some sufferer bending o'er a soldier's grave;
> How would that scene, with grief and horror fraught,
> Chill the warm glow, and check th' exulting thought!
>
> (104, 105)

This passage seems meant as a bridge: having chastened England's victory celebrations, Hemans proceeds to evoke Napoleon as 'Ambition', exercising the 'Power of the ruthless arm, the deathful spear, / Unmov'd, unpitying in [his] dread career' (106). Yet by characterizing England's exulting 'laureate Victor' as blind to the human costs of war, Hemans implicitly connects his figure to that of Napoleon. The apparent bridge comes to seem more like the loop in a roller coaster: the passage turns the givens of military glory on their heads, offering a glimpse of the two armies as parallel in destruction.

In some senses, this near reversal is paradigmatic for Hemans's patriotic verse. Throughout her career, she ransacked extensive readings in literature, folklore, and world history for exemplary narratives in which the threatened or actual dissolution of family ties intersected with the exercise of feminine national heroism. The result was a kind of vital, fragmented, and self-subversive catalogue of feminine patriotic subject positions – a body of work whose development often seems more centrifugal than linear and whose force seems to derive from its erratic course among and through contradictions, whether they are domestic and military values, Romantic and Enlightenment interpretations of patriotism, Christian pacifism and delight in military glory, or what John Lucas would call epic and pastoral modes of national poetry (4–7, 16–17).

What Victorian readers found in Hemans, then, was a fragmented, compelling, and complex range of patriotic positions, and the verses this audience favoured – such as the silly, sinister, and explosive 'Casabianca' (*Poetical Works* 398) – were often among the most disturbing. Like much of Hemans's work, 'Casabianca' commemorates an actual event. By setting the tactically unnecessary death of a child at the heart of Britain's victory in the Battle of the Nile, the poem suggests the powerful, unstable fusion of domestic and military values that helped render Hemans's poetry influential. For despite this poem's idealistic emphasis on filial loyalty and chivalric family honour, 'Casabianca' never fully defuses the horror of the history it evokes.

Young Casabianca, begging his unconscious father for release from a courageous, suicidal, and perhaps pointless exercise of military honour, is both patriotic martyr and senseless victim. The poem's didactic high point is its final lines: '. . . The noblest thing that perished there, / Was that young faithful heart'. The child embodies patriarchal family honour in the highest, most chivalric sense. Noble young Casabianca, 'beautiful and bright', is 'as born to rule the storm – / A creature of heroic blood, / A proud, though childlike form'. Indeed, the courageous child is father to the warlike man: while practical considerations of national political power or of personal ambition may taint the father's courage, the son brings to the battle only his 'young faithful heart'. His death thus upholds and extends the family – and the national – honour, by restoring military endeavour to its originary purity and innocence, its sources in the child's love of and blind faith in home and family. The more strategically useless such a willing death in battle, the more pure and poignant its symbolic significance. Surely young Casabianca's heirs rode in 'The Charge of the Light Brigade'.

The poem's emotional centre lies elsewhere, however, in the desperate child's reiterated 'Speak, Father!' and his question 'Must I stay?' Here the fusion of familial and national loyalties works on a different level. The child's futile cry for his father evokes an experience of abandonment that is both primitive and deeply domestic. By terming Casabianca's heart the 'noblest thing' lost, Hemans divides this domestic embodiment of familial agony from the rest of the battle's costs and uses it to challenge, if not discredit, the 'nobility' of the battle's conscious, adult actors – and victors. The scene is a damning enactment of the brutal waste of war, of the deadly implications of patriarchal honour, and of the betrayal of familial ties by adults intent on that honour. For a few moments, Casabianca is the ultimate orphan of war, yet he is also in some sense its unwitting propagator, just as his father is his unwitting murderer.

From Spartan Mothers to Internal Enemies:
Hemans's Patriotic Heroines

Within what Helen Cooper, Adrienne Munich, and Susan Squier term the 'war narrative of the sexual trope, in which love figures as both sexual congress and sexual productivity' ('Arms' 9), twentieth-century criticism has tended to position Hemans's patriotic heroines somewhere between the Spartan mother and Tennyson's sweetly bloodthirsty Maud. Many of Hemans's verses bear an affinity to Maud's 'passionate ballad gallant and gay' (1052); they offer ample evidence of the extent to which the phrase 'arms and the woman' evokes activities that may be at once military, maternal and erotic (Cooper, Munich, and Squier, 'Arms' 9–10). While Hemans's verses deploy such a trope, however, they also point beyond it. In the poems most beloved by Victorians, the military struggle is often finished; what resonates is not a battle cry but the voice of a lone 'sufferer bending over' a soldier's body or 'grave' ('War and Peace'; *'Domestic Affections'* 105). This feminine patriotism still stands in primary relation to soldiers' bodies, but that relation, which need be neither maternal nor erotic, is mediated by death rather than birth. In reaching out towards the dead — whether to hold, accuse, or mourn them — Hemans's heroines and speakers give the phrase 'arms and the woman' new meaning.

In *Phenomenology of Spirit*, Hemans's contemporary G. W. F. Hegel explores the cultural connections between femininity and the military dead, in terms of classical tragedy and of nineteenth-century conceptions of the state's relations to domesticity. The power of 'divine law' is governed by femininity, he asserts, and it is this law that rules burial. Alive, soldiers belong to the state; dead, they must be 'wed' to the 'lap of the earth', returned to 'elementary, eternal individuality'.[6] For Hegel, the central feminine national figure is Antigone. If considered in the context of nation, he asserts, her rebellion would take on a new significance for the relations between femininity and the power of the state:

> Taken in this form, [Antigone's action], which had been conceived as a simple movement of individualized pathos, discloses another aspect, and both the crime and the resulting destruction of the community disclose the actual form of their existence. Thus, human law in its general existence, the community, which in its effectivity altogether is masculinity and in its actual effectivity is the government, moves and maintains itself by wrenching into itself the special status of the household gods or the autonomous individuation into families, of which femininity is in charge, and by holding them in the continuity of its fluidity. Simultaneously, however, the family is its element altogether, and the individual consciousness is its general operative basis.[7]

To assert its communal, impersonal jurisdiction, the law governed by masculinity ('human law', in Hegel's terms) must forcibly absorb and subdue its own 'element'. Masculinity may not allow the 'divine law' governed by femininity to exercise autonomous authority but dare not deny its power altogether.

> To the extent that the community retains its existence only through the disruption of familial happiness and through the dissolution of self-awareness within the general [awareness], [the community] engenders itself through what it oppresses and through what is at the same time essential to it — [and thus engenders] in femininity altogether its internal enemy.[8]

The 'fluid' state contains feminine authority as if by chemical suspension, immersing and yet not dissolving it. As the representative of 'divine law' and of the 'law of weakness and darkness', femininity is both sacred and dangerous.[9] Like civil law in wartime, it must be remembered and revered, but for safety's sake it cannot be obeyed. Whereas martial law is theoretically an anomaly of national history, however, masculine law may represent history itself. In Hemans as in Hegel, masculine law has always already 'suspended' feminine authority. Life is war: the weak, dark, divine law of femininity must await the peace of the millennium. Until then, femininity must remain the 'eternal irony of the community', a site of resistance that is as symbolically indispensable as it is practically futile.[10]

At points in her work, Hemans seems allied with Hegel. These moments glorify, mourn and accept the need of the state to engender itself by what it oppresses: they attempt to mobilize the 'domestic affections' to the service of militaristic patriotism. At other points, however, often in confrontations with the real or imagined bodies of the dead, such attempts seem to falter. Hemans may collapse distinctions between the powers of domesticity and of war, creating chillingly ruthless heirs of the Spartan mother, or she may chart a deadly collision course between female figures and a state whose brutality is implicitly unveiled as senseless. Poems in which despair jostles with energetic expressions of straightforward militarism, of feminist sexual politics, and of pacifism raise the spectres of feminine 'internal enemies' who refuse either to continue fighting for 'divine law' or to reconcile themselves to failure.

Nineteenth-century women poets' grappling with issues of national identity has yet to be fully explored, but the verses of Elizabeth Barrett Browning, Frances E. W. Harper, Alice Meynell, and Lydia Sigourney indicate that Hemans's mournful patriotism is central to a complex poetic tradition.[11] As Hemans's work demonstrates, the 'complementary but more often contradictory awarenesses' of national identity and of gender are inseparable (Lucas 7). Hemans's work suggests that national awarenesses are paradoxical and inescapably gendered and that gender is shaped by its own contradictory awarenesses, including conceptions of national identity. Establishing feminine melancholy as something akin to a patriotic duty, Hemans's verse endows the 'nightingale's burden' of nineteenth-century women's poetry with national meaning (Walker 21–7). Her heroines' Victorian heir is less Tennyson's joyous Maud than the lachrymose Amelia of William Makepeace Thackeray's *Vanity Fair*.[12]

Hemans's deeply international (if culturally homogenized) patriotic heroines can be efficiently, if somewhat arbitrarily, divided into three groups.[13] Each group derives in some sense from the 'lofty' Spartan mother whose 'heroic worth' Hemans's early poems repeatedly praise (*Modern Greece* 28), and each establishes a connection between femininity and patriotism only to undermine it. The most striking, given Hemans's Victorian reputation for decorous calm,[14] are the desperate protagonists of narrative poems that recount clearcut actions resembling those in newly recovered folk ballads. These poems explore and exoticize feminine modes of what Lucas would call epic heroism: violent, revolutionary, disruptive – and, not incidentally, ambiguously related to patriarchal power.

As purely righteous as religious martyrs, figures such as the Suliote mother, the wife of Asdrubal, the bride of the Greek isle, or the widow of Crescentius commit murder, suicide, or both as an ultimate expression of duty ('*Forest*' 179–81; *Tales* 189–96; '*Records*' 21–34; *Tales* 1–49). Their deadly energy derives from the political disruption of merged domestic and national order. As Asdrubal's wife cries before stabbing her children, '[T]he arms that cannot save / Have been their cradle, and shall be their grave' (*Tales* 196). These women have no choice: for them, as Hemans writes in *Modern Greece*, 'all [is] lost – all, save the power to die / The wild indignant death of savage liberty' (26). Yet the exhilaration with which they enact as well as avenge their families' dissolution often blurs the line between self-sacrifice and rage. The Suliote's leap is perhaps too much like that of Hemans's Sappho, for example, (*Poetical Works* 532); Asdrubal's wife, for all her noble classical motives, looks suspiciously like the allegedly more primitive protagonist of 'Indian Woman's Death-Song' ('*Records*' 104–8), who drowns herself and her child to escape 'woman's weary lot' (107); and while the bride of the Greek isle, last seen on a burning deck, avenges the death of her compatriots and groom, she also brilliantly reenacts her earlier anguish at separation from her mother, who must watch the conflagration from shore ('*Records*' 32–4). Indeed, Hemans's evocation of suttee in this poem suggests that the bride may stand as a torch to marital misery, an embodiment of preemptive self-sacrifice.[15]

These are figures in extremis; they are heroines, but for Hemans they are also women whose sanity, and perhaps even humanity, is questionable. Asdrubal's wife, for example, is 'frantic ... frenzied', a 'being more than earthly, in whose eye / There dwells a strange and fierce ascendancy':

> The dark profusion of her locks unbound,
> Waves like a warrior's floating plumage round;
> Flush'd is her cheek, inspired her haughty mien,
> She seems th' avenging goddess of the scene.

> (*Tales* 194)

The widow of Crescentius is scarcely more reassuring. A sinister answer to the cross-dressing 'Cesario' of Shakespeare's *Twelfth Night*, she uses her minstrel disguise to serenade and then poison the man who is her country's enemy and husband's killer. 'Oh! there are sorrows which impart / A sternness foreign to the heart', she warns:

> And rushing with an earthquake's power,
> That makes a desert in an hour;
> Rouse the dread passions in their course,
> As tempests wake the billows' force!

The widow is a Byronic figure:

> 'He died, and I was changed – my soul,
> A lonely wanderer, spurn'd control.
> From peace, and light, and glory hurl'd,
> The outcast of a purer world,
> I saw each brighter hope o'erthrown,
> And lived for one dread task alone.'
>
> *(Tales* 28, 29, 36)

Seeing himself bereft of 'freedom to fight for at home', Byron went off to fight for the freedom of his 'neighbours'. For Hemans, in contrast, revolutionary nationalism remained either the neighbours' business or the subject of nostalgia or of fantasy.[16]

Closest to many Victorian critics' hearts was another group of heroines – women like Ximena of 'The Siege of Valencia: A Dramatic Poem' or Frau Stauffacher, the title character of 'The Switzer's Wife' ('*Records*' 37–43). Meek, devout, and Madonna-like, the Switzer's wife mediates between epic and pastoral modes. Armed by the 'sweet memory of our pleasant hearth', her husband has 'strength – if aught be strong on earth'; her (good) name is 'armour' for his 'heart' (42, 43). Hemans is closing her Byron here. Behind a series of such poems stands her admiration for Goethe's glorification of women who send their warriors off with prayers and tearful smiles and often then languish and fade alone. Through the Switzer's wife, Hemans also edges toward home, for as her letters and verses make clear, the poet felt a strong bond to the Swiss. She paralleled their mountain independence with that of the Welsh; she identified their famous *Heimweh*, 'homesickness', with her own (Owen 172); and perhaps above all, she seems to have seen in Switzerland a small, safe model of the interconnecting traditions of national independence and individual liberty that she envisioned for 'Albion'.[17] Intellectually and structurally, the Switzer's wife is an intermediate figure between revolutionary and domestic heroines. Indeed, she may have helped to mediate not only between pastoral and epic poetry but also between conceptions of Britain as an isolated, independent folk entity and as an imperial power (Ross, 'Romancing' 56–7). Certainly mid-century readers failed to register any difference between the Swiss woman's release of her husband to protect a family home and a British woman's sacrifice in sending her husband off to defend an empire. Never mind that Switzerland was the nonimperial country par excellence (despite the Swiss mercenaries in whom homesickness was first diagnosed [Hobsbawm 137]); never mind that Frau Stauffacher's prayerful surrender of domestic happiness springs from the same revolutionary grounds as the actions of Hemans's violent heroines. The Switzer's wife could be appreciated by Victorians as an honorary English national heroine – an association that gave domestic courage a touch of glory, even while annexing the moral force of the local freedom fighter to imperial ends.

Where Frau Stauffacher acts, other heroines of domestic patriotism endure. Their narratives often begin with the warrior gone and cast women's national loyalty as synonymous with more or less passive acquiescence to the suffering caused by separation through war. Often that suffering is fatal. Once the poet and soldier Körner lies in a 'hero's tomb', for example, his 'faithful-hearted' sister seeks only '[d]eath, death, to still the yearning for the dead' ('Körner and His Sister'; *Records* 246–9). 'Thou hast thine oak, thy trophy: – ' Hemans assures Körner, 'what hath she? – / Her own blest place by thee!' In 'Troubadour Song', such fading takes on a more sinister aspect (*Poetical Works* 383). A warrior, having eluded 'a thousand arrows', returns home to find that his beloved has died 'as roses die'. 'There was death within the smiling home – / How had death found her there?'

Here, too, however, Hemans's poems undercut one another. Just as the patriotic violence of Asdrubal's wife has its subversive counterpart in the Indian woman's killing of herself and her child, so the sacrifice of the Switzer's wife has an exotic counterpart in nonpatriotic submission: that of the heroine of 'The Hebrew Mother', who surrenders her son to be educated by the male authorities of her religion (*Poetical Works* 400–1). Like the Indian woman, the Hebrew mother appears in a context that stresses the sexual-political implications of her action rather than the patriotic ones.

Hemans also provides a deadly, if sympathetic, exoticized counterfigure to the Switzer's wife: a pious, dovelike Muslim woman whose eloquence and maternal passion lead to the senseless devastation of an idyllic city in India ('The Indian City'; *Records* 83–96). To be sure, this heroine's actions do not precisely parallel those of her more famous sister. Had she not left home in pilgrimage, the Indians would not have slaughtered her son; and had she not sought vengeance, the lost Indian city would have continued to stand. Still, this mother is a disturbing reminder that good women may support or even inspire bad wars.

Hemans's famous 'Woman on the Field of Battle' features a member of the poet's final group of heroines (*'Songs'* 123–6). 'Strangely, sadly fair', the protagonist lies beside a 'banner and shiver'd crest', proof that 'amidst the best / [Her] work was done'.

> Why? – ask the true heart why
>   Woman hath been
> Ever, where brave men die,
>   Unshrinking seen?
>
> Unto this harvest ground
>   Proud reapers came, –
> Some, for that stirring sound,
>   A warrior's name;
>
> Some, for the stormy play
>   And joy of strife;
> And some, to fling away
>   A weary life; –
>
> But thou, pale sleeper, thou,
>   With the slight frame,
> And the rich locks, whose glow
>   Death cannot tame:
>
> Only one thought, one power,
>   *Thee* could have led,
> So, through the tempest's hour,
>   To lift thy head!

The power, of course, is love, which wrenched this figure, like young Casabianca, from domestic safety to death in battle. Domestic affection justified not only military ardour but also action: love won the heroine 'a place' in the 'harvest' of the 'haughty Dead', the 'reapers' who beat the Grim Reaper himself by grasping honour, sport, or surcease from weariness. So far, this poem seems merely to unite the virtues of Hemans's desperate and domestic heroines. The final verse, however, strikes a new and disquieting note. What drove the heroine to the battlefield was love of a particular kind:

> Only the true, the strong,
> The love, whose trust
> Woman's deep soul too long
> Pours on the dust!

Instead of being mutually reinforcing, the sacrifices of domesticity and of nationalism become mutually subversive. Is this a Christian scene? Certainly no pacific afterlife arises to redeem the spilling of this figure's blood or of her love. As both are poured out 'on the dust', apparently in vain, families and empires implicitly blend in an image of pagan ritual (self-)slaughter 'too long' retained.

This point leads to the heart of a nineteenth-century critical controversy: does Hemans's overwhelming melancholy cast doubt on her faith in redemption, whether of soldiers' blood or of women's love (including love of poetry)?[18] Proponents of both sides might well have turned to the third group of Hemans heroines for support. Faltering or failed Spartan mothers, the protagonists of Hemans's dramas and of associated works such as 'The Abencerrage' (*Tales* 51–156) are torn apart by conflicts between national loyalties (including adherence to patriotically defined family honour) and bonds of familial or romantic love; the characters' position as Hegelian internal enemies is agonized and perhaps unstable.

At their most helpless, these heroines may be fully disoriented and victimized, like Moraima, in 'De Chatillon' (*Poetical Works* 611–37), who says in confusion 'Who leads the foe? . . . I meant – I mean – my people' (618). At their most aggressive, they may echo Elimina, in 'The Siege of Valencia' ('*Siege*' 91–247), who curses not only the Moors, for holding her sons hostage, but also her husband, for being willing to sacrifice the captives. She tells him that she hopes he comes to sit alone 'within [his] vast, forsaken halls' and to learn too late that 'dim phantoms from ancestral tombs . . . all – all *glorious*' – can never 'people that cold void' left by the loss of living children. Elmina's rebellion is explicitly feminine:

> Oh, cold and hard of heart!
> Thou shouldst be born for empire, since thy soul
> Thus lightly from all human bonds can free
> Its haughty flight! – Men! men! Too much is yours
> Of vantage; ye, that with a sound, a breath,
> A shadow, thus can fill the desolate space
> Of rooted up affections, o'er whose voice
> Our yearning hearts must wither! – So it is,
> Dominion must be won!

(122, 112–13)

Though traitorous, Elmina's cry echoes throughout Hemans's work, most often in the voice of an internal enemy whose feminine pacifism resigns itself to war on earth by hoping for a peaceable kingdom to come.[19]

In 'The Image in Lava', a particularly powerful example of Hemans's feminine antiwar writing (*'Records'* 307–10), the discovery at Herculaneum of the stone imprint of a mother's breast inspires an overt competition between the powers of the state and of the home:

> Temple and tower have moulder'd
> Empires from earth have pass'd, –
> And woman's heart hath left a trace
> Those glories to outlast!
>
> And childhood's fragile image
> Thus fearfully enshrin'd,
> Survives the proud memorials rear'd
> By conquerors of mankind.

What could have been a simple moral becomes increasingly complex as the brief poem progresses. Hemans's Herculanean mother, whose form was set as 'a mournful seal' by 'love and agony', may have chosen death. 'Perchance all vainly lavish'd / [Her] other love had been'; she might have found it 'far better . . . to perish' than to risk losing the only person she had left to love. Thus, what imprinted itself 'upon the dust', outliving 'the cities of renown / Wherein the mighty trust', may be an expression of isolation and deprivation as well as of maternal love. Perhaps domestic affections have been no real alternative to the powers of empire, after all. Perhaps the image in lava memorializes not only the triumph but also the inadequacy of such love:

> Immortal, oh! immortal
> Thou art, whose earthly glow
> Hath given these ashes holiness –
> It must, it *must* be so!

It must be so, Hemans seems to imply, because it would be too terrible if it were not. 'The Illuminated City' (*'Records'* 283–5), a poem much admired by Victorian critics, offers a more secular echo of Elmina's feminine suspicion of military glory. Drowned in the 'music of victory', which shakes its streets 'like a conqueror's car', Hemans's dazzling city is an emblem of the 'proud mantle' obscuring both the dead on the battlefield and their mourners at home, '[t]he things thou shouldst gaze on, the sad and true.'[20] In her intimate tone, the isolated, wandering speaker in 'The Illuminated City' unmistakably resembles the Cassandra-like speaker of 'Second Sight' ('*Songs*' 249–51). The confessional opening line of the poem, 'A mournful gift is mine, O friends!' proposes that the ability to pierce the veil of military glory is less a skill than a curse. Just as the speaker hears

> the still small moan of Time,
> Through the ivy branches made,
> Where the palace, in its glory's prime
> With the sunshine stands array'd

she sees the 'blood-red future stain / On the warrior's gorgeous crest' and 'the bier amidst the bridal train / When they come with roses drest'. 'Second Sight' juxtaposes the deaths of empires, soldiers, and brides in the visions of a speaker who must remain homeless, short of heaven.

Domesticating the Empire: The Powers of Patriotic Graves

Much of this catalogue of heroines belongs to the Romantic Hemans, from whose complex, passionate body of patriotic verse were winnowed the works that mid-century admirers made 'British classics', grown 'deep into the national heart' (Archibald Alison, quoted in Moulton 260). Collected and genteel, this Victorian verse constitutes the pastoral Hemans, the Hemans whose Englishness is both stable and exemplary. It also represents the imperial Hemans, whose poetry helped put to rest what Ross calls 'a specter haunting Britain at the verge of the nineteenth century . . . on the threshold of Britain's modernization of itself as a nation-state': the question of how to consolidate the notion of Englishness as an organic, indigenous national identity while simultaneously justifying imperial expansion beyond British home territory ('Romancing' 56, 57). Paradoxically, Hemans's attempt to mediate between rationalist and organic notions of national identity may have given rise to one of the greatest sources of her power as a Victorian patriotic poet: her emphasis on reverence for patriots' graves.

On the battlefield, soldiers' corpses may mock or challenge Hemans's victory celebrations, but in the (symbolically) domestic settings of her heroes' graves, military honour and family loyalty meet in peace. No longer at odds, mothers and military authorities join in reverence for the dead and in obedience to 'divine law'. Here alone the martial law of earthly existence may be safely superseded.

Conceived both as metaphors and as concrete objects, the graves of what Hemans loved to call the 'honoured dead' could symbolize the general fact of loss and the specific battles of national heroes; these sites could render the

rational and universal impulse of patriotism local and spiritual. Unambigu-
ously marking the merging of a people and a place, they served as points at
which patriots literally became one with the land. Even one's 'rational and
moral nature' (Hazlitt 67) might well demand specific attachment to a plot
where 'earth's most glorious dust, / Once fired with valour, wisdom, song, /
Is laid in holy trust' (Hemans, 'The English Boy'; *Poetical Works* 502–3). In
focusing local reverence for the literal and symbolic remains of patriotic
heroism, then, heroes' graves not only unified distinct national folk com-
munities but also bound those communities to the rest of the world by
evoking the universal love and sorrows of liberty.

Capable of uniting local loyalties with rationalist internationalism and of
joining the state with its feminine internal enemy, graves in Hemans could
also serve as the sources of national poetry. Lying on a mountain that is both
the Welsh Parnassus and 'the birth-place of phantoms', the first-person
speaker of 'The Rock of Cader-Idris' (*Selection* 12) risks madness to face the
'deep presence' not merely of the embodied 'powers of the wind and the
ocean' but also of the 'mighty ages departed'. Only after looking the dead in
the eye does the speaker awaken, 'as from the grave . . . to inherit / A flame
all immortal, a voice and a power!' If there is a 'sense' that 'gives soul to'
nature's beauty, investing a landscape with mythic power, Hemans suggests,
that soul arises from human connections with the dead.

Is Hemans the poet on the Welsh rock? If memory and graves claim a
land, as she often implied, she claimed Wales, the ground of her 'childhood,
[her] home, and [her] dead' ('A Farewell to Wales'; *Poetical Works* 474). Yet
she was not born there, and she did not think of herself as Welsh. In fact,
even as she celebrates the Welsh bards' national identity, constituting herself
as their heir, Hemans colludes in the dispersion of that identity. To Mary
Russell Mitford, for example, she describes the 'Welsh character' as not 'yet
merged in the English' character (Chorley 1: 127) – rather as if any regional
specificity were doomed; and even her nationalistic 'Welsh melodies' impli-
citly assign a 'brighter lot' to Wales during the period of England's
predominance ('The Mountain Fires'; *Selection* 54).

As Hemans's relation to Wales suggests, then, while her attempt to bind
abstract nation, physical land, and human affection through graves may
indeed resolve some of the issues raised by efforts to unite rationalist and
organic visions of patriotism, it poses other problems. Does honouring of the
national dead constitute identity? By tending a country's graves, metaphori-
cally and actually, may one claim to be a true heir to its bards? And if the
English love a land they have colonized – even honour the valour of those
who fought against them in defence of that land – have they thereby assumed
or appropriated the country's national identity? Perhaps the graves of the

honourable dead help dissolve national identities into mythic forms that are endlessly capable of appropriation. If so, it is not strange that Hemans's conception of graves as sites for the establishment and maintenance of national identity should have found tremendous resonance within Victorian imperialist discourse. 'We cannot be *habitually* attached to places we never saw, and people we never heard of . . .', Hazlitt writes. 'Are the opposite extremities of the globe our native place, because they are a part of that geographical and political denomination, our country? Does natural affection expand in circles of latitude and longitude?' (67). Hemans's poetry offers a clear answer to Hazlitt's scepticism, for if anything can create a habitual attachment to a place one has never seen, it is the grave of a loved one.

It is probably no accident that in 1823, some six years before Christopher North made his famous assertion that the sun never sets on the British empire, Felicia Hemans wrote that 'wave may not foam, nor wild wind sweep, / Where rest not England's dead' ('England's Dead'; *'Siege'* 308–10). Nor should the similarity between the titles of two of her most popular patriotic poems, 'England's Dead' and 'The Homes of England', come as a surprise. For just as domestic mourning makes the empire into a home, expanding affection in terms of latitude and longitude, until it reaches and symbolically appropriates the final resting place of the beloved and honoured dead, so domestic love makes the home into an empire.

'The Homes of England' is Hemans's most famous work on this subject and one of her best-known pieces altogether (*'Records'* 169–71). When the poem first appeared, in the April 1827 edition of *Blackwood's*, it had an epigraph from Joanna Baillie beginning, 'A land of peace . . .'. In volume form, however, 'The Homes of England' has a new epigraph, from *Marmion*: 'Where's the coward that would not dare / To fight for such a land?' Sentimental, reactionary pastoral fantasy at its crudest, 'The Homes of England' links 'stately', 'merry', and 'cottage' dwellings within a harmonious national hierarchy whose unity of 'hut and hall' seems as much defensive as organic. Hemans's verse constitutes domestic harmony, whether national or familial, as not only a form of defence but also an incentive for aggressive striving after glory, be it in the battlefield or the marketplace. Woman's empire is the hearth, as one of Hemans's great admirers notes (Preface, 1836 ix), and in an imperialist country, Hemans suggests, the hearth must be an imperialist site.

Hemans's engagement in the elaboration of such discourse is far from inadvertent. Though the word *imperialist* was not used to designate an advocate of imperialism until after Hemans died, by the time she was fifteen she had constructed an Albion whose world domination was moral, military, economic and perhaps sexual. 'Hail ALBION', she writes in *England and Spain*,

                              hail, thou land of freedom's birth!
                    Pride of the main, and Phoenix of the earth!
                    Thou second Rome, where mercy, justice, dwell,
                    Whose sons in wisdom as in arms excel!
                    Thine are the dauntless bands, like Spartans brave

          .   .   .   .

                    Hail, ALBION hail! to thee has fate denied
                    Peruvian mines and rich Hindostan's pride;

          .   .   .   .

                    Yet fearless Commerce, pillar of thy throne,
                    Makes all the wealth of foreign climes thy own;

          .   .   .   .

                    Look down, look down, exalted Shades! and view
                    Your ALBION still to freedom's banner true!

          .   .   .   .

                    See her secure in pride of virtue tow'r,
                    While prostrate nations kiss the rod of pow'r!

                                                                (4–8)

Hemans's conception of the home as both separate empire and the prerequi-
site for empire was also early and explicit. By 1812, in 'The Domestic
Affections' ('*Domestic Affections*' 148–72), she personified 'domestic affections'
as a female figure who 'dwells, unruffled, in her bow'r of rest, / *Her* empire,
home!' while 'war's red lightnings desolate the ball, / And thrones and
empires in destruction fall' (150). Here homesickness is already a soldier's
essential ration. Domestic memories alone 'cheer the soldier's breast / In
hostile climes, with spells benign and blest', arming him to face the dangers
of 'victory's choral strain', as well as of the 'ensanguin'd plain' and the
'armour's bright flash' (154). The 'spells of home' (a favourite Hemans phrase)
thus both fuel victory and temper the callousness triumph can instill; they
endow soldiers with the power to kill enemies and to sympathize with the
mourners whose love, memories, and sorrow hold together the home empire
and its extension in the graves of the beloved, honourable dead.[21]

  By the end of the century, deployment of the dead as outrunners of empire
had become self-conscious enough to be the source of cynical humour. In
Anthony Hope's *The God in the Car* (1895), for example, an investor reporting
on the progress of his central African scheme comments, 'Everything's going
very well. They've killed a missionary.' '[R]egrettable in itself', he says, the
action is 'the first step toward empire' (Brantlinger 182). Rudyard Kipling's
verse testifies, however, that the dead retained much of their imperial force.
'Never the lotus closes, never the wild-fowl wake', reads his popular 'The
English Flag',

But a soul goes out on the East Wind that died for England's sake –
Man or woman or suckling, mother or bride or maid –
Because on the bones of the English the English flag is stayed.

$(146)^{22}$

In its combination of the grisly and the celebratory, Kipling's verse outdoes even Hemans's. For her, in 'Casabianca', for instance, the connection between reverence for the courage of the dead and sanctification of the circumstances of their deaths remains only implicit; for him, critics of imperial actions are worse than hyenas, unearthing corpses they cannot eat ('Hyenas'). In other respects, however, Kipling is as far from Hemans as is his Kim from young Casabianca; indeed, Kipling's view of empire as what Daniel Bivona calls a 'privileged realm of play' can be fiercely antidomestic (36). If Hemans has a patriotic heir, it is rather Rupert Brooke, whose speaker in 'The Soldier' returns not merely to dust but to 'a richer dust . . . a dust whom England bore', creating a 'corner of a foreign field / That is for ever England'.

Even before Brooke, however, the Victorian discourse of imperial domestication was crumbling, along with the title character of Thomas Hardy's 'Drummer Hodge', who, no longer English in any sense, is laid to rest in an unmarked South African grave where 'his homely Northern breast and brain / Grow to some Southern tree'. Indeed, 'The Soldier' may mark both the culmination and the beginning of the end of Hemans's vision of domesticating patriotic graves. Such glorifications were powerless against attacks from the likes of Siegfried Sassoon, whose 'doomed, conscripted, unvictorious ones' rise to deride their memorial at Menin Gate as a 'sepulchre of crime' ('On Passing'), and whose speaker in 'Glory of Women' might be addressing admirers of 'Casabianca' when he says accusingly, 'You believe / That chivalry redeems the war's disgrace'.

The number of new editions of Hemans's work dropped off suddenly with the end of the Victorian era (Reiman). It is only fair to Hemans, however (and perhaps to some of her Victorian admirers), to note that her role as a poet of imperial mourning is no more stable than any of her other patriotic positions. 'The Indian with His Dead Child', for example, (*'Songs'* 48–51), acknowledges the violence and racism of imperialism, even the domesticating imperialism of the dead. Having sat 'alone, amidst [the] hearth-fires' of white settlers, who are indifferent to his sick 'child's decay', the speaker must raise his son from the 'grave-sod . . . defiled' by the colonists and carry him hundreds of miles to escape the 'spoiler's dwellings'.

A community that attempts to prevent its members from returning the dead to the 'lap of the earth', to 'elementary, eternal individuality', destroys itself, Hegel writes (*Phänomenologie* 258).[23] For all Hemans's piety, what her speakers sometimes suggest – though do not endorse – is a fear even greater than the thought that they are living in such a community. What if no philosophical or religious principle makes order of such destruction? What if the virtuous power of the internal enemy is not guaranteed? What if it is not enough?

In her tremendously popular 'The Graves of a Household' ('*Records*' 299–301), Hemans evokes a vacant British family graveyard that is the mirror image and perhaps the inevitable corollary of the burial ground in Hardy's 'Drummer Hodge', 'Sever'd, far and wide, / By mount, and stream, and sea', the graves of the family's children are flung throughout the empire and perhaps beyond. These dead are explicitly linked neither to imperial glory nor to one another: geographically separated, they may have lost even their connection in the memory of a 'fond mother'. Perhaps the resurrection will reunite them; certainly Hemans's Christian faith would insist on this. And yet the poem makes no promises. 'Alas! for love', read its final lines, 'if *thou* wert all, / And nought beyond, oh earth!' The true title of 'The Graves of a Household' might be 'The Grave of a Family', for the poem signals the end not only of the possibility but of the memory of living domestic love. On the other side of Hemans's imperial appropriation through burial stands the dissolution of domestic identity, familial and national. And with this, one returns to 'Casabianca', for a final reminder of what is left at the end of that poem: fragments, a paradigm of chivalric self-sacrifice, and the story of a courageous child's futile call for release.

NOTES

1 For Nemoianu, Hemans's 'obsolete ideologies' and unremitting noncanonical 'conservatism' could thwart radical pedagogy and endanger more canonical writers' tradition of critical thinking (1991: 240, 246).

2 On liberty and eighteenth-century patriotism see Lucas 1990: 23–32, 39–48, Cunningham 1989: 57–62, and Colley 1989. See Ross 1991: 56–7, and Woodring on 'English poetic nationalism' (1970: 45).

3 Jeffrey, for example, praises Hemans for omitting the 'revolting or extravagant excesses' of countries and periods besides her own and for retaining 'much of what is most interesting and peculiar' in their legends (1829: 35).

4 When I refer to femininity, I mean a condition that is not biological but culturally constructed and historically contingent. In dominant nineteenth-century British and American writings on the subject, womanhood is only truly embodied by married or marriageable 'Anglo-Saxon' gentlewomen – and not even by all of them.

5 'Some' was an understatement. As her biographer Henry Chorley notes, Hemans's 'mind wrought incessantly upon scenes of heroic enterprise and glory' (1836: 1, 21).

6   '[D]ie Familie ... vermählt den Verwandten dem Schoße der Erde, der
     elementarischen unvergänglichen Individualität' (Hegel 1990: 245). This trans-
     lation, like all the English versions of Hegel, is my own. For a translation of the
     context, see Hegel 1977: 271.

7   'In dieser Form genommen, erhält das was als einfache Bewegung des indivi-
     dualisirten Pathos vorgestellt wurde, ein anderes Aussehen, und das Verbrechen
     und die dadurch begründete Zerstörung des Gemeinwesens die eigentliche Form
     ihres Daseyns. – Das menschliche Gesetz also in seinem allgemeinen Daseyn,
     das Gemeinwesen, in seiner Bethätigung überhaupt die Männlichkeit, in seiner
     wirklichen Bethätigung, die Regierung ist, bewegt und erhält sich dadurch, das
     es die Absonderung der Penaten oder die selbständige Vereinzelung in Familien,
     welchen die Weiblichkeit vorsteht, in sich aufzehrt, und sie in der Continuität
     seiner Flüssigkeit aufgelößt erhält. Die Familie ist aber zugleich überhaupt sein
     Element, das einzelne Bewußtseyn allgemeiner bethätigender Grund' (1990:
     258). See also Hegel 1977: 287–8.

8   'Indem das Gemeinwesen sich nur durch die Störung der Familienglückseligkeit
     und die Auflösung des Selbstbewußtseyns in das allgemeine, sein Bestehen gibt,
     erzeugt es sich an dem, was es unterdrückt und was ihm zugleich wesentlich
     ist, an der Weiblichkeit überhaupt seinen innern Feind' (1990: 258–9). See also
     Hegel 1977: 288.

9   Divine law is 'das Gesetz der Schwäche und der Dunkelheit' (Hegel 1990: 257).
     See also Hegel 1977: 286. 'What Hegel defines as "Divine Law",' Solomon
     notes, derives from 'the structure of bourgeois society at the turn of the
     nineteenth century' (1983: 542).

10 Femininity is 'die ewige Ironie des Gemeinwesens ...' (Hegel 1990: 259; see
     also 1977: 288). Cooper, Munich and Squier write that classical epic also
     presents 'the dualities of man/woman, war/peace' and in so doing 'both
     establishes the conception of the war narrative informing western literary
     tradition and allows a questioning of those dualities' (1989: 10). *Arms and the
     Woman* strongly suggests how such dualisms may still authorize war narratives'
     reliance on a domesticity whose feminine representatives accept responsibility
     for preserving familial bonds and for submitting to the military destruction of
     those bonds. Bound as it is to what Hegel calls divine law, femininity both
     ensures the continuity of pacifist ideals and accedes to or assists in the
     downgrading of pacifism to weak utopianism. Freeman asserts, for example, that
     contemporary femininist pacifists who attempt to shift full responsibility for
     war to men or masculinity may merely participate 'in the framework that allows,
     indeed is indispensable to, the conflict in the first place', Femininity, even in its
     association with pacifism, remains 'the secondary term that copulates with ...
     and enables' masculinity (308).

11 Browning, the former 'poet laureate of Hope End', mockingly imagines herself
     laureate of England, 'cursing the Czar in Pindarics very prettily' (1898: 171),
     but she echoes Hemans in taking the national (and international) duties of
     womanhood seriously. An African American, Harper speaks as an internal enemy
     in poems such as 'Home, Sweet Home' or 'Do Not Cheer ...', but her 'Appeal

to My Countrywomen' challenges that stance's racial and political limits (1988: 185–6, 197–8, 193–5). Meynell, whose patriotic poetry was inspired by World War I, also appropriates and alters mournful patriotism, though for reasons different from those of the other poets named. See Baym 1992, on Sigourney.

12   In the hours before Waterloo, Mrs O'Dowd, in *Vanity Fair*, appears as a comic Venus outfitting her Mars, while Becky Sharp evinces 'quite a Spartan equanimity' (1987: 363, 365). Amelia, however, has no classical model. In spotless white, with a crimson sash bleeding down her breast, she embodies the new patriotic femininity of the Hegelian internal enemy: though she is useless to her husband for practical purposes, she embodies an innocent pain whose symbolic force is capable of driving him to remorse, to prayer – and to the battlefield (359–60, 371–2).

For a revealing (and hilarious) evocation of the mid-century association of Hemans with feminine patriotism and melancholy, see Thackeray 1855: 253–70.

13   Such a division must remain rough. It creates no clear space, for example, for the title character of 'The Sicilian Captive' (*'Records'* 172–9), who sings herself to death from homesickness, or for the shepherd-poet's sister, who leaves off pining at home to lead her people to battle ('The Shepherd-Poet of the Alps'; *Poetical Works* 485–7).

14   See the unsigned preface to the 1836 edition of Hemans's *Poetical Works* for early praise of her calmness (Preface vi). The anonymous preface to the 1854 *Poetical Works* contains a good mid-century example (Preface 3–8).

15   As Baym notes, nineteenth-century glorifications of feminine self-sacrifice could deny 'that women are submissive by nature and assert . . . that submission is the means by which a woman can overcome or at least check her chief adversary, God' (1978: 166). If destruction was inevitable, one could at least seize the sacrificial moment, positioning oneself as martyr rather than victim.

16   Revealingly, Hemans's celebrations of Welsh (and Scottish) patriotism all concern the past actions of men. 'Savage liberty' seems no longer required, especially of British women. See Lucas 1990 esp. 4–5, 16–17, on historical distancing from epic virtues in English poetry as a whole.

17   The significantly entitled 'The Spells of Home' (*'Records'* 286–8), for example, more or less generically associates the 'freeman' with 'the mountain-battles of his land'. Homesickness is a recurrent theme in Hemans's personal writing and verse. For a discussion of the 'tautological turn by which the domestic encapsulates nostalgia for itself', see Brown 1989: 288.

18   'Felicia Hemans' 75; 'Religious Character' 25–30. See also Browning's 'Felicia Hemans', which attempts to refute Letitia E. Landon's 'Stanzas'. Landon, whose readings of Hemans's melancholy could be ambiguous (1835: 428–32), offers her own bleak vision of life as war in 'The Battle Field'.

19   See Ross's revealing discussion of conflicts between familial and state values in 'The Siege of Valencia' (1989: 274–5).

20   In *Vanity Fair*, Thackeray provides a famous Victorian version of this stance (1987: 381, 385).

21 See Browning's opposing alignment of domestic and national virtues in the preface to *Poems before Congress*.

22 'If blood be the price of admiralty', sing the English dead in another of Kipling's verses, 'Lord God, we ha' bought it fair!' (1909: 11, 187).

23 'Der Todte, dessen Recht gekränkt ist, weiß darum für seine Rache Werkzeuge zu finden ... Diese Mächte sind andere Gemeinwesen ... Sie machen sich feindlich auf, und zerstören das Gemeinwesen, das seine Krafft, die Pietät der Familie, entehrt und zerbrochen hat' (Hegel 1990: 258; see also 1977: 287).

2

From *Patria* to *Matria*: Elizabeth Barrett Browning's Risorgimento

SANDRA M. GILBERT

Then Lady Reason . . . said, 'Get up, daughter! Without waiting any longer, let us go to the Field of Letters. There the City of Ladies will be founded on a flat and fertile plain . . .'

Christine de Pizan, *The Book of the City of Ladies* 16

Our lives are Swiss –
So still – so Cool –
Till some odd afternoon
The Alps neglect their Curtains
And we look farther on!

Italy stands the other side!
While like a guard between –
The solemn Alps –
The siren Alps
Forever intervene!

Emily Dickinson, no. 80

Our insight into this early, pre-Oedipus phase in the little girl's development comes to us as a surprise, comparable in another field with the discovery of the Minoan-Mycenaean civilization behind that of Greece.

Sigmund Freud, 'Female Sexuality' 195

And now I come, my Italy,
My own hills! Are you 'ware of me, my hills,

> How I burn toward you? do you feel to-night
> The urgency and yearning of my soul,
> As sleeping mothers feel the sucking babe
> And smile?
>
> *Aurora Leigh* 5.1266–71[1]

When in 1860 Elizabeth Barrett Browning published *Poems before Congress*, a frankly political collection of verses that was the culmination of her long commitment to Italy's arduous struggle for reunification, English critics excoriated her as unfeminine, even insane. 'To bless and not to curse is woman's function', wrote one reviewer, 'and if Mrs Browning, in her calmer moments, will but contrast the spirit which has prompted her to such melancholy aberrations with that which animated Florence Nightingale, she can hardly fail to derive a profitable lesson for the future' ('Poetic Aberrations' 494). Interestingly, however, the very first poem in the volume depicts Italy as a friendless, powerless, invalid woman, asking if it is '. . . true, – may it be spoken, – ' that she is finally alive

> . . . who has lain so still
> With a wound in her breast,
> And a flower in her hand,
> And a grave-stone under her head,
>   While every nation at will
> Beside her has dared to stand,
> And flout her with pity and scorn . . .
>
> ('Napoleon III in Italy' 111–18, *Poetical Works* 412)

Creating an ostensibly 'unfeminine' political polemic, Barrett Browning consciously or unconsciously seems to adopt the persona of a nurse at the bedside of an imperilled relative, almost as if she *were* a sort of literary-political Florence Nightingale. Putting aside all questions about the inherent femininity or unfemininity of political poetry, I will argue that this English expatriate's visions of *Italia Riuníta* had more to do with both her femaleness and her feminism than is usually supposed. In fact, where so magisterial a reader as Henry James believed that Barrett Browning's commitment to 'the cause of Italy' represented a letting down of 'her inspiration and her poetic pitch' (quoted by Markus, in *Casa Guidi Windows* xvi–xvii), I believe instead that, as Flavia Alaya has also observed, Italy became for a complex of reasons both the embodiment of this woman poet's inspiration and the most vivid strain in her 'poetic pitch'.[2]

Specifically, I will suggest that through her involvement with the revolutionary struggle for political identity that marked Italy's famous risorgimento, Barrett Browning enacted and reenacted her own personal and artistic struggle for identity, a risorgimento that was, like Italy's, both an insurrection and a resurrection. In addition, I will suggest that, by using metaphors of the healing and making whole of a wounded woman/land to articulate both the reality and fantasy of her own female/poetic revitalization, Barrett Browning figuratively located herself in a re-creative female poetic tradition that descends from Sappho and Christine de Pizan through the Brontës, Christina Rossetti, Margaret Fuller and Emily Dickinson to Renée Vivien, Charlotte Perkins Gilman, H.D. and Adrienne Rich. Infusing supposedly asexual poetics with the dreams and desires of a distinctively sexual politics, these women imagined nothing less than the transformation of *patria* into *matria* and thus the risorgimento of the lost community of women that Rossetti called the 'mother country' – the shadowy land, perhaps, that Freud identified with the mysterious 'Minoan-Mycenaean civilization behind that of Greece'. In resurrecting the *matria*, moreover, these women fantasized resurrecting and restoring both the *madre*, the forgotten impossible dead mother, and the *matrice*, the originary womb or matrix, the mother-matter whose very memory, says Freud, is 'lost in a past so dim . . . so hard to resuscitate that it [seems to have] undergone some specially inexorable repression' ('Female Sexuality' 195).[3]

Not surprisingly, then, Barrett Browning begins her covertly political 1857 *Kunstlerroman, Aurora Leigh*, with a meditation on this lost mother, using imagery that dramatically foreshadows the figure with which the poet opens her overtly political *Poems before Congress*. Gazing at a portrait of her mother that was (significantly) painted after the woman's death, young Aurora sees the maternal image as embodying in turn all the patriarchal myths of femaleness – muse, Psyche, Medusa, Lamia; 'Ghost, fiend, and angel, fairy, witch, and sprite' (1.154). But most heartrendingly she sees her as 'our Lady of the Passion, stabbed with swords / Where the Babe sucked' (1.160–1): the only *maternal* image of the lost mother dissolves into the destroyed woman/country from *Poems before Congress*, 'who has lain so still, / With a wound in her breast' while 'every nation' has flouted her 'with pity and scorn'.[4]

Among eighteenth-, nineteenth- and early twentieth-century English and American writers, tropes of Italy proliferated like flowers in Fiesole, so much so that the country, as its nationalist leaders feared, would seem to have had no reality except as a metaphor. As far back as the sixteenth but especially in the late eighteenth century, English romancers had exploited what Kenneth Churchill calls 'the violence-incest-murder-prison paradigm of Gothic Italy' (66). More seriously, from Gibbon to Byron and Shelley to John Ruskin, George Eliot, Henry James, Edith Wharton and D. H.

Lawrence, English-speaking poets and novelists read the sunny, ruin-haunted Italian landscape as a symbolic text, a hieroglyph, or, perhaps more accurately, a palimpsest of western history, whose warring traces seemed to them to solidify in the stones of Venice and the bones of Rome. Shelley, for instance, reflecting on the ancient city where Keats died seeking health, sees it both as 'that high Capital, where kingly Death / Keeps his pale court in beauty and decay' and as 'the Paradise, / The grave, the city, and the wilderness' ('Adonais' 55–6, 433–4) – a place whose ruins, building on and contradicting one another, suggest the paradoxical simultaneity of the originary moment (paradise) and the fall from that moment (the grave), the invention of culture (the city) and the supervention of nature (the wilderness). In 'St Mark's Place', Samuel Rogers is less metaphysical, but he too elaborates a vision of Italy as text, asserting that 'Not a stone / In the broad pavement, but to him who has / An eye, an ear for the Inanimate World, / Tells of past ages' (301), and George Eliot develops a similar perception when she writes in *Middlemarch* of 'the gigantic broken revelations' of Rome (book 2, chapter 15). Finally, emphasizing the dialectic between culture and nature that, as Shelley also saw, underlies all such statements, Edith Wharton summarizes the point most simply: Italy, she writes, is 'that sophisticated landscape where the face of nature seems moulded by the passions and imaginings of man' (3).

Interestingly, however, as post-Renaissance Italy sank ever further into physical decay and political disarray, lapsing inexorably away from the grandeur that was imperial Rome and the glory that was fourteenth-century Florence, both native and tourist poets increasingly began to depict 'her' as a sort of fallen woman. In Byron's famous translation, for example, the seventeenth-century Florentine patriot Vincenzo da Filijaca imagines 'Italia' as a helpless naked seductress, while Byron himself writes of Venice as 'a sea Cybele' and Rome as the 'Lone mother of dead Empires', 'The Niobe of nations!' (*Childe Harold's Pilgrimage*, canto 4, stanzas 2, 78, 79).[5] Similarly, Ruskin, who sees Venice as 'the Paradise of cities', the positive of Shelley's more equivocal Rome, hints that 'her' charm lies in her seductive femininity (*Diaries* 1: 183, *Letters* 128), and the expatriate novelist Ouida writes of her adopted city that 'in Florence [the past is] like the gold from the sepulchres of the Aetruscan kings that shines on the breast of some fair living woman' (*Pascarel*, quoted in Churchill 163).[6] The trope of Italy or of one of 'her' city-states as a living, palpable, and often abandoned woman had become almost ubiquitous by the time Barrett Browning began to write her poems about the risorgimento, and of course it derived from a traditional grammatical convention that tends, at least in most Indo-European languages, to impute metaphorical femaleness to such diverse phenomena as countries, ships and hurricanes. As applied to Italy, however, this metaphor of gender was often so intensely felt that, most notably for women writers, it frequently evolved from figure to fantasy, from speculation to hallucination. This Italy as art object 'moulded by the passions and imaginings of man' becomes Italy as Galatea and, worse still, a Galatea seduced and betrayed by her creator,[7] while Italy as destroyed motherland becomes Italy as wounded mother, Madonna of the sorrows whose restored milk and honey might nourish errant children, and especially daughters, of all nations. Ultimately, then, such women writers as Christina Rossetti and Elizabeth Barrett Browning revise and revitalize the dead metaphor of gender that is their literary and linguistic inheritance, using it to transform Italy from a political state to a female state of mind, from a problematic country in Europe to the problem condition of femaleness. Redeeming and redeemed by Italy, they imagine redeeming and being redeemed by themselves.

More specifically, as artists like Rossetti and Barrett Browning (and Emily Dickinson after them) struggle to revive both the dead land of Italy and the dead metaphor of 'her' femaleness, they explore five increasingly complex but always interrelated definitions of this lost, fragmented woman-country: (1) Italy as a nurturing mother – a land that feeds, (2) Italy as an impassioned sister – a land that feels, (3) Italy as a home of art – a land that creates, (4) Italy as a magic paradise – a land that transforms or integrates, and (5) Italy as a dead, denied, and denying woman – a land that has been rejected or is rejecting.

Christina Rossetti's ostensibly religious lyric 'Mother Country' is the most visionary statement of the first definition, for in it this poet, who was (paradoxically enough) fully Italian only on her father's side, mourns her exclusion from a dreamlike, distinctively female Mediterranean queendom:

> Not mine own country
> But dearer far to me?
> Yet mine own country,
> If I may one day see
> Its spices and cedars
> Its gold and ivory.
>
> (245)

Glamorous, rich and giving, such a maternal paradise is opposed to *this* (implicitly patriarchal) country, in which 'All starve together, / All dwarfed and poor' (245), and the metaphorical climates of the two locales strongly suggest that the luxurious mother country is Italy while the impoverished fatherland – 'here' – is England. As if to support such an interpretation with matter-of-fact reportage, Elizabeth Barrett Browning writes countless letters from Pisa and Florence, praising the nurturing maternal land to which she has eloped with Robert Browning after her perilous escape from the gloomily patriarchal household at 50 Wimpole Street. Food, in particular, seems almost eerily ubiquitous. Barrett Browning never tires of describing great glowing oranges and luscious bunches of grapes; the Italian landscape itself appears largely edible, the scenery deliciously beautiful. As for 'real' meals, they continually materialize at her table as if by magic. In Florence, she reports that 'Dinner, "unordered", comes through the streets and spreads itself on our table, as hot as if we had smelt cutlets hours before', while more generally, in another letter, she observes that 'No little orphan on a house step but seems to inherit naturally his slice of watermelon and bunch of purple grapes' (*Letters* 1: 341, 343).[8]

This land that feeds is also a land that feels. As both a mother country and, again in Rossetti's words, a 'sister-land of Paradise' (377), female Italy neither contains nor condones the super-egoistic repressions that characterize patriarchal England. Literary visions of Italy had always emphasized the passion and sensuality of 'her' people, but where Renaissance playwrights and Gothic romancers had dramatized the stagey strangeness of violent Italians, women writers like Barrett Browning, Rossetti and later Dickinson wistfully set the natural emotiveness of this mother country against the icy artifice of the Victorian culture in which they had been brought up. Indeed, from Barrett Browning's Bianca in 'Bianca among the Nightingales', who freely expresses her fiery rage at the cold Englishwoman who has stolen her lover away (*Poetical Works* 428–30), to Rossetti's Enrica, who 'chill[s]' English-women with 'her liberal glow' and 'dwarf[s]' them 'by her ampler scale' (377–8), the women who represent Italy in women's writing increasingly seem like ennobled versions of *Jane Eyre*'s Bertha Mason Rochester: large, heated, dark, passionate foreigners who are wholly at ease – even at one – with the Vesuvius of female sexual creativity that Dickinson was later to find *un*easily 'at home' in her breast (no. 1705).

Together, in fact, such heroines as Barrett Browning's Bianca, her Laura Savio of 'Mother and Poet' (*Poetical Works* 446–8), and Rossetti's Enrica seem almost to propose an ontology of female power as it might be if all girls were not, in Rossetti's words, 'minted in the selfsame [English] mould' (377). That most of these women are in one way or another associated with a violent uprising against the authoritarian rule of Austria and the patriarchal law of the pope, with Enrica (according to William Michael Rossetti) based on a woman who knew both Mazzini and Garibaldi, further cements their connections with Brontë's rebellious Bertha, but with a Bertha revised and transformed so that she, the alien, is free, and English Jane is trapped. As if to demonstrate this point, Christina Rossetti was 'en route' to Italy ('Italy, Io Ti Saluto') when she imagined herself as 'an "immurata" sister' helplessly complaining that

Men work and think, but women feel,
And so (for I'm a woman, I)
And so I should be glad to die,
And cease from impotence of zeal . . .

(380)

For, as Barrett Browning (and Charlotte Brontë) also knew, that 'Italian' speech of feeling was only 'half familiar' and almost wholly inaccessible to Englishwomen.

What made the inaccessibility of such speech especially poignant for poets like Rossetti and Barrett Browning, besides Italy's role as a feeding, feeling mother-sister, was 'her' special status as the home, even the womb, of European art; this mother-sister became a muse whose shapes and sounds seemed to constitute a kind of primal aesthetic language from which no writer should allow herself to be separated. In Florence, Barrett Browning imgines that she is not only in a city that makes art, she is in a city that *is* art, so much so that, as in some Edenic dream, the solid real and the artful unreal merge uncannily: 'The river rushes through the midst of its palaces like a crystal arrow, and it is hard to tell . . . whether those churches . . . and people walking, in the water or out of the water, are the real . . . people, and churches' (*Letters* 1: 332). That the art of Florence is almost entirely male — Michelangelo's monuments of unageing intellect, Ghiberti's doors — appears oddly irrelevant, for living in Florence Barrett Browning begins to believe, if only briefly, that she might live in, even inherit, this art; insofar as art is Italy's and Italy might be her lost and reclaimed self, art itself might at last be her own.

In allowing herself such a dream, the author of *Aurora Leigh* was tacitly acknowledging the influence of a foremother she greatly admired, Mme de Staël, whose *Corinne ou l'Italie* was 'an immortal book' that, said Barrett Browning, 'deserves to be read three score and ten times — that is, once every year in the age of man' (*Elizabeth Barrett* 176). For not only is *Corinne*, in the words of Ellen Moers, 'a guidebook to Italy', it is specifically a guidebook to an Italy that is the nurturing *matria* of a 'woman of genius', the enchanting *improvisatrice* Corinne, whose brilliant career provided a paradigm of female artistry for countless nineteenth-century literary women on both sides of the Atlantic.[9] Like Aurora Leigh, Staël's poetic heroine is the daughter of an Italian mother and an English father, and, like Barrett Browning herself, she transforms the Italy dominated by relics of such great men as Michelangelo and Ghiberti into a land of free women, a female aesthetic utopia. Corinne herself, writes Staël, is 'l'image de notre belle Italie' (book 2, chapter 2, 50). Triumphing as she improvises on the theme of Italy's glory, dances a dramatic tarantella, and translates *Romeo and Juliet* into 'sa langue maternelle' (book 7, chapter 2, 183), Corinne becomes not only a symbol of redemptive Italy but also a redemptive emblem of the power of symbolization itself, for, observes Staël, 'tout étoit langage pour elle' (book 6, chapter 1, 141). No wonder, then, that Barrett Browning, *Corinne*'s admirer, seems secretly to imagine an Italian heaven of invention whose speech constitutes a different, mystically potent language, a mother tongue: as if to balance Rossetti's remark that 'our [English] tongue grew sweeter in [Enrica's] mouth', she writes wistfully of the way in which 'the Tuscan musical / Vowels . . . round themselves as if they planned / Eternities of separate sweetness' (*Casa Guidi Windows* 1.1188–90).

Such a sense that even Italian speech encompasses 'eternities of . . . sweetness' inevitably translates itself into a larger vision of Italy as earthly paradise, a vision that brings us back to the 'green golden strand' of Rossetti's mother country and the vehement '*Italy*' of Dickinson's 'Our lives are Swiss – '. In this fourth incarnation, however, Italy is not just a nurturing mother country, she is a utopian motherland whose glamour transforms all who cross her borders, empowering women, ennobling men, and – most significantly – annihilating national and sexual differences. Describing the hopeful celebration of Florentine freedom that miraculously took place on the Brownings' first wedding anniversary in 1847, Barrett Browning writes about a jubilant parade: 'class after class' took part, and 'Then too, came the foreigners, there was a place for them' (*CGW* 66). She notes that 'the people were *embracing* for joy' (*CGW* 66) and expressing 'the sort of gladness in which women may mingle and be glad too' (*CGW* 67). In this setting, both sexes and all nationalities become part of the newer, higher nationality of Florence, so that expatriation turns, magically, into expatriotism. Less mystically and more amusingly, Virginia Woolf makes a similar point about Italy as utopia in *Flush*, her biography of the Brownings' dog. Arriving in Pisa, this pedigreed spaniel discovers that 'though dogs abounded, there were no ranks; all – could it be possible? – were mongrels.' At last inhabiting a classless society, he becomes 'daily more and more democratic . . . All dogs were his brothers. He had no need of a chain in this new world' (75, 78–9).

Finally, however, as Rossetti's 'Mother Country', 'Enrica', and 'An "Immurata" Sister' suggest, women writers from Barrett Browning to Dickinson are forced to admit that the nurturing, utopian, artful, feelingful, female land of Italy is not their own. Bred in what Barrett Browning and, after her, Rossetti call 'the rigid North', such writers are forever spiritually if not physically excluded from 'the sweet South', forever alienated from Italy's utopian redemption, if only by symbolic windows like those of Casa Guidi, which mark Barrett Browning's estrangement from Florence's moment of regeneration even while they allow the poet to view the spectacle of that rebirth.[10] As the poets make this admission, maternal Italy, guarded by the intervention of the 'solemn Alps' and 'the bitter sea', lapses back into the negated and negating woman whose image opens both *Poems before Congress* and *Aurora Leigh*. Dead, she is denied and denying: as Aurora leaves for England, her mother country seems 'Like one in anger drawing back her skirts / Which suppliants catch at' (1.234–5), and Christina Rossetti, exclaiming 'Farewell, land of love, Italy, / Sister-land of Paradise', summarizes the mingled regret and reproach with which these English daughters respond to the drastic loss such denial enforces:

> Wherefore art thou strange, and not my mother?
> Thou hast stolen my heart and broken it:
> Would that I might call thy sons 'My brother',
>   Call thy daughters 'Sister sweet';
> Lying in thy lap, not in another,
>   Dying at thy feet.
>
> ('En Route', *Works* 377)

For Rossetti, the despair these lines express becomes a characteristic gesture of resignation; the mother country is not to be found, not in this world at any rate, and so she immures herself in the convent of her soul, for 'Why should I seek and never find / That something which I have not had?' (380). For Barrett Browning, however, the struggle to revive and re-approach, rather than reproach, the lost mother country of Italy becomes the narrative project to which she devotes her two major long poems, *Casa Guidi Windows* (1851) and *Aurora Leigh*.

Though explicitly (and successfully) a political poem that meditates on two carefully defined historical occasions, *Casa Guidi Windows* is also a preliminary working through of important psychological materials that had long haunted Barrett Browning; as such, it is a crucial preface to the poet's more frankly confessional *Aurora Leigh*. To be specific: even while Barrett Browning comments in part 1 on the exuberant 1847 demonstration with which the Italian and 'foreign' citizens of Florence thanked Duke Leopold II for granting them the right to form a militia, and even while she mourns in part 2 the temporary failure of the risorgimento when in 1849 the Austrians defeated the Italians at Novara, she tells a more covert story – the story of Italy's and her own seduction and betrayal by the brutality, indifference and greed of patriarchal history. From this betrayal, this fall into the power of powers not her own, Italy/Barrett Browning must regenerate herself, and she can only do this, the poet's metaphors imply, through a strategic deployment of female, especially maternal, energies. By delivering her children both to death (as soldiers) and life (as heirs), she can deliver herself into the community of nations where she belongs.

For Barrett Browning this plot had distinctively personal overtones. 'After what broke [her] heart at Torquay' – the drowning of her beloved alter ego 'Bro' – she herself, as she later told her friend Mrs Martin, had lived for years 'on the outside of my own life . . . as completely dead to hope . . . as if I had my face against a grave . . .' (*Letters* 1: 288). Immuring herself in her room at 50 Wimpole Street, she had entrusted her future entirely to the will and whim of her notoriously tyrannical father, so much so that, as she also told Mrs Martin, employing a strikingly political metaphor, 'God knows . . . how utterly I had abdicated myself . . . Even my poetry . . . was a thing on the outside of me . . . [a] desolate state it was, which I look back now to [as] one would look to one's graveclothes, if one had been clothed in them by mistake during a trance' (*Letters* 1: 288). Clearly, in some sense, the drowning of the younger brother who was Barrett Browning's only real reader in the family and for whose death she blamed herself, caused a self-alienation so deep that, like Emily Brontë's Catherine Earnshaw Linton mourning the absence of *her* male alter ego, Heathcliff, she felt the world turn to 'a mighty stranger'. Invalid and isolated, she herself became a figure like Italy in part 1 of *Casa Guidi Windows*, who

> Long trammeled with the purple of her youth
> Against her age's ripe activity,
> Sits still upon her tombs, without death's ruth,
> But also without life's brave energy.

(171–4)

Yet just as the Italy of *Casa Guidi Windows*, part 1, trusts 'fathers' like Leopold II and Pio Nono to deliver 'her' from her living death, Barrett Browning expected her father to care enough to cure her illness; and just as Italy is duped by 'her' faith in these patriarchs, Barrett Browning was deceived by her faith in her father, who refused to send her south (significantly, to Italy) for her health, so that she was 'wounded to the bottom of my heart – cast off when I was ready to cling to him' (*Letters* 1: 291). But the plot thickens as the poet quickens, for, again, just as in Barrett Browning's own life a risorgimento came both from another younger brother figure – Robert Browning – and from the female deliverance of motherhood, so, in *Casa Guidi Windows*, promises of resurrection are offered wounded Italy both by the hope of a sturdy male leader who will 'teach, lead, strike fire into the masses' and by the promise of 'young children lifted high on parent souls', children whose innocence, fostered by maternal grace, may unfold 'mighty meanings' (2.769, 741).

Given the personal politics embedded in this story, it is no wonder that
Barrett Browning prefaces the first edition of *Casa Guidi Windows* with an
'advertisement' in which she takes especially intense 'shame upon herself that
she believed, like a woman, some royal oaths'; that in part 2 she reproaches
herself for her 'woman's fault / That ever [she] believed [Duke Leopold] was
true' (64–5); and that she also asks 'what woman or child will count [Pio
Nono] true?' (523). It is no wonder, either, that, in aligning herself with the
revolutionary cause of Italy, Barrett Browning aligns herself against the
strictures and structures of her fatherland, England, whose 'close, stifling,
corrupt system', like her imprisoning room in Wimpole Street, 'gives no air
nor scope for healthy . . . organization' (*Letters* 2: 190), a country for which
'nothing will do . . . but a good revolution' (*Letters* 2: 193). As magisterial
and patriarchal as Edward Moulton Barrett, England has 'No help for women,
sobbing out of sight / Because men made the laws' and 'no tender utterance
. . . For poor Italia, baffled by mischance' (*CGW* 2.638–9, 649–51). What is
more remarkable in *Casa Guidi Windows*, however, and what more directly
foreshadows the Italian dream of *Aurora Leigh* is the way in which Barrett
Browning, dreaming behind the mediation of her windows, imagines Italy
ultimately redeemed by the voices and visions of mothers and children: part
1 begins, after all, with 'a little child . . . who not long had been / By
mother's finger steadied on his feet' (11–12), singing '*O bella libertà, O bella*',
and part 2 ends with the poet's 'own young Florentine, not two years old',
her 'blue-eyed prophet', transforming society with a clear, unmediated gaze
not unlike Wordsworth's 'eye among the blind'. In between these epiphanies,
Miriam the prophetess appears, clashing her 'cymbals to surprise / The sun'
(1.314–16), and Garibaldi's wife outfaces 'the whistling shot and hissing
waves, / Until she [feels] her little babe unborn / recoil within her'
(2.679–83).

But what is finally perhaps most remarkable and, as Julia Markus points
out, 'most daring' about *Casa Guidi Windows* is the way in which, as Barrett
Browning meditates on the plight of wounded 'Italia', the poet finally
presents herself, against the weight of all the literary history she dutifully
recounts throughout the work, as 'the singer of the new day':

> And I, a singer also, from my youth,
> Prefer to sing with those who are awake,
>   With birds, with babes, with men, who will not fear
> The baptism of the holy morning dew . . .
> . . . .
> Than join those old thin voices with my new . . .
>
> (1.155–62)

Crossing the Anglo-Italian frontier represented by Casa Guidi windows, Barrett Browning gains her strongest voice in Italy and regains, as we shall see, a vision of her strengthened self from and as Italy, for the female artistic triumph that this passage describes points directly to the triumphant risorgimento of the woman poet that *Aurora Leigh* enacts.

As its title indicates, *Aurora Leigh* is a mythic narrative about 'the baptism of the holy morning dew' that Barrett Browning proposed to sing in *Casa Guidi Windows*. But before she and her heroine can achieve such a sacrament or become true singers of 'the new day' and of the renewed *matria/matrice* that day implies, both must work through precisely the self-division that left 'Italia' (in *Casa Guidi Windows*) and Barrett Browning (in Wimpole Street) living 'on the outside' of their own lives. Significantly, therefore, the tale of the poet-heroine's risorgimento, which parallels the plot of the poet-author's own insurrection-resurrection, begins with a fragmentation of the self that is both symbolized and precipitated by a shattering of the nuclear family, a shattering that leads to a devastating analysis of that structure. Just as significantly, the story ends with a reconstitution of both self and family that provides a visionary new synthesis of the relationships among men, women and children.

As if to emphasize the larger political issue involved in these emotional dissolutions and resolutions, the heroine's self and family are defined by two *paysages moralisés*, her mother country of Italy and her fatherland of England, between which (although at one point Aurora claims that 'a poet's heart / Can swell to a pair of nationalities, / However ill-lodged in a woman's breast' [6.50–2]) she must ultimately choose. Both in its theatrical, sometimes hectically melodramatic plot, then, and in its intensely symbolic settings, *Aurora Leigh* continually reminds us that it is not only a versified *Kunstlerroman* which famously aims to specify the interaction between an artist and the particular 'full-veined, heaving, double-breasted Age' (5.217) that created her, it is also an 'unscrupulously epic' (5.215) allegory of a woman artist's journey from disease toward what Sylvia Plath once called 'a country far away as health' ('Tulips', *Ariel* 12).

Not surprisingly, given these geographical and dramatic imperatives, *Aurora Leigh* begins and ends in Italy, the lost redemptive land that must be redeemed in order for both poet-heroine and poet-author to achieve full selfhood. Here, in book 1, Aurora encounters and is symbolically rejected by her dead mother, 'a Florentine / Whose rare blue eyes were shut from seeing me / When scarcely I was four years old' (29–31), and here, even as she comes to terms with 'a mother-want about the world' (40), her father dies, leaving her suddenly awake 'To full life and life's needs' (208–10). While the mother seems irremediably gone, however, the father, 'an austere Englishman' (65), is quickly replaced by 'A stranger with authority' (224) who tears the child so abruptly from the land which has come to represent her mother that, watching 'my Italy', / Drawn backward from the shuddering steamer-deck, / Like one in anger drawing back her skirts' (232–4), she is uncertain whether the mother country has been rejected ('drawn back') or is rejecting ('drawing back').

This violent, neo-Wordsworthian fall into division from the mother and into 'my father's England', home of alien language and orphanhood, is followed by a more subtle but equally violent fall into gender. Arriving in patriarchal England at the crucial age of thirteen, Aurora discovers that she is a *girl*, destined to be brought up in 'A sort of cage-bird life' (1.305) by a new and different 'mother' – her 'father's sister', who is her 'mother's hater' (1.359–60), for 'Italy / Is one thing, England one' (1.626–7); inexorably parted, the two nations are irrevocable emblems of separation. Hence, as many feminist critics have pointed out, the girl is coerced into (at least on the surface) accepting a typical Victorian education in 'femininity', reading 'a score of books on womanhood / To prove, if women do not think at all, / They may teach thinking' (1.427–9), learning 'cross-stitch', and so forth. That she has 'relations in the Unseen' and in Nature, which romantically persist and from which she draws 'elemental nutriment and heat . . . as a babe sucks surely in the dark' (1.473–5), and that she darkly remembers 'My multitudinous mountains, sitting in / The magic circle, with the mutual touch / Electric . . . waiting for / Communion and commission' (1.622–6) – another striking image of the mother's nurturing breasts – are the only signs that somewhere in the shadows of her own psyche her mother country endures, despite the pseudo-oedipal wrenching she as undergone.

As Aurora grows into the fragmentation that seems to be (English) woman's lot, things go from bad to worse. Exiled from the undifferentiated unity of her mother country, the girl discovers that her parents have undergone an even more complicated set of metamorphoses than she at first realized, for not only has her true dead southern mother been replaced by a false and rigid northern stepmother – her 'father's sister' – but her true dead father, after being supplanted by 'a stranger with authority', has been replaced by a false and rigid northern stepfather, her cousin Romney Leigh, who, upon her father's death, has become the putative head of the family. To be sure, as Aurora's cousin, Romney has the potential for becoming a nurturing peer, an empowering 'Bro' rather than a debilitating patriarch. But certainly, when the narrative begins, he is a symbolic father whose self-satisfied right and reason represent the masculine 'head' that inexorably strives to humble the feminine 'heart'.

'I am not very fond of praising men by calling them *manly*; I hate and detest a masculine man', Barrett Browning told one correspondent (*Letters* 1: 134), and clearly by 'masculine' she did not mean 'virile' but 'authoritarian'. Yet such (implicitly patriarchal) authoritarianism is exactly what character- izes Romney Leigh at the cousins' first meeting, for his, says Aurora, was 'The stranger's touch that took my father's place / Yet dared seem soft' (1.545–6), and she adds 'A godlike nature his' (1.533). That Aurora has evidently been destined to marry this man makes the point even more clearly. Drawn away from the natural lore and lure of the mother, she has been surrendered to what Lacan calls the law of the father, inscribed into a patrilineal kinship system where she is to be doubly named by the father, both as daughter-Leigh and as wife-Leigh, just as Elizabeth herself was originally named Elizabeth Barrett Barrett. That Romney refuses to read her poetry, claiming that her book has 'witchcraft in it' (2.77), clarifies the point still further. Her work is either 'mere' or 'magical' 'woman's work' (2.234) because she exists 'as the complement / Of his sex merely' (2.435–6), an (albeit precious) object of exchange in a network of marital transactions that must by definition deprive her not only of her autonomy but, more importantly, of her desire.

Nevertheless, Aurora insists on continuing to transcribe the texts of her desire, poems whose energy is significantly associated with her inner life, her 'relations in the Unseen', and her mother country. At the same time, because she has been exiled in her fatherland, she must inevitably write these works in her father tongue. Inevitably, therefore, because she is struggling to find a place in traditions created by that masculine (and masculinist) language, she must study her father's books. Creeping through the patriarchal attic 'Like some small nimble mouse between the ribs / Of a mastodon' (1.838–9), she finds a room 'Piled high with cases in my father's name' (1.835) and 'nibbles' fiercely but randomly at what amounts to a paradigmatic library of western culture. Most inevitably, however, this furtive self-education, which both parallels and subverts her aunt's effort to educate her in 'femininity', leads to further self-division. She can and does reject both Romney's offer of marriage and the financial legacy he tries with magisterial generosity to bestow on her, but once she has internalized – nibbled, devoured – the texts that incarnate patriarchal history, she is helplessly implicated in that history, so that even her 'own' poetry is tainted, fragmented, impure.

How, then, is Aurora to rectify and clarify both her art and her self? Barrett Browning's 'unscrupulous' epic seeks to resolve this crucial issue, and perhaps paradoxically, the author begins her curative task by examining the ways in which her other major characters are just as fragmented and self- alienated as her heroine. To start, for instance, she shows that, despite (or perhaps because of) his super-egoistic calm, Romney too is self-divided. This 'head of the family', she quickly suggests, is no more than a 'head', abstractly and, as his abortive wedding to Marian Erle will prove, ineffectually espoused to 'social theory' (2.410). In fact, he is not just a false father because he has replaced Aurora's 'true' father, he is a false father because, as Barrett Browning decided after her long imprisonment in Wimpole Street, all fathers are in some sense false. Indeed, the very idea of fatherhood, with its implications of social hierarchy and psychic fragmentation ('man with the head, woman with the heart' [Tennyson, *The Princess* 5.439]), is dangerously divisive, not only for women but for men. As a brother like her own 'Bro', Romney might be able to 'read' (and thus symbolically unite with) the texts of female desire that transcribe Aurora's otherness, but as a father he is irremediably blind to them. As a brother, moreover, he might more literally unite himself to the social as well as sexual others from whom his birth and breeding separate him, but as a father or 'head', he is, again, hopelessly estranged from most members of the 'body' politic.

That Romney craves a union with both social and sexual others is, however, a sign that, like Aurora, he is half consciously struggling toward a psychic reunification which will constitute as much of a risorgimento for him as it will for her. His ill-fated and 'mis-conceived' proposal to Aurora suggests his intuition of his own need even while the fact that she 'translates' him 'ill' emphasizes the impossibility of communion or communication between them. In addition, his eagerness to go 'hand in hand' with her among 'the arena-heaps / Of headless bodies' (2.380–1) till, through her 'touch', the 'formless, nameless trunk of every man / Shall seem to wear a head with hair you know, / And every woman catch your mother's face' (2.388–90) implies that, at least metaphorically, he understands the self-division that afflicts both him and his cousin, even while Aurora's reply that since her mother's death she has not seen 'So much love . . . / As answers even to make a marriage with / In this cold land of England' (2.398–400) once again outlines the geography of 'mother-want' in which both characters are situated. Similarly, his subsequent plan to 'take [a] wife / Directly from the people' (4.368–9) reveals once more his yearning to heal in his own person the wounds of the body politic, even while Aurora's recognition that his scheme is both artificial and divisive, 'built up as walls are, brick by brick' (4.353), predicts the project's failure. For Romney, who feels himself 'fallen on days' when marriages can be likened to 'galley-couplings' (4.334), redemption must come not from the outward ceremony of marriage but from an inward metamorphosis that will transform him from (false) father to (true) brother, from (false) 'god' to (true) groom.

Despite its misguided formulation, however, Romney's impulse to wed Marian Erle does begin the crucial process of metamorphosis, for this 'daughter of the people' (3.806), an 'Erle' elf of nature rather than an 'earl' of patriarchy, has a history that parallels his and Aurora's history of fragmenta-

tion at the same time that she is an essential part of the reunified family/
being he and Aurora must become.[12] Ignored and emotionally abandoned by
a drunken father who beat her and a bruised mother who tried to prostitute
her to a local squire, this 'outcast child . . . Learnt early to cry low, and walk
alone' (3.874–7). Her proletarian education in alienation offers a darkly
parodic version of Aurora's bourgeois education in femininity. Reading the
'wicked book' of patriarchal reality (3.952) with the same fervour that
inspired Aurora's studies of her father's patriarchal texts, Marian imagines a
'skyey father and mother both in one' (3.899) just as Aurora imagines
inscribing her desire for her motherland in her father's tongue. Finally, too
the shriek of pain Marian utters when her mother tries to sell her to the
squire – 'God, free me from my mother . . . / These mothers are too dreadful'
(3.1063–4) – echoes and amplifies Aurora's impassioned protest against the
'Keeper's voice' (2.561) of the stepmother-aunt, who tells her that she has
been 'promised' to her cousin Romney: 'I must help myself / And am alone
from henceforth' (2.807–8). Repudiating the false mothers of patriarchal
England both these literally or figuratively orphaned daughters cry out, each
in her own way, the intensity of the 'mother-want' that will eventually unite
them, along with Romney and with Marian's child, in the motherland of
Italy, where each will become a nurturing mother country to the other.

When Marian and Aurora first meet, however, both are stranded in the
alienating cityscape of nineteenth-century London, where each lives in an
attic that seems to symbolize her isolation from world and self alike. Though
Aurora has ostensibly become a successful poet, her ambition continually
reminds her of her failure, since it constantly confronts her with fragmented
verses whose 'heart' is 'Just an embryo's heart / Which never yet had beat'
(3.247–8), while Marian, though her 'heart . . . swelled so big / It seemed to
fill her body' (3.1083–5), lives up a 'long, steep, narrow stair, 'twixt broken
rail / And mildewed wall' (3.791–2). Parts of a scattered self – the one
heartless, the other too great-hearted – this pair of doubles must be unified
like the distant and dissonant city-states of Italy, and ultimately, of course,
the two are brought together by Romney's various though similar desires for
them. To begin with, however, they are united by the visits of yet another
potential wife of Romney's – Lady Waldemar – to their parallel attics.

Voluptuous and vicious, the figure of Lady Waldemar offers a further
comment on nineteenth-century ideals of 'femininity'. In fact, as we shall
see, she is the (false) wife/mother whose love the (false) father must reject if
he is to convert himself into a (true) brother. At the same time, though, her
beckoning sexuality both initiates and instigates the 'plot' proper of *Aurora
Leigh*, emblematizing a fall into heterosexual desire with which Aurora and
Marian must variously struggle before they can become whole. Almost at
once, Aurora perceives this fashionable aristocrat as a male-created, socially

defined 'lady' – 'brilliant stuff, / And out of nature' (3.357–8) – a perception Lady Waldemar's name reinforces with its reminiscences of generations of Danish kings. But even while Aurora defines her as 'out of nature' in the sense that she is an antinatural being, a cultural artifact, this 'fair fine' lady defines herself as being 'out of nature' in the sense that she is *from* nature, nature's emissary. For, confessing that she has 'caught' love 'in the vulgar way' (3.466), Lady Waldemar instructs the poet-heroine that 'you eat of love, / And do as vile a thing as if you ate / Of garlic' (3.450–2) since 'love's coarse, nature's coarse' (3.455). Two books later, when she reappears at a party Aurora attends, the very image of Lady Waldemar's body reiterates her 'natural' sexuality. Gorgeously seductive, 'the woman looked immortal', (5.618), her bare breasts splitting her 'amaranth velvet-bodice down / To the waist, or nearly, with the audacious press / Of full-breathed beauty' (5.622–4).

As emblems of nurturing maternity, breasts have obsessed both author and heroine throughout *Aurora Leigh*, but this is the first time their erotic potential is (quite literally) revealed, and tellingly the revelation is associated with Aurora's growing sense of artistic and sexual isolation: 'Must I work in vain, / Without the approbation of a man?' (5.62–3); with her confession of 'hunger . . . for man's love' (5.498); and, most strikingly, with her feeling that her 'loose long hair [has begun] to burn and creep, / Alive to the very ends, about my knees' (5.1126–7). Furthermore, Lady Waldemar's eroticism is associated with – indeed, causes – Marian's betrayal into sexuality, a betrayal that leads to both a 'murder' and a rebirth, while Aurora's mingled fear of and fascination with Lady Waldemar's erotic presence finally drive the poet back to her motherland of Italy, where she is ultimately to be reunited with both Marian and Romney. In fact, what have often been seen as the awkward or melodramatic turns of plot through which Barrett Browning brings these three characters back together in a sort of Florentine paradise are really important dramatic strategies by which the author herself was trying to work out (and out of) the 'problem' of female sexuality by first confronting the engendered world as it is and then reengendering and reconstituting it as it should be.

Trusting the duplicitous Lady Waldemar, who 'wrapped' the girl in her arms and, ironically enough, let her 'dream a moment how it feels / To have a real mother' (6.1001–3), Marian is treacherously brought to France by the servant of this false 'mother', placed in a brothel where she is drugged and raped, and thereby sold into sexual slavery – a deed that, as Marian herself notes, was 'only what my mother would have done' (7.8–9). At the same time, Aurora – missing her 'woodland sister, sweet maid Marian' (5.109), and convinced that Romney is about to marry the 'Lamia-woman', Lady Waldemar (7.152) – finally decides to return to the Italy that she had long heard 'crying through my life, / [with the] piercing silence of ecstatic graves' (5.1193–4). Not coincidentally, she plans to finance her trip by selling the 'residue / Of my father's books' (5.1217–18), a crucial first step in what is to be a definitive renunciation of the power of the fatherland. Her journey to the mother country, however, is impelled as much by desire as by denial, for, in the passage I have used as an epigraph to this essay, she 'burns' toward her 'own hills' and imagines that they desirously reciprocate her 'yearning . . . As sleeping mothers feel the sucking babe / And smile' (5.1268–71). Thus, when en route she encounters the lost Marian in a Paris flower market, she begins the process of reunification that will regenerate both these wounded daughters. For the 'fallen' Marian, whose face haunts Aurora like the face of a 'dead woman', has become a mother whose assertion of what J. J. Bachofen was later in the century to call 'mother right' – 'I claim my mother-dues / By law' – proposes an empowering alternative to 'the law which now is paramount', the 'common' patriarchal 'law, by which the poor and weak / Are trodden underfoot by vicious men, / And loathed for ever after by the good' (6.665–9). Becoming such a powerful figure, moreover, she has become a creative authority whose maternal eroticism speeds the two women toward the unfallen garden of female sexuality that they will plant in the richly flowering earth of Florence. There Marian's 'unfathered' child will 'not miss a . . . father', since he will have 'two mothers' (7.124), there Aurora will set Marian like a 'saint' and 'burn the lights of love' before her pure maternity (7.128), and there in a revision of her own eroticism, Aurora will exorcise the haunting vision of what she now comes to see as Lady Waldermar's distorted (Lamia-like) sexuality.

For when she returns to her motherland with Marian as her sister/self, Aurora returns transformed. No longer merely an aching outcast daughter crying her inchoate 'mother-want', she has become herself, symbolically at least, a mother, since she is one of the 'two mothers' of Marian's child. In addition, transformed into a hierophant of 'sweet holy Marian' (6.782), she has learned to devote herself to the specifically female theology of the Madonna, the Queen of Heaven whom the Florentine women worship and whose rituals facilitate Aurora's increasing self-knowledge. Finally, she has become a poet, an artist-heroine who can not only weep but word her desire, in a language that through her interaction with Marian she has begun to make into a mother tongue. In fact, as she learns some weeks after her arrival in Florence, people in England have finally begun to 'read' her. Her new book, writes her painter friend Vincent Carrington, 'Is eloquent as if you were not dumb' (7.553), and his fiancée, who has Aurora's verses 'by heart' more than she has her lover's words (7.603), has even insisted on having a portrait painted with 'Your last book folded in her dimpled hands / Instead of my brown palette as I wished' (7.607–8).

That Marian's child is 'unfathered' contributes in yet another way to the regenerative maternity both women now experience, for, after all, the baby is only figuratively unfathered; literally, he was fathered by some nameless customer in a brothel. To call him 'unfathered', therefore, is to stress the likeness of his mother, Marian, not only to the fallen woman Mary Magdalen but also to the blessed Virgin Mary, whose immaculate conception was the sign of a divine annunciation. That Barrett Browning surrounds Marian's maternity with the rhetoric of Mariolatry implies the theological force she wants to impute to this 'maiden' mother's female energy. As opposed to the often sentimentally redemptive power ascribed to such Victorian 'mothers' boys' as Gaetano (in Browning's *The Ring and the Book*), Leonard (in Mrs Gaskell's *Ruth*), or Paul Dombey (in Dickens's *Dombey and Son*), Marian's son has an austerely religious significance. Nameless but beautiful, he is hardly ever characterized as a real child might be. Rather, when Marian explains that, in her despair after her rape, 'I lived for him, and so he lives, / And so I know, by this time, God lives too' (7.112–13), the ambiguity of her language – does she believe that he is the 'God' who 'lives' or does his survival mean that 'God lives'? – argues that he is in some sense a divine child, a baby god whose sacred birth attests to the divinity of his mother. Thus, even while she revises the story of the annunciation to question the brutality of a male God who uses women merely as vessels for his own ends, Barrett Browning suggests that the female creativity 'holy' Marian and reverent Aurora share can transform the most heinous act of male sexual brutality, a rape, into a redemption. At the same time, by demonstrating the self-sufficient strength of Marian and Aurora's mutual maternity, she interrogates the idea that there is anything more than a momentary biological need for fathers or fatherhood.

It is noteworthy, then, that when she returns to Italy Aurora keeps reminding herself that she has returned to the land where her father is buried, the land of her mother's birth and her father's tomb, her 'father's house / Without his presence'. Though both her parents are buried near Florence, it is, curiously enough, evidence of only her father's disappearance that Aurora seeks and finds; when she revisits 'the little mountainhouse' where she had lived with him, she discovers that it has been effaced by female fertility symbols – 'lingots of ripe Indian corn / In tessellated order and device / Of golden patterns' (7.1124–6) – so that 'not a stone of wall' can be seen, and a black-eyed Tuscan girl sits plaiting straws in the doorway, as if forbidding entrance. While Aurora's mother lives on in the Italian mother-land, her father is as irretrievably dead as Marian's child's father is nonexistent.

But how are both Aurora and Barrett Browning to deal with the wished-for but unnerving fate of the dead father? Freud famously argued that anxiety about the murder of this mythic figure ultimately constituted a social order in which 'his' absent will was internalized as the superego that creates the law (see *Totem*, esp. 915–19). Barrett Browning, however, as if responding in advance to Freud's hypothesis, implicitly suggests that man as father must be exorcised rather than internalized and that, in a risorgimento of matriarchal law, he must be replaced with man as brother or man as son. For, unlike such a precursor as Christine de Pizan (in *City of Ladies*) or such a descendant as Charlotte Perkins Gilman (in *Herland*), Aurora does not envision an all-female paradise. Rather, she longs for a mother country or 'sisterland to Paradise' in which women *and* men can live together free of the rigid interventions and interdictions of the father.

Thus, even when she and Marian and Marian's child have been securely established in 'a house at Florence on the hill / Of Bellosguardo' (7.515–16), from which, like goddesses surveying past and future, they can see sunrise and sunset, 'morn and eve . . . magnified before us' (7.525–6) – a scene that recalls Marian's 'skyey father and mother both in one' – Aurora yearns obsessively for Romney. 'Like a tune that runs / I' the head' (7.960–1), the erotic longing for her cousin that was first signalled by the appearance of Lady Waldemar has made her, she admits at last, just what Lady Waldemar confessed herself – a 'slave to nature' (7.967). In addition, that longing reveals Aurora's radical sense of incompleteness, a feeling of self-divison which suggests that, for Barrett Browning as for her heroine, a *matria* without men might become madly and maddeningly maenadic. As she sinks into a sort of sexual fever, Aurora notes that even her beloved Florence 'seems to seethe / In this Medæan boil-pot of the sun' (7.901–2) and ruefully confesses that, in the absence of the consort whom she desires because his presence would complete the new configuration of humanity toward which she aspires, even her old 'Tuscan pleasures' seem 'worn and spoiled' (7.1041).

In endowing a woman named *Aurora Leigh* with such erotic feeling for a cousin whom she wishes to remake in the image of a brother, however, Barrett Browning must at least half consciously have understood that her wish to provide her protagonist with a fraternally understanding and erotically egalitarian lover might oblige her to risk retracing the outlines of the nineteenth century's most notorious brother-sister incest plot: Byron's affair with his half-sister, *Augusta Leigh*. Unlike such 'realistically' depicted sister-brother pairs as Tom and Maggie Tulliver in *The Mill on the Floss*, but like Romney and Aurora, Byron and Augusta rarely met until they were young adults, when both couples discovered and resisted similar mutual attractions. To be sure, the socially illicit Byronic duo made a far weaker effort at resistance than Barrett Browning's socially 'legitimate' pair of cousins. Nevertheless, what Leslie Marchand says of Byron and Augusta is equally true of Romney and Aurora: 'in their formative years they had escaped the rough familiarity of the brother-sister relationship', so that 'consanguinity', with all the equality it might imply for peers of the same generation, was 'balanced by the charm of strangeness' (1: 396). But Barrett Browning, who as a girl had dreamed of dressing in boy's clothes and running away to be Lord Byron's page, grew up to become, if not as censorious as her friend Carlyle was toward the hero of Missolonghi, at least ambivalent toward him. Even while insisting that her 'tendency' was 'not to cast off my old loves', she wrote that Byron's poems 'discovered not a heart, but the wound of a heart; not humanity, but disease' (for EBB's ambivalent feelings toward Byron, see Taplin 15, 103). In addition, she was close to both the 'wronged' Lady Byron's friend Anna Jameson and to Harriet Beecher Stowe, author of *Lady Byron Vindicated*, both of whom would have reminded her of the masculine exploitativeness involved in Byron's sexual exploits.

Simultaneously inspired and exasperated by the Byron story, therefore, Barrett Browning had to rewrite it to gain strength from it. Thus the seductive and antipoetic Augusta Leigh becomes the pure poet Aurora Leigh, and the morally corrupt but sexually devastating and romantically self-dramatizing Byron becomes the morally incorruptible but physically devastated and romantically diffident Romney. Furthermore, the sexual inequities implied by Byron's sordid secret affairs and by Romney's one-time authority as 'head' of the Leigh family are eradicated both by Aurora's purity and by her recently achieved matriarchal strength. Newly defined 'brother' and 'sister' can unite, and even unite erotically, because the Byron episode has been reenacted on a 'higher' plane, purged of social disorder and sexual disease.

The humbled Romney's arrival in Florence does, then, complete both the reconfiguration of the family and the regeneration of the motherland that poet-author and poet-heroine have undertaken. Blinded in a fire that recalls yet another famous nineteenth-century plot — the denouement of *Jane Eyre* — this former patriarch seems to have endured the same punishment that Brontë's Bertha dealt Rochester, although in personality Romney is closer to Jane Eyre's austere cousin St John Rivers than to that heroine's extravagant 'master'. Significantly, however, Barrett Browning — who seems vigorously to have repressed her memory of the *Jane Eyre* episode, no doubt so she could more freely revise it — swerved from Brontë in having Romney's injury inflicted not by a mad wife but by a bad father; William Erle, the tramp and poacher who began his career of destructiveness by bruising and abusing his daughter, Marian. Women do not need to destroy the fatherland, Barrett Browning implies by this revision, because it will self-destruct. Again, Barrett Browning swerves from Brontë in allowing her disinherited patriarch to rescue one item from the house of his fathers — a portrait of the lady from whom Aurora inherited her mouth and chin. A woman, she implies by this revision, may be an inheritor. In the end, therefore, as Romney describes 'the great charred circle' where his ancestral mansion once stood with its 'one stone stair, symbolic of my life, / Ascending, winding, leading up to nought' (8.1034–5), his saving of the picture suggests also that the power of the Leighs has not been destroyed but instead transferred to 'a fairy bride from Italy' (9.766), who has now become the true heir and 'head' of the family.

That Aurora has successfully become a 'head' of the family, the figure both Romney's father, *Vane* Leigh, and Romney himself only vainly strove to be, is made clearest by her blinded cousin's revelation that he has at last really read and recognized her work. Seeing through and because of his blindness, like wounded father figures from Oedipus and Gloucester to Rochester, Romney receives and perceives Aurora's prophetic message – 'in this last book, / You showed me something separate from yourself, / Beyond you, and I bore to take it in / And let it draw me' (8.605–8) – and that message, 'Presented by your voice and verse the way / To take them clearest' (8.612–13), elevates her to the 'dearest light of souls, / Which rul'st for evermore both day and night!' (9.831–2). Finally too, therefore, he has become, as both 'Bro' and Robert Browning were for Barrett Browning herself, a 'purely' attentive brother-reader who can at last comprehend the revisionary mother tongue in which the woman poet speaks and writes. It is no coincidence, surely, that Barrett Browning has Aurora, who never before associated Romney with the ocean, envision her lost lover as arising from beneath the bitter waters that had engulfed her lost brother and standing before her like a 'sea-king' while 'the sound of waters' echoes in her ears (8.59–60).[14] Deciphering the texts of Aurora's desire, Romney has accomplished his own transformation into an ex-patriarch who entrusts himself and his sister-bride to the 'one central Heart' (9.890) of love that may ultimately unify all humanity by eradicating the hierarchies and inequities of patriarchy. At the same time, emigrating from the rigid north of the Leighs to the warm south ruled by his 'Italy of women' (8.358), he has become both an expatriate and an ex-patriot, a dweller in the new *matria* where, in a visionary role reversal, the empowered Aurora will 'work for two' and he, her consort and cohort, 'for two, shall love' (9.911, 912).

Romney's violent metamorphosis reminds us of Barrett Browning's implicit belief that, as in *Casa Guidi Windows* (where the poet advocates the self-sacrifice of Italian men), only the devastation of the fatherland can enable the risorgimento of the mother country.[15] Both Marian and Aurora too, however, have experienced violent metamorphoses, Marian literally, in the rape she describes as a 'murder', and Aurora figuratively, in her passionate struggle to come to terms with the eroticism Lady Waldemar incarnates and with the murderous rage 'the Lamia-woman' evokes. Now, though, after all this violence, these characters are brought together in a symbolically reunified family of brother/husband and sister/wife and mother and son. Is Aurora the

dawn in which Marian and Romney can be reborn? Is Marian the womb that
gives new life to Aurora's and Romney's light? Is Romney the lover who can
read their new roles rightly in the 'bittersweet' darkness of his visionary
blindness? Is Marian's child the redemptive son whose coming signals a new
day? There is certainly a temptation to define each member of this prophetic
quartet allegorically. But even without stipulating meanings that the epic
'unscrupulously' leaves in shadow, it is clear that in its final wholeness this
newly holy family integrates what the writer called 'Philosophical Thought'
with what she called 'Poetical Thought' and unifies both with the powerful
dyad of mother and child, womb and womb fruit (see 'A Thought on
Thoughts', *Complete Works* 6: 352–9). Eastering in Italy, moreover, these four
redeemed beings begin to make possible the 'new day' that their author
imagined in, for, and through the country she chose as her *matria*. For among
themselves they constitute – to go back to the qualities women writers have
sought in Italy – a land that feels, that feeds, that makes art, and that
unmakes hierarchies. In mythologizing them as she does, Barrett Browning
sets against the exhaustion of belatedness that she thought afflicted contem-
porary (male) poets 'who scorn to touch [our age] with a finger tip' a
matriarchal future that she hoped would be sacramentally signalled by 'the
holy baptism of the morning dew'.

In its ecstatic delineation of a female risorgimento, the redemption of Italy
that Barrett Browning began to imagine in *Casa Guidi Windows* and fully
figured in *Aurora Leigh* was both predictable and precarious. Given the long
history of Italy as a literary topos, together with the country's personal
association for this woman poet, it is not surprising that that embattled
nation would come to incarnate both a mother's desire for *bella libertà* and a
daughter's desire to resurrect the lost and wounded mother. Certainly Barrett
Browning's American contemporary Margaret Fuller imagined the country
in a similar way. 'Italy has been glorious to me', she wrote Emerson in 1847,
explaining that her expatriate experience had given her 'the full benefit of [a]
vision' of rebirth 'into a state where my young life should not be prematurely
taxed'. In an 1848 dispatch to the *Tribune*, she added that in Rome 'the sun
and moon shine as if paradise were already re-established on earth. I go to
one of the villas to dream it is so, beneath the pale light of the stars' (quoted
in Chevigny 435, 453).

Part of this visionary passion no doubt arose from Fuller's revitalizing and
egalitarian romance with Angelo Ossoli, in whom, as one observer put it, she
loved 'an imagined possibility in the Italian character' much as Aurora, in
loving Romney (and Elizabeth Barrett, in loving Robert Browning), loved
'an imagined possibility' in the English character.[16] At the same time,
however, Fuller's dream of an Italian paradise was not just energized by her

hope for a utopian future that the risorgimento might make possible; it was also shaped by her sense that behind Italy's 'official' history of popes and patriarchs lay another history, the record of a utopian, and specifically matriarchal, past. Visiting 'an Etrurian tomb' in 1847, she noted that 'the effect . . . was beyond my expectations; in it were several female figures, very dignified and calm . . . [whose] expression . . . shows that the position of women in these states was noble.' Later, passing through Bologna, she remarked that 'a woman should love' that city 'for there has the spark of intellect in woman been cherished with reverent care', and she made similar points about Milan, as well as, more generally, about the Italian 'reverence to the Madonna and innumerable female saints, who, if like St. Teresa, they had intellect as well as piety, became counsellors no less than comforters to the spirit of men' (Chevigny 427–8).

But in particular Fuller's analysis of Etruscan tomb paintings, like the novelist Ouida's apparently casual likening of Florence's past to 'gold from the sepulchres of the Aetruscan kings . . . on the breast of some fair living woman', should remind us that as early as the 1840s, in just the years when both Fuller and Barrett Browning were imagining the risorgimento of an Italian *matria*, the Swiss jurist J. J. Bachofen was visiting Etruscan tombs outside Rome, where his discovery of a painting depicting 'three mystery eggs' led him to speculate that in 'Dionysian religion . . . the supreme law governing the transient world as a *fatum* [is] inherent in feminine matter' and that 'the phallic god striving toward the fertilization of matter' stands merely 'as a son' to 'the maternal womb' (28–9). This speculation, published only two years after *Aurora Leigh* in Bachofen's 1859 *Essay on Mortuary Symbolism*, led in turn to the even more radical hypotheses of his *Mother Right* (1861), in which he presented the first strong argument that matriarchy was the primordial form of social organization.

In visiting, studying and 'reading' Etruscan tombs (as Freud too would do some fifty years and D. H. Lawrence some eighty years later), Bachofen was in one sense 'reading' the palimpsest of Italy the way travellers like Shelley, Rogers and Ruskin did in the archaeological metaphors I quoted earlier. Unlike them, however, and like both Fuller and Barrett Browning, he was 'reading' beyond or beneath the patriarchal history western tourists had always expected to find among the ruins of Rome and the monuments of Florence and interpreting his reading as Freud did his reading of the 'Minoan-Mycenaean' age. Thus Bachofen too was preparing at least his female audience to resurrect the old lineaments of a 'new, near Day' (*Aurora Leigh* 9.956) just as the newly matriarchal Aurora does at the end of Barrett Browning's epic when, in a revisionary swerve from Shelley and Ruskin, Barrett Browning has her 'read' an Italian sunrise for Romney in the language of Apocalypse: 'Jasper first . . . And second, sapphire; third, chalcedony; / The rest in order:

– last, an amethyst' (9.962–4). Through such revisionary readings, moreover, both writers (along with Fuller) were preparing the way for such a descendant as H.D.: her *Tribute to Freud* ends with a reading of Goethe's 'Kennst du das Land', the German poet's vision of Italy as sister land to paradise, a vision that makes the American modernist think of 'the *Ca d'Oro*, the Golden House on the Grand Canal in Venice . . . the *domus aurea* of the Laurentian litany' (111). That it was Goethe who sought also to understand the *Ewige Weibliche* and whose injunction to 'go down to the Mothers' deeply influenced Bachofen (see *Faust* 2.1.6215–21) would have surely given extra richness to the regenerated Italy of his (and H.D.'s) 'Land wo die Zitronen blühn . . .'. Guarded by siren mountains and a bridge of clouds, as Emily Dickinson also believed, the regenerated *matria* of Italy stands 'on the other side' of patriarchal history.

Yet both Goethe's poem and H.D.'s *Tribute* end with Mignon's equivocal plea: 'o Vater, lass uns ziehn!' For both the female poet and her German precursor, the journey to the magic land can only be accomplished with the guidance of the father. If he permits, the *matria* will be revealed; if not, the Alps and clouds, emblems of despair as well as desire, must, in Dickinson's words, 'forever intervene'. Similarly, Barrett Browning's visions of female regeneration are subtly qualified, for even while the plots and characters of *Aurora Leigh* and *Casa Guidi Windows* propose matriarchal apocalypses, the poet acknowledges that such consummations, though devoutly wished, require (in this world) male cooperation – Romney's abdication, the sacrifices of Italian men – and (in heaven) the grace of God the Father, who, with masculine wisdom, will build into 'blank interstices' (*CGW* 2.776) and 'make all new' (*AL* 9.949). By the time she wrote *Poems before Congress*, Barrett Browning's quasi-feminist vision had darkened even further. In just the poem whose image of Italy as an invalid woman echoes and illuminates Aurora's vision of her dead mother as 'Our Lady of the Passion, stabbed with swords', the author imagines the redemption of her *matria* by, and only by, the grace of the French ruler Louis Napoleon, whose feats of male military bravery will make him 'Emperor/Evermore'. And, in fact, Italy's risorgimento was finally achieved only by the manoeuvres of traditionally masculine 'heroes' like Louis Napoleon, Mazzini, Garibaldi, Victor Emmanuel, Charles Albert, and – most of all – the Machiavellian statesman Cavour.[18] Thus the specifically matriarchal risorgimento of *Aurora Leigh* is ultimately almost as momentary and provisional as the brief hopeful revelation of the 'mercy Seat' behind the 'Vail' that ends *Casa Guidi Windows*. For inevitably the reality of patriarchal history, with its successes and successions, obliterated Barrett Browning's implicit but impossible dream of a *matria*.

Though Barrett Browning was disturbed by the unfavourable comparison one English reviewer made between her and Florence Nightingale, then, she might have sympathized with the view that unfairly stereotyped 'lady with a lamp' expressed in a book the author of *Aurora Leigh* probably never read. As if commenting on the marriage of true minds Barrett Browning's epic envisions at its close, Nightingale argued in *Cassandra* (written in 1852 and privately printed in 1860) that 'the true marriage – that noble union, by which a man and woman become together the one perfect being – probably does not exist at present upon earth' (44). Indeed, this woman, whose Christian name – Florence – was intended to honour the very city in which Barrett Browning found a modicum of *bella libertà* and who hoped that the 'next Christ' might be, like the redemptive Aurora, a 'female Christ', used a specifically Italian metaphor to describe the enchained reality of nineteenth-century woman: 'She is like the Archangel Michael as he stands upon Saint Angelo at Rome. She has an immense provision of wings . . . but when she tries to use them, she is petrified into stone' (50).

Perhaps, given the power and pressure of history, a woman who is 'nobody in the somewhere of patriarchy' can only, as Susan Gubar has observed, be 'somebody in the nowhere of utopia' (140), for even a land like Italy, with all the metaphorical possibilities that give it strength as a matriarchal topos, is inextricably part of the larger topos of European time. As such, it is a text whose usefulness to women can be countered by masculinist rereadings that redeem it for both the father and the phallus. Even Bachofen, the theorist of matriarchy, was to argue that 'mother right' must historically be transformed and transcended by 'father right', and sixty years after Barrett Browning imagined Italy as a *matria*, D. H. Lawrence claimed the land as a metaphorical *patria*, asserting that 'To the Italian the phallus is the symbol of individual creative immortality, to each man his own Godhead' (44). Even the word *matria*, moreover, which I have used throughout this essay to describe the visionary country sought by women like Fuller, Rossetti, Barrett Browning and Dickinson, is nonexistent. The real Italian word for 'motherland' is *madrepatria*, a word whose literal meaning – 'mother-fatherland' – preserves an inexorably patriarchal etymology. In Italian linguistic reality there is no matriarchal equivalent to patriarchal power: one can only imagine such an antithetical power in the 'nowhere' of a newly made vocabulary.

It is no wonder, then, that Barrett Browning appointed Louis Napoleon 'Emperor/Evermore' and that in the last poem she ever wrote, entitled 'The North and the South', she came full circle back to Aurora's self-divided beginnings, admitting the dependence of the matriarchal south on the patriarchal language of the rigid north. While the north sighs for the skies of the south 'that are softer and higher', the south sighs 'For a poet's tongue of baptismal flame, / To call the tree or the flower by its name!' (*Poetical Works* 450).[19] Though she had enacted and examined a vision of female redemption far more radical than any Rossetti had allowed herself to explore, Barrett Browning would have conceded that, along with Rossetti, she was chained like Nightingale's angel to the rock of patriarchal Rome, and, along with Rossetti, she finally had to bid farewell to the Italy both had dreamed might be a sister land to paradise. As Christine de Pizan and Charlotte Perkins Gilman knew, in the world as it is the City of Ladies can only be built on 'the Field of Letters'.

NOTES

1   All the quotations from *Aurora Leigh* in this essay come from the edition introduced by Cora Kaplan. All references to *Casa Guidi Windows* are to the edition by Julia Markus.
   I am deeply grateful to Elliot Gilbert for critical insights that have been helpful throughout this essay. In addition, I am grateful to Susan Gubar and Dorothy Mermin for useful comments and suggestions. Finally, I want to thank my mother, Angela Mortola, for inspiring me to think about Italy. This paper is dedicated to her, with love.

2   In a brilliant essay on the Brownings and Italian politics, Flavia Alaya notes the connections among the regeneration of Aurora Leigh, the reunification of Italy, and EBB's personal sense of rebirth after her flight with Browning from England to Italy. But Alaya's study emphasizes the literary dialectic between two major poets who were, as she puts it, 'quite literally political bedfellows', for she shows through a close reading of *The Ring and the Book* how Browning's Pompilia constitutes a re-vision of both Elizabeth and Italy, so that the husband's complex set of dramatic monologues is in some sense a response to the wife's earlier, apparently more naive and personal epic of a heroine's risorgimento. In addition, through close readings of Barrett Browning's letters and some of her poems, Alaya vigorously defines and defends this woman poet's often misunderstood (and frequently scorned) political stance.

3   Though Alaya sees Browning/Romney as the 'father' of Elizabeth/Aurora's reborn self, an opinion I disagree with, she does also suggest that 'a mother-quest played a much more dominant role in [Barrett Browning's] psychic life' than is usually thought (1978: 30, n. 18).

4   For a discussion of Aurora's vision of her mother's portrait, see Gilbert and Gubar 1979: 18–20.

5   Alaya also discusses this pervasive trope of Italy as a tragic woman and the political function of the image in the risorgimento (1978: 14–16).

6   Significantly, Ruskin describes the way the pillars of the porches of San Marco 'half-refuse and half yield to the sunshine, Cleopatra-like, 'their bluest veins to kiss' . . . (1955: 128).

7   For a discussion of woman as Galatea, see Gilbert and Gubar 1979: 12–13.

8   Elsewhere, Barrett Browning remarks that '[we] can dine our favourite way . . .

with a miraculous cheapness . . . the prophet Elijah or the lilies of the field took as little thought for their dining, which exactly suits us' (1899: 1, 303).

9   For an extraordinarily useful analysis of *Corinne*'s significance to nineteenth-century women writers, and especially to EBB, see Moers 1976: 173–210. On *Corinne*'s Italy as a 'land of women', see Gutwirth 1978: 208–15 and Peel 1982: esp. 34–64. I am grateful to Ellen Peel for sharing this material with me.

10 For 'the rigid North', see 'Enrica' and *Casa Guidi Windows* 1.1173; it is possible, even likely, that Rossetti borrowed the phrase from Barrett Browning. For 'the sweet South', see Rossetti's 'Italia, Io Ti Saluto', 378–9.

11 Until recently, few critics have dealt directly with *Aurora Leigh*; major modern writers on the subject include Virginia Woolf, '*Aurora Leigh*'; Ellen Moers, esp. 201–7; Helen Cooper; Cora Kaplan, introd., *Aurora Leigh*; Barbara Gelpi; Virginia Steinmetz; and Dolores Rosenblum.

12 The name Marian Erle evokes Goethe's 'Erlkönig', the uncanny and elfish forest spirit who is a manifestation of nature rather than of culture.

13 See Kaplan 1978: 23–4, in *Aurora Leigh*. Dorothy Mermin has pointed out to me the resemblances between Romney Leigh and St John Rivers, a likeness Taplin also takes up (316–17). Interestingly, as Romney becomes more like Rochester, he also becomes, in a sense, more Byronic; at the same time, however, his kinship to St John Rivers mutes (and thus makes acceptable) his Byronic qualities.

14 Immersed in Browning's very name is a wordplay on 'Bro's' fate: 'Browning' suggests a conflation of 'Bro' and 'drowning'.

15 See *Casa Guidi Windows* 2.399–405:

> I love no peace which is not fellowship,
>   And which includes not mercy. I would have
> Rather, the raking of the guns across
>   The world, and shrieks against Heaven's architrave;
> Rather the struggle in the slippery fosse
>   Of dying men and horses, and the wave
>   Blood-bubbling . . .

16 Chevigny ascribes this comment to W. H. Hurlbut, who thought Ossoli an 'underdeveloped and uninteresting Italian' (1976: 375). In any case, the parallels between Barrett Browning and Fuller are interesting. Although Barrett Browning makes Romney older than Aurora, both Ossoli and Browning were considerably younger than their mates, as though Fuller and Barrett Browning had each half-consciously decided that in a utopian rearrangement of the relationship between the sexes men should be younger than their wives in order symbolically to free women from the bonds of daughterhood. In addition, both Fuller and Barrett Browning, quite late in life and rather unexpectedly, had children in Italy, and the private experience of maternity may well have reinforced their mutual hopes for a public experience of matriarchy.

17 As Susan Gubar has pointed out to me, the conclusion of George Eliot's *Romola*

(1863) imagines a kind of private matriarchy secretly existing behind the patriarchal facade of fifteenth-century Florence.

18   As Chevigny notes, Fuller's experiences during the risorgimento were marked by similar – and more dramatically personal – ambiguities, for motherhood simultaneously empowered and weakened her. While Ossoli was fighting in Rome, she was in Rieti, absorbed in child care, and 'in their letters [during this period] they came near assuming conventional sex roles' (385).

19   It is interesting that she wrote this poem to honour a literary man, Hans Christian Andersen, who had produced such visions of redemptive (but self-renouncing) femaleness as 'The Snow Queen' and 'The Little Mermaid'.

3

The Embodied Muse: Elizabeth Barrett Browning's *Aurora Leigh* and Feminist Poetics

Joyce Zonana

At the conclusion of her 'unscrupulously epic' feminist poem *Aurora Leigh*, Elizabeth Barrett Browning offers a striking image of a woman artist who is simultaneously poet and muse. Empowered by her acknowledgement of her love for her cousin Romney, the poem's narrator-heroine, Aurora Leigh, dictates to her blind lover words that constitute a vision of the New Jerusalem only she can actually see. From the terrace of her Italian tower, she looks out towards the east, where

> Beyond the circle of the conscious hills,
> Were laid in jasper-stone as clear as glass
> The first foundations of that new, near Day
> Which should be builded out of heaven to God.
>
> (9, 954–7)[1]

Like the Muses whom Hesiod reports having met on Helikon, Aurora has heavenly knowledge, even as she stands on a 'promontory of earth' (9.847). The blind man, listening to her, sees with 'inscient vision' (9.913). As he asks Aurora to 'breathe thy fine keen breath along the brass' (9.931), Romney calls to mind both ancient and modern examples of the inspired blind poet, listening to the divine song of a muse: Homer, Demodokos, Thamyris, Milton. Aurora simultaneously sees, names, and is the dawn for this man who has asked her to 'fulfil' (9.910) his inadequacy:

'Jasper first,' I said;
'And second, sapphire; third, chalcedony;
The rest in order: – last, an amethyst.'

(9.962–4)

Aurora here takes her place as a triumphant goddess, embodying through her
words the promise of her name, conclusively demonstrating that the woman
artist can both see and sing, by her own eyes inspired.

While Barrett Browning's figuring of Aurora as muse seems unmistakable,
none of the many fine, recent feminist readings of the poem has even
considered this possibility. Instead, critics interested in Browning's treatment
of inspiration have argued either that the blind Romney is Aurora's male
muse, 'both infant son and father/lover', or that Marian Erle, 'the unmention-
able, fallen other woman of Victorian society', is a female sister or mother
muse.[2] These readings suggest that, as a female poet, Barrett Browning
challenges partriarchal poetry's vision of the muse as the passive female object
of the active male poet's quest, but they do not consider that she might
question the more basic – and equally patriarchal – premise that the muse
must be external and other to the poet, the 'object' of a quest. To believe
that the muse must be an objectified other is to ignore not simply the claims
of numerous feminist critics and poets but the words of Aurora herself, who
insists that 'life develops from within' (2.485) and who throughout the poem
emphasizes the importance of internal inspiration and urges an abolition of
the subject/object dichotomy.[3] One might argue that to figure the muse as
other is simply to project an internal aspect of the self, but, as I shall hope to
show below, even this seemingly innocent form of self-division is contrary to
Aurora's theology and aesthetic.

Among the critics who have taken Romney to be Aurora's male muse,
Helen Cooper has offered the most subtle analysis, arguing that Aurora must
first overcome Romney's inhibiting gaze, the gaze of the 'composite precursor'
who can silence and objectify the woman poet seeking to claim and speak her
own subjectivity. Cooper views Marian as the instrument of Aurora's
transformation into a poet who reconciles being a woman with being an
artist, and she suggests that Marian's child serves as a transitional muse for
Aurora, who becomes empowered as she assumes a maternal rather than a
daughterly relation to her inspiration. Because Romney, after his blinding,
'becomes dependent on Aurora . . . as a young child, dependent on his
mother', he too can become a positive muse, even while he continues to
function as 'father/lover', an 'authoritative prescursor' who recalls the 'blind
Milton writing of the old Eden' (187).

Cooper recognizes (and even insists on) the parallel between Romney and
the blind Milton; yet she claims it is Romney who is the muse, although it

clearly is Aurora who dictates words to him. Cooper criticizes one aspect of Harold Bloom's model of poet, muse and precursor poet engaged in a 'triangular oedipal struggle' when she argues that the 'preoedipal figuration between parent and infant' may be a more appropriate model for Barrett Browning's (and other poets') construction of the muse (187). Yet she seems uncritically to accept Bloom's psychosexual model of gender and creativity: if a male poet depends on a female muse, then a female poet must depend on a male muse; or, in Jungian terms, if a male must draw on his anima for creativity to flourish, then a female must turn to her animus, discovering what Barbara Gelpi has called the 'man within'.[4]

Angela Leighton avoids the patriarchal (and heterosexist) presumptions of Jungian anima-animus psychology when she persuasively argues that Aurora, after her 'emancipation' from 'the long shadow of the father muse' (140), takes the female Marian to be her liberating sister muse of 'contemporaneity and commitment' (154). Leighton's argument is compelling, even exhilarating, particularly when she suggests that Aurora's mature voice no longer speaks a 'poetics of the daughter, but of the woman' who daringly allies herself with her fallen sister (154). But Leighton stops just short of an even more emancipatory vision of female poetic authority: that the poet finds her voice within herself, that the muse as well as the poet is liberated from her status as object to become a fully empowered subject.

If Aurora's identification with Marian is to be the radically feminist act Leighton (I think correctly) takes it to be, then Marian must cease to be an object to Aurora. And if she is the muse, then she must be a new kind of muse, one who is fully integrated with the poet, a subject in her own right. Aurora moves from her rediscovery of Marian in Paris to her discovery of her self in Italy. Marian helps her along her path, for she is, as Leighton, Cooper, Rosenblum and others have shown, an essential mirror in Aurora's process of self-discovery. But it is trivializing Marian to see her only as an 'instrument' of Aurora's growth. If Marian teaches anything to Aurora, it is that all individuals must be perceived as subjects, never as objects in other people's social schemes or literary representations. Thus, in the final pages of the poem, Marian vanishes from the narrative, for Barrett Browning refuses to place her in any position in relation to Aurora. Aurora must speak her own truth, affirming – and naming – a muse (the dawn) who is nothing less than her very self.

The reluctance of feminist critics to read *Aurora Leigh*'s concluding lines as a portrayal of Aurora as muse is understandable. To regard the female poet as a muse appears to be a denial of her subjectivity, a negation of her quest to be a poet rather than the object or inspirer of male poetry.[5] Yet such conclusions are necessary only if we are confined to the traditional, Christian and patriarchal, conception of the 'heavenly' – and 'otherly' – female muse. We might be persuaded otherwise if we could see that Elizabeth Barrett

Browning began the process (which has perhaps reached its apex in the recent work of Mary Daly) of reclaiming the muse as a powerful image of female divinity, creativity and sexuality – for women as well as for men.[6] Aurora is an earthly not a heavenly muse: what enables her to function as a muse is her full subjectivity, her radical embodiment, her complete acceptance of herself as woman and artist. Elizabeth Barrett Browning abandons the idealization and objectification of the female that have been a part of the western tradition of the muse since the overlay of Christian neoplatonism on ancient Greek myth, offering instead a corporeal muse who has 'herself a sort of heart' (9.27).[7] Aurora is not a transcendent, disembodied, heavenly figure who can only be apprehended by a poet who has closed his senses to earthly temptations and distractions. Nor is she a Victorian Angel in the House, the nineteenth century's version of Milton's Urania. Instead, she is an immanent, embodied, earthly woman who teaches that the only 'way' to heaven is through a complete valuation of 'the despised poor earth, / The healthy, odorous earth' (9.652–3).

The proper conceptualization and function of both poet and muse is a focus of much of Barrett Browning's poem. Beginning with Aurora's celebrated analysis of her mother's portrait, the term 'Muse' is introduced early in book 1, and it recurs throughout the poem, reminding us that we are in an epic environment where one might legitimately expect to encounter muses. As Hesiod had observed in the *Theogony*, at the opening of the western tradition of epic, the Muses had instructed him 'always to put [them] at the beginning and end of my singing', and so most male poets had complied.[8] But in Barrett Browning's 'unscrupulously epic' work (5.214), the poet and the reader must learn to 'let go conventions' (1.852). Aurora meditates:

> What form is best for poems? Let me think
> Of forms less, and the external. Trust the spirit,
> As sovran nature does, to make the form;
> For otherwise we only imprison spirit
> And not embody.
>
> (5.223–7)

Aurora may refer to the Muses but only in ways that will 'embody' rather than 'imprison' her poetic spirit.

Thus there are no explicit invocations to the muse in the poem. At the outset of her nine-book epic, Aurora begins with a brash self-confidence: 'I . . . / Will write my story', she proclaims, 'for my better self' (1.2–4). She has no need for a muse because she is writing of what she knows; muses had primarily functioned as guarantors of poetic truth for poets writing about historical or cosmic subjects for which they required authoritative witnesses. Milton places his trust in a muse that 'from the first / Wast present'; Homer appeals to muses who 'know all things'; and Virgil calls on goddesses who 'remember' and 'can tell'.[9] In contrast to these epic singers, Aurora is her own authority, and she places herself at the beginning and end of her epic. In doing so, she goes even further than her recent precursor Wordsworth in a romantic revision of classical tradition, for Wordsworth, also writing an autobiographical epic, nevertheless maintained his dependence on the 'correspondent breeze' in *The Prelude*, and in his 'Prospectus' to the *Excursion* he called on a muse 'greater' than Milton's Urania.

In another contrast with her male predecessors, particularly in the English tradition, Aurora is content to sing from a vantage point on earth. Not only does she not require an external muse for authoritative knowledge, she also does not ask to fly or be raised as both Milton and Wordsworth had requested. Rather, she deliberately insists that to write effectively and authentically, she must stand – or at times even lie – on the earth.

Aurora's full acceptance of her position as an earthly singer comes late in the poem. At first, following the patriarchal tradition she has imbibed in her father's books, she envisages inspiration as elevation and transcendence of the senses, imagining that Zeus's eagle has ravished her

> Away from all the shepherds, sheep, and dogs,
> And set me in the Olympian roar and round
> Of luminous faces for a cup-bearer.
>
> (1.92–3)

A moment later, however, she 'drop[s] the golden cup at Herè's foot' and 'swoon[s]' back to earth, where she finds herself 'face-down among the pine-cones, cold with dew' (1.929–31). Eventually Aurora will not have to fall but will choose to lie among the pine-cones.

Aurora's vision of inspired flight recalls Eve's dream in *Paradise Lost*; she has moved up to the realm of the gods too quickly, failing to recognize what Romney will later emphasize:

> 'You need the lower life to stand upon
> In order to reach up unto that higher;
> And none can stand a-tiptoe in the place
> He cannot stand in with two stable feet.'
>
> (4.1207–10)

Or, as Aurora herself puts it,

> No perfect artist is developed here
> From any imperfect woman. Flower from root,
> And spiritual from natural, grade by grade
> In all our life. A handful of the earth
> To make God's image!
>
> > (9.648–52)

Heaven is to be gained not by abandoning but by embracing earth. As Milton expressed it in *Paradise Lost*, humans can only 'put on' divinity through a full acceptance of their mortal limits. Yet while this is the thematic import of the action in *Paradise Lost*, the epic narrator needs to soar, 'upheld' by Urania, in order to report that truth properly. In contrast, Aurora moves closer to the earth, deeper into her own embodied spirit, as her poem articulates its own transforming truth, 'which, fully recognized, would change the world / And shift its morals' (7.856–7).

Before considering some aspects of the process by which Aurora arrives at the full knowledge of her 'truth' and her muse, it may be helpful to examine briefly some of the central tenets of her philosophy and their implications for her poetics. Most simply stated, Aurora's mature message, presented in book 7 of the poem, is that 'a twofold world / Must go to a perfect cosmos' (7.762–3). The material and spiritual worlds are so intimately and necessarily intertwined, she claims, that 'who separates those two / In art, in morals or the social drift, / Tears up the bond of nature and brings death' (7.764–6). For Aurora, it is the division of spirit and flesh, not disobedience to Reason or God, that constitutes the Fall, bringing death into this world. As she states, to 'divide / This apple of life' – 'The perfect round which fitted Venus' hand' – is to destroy it 'utterly as if we ate / Both halves' (7.769–73).

Aurora condemns both those who value only spirit and those who believe that only the material is real. Yet while the world is twofold, spirit and flesh inextricably intermingled, epistemologically and developmentally the material is primary. One cannot apprehend spirit except through flesh. Thus, the artist 'holds firmly by the natural, to reach / The spiritual beyond it' (7.779–80). And hence Aurora's epic will be grounded in the 'natural' world of the poet's life; she will tell a story of contemporary experience, and she will rely on highly concrete 'woman's figures' (8.1131) to communicate her twofold truth that

> Without the spiritual, observe,
> The natural's impossible – no form,
> No motion: without sensuous, spiritual
> Is inappreciable, – no beauty or power.
>
> > (7.773–6)

That an embodied, visible muse will preside over the work of a poet with such a message and such a technique should not surprise the reader.

Aurora's conviction of the 'twofold man' living in 'this twofold sphere' (7.777) is rooted in a typological, Christian perception of the cosmos. As she says, 'nothing in the world comes single' (7.804); all things are 'patterns of what shall be in the Mount' (7.806). Or, even more explicitly, she insists that the artist 'fixes still / The type with mortal vision, to pierce through, / With eyes immortal, to the antitype' (7.780–2). Yet Aurora goes much further than her contemporaries in her application of typology. She uses it to challenge the traditional Christian mind-body dualism, to overturn the view of woman's flesh as evil, and to criticize Miltonic hierarchy and division. In the end, she sounds far more like a twentieth-century feminist or ecologist than a Victorian divine.[11]

In the passage that functions as the centrepiece of the exposition of her aesthetics, Aurora explains that the truth that 'would change the world' is a constant awareness of 'the spiritual significance burn[ing] through / The hieroglyphic of material shows' (7.860–1). If the artist's audience could perceive this, then each individual would

> paint the globe with wings,
> And reverence fish and fowl, the bull, the tree,
> And even his very body as a man –
> Which now he counts so vile, that all the towns
> Make offal of their daughters for its use . . .
>
> (7.862–6)

With these strong words, Aurora makes plain her profound valuation of the earth, the natural world, the human body, and especially the female body. She points to the abuse of women and argues that it is the result of a failure to see spirit in matter; she dramatically concludes her meditation on art with an image of woman treated as 'offal'. This, then, is the 'death', the rift in the 'bond of nature' that makes God 'sad in heaven' (7.867) and that her work is intended to correct. Again the reader can see why, to communicate this truth, she would choose a female muse who dwells on the earth and who demonstrates in herself the infusion of all body with spirit.

Early in her life, before she turns to poetry as a compensation for her loss, Aurora does have an experience of such an earthly female muse. This muse is her mother, a woman who is consistently characterized in terms that evoke the traditional muses even as they insist on her physical embodiment. When the father first encounters the mother in Italy he is 'transfigur[ed] . . . to music' (1.89) by her face, which 'flashed like a cymbal on his face' (1.87). Shaken with 'silent clangor' (1.88), the father 'throw[s] off the old conventions' (1.177) of his 'provisioned and complacent' (1.69) English past, entering into a deep, transforming love. The words and images Aurora uses to characterize her mother's effect on her father recur later in the poem, applied to poetry and to the poet. When she first encounters poetry, Aurora's soul 'let[s] go conventions' (1.852). Choosing to be a poet, she compares herself to the Biblical Miriam, touching cymbals (2.175); when Romney has finally come to hear her song, he calls her 'My Miriam' (8.334). And, as I shall show more extensively below, Aurora paradoxically chooses a form of 'silence' as the most evocative and significant of her 'songs'.

Aurora's mother dies while her child is still young, and so Aurora is denied the permanent experience of this earthly muse who 'might have steadied the uneasy breath, / And reconciled and fraternized my soul / With the new order' (1.37–9). Instead, she is left with a portrait of the dead mother, a portrait in which she finds:

> Ghost, fiend, and angel, fairy, witch, and sprite,
> A dauntless Muse who eyes a dreadful Fate,
> A loving Psyche who loses sight of Love,
> A still Medusa with mild milky brows
> All curdled and all clothed upon with snakes
> Whose slime falls fast as sweat will; or anon
> Our Lady of the Passion, stabbed with swords
> Where the Babe sucked; or Lamia in her first
> Moonlighted pallor, ere she shrunk and blinked
> And shuddering wriggled down to the unclean;
> Or my own mother . . .

> (1.154–64)

In her childhood experience of the portrait, Aurora sees how the apparently competing images of woman as heavenly and earthly cohere; she notes that the face, though coloured by varying perspectives, 'did not therefore change, / But kept the mystic level of all forms, / Hates, fears, and admirations' (1.151–3). Thus, although a nineteenth-century critic found the passage to be a 'perfect shoal of mangled and pompous similes', and twentieth-century critics read the passage as a representation of 'male-defined masks and costumes', Aurora as a child does not have difficulty accepting the complex of images.[12]

The images of womanhood that Aurora finds in her mother's portrait are of course the traditional, highly bifurcated images of western patriarchal literature – as Aurora herself acknowledges. Yet these images serve as appropriate characterizations of the mother and function to define the possibilities of womanhood for Aurora; the mistake she makes is not that she accepts these 'male-defined' images but that she believes they cannot coexist in one being. For, indeed, a truly 'twofold' woman or muse will include in herself all the characteristics of womanhood, positive and negative, heavenly and earthly, male-defined and female-identified. Aurora is correct to see that her mother contains Lamia, Medusa, Madonna and Psyche. To the sister-in-law in England, Aurora's aunt, the mother was a seductive and dangerous, fleshly Lamia, taking her brother away from his duty. Like 'Our Lady of the Passion', the mother was 'stabbed with swords / Where the Babe sucked': 'the mother's rapture slew her' (1.35). In death, she 'petrifies' both husband and daughter, and, as a model of a 'loving Psyche', she causes Aurora, identifying herself as pure spirit, temporarily to lose 'sight of Love'.

Although as a child Aurora uses her mother's portrait to hold together competing visions of woman, as she matures she learns the lessons of her culture and begins to split the once-coherent image, projecting its various fragments on to the different women in her life. She suffers a double loss of her mother: first in life then in imagination. But in her nine-book poem of self-portrayal, Aurora undergoes a healing gestation, giving birth anew to the mother with whom she can finally identify herself. In recreating her mother in herself, Aurora becomes a fully embodied, earthly muse. But first she must experience division and disembodiment, becoming what her culture has called 'heavenly'.

Beginning with the garden scene in book 2, Aurora identifies herself as a disembodied, spiritual muse or Psyche, teaching truths to a world led astray by materialism. Though she rejects Romney's attempts to make her into the Angel in his House, she becomes an angel all the same – the Angel in the House of poetry. While Romney, with what he later calls 'male ferocious impudence' (8.328), insists on the importance of attending to mankind's material needs, Aurora aligns herself with a purely spiritual principle, the Victorian poet's 'feminine ideal'. As E. L. Bryans was to put it some fifteen years later, the Victorians believed that women more than men possess 'natural gifts particularly adapted' for the production of poetry: pity and love, and the capability of 'dwelling on the unseen'.[13] It is not so much 'unfeminine' to be a poet as it is 'unmasculine'; in choosing to be a poet, Aurora does not so much challenge her century's gender rules as confirm them.

Thus, though Helen Cooper has argued that after book 2 Aurora imagines herself as male, I would claim rather that she continues to see herself as a woman, but as a disembodied, spiritual woman – the 'heavenly' female whose guises include the Christian muse and the Victorian angel. Cooper believes that because Romney scorns women's poetry, Aurora, to maintain her identity as poet, must redefine herself as male. Cooper reads Aurora's quest in the second half of her poem as the reclaiming of her female identity. Aurora, however, never abandons her female identity; she simply focuses on one aspect of the female (or any human) self – the spiritual. Her quest is to reclaim the material as an integral aspect of her already female, 'heavenly' being.

Romney in the garden does not simply argue against 'woman's verses' (2.831); he questions the value of any commitment, poetic or feminine, to spiritual truths. He insists that his allegiance as a man is to the earth and to other men:

> 'But I, I sympathize with man, not God
> (I think I was a man for chiefly this),
> And when I stand beside a dying bed,
> 'Tis death to me.
>
> . . . .
>
> And I, a man, as men are now and not
> As men may be hereafter, feel with men
> In the agonizing present.
>
> (2.294–7; 302–4)

Romney's view of 'man' is that he is a virile actor in the world. In the face of Romney's gendered commitment to the material, Aurora makes an equally gendered choice for the spiritual. As Romney chooses the male path of the body and Aurora the female path of the spirit, each divides and destroys the twofold 'apple of life'. Here in the garden is Elizabeth Barrett Browning's version of the Fall, the division between spirit and flesh, female and male, heaven and earth that will be 'restored' in books 8 and 9 when Romney and Aurora acknowledge their love and the 'twofold' nature of reality.

Because by her own and her culture's definition, poetry is a 'feminizing', 'angelic' pursuit, Aurora moves, as poet, towards an excruciatingly disembodied experience of herself. Her contemporaries address her as the Muse and she does not contradict them.[14] She visualizes the landscape of the muse as a 'melancholy desert' (1.1021), and she takes this desert to be her home, seeing herself as a 'palm' that 'stands upright in a realm of sand' (2.519) and feeling 'the wind and dust / And sun of the world beat blistering in my face' (5.421–2). In imagining the muse's (and her own) realm as a desert, Aurora does violence to the memory of her mother, who had 'drowned' (1.70) and 'flooded' (1.68) Aurora's father with passion. The classical Muses too had always been associated with water, singing, as Hesiod tells us, 'by the dark blue water / of the spring' (*Theogony*, 2. 3–4). Aurora goes further than her male precursors in making the muse a disembodied, infertile female figure. She must exaggerate the myths of patriarchy in order finally to free herself from them.[15]

As Aurora becomes a disembodied muse/Psyche, so she perceives the other women in her life as each representing separate aspects of the once composite image. Her English aunt becomes a deadening Medusa, Lady Waldemar a threatening Lamia ('that woman-serpent' – 6. 1102), and Marian a suffering Madonna. Each of these categorizations allows Aurora to distance the other women she encounters, to see them as different from, and potentially destructive to, her own 'spiritual' essence as Psyche or muse. Yet eventually she discovers that she has in herself, as her mother's daughter – as a woman – the very qualities she has denied and projected onto others.[16]

In book 5, she is startled to discover her hair beginning 'to burn and creep, / Alive to the very ends' (5. 1126–7); she is beginning to recognize herself as a Medusa that has transfixed Romney, even as she repressed her desire for him. To escape this perception, she flees to Italy, only to encounter in France Marian Erle (a lower-class woman who had been betrothed to Romney but who fled from him when she became persuaded that he was marrying her out of charity rather than love). To some extent, she begins to identify with Marian, insisting that together they will be 'two mothers' (7. 124) for Marian's unnamed fatherless child. At the same time, however, she distances Marian by making of her a Madonna:

> And in my Tuscan home I'll find a niche
> And set thee there, my saint, the child and thee,
> And burn the lights of love before thy face,
> And ever at thy sweet look cross myself
> From mixing with the world's prosperities.
>
> (7. 126–30)

In setting up Marian as a saint, Aurora promises to strengthen her already well-developed alienation from her physical self and from her world.[17]

Aurora's final maturation as woman and poet comes when she acknowledges and articulates her love for Romney, the 'sea-king' (8. 60) risen from the depths of her desire. Significantly, Romney appears on a night when Florence appears to Aurora as 'flooded' (8. 37) and 'drowned' (8. 38) in shadows. Aurora is no longer in an arid desert; the muse is returning to her source. In the course of admitting to herself and to Romney the nature of her feelings, Aurora unites herself with the women she had previously distanced:

> Now I know
> I loved you always, Romney. She who died
> Knew that, and said so; Lady Waldemar

> Knows that; . . . and Marian. I had known the same,
> Except that I was prouder than I knew,
> And not so honest.
>
> (9. 684–9)

The Medusa, the Lamia and the Madonna all know the muse better than she knows herself; Aurora does not so much penetrate beneath the 'masks' of womanhood as incorporate them into herself. Muse, Medusa, Madonna, Psyche and Lamia need no longer be opposed as conflicting aspects of the female. The muse can be both spirit and flesh, heavenly and earthly, taking on a role not merely as the mediator between two realms but as their manifold embodiment.

Aurora offers an especially striking image of the 'twofold' union of spirit and flesh in book 5 during her meditation on her goals as a poet. Articulating her desire to 'speak' her poems 'in mysterious tune / With man and nature' (5. 2–3), Aurora enumerates various aspects of the world she hopes her art will express. Among these are 'mother's breasts / Which, round the new-made creatures hanging there, / Throb luminous and harmonious like pure spheres' (5. 16–18). The poet seeks to 'tune' her verse, not to the harmony of the inaccessible heavenly spheres, but to the music of these very earthly, tangible and visible spheres of the female body. In just three lines of concentrated imagery, Barrett Browning offers a compelling alternative to the centuries-long tradition of cosmic harmony associated with disembodied and ethereal muses.[18] The idea and the image are echoed when, joined in an embrace with Romney, Aurora feels 'the old earth spin, / And all the starry turbulence of worlds / Swing round us in their audient circles' (9.838–40). Through physical passion the female Aurora is suddenly surrounded by the harmony once considered accessible only to males who had transcended their fleshly, mortal limits.

Intimately related to Aurora's ability to hear celestial harmony in mothers' breasts and through her own passion is her linking of the rhythm of blood with the rhythms of her verse – again, a radical alteration of tradition. She reports that, as a young woman, her 'pulses set themselves / For concord', that the 'rhythmic turbulence / Of blood and brain swept outward upon words' (1.896–8). Later as she articulates her mature poetic theory, she insists, while

> (glancing on my own thin, veinèd wrist)
> In such a little tremor of the blood
> The whole strong clamor of a vehement soul
> Doth utter itself distinct.
>
> (7.818–21)

Aurora here espouses what contemporary feminists have defined as a poetics of the body, and she takes this poetics to its extreme when, dropping her head on the 'pavement' of an Italian church, she prays that God

> would stop his ears to what I said,
> And only listen to the run and beat
> Of this poor, passionate, helpless blood – And then
> I lay, and spoke not: but He heard in heaven.
>
> (7.1269–72)

Aurora, the poet, silences her voice, allowing her blood to speak.

The reader may object: Aurora's God may hear the beat of her blood, but can a reader? The poetics of the body seems to be a poetics of silence, Aurora's denial of her ambition to speak, a return to the dumbness imposed on women by patriarchy. But in its context, this is an expressive silence, signifying far more than what Aurora elsewhere calls the 'full-voiced rhetoric of those master-mouths' (4.1108), the 'pregnant thinkers of our time' (4.1098). Aurora's silence in the church recalls the 'green silence of the woods' (4.164), the silence of nature that she hears 'open like a flower' (1.683). It is a silence actively opposed to the noise of the 'master-mouths', a writing with white ink that articulates the truths of what we perhaps should call 'mistress-bodies'.[19]

In her espousal of silence, Aurora, prostrate on the floor of an Italian church, mimes the prostration of other women (legendary and contemporary) she has referred to throughout the poem. Specifically, she recalls her own allusions to descriptions of rape victims, whether they be the mortal women figuratively ravished by Zeus or the mortal woman – Marian – literally subjected to 'man's violence' (6.1226). These problematic descriptions and associations force us to ask if Aurora (and through her Elizabeth Barrett Browning) in fact associates poetic inspiration with sexual possession or, indeed, rape by a male muse. In several discussions of art and the artist, Aurora pointedly refers to two classical rape stories, that of Danae and the shower of gold and of Io and the gad-fly. While each story appears at first to suggest that Aurora imagines her inspirer to be a male divinity – of even, perhaps, her male lover-to-be Romney – closer analysis, supplemented by a consideration of Marian's rape, reveals that Aurora's comparisons of herself to these ravished maidens may lead us to see the female body itself – not the male divinity – as the ultimate source of poetic truth and power.

The first story of divine rape is that of Danae. The painter Vincent Carrington introduces it into the narrative when he asks Aurora to help him judge two new sketches:

'A tiptoe Danae, overbold and hot,
Both arms aflame to meet her wishing Jove
Halfway, and burn him faster down; the face
And breasts upturned and straining, the loose locks
All glowing with the anticipated gold.
Or here's another on the self-same theme.
She lies here – flat upon her prison-floor,
The long hair swathed about her to the heel
Like wet seaweed. You dimly see her through
The glittering haze of that prodigious rain,
Half blotted out of nature by a love
As heavy as fate.'

                                                      (3.122–33)

The passage is resonant with echoes and anticipations of other significant moments and images in the poem. The 'tiptoe' Danae may remind us of the Aurora who sought in book 1 to fly up to heaven, the same Aurora who would later hear Romney insisting that 'none can stand a-tiptoe in the place / He cannot stand in with two stable feet' (4.1209–10). Other aspects of the passage strike other chords, revealing the centrality of the Danae figure to Aurora's understanding of herself as woman and artist.

Both Carrington and Aurora prefer the second sketch, Carrington because it '"indicates / More passion"' (3.134–5), Aurora because

                         Self is put away,
And calm with abdication. She is Jove,
And no more Danae – greater thus. Perhaps
The painter symbolizes unaware
Two states of the recipient artist-soul,
One, forward, personal, wanting reverence,
Because aspiring only. We'll be calm,
And know that, when indeed our Joves come down,
We all turn stiller than we have ever been.

                                                      (3.135–43)

Aurora's preference for the second sketch is unsettling, suggesting a passivity that ill accords with the determined activity we know to be necessary for the fulfilment of her 'vocation'. Yet the Danae 'half blotted out of nature by a love / As heavy as fate' recalls the 'dauntless Muse who eyes a dreadful Fate' in the mother's portrait. The Danae overcome by Jove is transformed; she has what the figure in the first sketch can only aspire to. Divinity burns – and drowns – her, making her into a resonant image of the 'twofold world' Aurora wants her art to reveal. In Carrington's Danae we literally see 'the spiritual significance burn[ing] through / The hieroglyphic of material shows' (7.860–1). Danae is the artist/muse who embodies the truth of her art.

The 'prodigious rain' that falls on the prostrate Danae has affinities with other 'rains' in Aurora's narrative. In book 1 she recalls how once, Romney 'dropped a sudden hand upon my head / Bent down on woman's work, as soft as rain – / But then I rose and shook it off as fire' (1.543–5). Romney's hand is alternately rain and fire, a fragmented version of the fiery rain that will be Jove. But Aurora will not allow Romney's hand to 'calm' her; she awaits, not her mortal lover, but her Jove. And, as Romney later tells her, her Jove has come down, entering into her poetry and finally into him:

> 'this last book o'ercame me like soft rain
> Which falls at midnight, when the tightened bark
> Breaks out into unhesitating buds
> And sudden protestations of the spring.
>
> . . . .
>
> in this last book,
> You showed me something separate from yourself,
> Beyond you, and I bore to take it in
> And let it draw me.'
>
> (8.595–8; 605–8)

Aurora becomes the vehicle for a truth that transfigures Romney just as Jove transfigures Danae. Aurora herself becomes the 'prodigious', fertilizing rain that, in the ancient myth, generates the hero Perseus. It is Perseus who kills the Medusa, whose blood, transformed into Pegasus, ultimately gives rise to Hippocrene, the spring that sustains the Muses.

Of course the most dramatic echo of Danae 'flat upon her prison floor' is the moment, already referred to, when Aurora flattens herself on the pavement of the Italian church, no longer striving, no longer reaching up to God, but submitting in silence to the 'run and beat' of her own blood. As we have noted, this is a passive Aurora, who has finally given in to the impulses of her own body, the impulses of desire and love. She does not give in to Romney's desire, for at this point she believes him to be married to Lady Waldemar. Rather, she accepts and acknowledges her own passion, taking it to be, finally, divine. Her 'blood', then, becomes the equivalent of Danae's 'Jove'. This is the divinity to which she submits, not to any male within or without. And it is a divinity that has been 'in' her all along.

The point is made more explicitly earlier in book 7 when Aurora uses the story of Io and Jove to figure her experience as an artist. She explains that she has felt the 'truth' expressed in her poetry to 'hound' her

> through the wastes of life
> As Jove did Io; and, until that Hand
> Shall overtake me wholly and on my head
> Lay down its large unfluctuating peace,
> The feverish gad-fly pricks me up and down.

(7.829–33)

The gad-fly image indicates that the truth Aurora has perceived (of the 'twofold world') has tormented her into expression. The 'Hand' she awaits seems to promise the reconciling stillness of death. But the Hand is the gad-fly transformed, the 'truth' deepened to a fuller experience:

> When Jove's hand meets us with composing touch,
> And when at last we are hushed and satisfied,
> Then Io does not call it truth, but love.

(7.895–7)

Aurora equates the 'truth' that has pursued her with 'love', the very experience her father had insisted on in his last words: '"Love – " / "Love, my child, love, love"'(1.211–12). Similarly, Jove's hand recalls her father's hand, the hand that as a young woman she had longingly remembered: 'O my father's hand, / Stroke heavily, heavily the poor hair down' (1.25–6). Romney had attempted to replace the father, and Aurora had rejected him. But the father's hand itself is a poor substitute for the dying mother's kiss, and the 'love' the father had urged on Aurora was only what his wife had taught him. The imagery of a male muse/raptor that seems to pervade Aurora's figure of Jove as gad-fly/hand resolves into its female substrate, the love made manifest by Aurora's mother. And so we may also speculate about why Barrett Browning, who knew her classics well, apparently mistakes the identity of the gad-fly. In the story of Io as told by Ovid and others, the gad-fly is not Jove at all but a creature sent by the jealous Juno to torment her husband's latest mortal mistress. By conflating male and female divinities, Barrett Browning – or her Aurora – appears to signal that the gender of the divinity is less important than its truth – a corporeal/spiritual love that makes manifest the divinity inherent in the body.[20]

It is in book 7 in the passages just discussed that Aurora offers the fullest articulation of her aesthetic, theological and social message. Significantly, these passages, as numerous critics have noted, occur after Aurora's reunion with Marian Erle. While Aurora first wrote these truths into the manuscript completed before leaving England (at the end of book 5), the presentation of these ideas after Aurora's reunion with Marian suggests that for the reader if not also for Aurora the full understanding of them is contingent on knowledge of what has happened to Marian. Marian has experienced complete profanation of the human body and shows what can and will occur to a woman when the body is treated purely as body, divorced from spirit. To exalt pure spirit (as Aurora had in her disembodied pursuit of poetry's 'spiritual' truth) or to embrace the material to the exclusion of spirit (as Romney had in his utilitarian attempt to improve society) is to create the conditions that caused Marian's rape. It is precisely because of the separation of spirit and flesh that, as Aurora puts it, 'the towns / Make offal of their daughters', and both Aurora and Romney are guilty of that separation. Even Marian's rape can be described as a consequence of Aurora's wilful denial of her own body and Romney's stubborn denial of his own spirit because their denial kept Aurora and Romney apart, leading Romney to choose Marian and Aurora initially to abandon her. Marian's rape serves as a crucial counterweight to Aurora's idealized visions of divine rape and must be considered in any attempt to understand them. Marian too is both Danae and Io, though her Jove is certainly no god.

Marian experiences two devastating betrayals in her life, one when she is sold to a man by her mother, the second when Lady Waldemar's former servant sells her to male desire. The first experience, a near-rape, identifies Marian with Danae; the second, an actual rape, links her with Io. Aurora reports how 'one day' Marian's mother,

> snatching in a sort of breathless rage
> Her daughter's headgear comb, let down the hair
> Upon her like a sudden waterfall,
> Then drew her drenched and passive by the arm
> Outside the hut they lived in.

> (3.1044–8)

'Blinded' by 'that stream / Of tresses', Marian finds herself confronted by a man 'with beast's eyes' (3.1049–50),

> That seemed as they would swallow her alive
> Complete in body and spirit, hair and all, –
> And burning stertorous breath that hurt her cheek,
> He breathed so near.

> (3.1051–4)

Characterized in terms that recall Carrington's second Danae, Marian flees from this horribly material 'Jove', whose heavy breath seems a parody of the longed-for 'breathings' of a muse.

In her next encounter with female betrayal and male lust, Marian cannot escape:

> 'Hell's so prodigal
> Of devil's gifts, hunts liberally in packs,
> Will kill no poor small creature of the wilds
> But fifty red wide throats must smoke at it,
> As HIS at me . . . when waking up at last . . .
> I told you that I waked up in the grave.'
>
> (6.1213–18)

Drugged and raped, she finds herself 'half-gibbering and half-raving on the floor' (6.1232), reduced like Io to the life of a beast. And like Io she takes to the road, 'hunted round / By some prodigious Dream-fear at my back' (6.1266–7), imagining as well 'some ghastly skeleton Hand' (6.1243) pursuing her through the landscape.

Marian's experiences of literal rather than figurative rape show Aurora that her own figures but weakly represent the truth she claims to perceive. Marian teaches in her own body the terrible cost of separating spirit and flesh – a lesson that Aurora claims to have known before, but only, we must admit, in her spirit. Through her experience with Marian she comes to know and acknowledge this truth fully in her body, submitting to 'the run and beat / Of this poor, passionate, helpless blood'.

Marian moves from being treated as pure body to spiritual redemption effected by her maternity, 'God's triumph' (7. 331). For Marian, utter physical abasement results in spiritual elevation, just as Aurora's spiritual elevation, as disembodied muse/artist, requires her descent to the level of her own blood. The two women are necessary counterparts of one another, graphically illustrating through their complementary experiences and language the 'twofold' world Aurora and her creator seek to make manifest. The stories of divine rape are completed by the reality of human rape, something that would not occur if the earth, the body and woman were valued as both material and spiritual. Similarly, the story of human or earthly rape is completed by the stories of divine rape: Marian comes to the fullest experience of divinity on earth through the birth of her child. She speaks of being 'beaten down / . . . into a ditch' (6.676–7) where she awakes to find 'bedded in her flesh / . . . some coin of price (6.679–81). She reports that God tells her: '"I dropped the coin there: take it you, / And keep it, – it shall pay you for the loss"' (6.683–4). Marian's 'coin of price' figure echoes the Danae imagery used earlier by Aurora. Yet what Marian calls God's 'coin' is the product of woman's normal biological capacity. It is Marian's female physiology, her 'blood', that becomes her token of divinity.

Rather than reifying or valuing the male muse/raptor, then, Aurora's figures of Danae and Io finally show that any 'earthly' women is, in herself, divine. She has no need for an external source of poetic or spiritual power but contains it within herself. This is the 'truth' ('Love') that inspires Aurora, the truth she utters and embodies as both poet and muse.

To read Aurora as the muse – for Barrett Browning, for herself, for Romney and, ultimately, for the reader – is, finally, to be in a better position to understand why Romney 'had to be blinded . . . to be made to see.'[21] Modern critics, following the lead of Barrett Browning's contemporary Anna Jameson, persist in reading Romney's blinding as analogous to (and perhaps even modelled on) Rochester's blinding in *Jane Eyre*, a 'punitive equaliser' insuring that this powerful Victorian man cannot 'reassert' his 'dominant functions'.[22] Such a reading ignores Barrett Browning's protest that she was not thinking of Charlotte Brontë's novel when she wrote her poem.[23] More importantly, it fails to take account of a far older cultural archetype that would have been present to Barrett Browning's imagination: the classical stories of a conflict between a mortal singer and the immortal Muses.

One of the most dramatic of such stories is the tale of Thamyris's blinding. As Homer tells the story in *The Iliad*, the poet Thamyris had 'boasted that he would surpass' the 'very Muses': 'these in anger struck him maimed and the voice of wonder / they took away, and made him a singer without memory.'[24] Early in *Aurora Leigh*, Romney rejects the transfiguring potential of poetry, claiming that he intends to 'impress and prove' that 'nature sings itself, / And needs no mediate poet, lute or voice, / To make it vocal' (2.1204–6). Romney assumes the role of Thamyris, claiming that the material world – without any spiritual dimension to it – can sing. Later, of course, after the failure of his schemes and after his blinding, he admits that he was wrong to view

> Our natural world too insularly, as if
> No spiritual counterpart completed it,
> Consummating its meaning, rounding all
> To justice and perfection, line by line.
>
> (8.617–20)

Romney admits that the poetry of earth can only emerge, 'line by line', if one believes that the material is infused with the spiritual. No mortal can sing without a muse who embodies the union of heaven and earth. Romney's blinding is his punishment, not for being a Victorian man, but for his presumption in challenging a goddess. At the conclusion of the poem he accepts Aurora as muse, a woman who will, in Aurora's terms, both 'be and do' (5.367). This goddess, unlike her precursors in the poetry of men, is made of earth and committed both to living upon it and transforming it.

NOTES

1　All citations from *Aurora Leigh*, documented parenthetically in the text, are from Elizabeth Barrett Browning, *The Poetical Works of Elizabeth Barrett Browning*, ed. Harriet Waters Preston (Boston: Houghton Mifflin, 1974).

2　Helen Cooper, 1988: 187; Angela Leighton, 1986: 156. (Subsequent references to Cooper or Leighton are cited parenthetically in the text.) In their focus on either Romney or Marian as muse, Cooper and Leighton epitomize the concerns of a good number of other critics of the poem. For earlier discussions of Romney as implicit or explicit muse, see Deirdre David, 1985: 113–36; Joanne Feit Diehl, 1978: 572–87; Barbara Charlesworth Gelpi, 1981: 35–48; and Virginia V. Steinmetz, 1981: 18–41. For discussions of Marian as muse, see Nina Auerbach, 1984: 161–73; Sandra M. Gilbert, 1984: 194–211; Dolores Rosenblum, 1983: 321–38; and Virginia V. Steinmetz, 1983: 351–67.

3　For a sustained argument that women poets may figure the muse as self, see Mary K. Deshazer, 1986. Examples of contemporary women poets who regard the self as muse include Adrienne Rich and May Sarton.

4　Gelpi 1981: 48. For a powerful commentary on the patriarchal assumptions embedded in Jung's theory, see Naomi Goldenberg, 1976: 443–9. Regarding the belief that a female poet's muse must be male, see Lillian Faderman and Louise Bernikow, 1978: 188–95.

5　See Dorothy Mermin, 1986b: 7–11, and 1986: 64–80, for eloquent expression of this view. Helen Cooper similarly argues that 'a female poet enacts her liberation by transforming herself from being the object of male narrative to being the subject of her own story' (1988: 145). My argument, simply, is that the muse too may be liberated by the female poet's quest.

6　See Mary Daly 1984: 301–3, and 1987: 147.

7　For a discussion of how the ancient Muses were appropriated by early Christian writers, see Ernst Robert Curtius, 1953. Two important texts in the development of the Christian muse are Macrobius, 1952 and Fulgentius, 1971. Macrobius links the Muses with the Pythagorean harmony of the spheres and insists that the heavenly music they make can be 'apprehended only in the mind and not by the senses' (196). Similarly, Fulgentius is advised by the Muse Calliope to 'let fade the whole mortal nature which is yours' (47), so that he might perceive her allegorical truths. Milton is heir to this tradition, and through his reliance on Urania, he makes it a central part of the English imagination. See also Leo Spitzer, 1963.

8 Hesiod, 1959: 34. Subsequent references are cited parenthetically in the text.

9 John Milton, 1957: 1, 19–20; Homer, 1951: 2. 485; Virgil, 1981: 9. 702.

10 Romney's formulation echoes and critiques Tennyson's description in *The Princess* (1969) of a conventional, idealized muse figure. Tennyson's Prince describes his mother:

> No angel, but a dearer being, all dipt
> In angel instincts, breathing Paradise,
> Interpreter between the gods and men,
> Who look'd all native to her place, and yet
> On tiptoe seem'd to touch upon a sphere
> Too gross to tread, and all male minds perforce
> Sway'd to her from their orbits as they moved,
> And girdl'd her with music.
>
> (7.301–8)

Although at first Aurora finds her earth 'too gross to tread', her 'music' will finally be rooted in earth, rather than suspended from heaven.

11 For a lucid exposition of Biblical typology and Victorian aesthetics, see George Landow, 1980. For an example of the contemporary union of feminism and ecology I have in mind, see Susan Griffin, 1978.

12 John Nichol, 1857: 401; Gilbert and Gubar, 1979: 19.

13 E. L. Bryans, 1871: 484. See Carol Christ, 1977: 146–62, for a careful analysis of the 'feminine' elements in Victorian (male) poets' self-representations. Dorothy Mermin explores the same issues, though she concludes that 'the association of poetry and femininity . . . excluded women poets' (1986: 68).

14 See, for example, 3.363; 3.77; 5.796; and 9.26.

15 Angela Leighton reads Aurora's 'desert' imagery as a positive definition of the place where 'true creativity' (1986: 127) can be found. Leighton thus ignores Aurora's own movement towards a more fertile landscape and towards an identity, not as a solitary poet, but as a poet in a vital relationship of love and community. Surely one of Elizabeth Barrett Browning's major achievements in *Aurora Leigh* is the revision of the Romantic (and Victorian) notion of the poet as a solitary, alienated quester, confined to mountaintops or what Leighton calls 'the imagination's desert plains' (1986: 155).

16 Helen Cooper (1988: 157) makes a similar argument, though she shares Gilbert and Gubar's view that Aurora must utterly reject – rather than integrate – these images of womanhood.

17 Sandra Gilbert has celebrated Aurora's identification with Marian, calling their domestic arrangement in Italy an 'unfallen garden of female sexuality . . . [planted] in the richly flowering earth of Florence' (1984: 204). But Aurora in her Italian tower is parched and dry, unable to blossom. Aurora experiences herself as excruciatingly – and destructively – isolated. Worship of her private Madonna may be the beginning of Aurora's development of a 'specifically female

theology', perhaps even her discovery of a 'mother tongue' (204), but Aurora must go even further if she is not to remain a disembodied muse locked in a high tower of her own creation.

18 Marjorie Stone, 1985: 748–70, remarks that Barrett Browning's use of the breast/sphere image invests the female body 'with cosmic rather than coy images' (767), contributing to a feminist 'revision' of traditionally phallogocentric signifiers. Susan Stanford Friedman, 1986: 203–28, also cites these lines, suggesting that this metaphor 'anticipates contemporary feminist aesthetics of the body' (211). May Sarton provides the clearest gloss on Aurora's revisionary aesthetic when she independently asserts in 'Contemplation of Poussin' that 'celestial harmony would never move / Us earthlings if it had not sprung from blood. / The source flows bright from every carnal love' (1984: 14).

19 For the concept of writing with white ink, or signifying with the female body, see Hélène Cixous, 1976: 875–93. The reader of Cixous's essay may well be struck by how many of her images have their analogues in Barrett Browning's own 'woman's figures.'

20 Io herself was, in the nineteenth century, identified as the moon, a priestess of Hera, or a form of Hera herself, the earth. 'The nymph is an epithet of the goddess', wrote Thomas Keightley (1838: 408). Thus we may discern an even more compelling reason for Aurora's identification with Io and for her appropriation of the gad-fly/hand as an image of love.

21 Elizabeth Barrett Browning, 1897: 2.242.

22 Cora Kaplan, Introd., *Aurora Leigh and Other Poems*, (1978: 24). See also Elaine Showalter, 1977: 24, and Mermin, 1986: 80.

23 1897: 2, 246; see also Julia Bolton Holloway, 1977: 130–3.

24 *The Iliad*, 2.597–600.

4

The Mother Planet

Stevie Davies

Wherever 'heaven' is located, it is inimical to God's. Emily Brontë turned her back on his Heaven because it could bear to enjoy its solipsistic bliss immune to the sufferings of the mother-planet. In a tender and intelligent poem of 1841, beginning 'I see around me tombstones grey' (A19), she explained why 'Heaven itself, so pure and blest / Could never give my spirit rest'. Pure of compassion and blest only by oblivion or indifference to the world's suffering, the inmates of Heaven were welcome to their self-regarding 'long eternity of joy'. Earth is personified as the mother-planet, careful of all her mortal children:

> No – Earth would wish no other sphere
> To taste her cup of sufferings drear;
> She turns from Heaven a careless eye
> And only mourns that *we* must die!

The mediation and atonement of Christ are irrelevant gestures, in the light of the orphanage of Creation. Heaven is morally reprehensible, in that it can bear to be happy in the face of the planet's pain. Other women have attested to the shameful character of the Christian Heaven, in the light of creaturely suffering. It is used as a metaphor for complacency, condescension and the imperviousness of the fortunate to the reality of life for the unfortunate. '[T]he real situation was this,' writes a twentieth-century African woman, Tsitsi Dangarembga. 'Babamukuru [the benefactor] was God, therefore I had arrived in Heaven. I was in danger of becoming an angel, or at the very least, a saint, and forgetting how ordinary humans existed – from minute to minute and from hand to mouth.'[19] Each author is reacting against the hierarchy of blame built into patriarchal Christianity. Emily Brontë's poem becomes, in response to earth's fellow-feeling with all creatures, both 'good' and 'evil', a manifesto of solidarity with and affiliation to the stricken mother-planet, against the Father God:

> Ah mother, what shall comfort thee
> In all this boundless misery? . . .
> Indeed, no dazzling land above
> Can cheat thee of thy children's love.
> We all, in life's departing shine,
> Our last dear longings blend with thine;
> And struggle still and strive to trace
> With clouded gaze, thy darling face.
> We would not leave our native home
> For *any* world beyond the Tomb.
> No – rather on thy kindly breast
> Let us be laid in lasting rest;
> Or waken but to share with thee
> A mutual immortality.

Tenderness for the natural world in all its weathers, seasons, lights and shades centred Emily Brontë's emotional and spiritual world: love of kin and love of earth were not distinct. This affinity with all that suffers takes the form of passionate endearedness such as a very young child feels for her mother, struggling to keep awake so as to avoid breaking the circuit of the gaze between one's own and the unique 'darling face'. The child desires that face and no other, guarantor of security. The Father's Heaven would blind the cheated eyes with its simulated perfection. The poem states a resolution to stick by the mother-world on any terms, whether that means sleeping with her or waking with her in the beauty of 'mutal immortality'. It is to that entirely merciful sleeping or waking that she confides her characters in *Wuthering Heights*.

Earth is one of the most recurrent words in the poetry:

'Earth lie lightly on that breast . . .' (1839)

Shall Earth no more inspire thee,
    Thou lonely dreamer thou . . . (1841)

In the earth, the earth, thou shalt be laid . . . (1843)

Cold in the earth, and the deep snow piled above thee . . . (1845)

None would ask a Heaven
More like this Earth than thine . . . (1841)

The earth that wakes *one* human heart to feeling
 Can centre both the worlds of Heaven and Hell. (?1847)

Earth as source, grounding and destination was uniquely charged with power and meaning for Emily Brontë. It had an almost talismanic status in her vocabulary, earthing her, assuring her of where she stood, and refreshing her with the detailed beauty of the place where she belonged. It recurs in many first and last lines of her poems as origin or destination; and of course it is the last word of *Wuthering Heights*. In her usage, even where she seems to imply little more specific than a synonym for 'world', 'globe', or 'landscape', the word carries a more than abstract quality. It meant peat, clay, fibre and stones, together with the vegetation which it sustains on the surface and the underworld into which the remains of life rot down and are recycled. Cathy's grave on the green slope, trespassed into befriendingly by the 'heath and bilberry plants' is almost buried in 'peat mould'. If *earth* was perhaps the most solid, stable and conclusive word in her lexicon, for it meant 'mother', at the same time it was a haunting-ground, for to it had reverted her own dead mother and sisters, together with all earth's children. Her vision is curiously 'Greek' in feeling, with something of the Eleusinian sense of compact between the nether world of the burial chamber, the surface growth and the over-arching skies. In the Eleusinian story, however, the mother-daughter seasonal myth celebrates the benefit of crops and the benefaction of culture; for Emily Brontë, it is the wildness and wilderness of the moorlands that speak of life-and-death matters. Non-human and beyond culture, they lead in to the realm of the spirit and of vision. Upper and nether earth seem in constant dialogue, like unconscious and conscious in a single, complex mind. The world of nature was at once a site of loss and decomposition and an area of reconstitution and composition.

Charlotte Brontë called her sister, justly, 'a native and nursling of the moors'. The image touchingly suggests the mother-child relationship of dependency and tenderness in which Emily Brontë stood to her native surroundings, which Charlotte pointed out were not idyllically beautiful to a conventional eye. The rough black heath, windswept at all seasons, and louring cloudscape, have little Romantic picturesqueness. But every aspect of weather, especially wind, climate, light and shade, and each particular of flora and fauna seem to have moved her. Her eye was alive and attentive to the most ordinary details. Common grass is generally accounted unremarkable. Emily Brontë thought otherwise:

> Only some spires of bright green grass
> Transparently in sunshine quivering
>
> (August 1837; D12, 20)

In this perfect imagist fragment, the eye witnesses sublimity in the common-place. Through the low light of morning or evening sun, a translucent green is revealed in 'spires' (not 'blades') with the sacramental quality of epiphany. The wind breathes in the grasses and, respiring there, it inspires them to respond in their 'quivering' motion. The poem teaches us a new vantage-point, from whose humility to view the proud beauty of the natural world. Lying flat on the earth, we may look up with fresh eyes into the marvel of the ordinary.

But grass is incomplete when viewed at surface-level: it is green intelligence from the underworld. Imaginatively she divined the state of things below in a vision of the fibrous entanglement of roots in the soil. In a Gondal poem beginning 'In the earth, the earth, thou shalt be laid'/(6 September 1843; B27), adverse voices argue. The first warns of death's defiling bed, 'Black mould beneath thee spread / And black mould to cover thee'. The second voice welcomes the prospect:

> 'Well, there is rest there,
> So far come thy prophecy;
> The time when my sunny hair
> Shall with grass-roots twinèd be.'

In that unconscious world of burial, a trace of lustre is implanted. The twining of 'sunny hair' with 'grass-roots' suggests the intricate pattern of the weaving of one life-form with another. The burial of fair hair takes down an implication of sunlight into the underlying darkness. Emily Brontë's conception of beauty is almost invariably elegiac. At the outset of her own life on earth she had lost so much that its solaces carried a quality of requiem. Another Gondal poem of the same year (1843) refocuses the splendour of sunlit grass over the blackness beneath:

> Upon the earth in sunlight
> Spring grass grows green and fair;
> But beneath the earth is midnight,
> Eternal midnight there.
>
> ('To A. S.', 1830'; B26)

Conscious day glows above unconscious night; green above black; life roots in death; the foliage in the trees derives from the eternal rocks beneath.

These oppositions and their identity were literally and in the deepest sense the mysteries upon which Emily Brontë's mind brooded, twisting fair hair with grass roots as Nelly twisted the fair and dark hair of Linton and Heathcliff into Cathy's locket and buried the woven opposites together, subversively and against both their wills (168). Donne's 'bracelet of bright haire about the bone'[20] may be more dazzling but is surely less tenderly magnificent than this braiding of dark with light, hair with root, heath with cliff. In the underworld which it is only natural to shun, Emily Brontë's imagination persistently moved, seeking accommodation.

In the event, she was not of course permitted burial in the mother-world but was committed to the vault beneath the floor of Haworth Church, taking her inscribed place on the mural tablet underneath the names of her mother and pre-deceased sisters and brother. 'Yesterday', wrote Charlotte in the raw letter, 'we put her poor, wasted, mortal frame quietly under the church pavement.'[21] Anne Brontë's poetry records how much they hated the 'cold,' damp stone' of the floor that covered the dead people they had loved.[22] Emily's bones had to rest in the building where Grimshaw had thundered and her father orated Sunday by Sunday. Deaf to such devotions, her corpse decayed under the floor of a church she had sought to desecrate and demolish in *Wuthering Heights* and her poems; the out-and-outer was locked in. She had lived for 30 years, nearly 27 of them bereaved. When at the age of three she had looked around for her mother, she had disappeared without trace. To her question, 'Where is she?' must have come the answer, 'She's in Heaven' and comforting words (contradicted by haggard looks?) to the effect that all was well with her. Emily Brontë had looked up into the godforsaken sky. Her mother was not in Heaven. Evidently that was a lie or delusion. Maria Brontë was nailed into a box, lowered into the church floor and covered with a flagstone. 'No, that is not your mother – only her body'. Where then was her mother? The second Maria, and then Elizabeth, sickened and died. Where were Maria and Elizabeth? In Heaven? Under the church floor? In what state were the beloved mother-figures and how could one communicate with them?

In her desolation in 1848, Charlotte assented to the finality of Emily's loss: 'Yes, there is no more Emily in time or on earth now'.[23] She acknowledged her absolute absence. She did not prevaricate. She knew. It appears to me that Emily Brontë never fully assented to or recognized her mother's and sisters' death as conclusive. Haunted by a numinous sense of presence, she tracked them; they haunted her. '"It's twenty years . . . twenty years, I've been a waif for twenty years!"' wails the girl-spirit, terrifyingly, piteously, at the window of the Heights (24). Heathcliff, the seeker, follows that lure throughout the second half of the novel and of his life. He describes in Biblical cadences, the sense of her proximity at the graveside.

'A sudden sense of relief flowed from my heart through every limb. I relinquished my labour of agony, and turned consoled at once, unspeakably consoled. Her presence was with me; it remained while I re-filled the grave, and led me home.'

(290)

The Biblical echo is not so much ironic as blasphemous. For this 'presence' is the antinomian version of the Holy Spirit, 'the Comforter', which Christ left behind him to believers. It relieves, consoles and guides. Yet it also baits and derides: '"I felt her by me – I could *almost* see her, and yet I *could not!*"' Heathcliff, that genetic mishap, is jeered at by the no-nonsense housekeeper for demanding '"always milk, milk for ever"' (211) and for the '"nursing he gives hisseln"' (212); but the mollycoddle is only expressing the universal need for mothering in a more literal way than his fellows. Heathcliff's violence and Cathy's hysteria are simply different languages for the same thirst.

In her poetry, Emily Brontë often presents the beauty of a wild and natural scene as deriving its life directly from loss:

> The linnet in the rocky dells,
> The moor-lark in the air,
> The bee among the heather-bells
> That hide my lady fair:
>
> The wild deer browse above her breast,
> The wild birds raise their brood;
> And they, her smiles of love caressed,
> Have left her solitude!
>
> ('The linnet in the rocky dells': 1 May 1844; B30)

Unvisited by human witnesses, the ballad-scene has a haunting privacy and introspection. We seem to look in from a distance, without disturbing the peaceful transactions of an environment which has its own coherence and integrity: the creatures of air (linnet, lark, bee) cohabit with the creatures of earth among the rocks, heather and grass. The gentle shock of the line which has the deer 'browse above her breast' comes of its suggestion of the buried woman's nursing of the wild creatures. A secret and unconscious communion links the living and the dead, above whose mound parent birds rear a new generation. The buried 'lady' of this delicate poem is as secret and silent as the earth-mother herself who seems to underlie the whole fabric of Emily Brontë's artistic creation. To the question *Where is she?* both *Wuthering Heights* and the poetry intimate that 'she' is in the not-seen, not-said, not-heard. This might be registered as a doctrine of literary despair; were it not that Emily Brontë's novel has a *trompe l'œil* cunning to persuade us to believe we have seen what we have not been shown. Silence can be very speaking, and *Wuthering Heights* is rich in such articulation. Few readers emerge aware of how little the moorlands have been described in the first half of the novel. Most narrated events take place indoors, whether within Wuthering Heights or Thrushcross Grange, the moor being the space beyond and between. That very absence of description is a secret of the mysterious sense of adjacent presence or being which the novel sets up. The moors are an 'other' world, a forcefield of silence on to which the characters move off the page to roam, out of our sight. If the heath is the magnetic centre of desire, yet that centre is best represented by the white margin of our book, which imagination is stimulated to charge with meaning and attraction. The unsaid is also the area of the unconscious mind, that inner wilderness. Emily Broneë not only had a concept of the unconscious mind, explored in the split and doubled personality, but also a Schellingesque association of the subconscious mind with unconscious nature. She also has the art, through what she writes and what she leaves unsaid, to activate the reader's unconscious mind to participate in this process. Language cultivates, domesticates, familiarizes; silence leaves wild and forbids entry. But where access is forbidden, we automatically want to go. Joseph can violate the children's tabernacle in the womb of the dresser, rending down their pinafore-curtain (19). We witness them being scrambled out of their special place and trounced. But no one follows them out on to the moors, their holy place. That sanctuary is not penetrated, even by the reader, for the outing is presented only as a plan which is never *on the page* fulfilled. We do not accompany the companions on to the heath and 'scamper' with them. The text preserves the excursion's confederate privacy, excluding the reader by a row of dots. Wayward children clamber out into the lawless 'holyday' of the unconscious, to err at will on the pathlessness where there is no right or wrong, God or Satan, and which 'centres both the worlds of Heaven and Hell'.

NOTES

19 Dangarembga 1988.
20 Donne 1977, 'The Relique'.
21 Charlotte Brontë to W. S. Williams, 25 December 1848, in Brontë 1932; 1980: 2. 295.
22 'Yes, thou art gone' (April 1844), in Anne Brontë 1979.
23 Charlotte Brontë to W. S. Williams, 25 December 1848, in Brontë, 1932; 1980: 2. 295.

5

Armgart – George Eliot on the Woman Artist

KATHLEEN BLAKE

A more indefatigable and psychologically adept husband-therapist of a woman's creative drive than George Henry Lewes cannot be imagined. George Eliot dedicated her *Legend of Jubal and Other Poems* (1871) 'To my beloved Husband, George Henry Lewes, whose cherishing tenderness for twenty years has alone made my work possible to me.' And yet *Jubal* contains the dramatic poem *Armgart*, which like *Middlemarch* and *Daniel Deronda* (1871–2, 1876) poses the incompatibility of love and art for the artist who is a woman.[1]

George Eliot confirms the representative ambivalence of the century's epic-scale portrait of the woman artist, Elizabeth Barrett Browning's *Aurora Leigh* (1857), whose poet-heroine is 'Passioned to exalt / The artist's instinct in me at the cost / Of putting down the woman's', while alternately believing that 'Art is much, but Love is more' (9. 645–7, 656). *Aurora Leigh* had some importance for Eliot. She was reading it during the crucial period of her return to England with Lewes in 1856–7, when she first attempted fiction under his encouragement. She also wrote a review of it for the *Westminster Review* in January of 1857.[2] She calls it Elizabeth Barrett Browning's longest and greatest poem, the characteristic femininity of which is its asset. We can infer particular meaning for Eliot in an extracted quotation: Aurora Leigh reflects that she might have been happier and better as a common woman, if she had forgone vocation in favour of love, 'To keep me low and wise'. Eliot does not treat this conflict in her own first works, but she returns to it in *Middlemarch* and *Daniel Deronda*, and it forms the dramatic centre of her interesting, neglected poem *Armgart*.

The theme reverberates curiously in relation to her own life. At the time she picked it out for notice in *Aurora Leigh* she had just committed herself to love *and* art. It seems clear that she questioned that *and*, and wondered if it might not become an *or*. Like Elizabeth Barrett Browning, George Eliot centres her portrayal of the woman artist in an antagonism that she herself almost totally evaded. Nothing could be stranger. And yet there may exist no more striking testimony to the deep embeddedness of ambivalence toward love in the woman artist's thinking about herself in the nineteenth century.

Lewes's record is impeccable as a compounder and not a divider of George Eliot's creativity. In one respect his fostering role was even more essential than Robert Browning's because Elizabeth Barrett was already a successful poet, if fallen into a morbid state, before Browning appeared to help her toward health and happiness and her best work. George Eliot did not write imaginative literature at all until after her liaison with Lewes. In her account he prodded her to try, and he judged her capable in an area where she felt wanting, dramatic power. He applauded her first title, he cried over her pathos, and he sent 'Amos Barton' to *Blackwood's*. From his 1852 *Westminster Review* article on 'Lady Novelists' he is known as an appreciator of the distinctive contribution of women writers. Ellen Moers contends in *Literary Women* that he set George Eliot reading Jane Austen as an apprenticeship to great things.[3]

Lewes provided an important sounding board. Until *Felix Holt* he was the only one to whom she read her works in progress. She benefited from his ideas, for instance, that Adam should be less passive in *Adam Bede*. However, her biographer Ruby Redinger believes that Lewes also knew how to withdraw as an adviser, recognizing Eliot's difficulty in resisting the influence of someone so close as himself. Lewes put his publishing experience at her service. Gordon Haight sees his influence in the negotiations with Blackwood for financial recognition after the success of *Adam Bede*. He worked out the unconventional eight half-volume part-issue for *Middlemarch*, to allow Eliot the scope she needed. In the last letter before his death he directs *Theophrastus Such* to Blackwood. Lewes helped Eliot in her research, for instance for *Romola* and *Daniel Deronda*. He also helped her to stop researching and start writing. His most important role was to hearten and activate her in the depressions that recurred with each book. She repeatedly doubted that her next would measure up to her last. He repeatedly battled those doubts. From the first he had figured out her 'shy, shrinking, ambitious nature', which he warned Blackwood not to criticize too much if he wanted more writing to ensue. Her fear of success, which Redinger makes central to her character, could not have found a more persistent counteractant. Or if the true character centre appears in the ambition rather than the shy shrinking, he ministered to that. Haight says Lewes's management of the priory's social activity shows how well he knew Eliot's need to be recognized and admired. 'He devoted the last decade of his life almost entirely to fostering her genius.'[4]

According to Redinger Eliot had realized that her relation with Herbert Spencer would not do because she wanted to work with a man and not for him as listener/secretary or nurse/housekeeper (211). If she had had a forecast of the danger of being overborne in her own vocation by masculine demands, it was resoundingly unforthcoming in her relation with Lewes. And yet, she returns to the conflict in her writing with unresolved vehemence.

The actress Madame Laure in *Middlemarch* is the crude model of the woman who cannot reconcile her career and marriage and so murders her husband with fatal onstage realism. The Princess Halm-Eberstein, the dramatic singer Alcharisi of *Daniel Deronda*, encounters the same conflict with less crudity and less finality. The most striking thing about the Alcharisi is her self-division. Her mind is breaking into several (5. 140).

Alcharisi has rebelled against being the Jewish woman expected by her father: sacrifice to heritage, 'makeshift link' between male generations (5. 132). Instead she married a man she could control, who would not interdict her career, and she disburdened herself of her child Daniel. She casts marriage and children as obstacles to ambition. She is 'not a loving woman' because love is subjection, and 'I was never willingly subject to any man' (5. 185). Alcharisi says that love encloses the self in another self for man or woman. However, her case and the rest of the novel show that the enclosure is straiter for a woman. The son and husband can include love with vocation; for the mother and wife they are mutually exclusive. Alcharisi lets love go, while Mirah, also a singer, gives up her career as she comes to love Daniel.

Because he is not a woman, even with his much-practised sympathy, Daniel Deronda has a hard time conceiving 'what it is to have a man's force of genius in you, and yet to suffer the slavery of being a girl' (5. 131). The novel gives Alcharisi more understanding than Daniel can. She represents the unredeemed and un-explained-away cost of Jewish and familial continuity. George Eliot makes Alcharisi reverse her former severance from her son and thereby give him his inheritance, which is also his vocation as a racial leader. But she does not make her repudiate her former rebellion. Alcharisi restores Daniel against her principles, out of unconsenting dread of her father's memory, growing on her as she nears death. In fact, the reversal may derive from her illness, not her strength (5. 138). On this the novel remains as divided as her own mind.

Armgart is also very divided about the female artist who is 'not a loving woman'. The poem is quite resolute in supporting Armgart against the threats posed by men and motherhood, but it introduces another version of the conflict of love and art for a woman, one even more foundering, and fascinating.

Armgart is a dramatic poem that Henry James thought the best of the four long poems in the *Jubal* collection but that, like the rest of Eliot's verse, is almost completely unrecognized by criticism. As James says, it is difficult not to overrate or underrate the poetry by measure of the fiction. The latter impulse has dominated. Swinburne says it would be unmanly to treat the poetry critically at all. A recent article called 'George Eliot's Great Poetry' is practically the only one to be found that promises to treat the subject, and it turns out to concern *The Mill on the Floss*.[5]

If *Armgart* is not great, it surely has great interest in respect to the double dilemma into which it plunges its laurelled prima donna. One develops from a proposal of marriage from Graf Dornberg, the other from the loss of voice in illness. Armgart rejects the Graf's addresses because he separates her art from herself as expendable. She disdains his various wooing arguments. One is that unlike men, women are what they are, not what they achieve:

> Men rise the higher as their task is high,
> The task being well achieved. A woman's rank
> Lies in the fullness of her womanhood.
> Therein alone she is royal.

Armgart receives this with irony:

> Woman, thy desire
> Shall be that all superlatives on earth
> Belong to men, save the one highest kind –
> To be a mother.

The Graf's second argument is that a woman not only suffers less but achieves more without her art, in 'home delights / Which penetrate and purify the world'. Armgart's rejecting irony is again bitter: should she sing in her chimney corner to inspire her husband at his newspaper? (10. 95, 97)

The Graf has attempted to set her artistry off against her womanhood, as if it were unnatural. The art of singing offers a fine riposte because a soprano voice comes from nature and is not furnishable by a man. Armgart refuses to recognize a conflict, except as one made by men:

> I am an artist by my birth –
> By the same warrant that I am a woman:
> . . . .
> . . . if a conflict comes,
> Perish, no, not the woman, but the joys
> Which men make narrow by their narrowness.

(10. 98)

The joys that must perish are those of love. Eliot dramatizes the conflict through a convoluted and convincing route of motivation. The Graf does not overtly demand that Armgart renounce her art to marry him, but she feels the pressure anyway from a man who grudgingly tolerates instead of rejoicing in her singing. The interdiction of art by love would come from within herself, 'My love would be accomplice of your will' (10. 101). So she will repress love and transform the pain into art.

It turns out that for Armgart to sacrifice her art is essential to her appeal to the Graf, though he doesn't say so outright. Armgart holds that his affection depends on all she has to give up for him: 'my charm / Was half that I could win fame yet renounce!' (10. 119). When she loses her voice he does not return to renew his suit. This vouches for Armgart's blame to men for setting love and art at odds for a woman. The poem seems to be with her.

I think it is with her in recognizing the intensity and ambition that the world so little credits in a woman. Some of the best passages of the poem concern Armgart's exaltation of celebrity. She revels in fame and impact on the multitude. She needs their applause and flowers and jewels to register her powerful self to herself: 'splendours which flash out the glow I make' (10. 87). Her ambition is treated seriously as a source of artistic identity and energy. The poem gives a deeply felt case for the artist's overweening pride. In the end it does turn out to be overweening, however, and sympathy for Armgart becomes divided.

Again the issue is love versus art, but recast into new terms. When Armgart loses her voice she cannot bear to live within the mediocrity that she sees as the common fate of women. She feels suicidal rebellion against 'woman's penury' (10. 130). Her cousin and attendant, the plain, self-effacing, hitherto almost unheeded Walpurga, now replaced Graf Dornberg in the argument over love and art. Walpurga contends that Armgart's glory as an artist had so removed her from the common lot that she despised it, so that the communication with the audience on which the singer exalted herself was at base factitious and cynical: natures like hers perform 'in mere mock knowledge of their fellows' woe, / Thinking their smiles may heal it' (10. 129). Walpurga tasks Armgart with egotistical lack of care for others, of the same sort that made her oblivious to Walpurga's own care for her; she dismisses that unobtrusive tenderness as petty, mere 'thwarted life', 'woman's penury' (10. 127). Eliot gives vent in Walpurga to the anger of the ordinary woman at being the measure of everything escaped by the extraordinary one. Walpurga defines one of the escapes as a loss: the loss of love. Walpurga has found a meaning for her monotone life in loving Armgart. She is impatient with Armgart's despair because it pridefully rejects as worthless what Walpurga has based her life on.

Therefore the poem presents a double critique of the conflict of love and art for a woman. It expresses indignation at the unnecessary sacrifices demanded by men of women in marriage. Armgart is right not to marry the Graf. But it also deepens the conflict until vindication is harder to come by. It seems that glory saps loving-kindness. This constitutes a particular liability for a woman artist because her glory is so exceptional in a world which devalues women's achievements (as the poem shows) that it exaggerates the gap between herself and her sex. Armgart is wrong to recoil utterly from the lot to which she is reduced because it is no better than the lots of millions of women like Walpurga.

The conclusion of the poem takes careful sorting. Marriage offers no compensation for a lost voice. Singing versus marriage was a falsely imposed set of alternatives to begin with. Armgart ends up teaching music in a small town. She thereby remains true to her art. She refuses to denigrate it by becoming a poor actress; instead she will help to form other fine singers. She also shows care for Walpurga because the small town is the home that Walpurga had left in order to serve Armgart. Love and art are here in some sense reconciled. The poem appears to say that this reconciliation is necessary for true art, and that for a woman artist love and art are destructively divided, but not so importantly in the relation one first thinks of, between the sexes. There the division must be suffered, because anything else means capitulation to the unfair demands of men. Rather the poem identifies the more dangerous result of the division of art and love as the woman artist's contempt for her own sex. This becomes a species of suicidal self-hatred when she suffers the common feminine lot herself, and it provides no basis for the best in art, because communication must be communion.

NOTES

1   Haight 1968: 437; *Armgart* and *Daniel Deronda* in George Eliot 1885; X, III–V – volume and page references will appear in parentheses in the text.
2   Haight 1968: 185; *Aurora Leigh* in Barrett Browning 1974; George Eliot 1857.
3   J. W. Cross in George Eliot 1885: XI, 335–8; Moers 1976: 47.
4   Haight 1968: 383, 265, 311; Redinger 1975: 372; Haight: 306f., 433–4, 514–15, 345, 472, 353, 240; Cross, letter to Blackwood, November 1856, in George Eliot 1885: XI, 343; Haight: 392–3.
5   James, review of *Jubal and Other Poems, North American Review*, 119 (1874), and Swinburne, from *A Note on Charlotte Brontë* (1877), both in Haight (ed.) 1965: 88, 125; Freeman 1970: 25–40.

6

Adelaide Procter's 'A Legend of Provence': The Struggle for a Place

GILL GREGORY

Adelaide Procter's reputation as a poet was established in 1858 with the publication of *Legends and Lyrics*, which went into its fourth edition a year later. Many of her poems were first published in *Household Words*, under the editorship of Dickens, and in 1865 Dickens wrote a warmly admiring Introduction to a posthumous edition of *Legends and Lyrics*. The year before, Adelaide had died of tuberculosis at the age of 38.

She was the eldest child of the poet Bryan Procter (Barry Cornwall) and Anne Skepper, the literary 'salon' hostess. Adelaide combined a busy literary and social life with philanthropic work, and in 1860 was involved in the establishment of a refuge for homeless women in East London. This was a Catholic refuge (Procter converted to Roman Catholicism at the age of 24), but admitted both Catholics and Protestants. 'A Chaplet of Verses', a collection of mostly religious lyrics by Procter, was published in 1862 to raise funds for it.

Procter was also involved with the Langham Place group of women (among them Bessie Parkes and Barbara Bodichon) who launched *The English Woman's Journal* in 1858. Her contributions to the *Journal* include poems, an account of a journey to the Lake District with a woman friend and a biography of the French salon hostess Juliette Recamier. She was also a key committee member of the 'Society for Promoting the Employment of Women'. Some of Procter's most rhetorically powerful poetry was published between 1858 and 1862 during the period of her philanthropic and campaigning work. The poem 'Homeless', for instance, is a passionate indictment of homelessness. A materialistic obsession with 'market' as opposed to human values is held responsible for the bundle in the street which is ignored and may be mistaken for 'goods':

> Nay; – goods in our thrifty England
> Are not left to lie and grow rotten,
> For each man knows the market value
> Of silk or woollen or cotton . . .
> But in counting the riches of England
> I think our Poor are forgotten.
>
> (Procter 1914:339)

The poems written during this period are also increasingly concerned with women's sexuality. For example, in 'A Woman's Answer' the speaker describes promiscuous desires which seek an existence beyong the confinement of an 'exclusive love': 'Dearest, although I love you so, my heart / Answers a thousand claims besides your own' (1914:251). The speaker ironically enumerates all her loves (the seasons, the stars, the flowers) and flatters her lover by linking these to her love for him. The poem satirically concludes with her assurance that she does love him 'more a thousand times than all the rest!' (1914:252).

Procter is also aware of the dangers of allowing sexual desire full expression. In the fine lyric 'Three Roses' (1858) a woman is shown to initiate a relationship with the gift of a rose: 'Just when the red June Roses blow / She gave me one, – a year ago.' The recipient gives her a rose in return and in the final stanza a rose is thrown on to the dead woman's coffin. Her initiative has led her to the grave:

> The red June Roses now are past,
> This very day I broke the last –
> And now its perfumed breath is hid,
> With her, beneath a coffin-lid;
>
> (1914:199–200)

The woman poet, Procter, sees the initiative subtly slip into a state of deadly initiation, as she observes a woman's vulnerability through the male speaker's eyes. She experiences his control and powerlessness in the face of an initiation which seems to hold a mesmeric power beyond the specificity of the exchange. 'Three Roses' powerfully depicts the terrain of sexuality as both a known and as a very 'foreign' ground.

Procter's concern with homelessness and her unconventional treatment of women's sexuality come together in the intensely lyrical narrative poem 'A Legend of Provence'. The poem is one of a series of narratives which make up 'The Haunted House', the title of the 1859 Christmas edition of *All The Year Round*, edited by Dickens, who wrote the frame narrative, 'The Mortals in the House'. The 'mortals' are friends of the protagonist, John, who is staying in an apparently 'haunted house', and who has invited them to visit so that they may test whether or not it is haunted. When they meet to report, the 'ghost' of each guest's room proves attributable either to the imagination or to the memory of the guest.

The narrator/Dickens describes the friends and includes a portrait of Belinda Bates, who is clearly Adelaide Procter:

> Belinda Bates, bosom friend of my sister, and a most intellectual, amiable, and delightful girl, got the Picture Room. She has a fine genius for poetry, combined with real business earnestness, and 'goes in' – to use an expression of Alfred's – for Woman's mission, Woman's rights, Woman's wrongs, and everything that is Woman's with a capital W, or is not and ought to be, or is and ought not to be. 'Most praiseworthy, my dear, and Heaven prosper you!' I whispered to her on the first night of my taking leave of her at the Picture Room door, 'but don't overdo it. And in respect of the great necessity there is, my darling, for more employments being within the reach of Woman than our civilisation has as yet assigned to her, don't fly at the unfortunate men, even those men who are at first sight in your way, as if they were the natural oppressors of your sex; for, trust me, Belinda, they do sometimes spend their wages among wives and daughters, sisters, mothers, aunts, and grandmothers; and the play is, really, not all Wolf and Red Riding-Hood, but has other parts in it.' However, I digress.
>
> (Dickens, *ATYR* 1859: 7)

'The Haunted House' concludes with Belinda/Procter and an anxious young man Alfred Starling becoming engaged. The narrator approves of the engagement as:

> a kind of union very wholesome for the times in which we live. He wants a little poetry, and she wants a little prose, and the marriage of the two things is the happiest marriage I know for all mankind.
>
> (*ATYR* 1859: 48)

This pairing and closure, designed to curtail the excesses Dickens associates with 'Woman's mission', contrasts with the poem Belinda narrates. It begins with a lead written by Dickens: 'Belinda, with a modest self-possession quite her own, promptly answered for this Spectre in a low, clear voice' (*ATYR* 1859: 19).

The suggested containment of Belinda's self is juxtaposed to the discontent figured in the opening lines of the poem: 'The lights extinguished; by the hearth I leant, / Half weary with a listless discontent.' The speaker sits in the dark and the fire momentarily lights up a picture showing 'The likeness of a Nun' (Procter 1914: 156–66. 1–11) which is described as being like a Rembrandt. The portrait triggers the memory of a legend the speaker once heard, and in a dreamlike state she is transported to Provence, where she meets a storyteller who narrates a legend relating to the nearby convent of 'Our Lady of the Hawthorns'. The convent's prized possession is a young orphaned woman, Sister Angela, who is described as virginal, childlike and accomplished in singing and flower arranging. Some soldiers wounded in a crusade seek aid in the convent and a young foreign knight is nursed by Angela. As he recovers, she recounts legends to him and describes various festivals. He reciprocally describes tournaments and pageants, and, amazed that the rumoured 'hideous charm' (163) of the world is absent from his descriptions of loveliness, she asks for more. She and the knight subsequently elope.

But Angela's fantasy is quickly dispelled by her realization that the knight's love for her is 'slight' and 'frail' (199). Disillusioned, she becomes an outcast (and perhaps a prostitute) and finally crawls back to the convent, where she begs to be admitted. Looking up, she sees 'Herself', now 'a grave woman, gentle and serene / The outcast knew it – *what she might have been*' (254–7). 'Herself' proves to be the Virgin Mary who has taken Angela's place in her absence. Angela resumes her old position, with only a 'shadow' of a difference: 'Not trouble – but a shadow – nothing more' (295). Before she dies, years later, she tells her story from her deathbed. The narrator concludes: 'But still *our place is kept*' (327). The poem unconventionally allows the fallen woman to resume her 'place' and she is not blamed for her fall.

The idea of the woman's place as shifting and unstable runs through this poem. At the beginning Belinda gazes at a picture of a nun which is in shadow:

> I seemed to trace
> A world of sorrow in the patient face,
> In the thin hands folded across her breast –
> Its own and the room's shadow hid the rest
>
> (11–14)

Likened to a Rembrandt, the picture lies in Rembrandt's shadow and lacks a definition of its own. It is compared with a priceless painting, but is not itself valued. It can hardly be seen and no provenance is given.

Like the painting, Angela, the orphan without a history, is depicted as both priceless and without value, lacking her own definition:

Of all the nuns, no heart was half so light,
No eyelids veiling glances half as bright,
No step that glided with such noiseless feet,
No face that looked so tender or so sweet,
No voice that rose in choir so pure, so clear,
No heart to all the others half so dear,
So surely touched by others' pain or woe,
(Guessing the grief her young life could not know,) . . .

(63–70)

The repetition of 'No' renders her almost absent, defined by others' lack, need and pain. Without any firm ground, she is a figure of infinite malleability:

She had known
No home, no love, no kindred, save their own.
An orphan, to their tender nursing given,
Child, plaything, pupil, now the Bride of Heaven

(73–6)

The most defined expression of her emotions may be seen in the flower imagery which provides her with a floral vocabulary:

Thus Angela loved to count each feast the best,
By telling with what flowers the shrine was dressed.
In pomp supreme the countless Roses passed,
Battalion on battalion thronging fast,
Each with a different banner, flaming bright,
Damask, or striped, or crimson, pink, or white,

.   .   .   .

Each evening through the year, with equal care,
She placed her flowers . . .

(87–98)

The passage has an obsessive quality which creates a sense of the intensity of Angela's involvement in her office. The placing of the flowers repeats the multiple moments of pleasure and simultaneously marshals her desires with military precision. The roses in battalions mirror the regimentation and strength of her arrangements, with the flaming roses suggesting passionate and triumphant love. To live *sub rosa* is also to live under an injunction to secrecy, which suggests the degree of containment that is taking place.

In Christina Rossetti's poem 'The Iniquity of the Fathers upon the

Children', the daughter of a fallen woman ponders what lies 'under the rose' where she was born: 'For I knew of something under / My simple-seeming state.' (Rossetti 1994:203). By contrast, Angela is depicted as being without a ground to delve into. To an extent she is the flowers, particularly the cut flowers laid on the shrine, suggesting artificiality and deadness.

The hawthorn wood which names and almost conceals the convent is more suggestive of an uncontrolled living nature with a potential for both pleasure and pain. The virginal impenetrability signified by the hawthorn ('May' or Mary's flower) is countered by the possibility of a thawing but the thorn also suggests martyrdom. The knight metaphorically cuts through the wood and thorns into Angela's contained and ritualized silence. He prompts her to an unfamiliar eloquence, and at this point in the narrative Procter employs humour and irony to question Angela's apparent naivety and innocence:

> What could she speak of? First, to still his plaints,
> She told him legends of the martyred Saints;
> Described the pangs, which, through God's plenteous grace,
> Had gained their souls so high and bright a place.
> This pious artifice soon found success –
> Or so she fancied – for he murmured less . . .
>
> (135–40)

Her question is teasingly rhetorical and the images of martyrdom suggest a poignant awareness of her ludicrous position. She enjoys her own loquacity as she proceeds to elaborate on the festivals, and a reference to the showering hawthorn in the Virgin Mary's procession sounds sexually provocative: 'They struck the hawthorn boughs, and showers and showers / Of buds and blossoms strewed her way with flowers' (155–6). Her access to speech frees her into the spontaneity of her desires.

In the folktale sources for this legend the nun's lover is either a cleric or devil in disguise, and the nun is often depicted as being subjected to temptation and succumbing to her seducer only after a struggle to control her desires. By excluding the temptation and struggle, Procter emphasizes the attraction of the knight's proposition and Angela's lack of guilt. Her sexual desire appears to be natural, and she responds to a man who is 'foreign' (127) but not a devil or seducer in disguise. She responds to the pageantry of 'Tourney, and joust' (159) which he describes to her, imagery which is mirrored in her flower arranging. Her erotic desires displaced on to the flowers are thus associated with the knight's ambitious desire for glory. In 'A Legend of Provence' Procter poses the problem of the ambitious desires of a young woman, whose 'place' is depicted as ephemeral and fragile, and whose desires are contained *sub rosa*.

Eventually she returns to a miraculous surrogate mother who is and is not herself, who is strange and intensely familiar:

> She raised her head; she saw – she seemed to know –
> A face that came from long, long years ago:
> Herself; yet not as when she fled away,
> The young and blooming novice, fair and gay,
> But a grave woman, gentle and serene:
> The outcast knew it – *what she might have been*.
> But, as she gazed and gazed, a radiance bright
> Filled all the place with strange and sudden light;
> The Nun was there no longer, but instead,
> A figure with a circle round its head,
> A ring of glory; and a face, so meek,
> So soft, so tender. . . . Angela strove to speak,
> And stretched her hands out, crying, 'Mary mild,
> Mother of mercy, help me! – help your child!'
> And Mary answered, 'From thy bitter past,
> Welcome, my child! oh, welcome home at last!
> I filled thy place
>
>   (252–68)

In G. Du Maurier's illustration Angela gazes up at herself/the Virgin Mary, framed by the branches of a dense wood (163). The wood (L. *materia*) in Freudian terms symbolizes the mother's body and creates a powerful sense of her materiality. Both daughter and mother are depicted as having temporarily consumed and incorporated each other. Angela moves from a wood associated with predatoriness, wolves and men to the wood or *materia* of the mother's body.

J. B. Pontalis, in *The Dream Discourse Today*, writes of the Freudian notion of the dream as the displaced maternal body: 'Dreaming is above all an effort to maintain the impossible union with the mother, to preserve an undivided totality' (1993: 113). The wood as signifier of the mother's body and the wood as Belinda's dream landscape doubly suggest the importance Procter places on establishing a ground for the exploration of the mother. She explores her relationship to a daughter who looks for a 'place' which will accommodate erotic and ambitious desires. By depicting Angela entering into her own body through the body of a mother on the threshold of the convent, there is an attempt to penetrate (the gateway is hymeneal) incestuous desire: the 'bar' of blood which cannot be passed (Rossetti 1994: 158).

It is an attempt to break the spell of the dream or phantasy of an impossible union with the mother. The paradoxically material and transparent body of the mother dissolves any notion of the safety of the mother's arms, and the recrossing of the threshold is destabilizing rather than reassuring. The threshold is less a point of return and reunion than a place where Angela faces the complex phantasy of *'what she might have been'* (257). The words resonate beyond her recognition of an 'other' self. They draw attention to the gap between her fallen and surrogate self, and to all the blank spaces in her life which have not been filled or filled in – her life prior to coming to the convent, her *sub rosa* existence and her life of destitution. The powerful incestuous desire for a mother's body to fill the gaps: ('I filled thy place' (268)) is faced. It is a moment of both joy and intense anxiety.

The penetration of the dream involves entering into this anxiety. Angela Leighton has referred to the threshold of the convent as signifying 'a threshold of the self':

> marking a split in consciousness which echoes the moral divisions of the age. If the place of the Romantic imagination is that of a border-line between the known and the unknown, the border-line of the Victorian female imagination is the same, but fraught with social and sexual anxieties . . .
>
> (1989: 118–19)

By merging Angela's virgin and fallen selves, which are known and unknown on either side of the threshold, Procter locates 'anxieties' relating to sexuality and desire on the borderline which separates and joins the selves. At the point of meeting and merger, the pure and the fallen, mother and daughter, come together for a moment. This moment of incorporation stops the projection of the deviant desires of mother and daughter on to the fallen woman outside. Incestuous desire for the mother and the deviant desire of the fallen woman are faced and allowed inside, and to this extent there is a move towards the ground of a more integrated and defined self.

The final retreat, however, is into passivity and death. By the conclusion Belinda has explored the shadow and Dickens's reduction of Belinda/Procter's feminism to a narrow obsession with 'everything that is Woman's with a capital W' has been contested. The single women, Belinda and Adelaide, and the virgin and fallen woman, Angela, are linked within their respective shadows and the unfulfilled desires which they suggest. Shadows gather around Belinda, and Angela is left with 'a shadow – nothing more' (295) at the end. Integration remains extremely problematic. Angela's unknown real mother (perhaps another fallen woman) is excluded from the picture – she is barely even a shadow.

The idea of the shadow, both visible and invisible, keeps reappearing in Procter's poetry. In the poem 'Homeless' a woman's exclusion from the home

and from recognition is absolute. There is no possibility of a return to a
'place' or to a mother. The vagrant 'sister-woman' is shown to exist, or hardly
exist, in a state beyond both law and criminality. She is a haunting figure,
whose pain cannot be accommodated – she can only pass the window pane –
and she has no 'place' either inside or outside the home:

> Look out in the gusty darkness –
> I have seen it again and again,
> That shadow, that flits so slowly
> Up and down past the window pane: –
> It is surely some criminal lurking
> Out there in the frozen rain?
>
> Nay, our Criminals all are sheltered,
> They are pitied and taught and fed:
> That is only a sister-woman
> Who has got neither food nor bed –
> And the Night cries 'sin to be living',
> And the River cries 'sin to be dead'.

(1914: 338)

7

Christina Rossetti's Poems

Jerome J. McGann

Christina Rossetti's work is dominated by a powerful mixture of certain specific social themes, on the one hand, and a set of characteristic symbolic modes, on the other. These themes, announced in her earliest work during the 1840s (and well before she met William Bell Scott),[10] focus on the psychological tensions recognized by a single woman experiencing and studying human love under specific social circumstances. Her all but obsessive studies of women in love have sanctioned, and helped to perpetuate, the largely misguided biographical searches for her own lost love. But what is important about Rossetti's work will not be elucidated by searching for that hypothetical man-she-loved-in-vain; rather, it will be revealed when we understand better the patterns of frustrated love as they appear in the works and the social and historical formations which those patterns dramatize.

Indeed, Christina Rossetti did not have to live through a merely personal experience of the failure of love. Her sensibility was larger than that, and she clearly recognized that the patterns of such failure surrounded her everywhere, in art as well as in life: in society at large, as the notorious life and death of Letitia Elizabeth Landon (for example) revealed,[11] and near at hand, in her early home life as well as in the later, disastrous love experiences which centred on her brother Dante Gabriel. The great value of Christina Rossetti's work – and in this she is like no other woman writer of the period – lies in its pitiless sense that the world is a scene of betrayal and that the betrayal appears most clearly, and most terribly, in the relations between men and women. Only Dante Gabriel Rossetti's vision of the world as the hell of love produces a comparable body of work (A. C. Swinburne's is different and much more benevolent). In Christina Rossetti's case, the poetry seizes the advantage of its alienation – that it was written by a single woman, a fact emphasized by her work and never to be forgotten by the reader – and it explores, more self-consciously than her brother had done (if no more passionately), the root patterns of betrayal.

Before we look more closely at these thematic aspects of her poetry, however, we have to examine, at least briefly, some of Rossetti's typical stylistic procedures. Deeply read, and even schooled, in Christian typology, Christina Rossetti possessed a sophisticated symbolic method and apparatus which she used repeatedly and self-consciously (see *The Face of the Deep*, for example, where she has some important discussions of these symbolic modes of expression).[12]

The central moral problem in a symbolically ordered world involves distinguishing between what seems and what is. For an artist, however, this moral problem can locate a set of expressive powers since it offers the artist opportunities for constructing multiple levels of statement. For a morally committed artist like Rossetti, these multiple levels form part of a structure which exercises and puts to the test the reader's powers of apprehension. Her poetic characters are themselves typically placed in situations where they are asked to distinguish the real from the illusory. This technique is so widespread that one need only cite a few of her most famous works – 'Sleep at Sea', 'The Lowest Room', 'The Hour and the Ghost', or 'Memory' – to see how fundamental the procedure is.

Let me give two examples of Rossetti's typical method. The first poem was called 'Two Choices' by Christina Rossetti (it is not in Crump's first volume, and William Michael Rossetti retitled it 'Listening'):[13]

> She listened like a cushat dove
> That listens to its mate alone:
> She listened like a cushat dove
> That loves but only one.
>
> Not fair as men would reckon fair,
> Nor noble as they count the line:
> Only as graceful as a bough,
> And tendrils of the vine:
> Only as noble as sweet Eve
> Your ancestress and mine.
>
> And downcast were her dovelike eyes
> And downcast was her tender cheek;
> Her pulses fluttered like a dove
> To hear him speak.

The sinister quality of this poem depends upon several ambiguous elements which radiate into a general problematic pattern. The scene presents, schematically, the figures of a man and a woman to whom he is speaking, obviously of his love. The event shows the woman being drawn into a state of thrilling trepidation and innocent dependency. The sinister overtones emerge because of the ambiguous nature of the poetic comparisons. The association of the woman with Eve is pivotal, for with that reference one begins to question the figural value of the scene's apparent innocence. Yet the verbal surface does not urge an inversion of the poem's appearances; on the contrary, it sustains these appearances even as it suggests the melancholy ambiguousness of the emblem.[14] Precisely in that tension does the poem achieve its principal effects. The female figure listens to the man, and her posture offers the reader a procedural sign for reading the poem: we too listen and try to detect the meaning of the words we encounter. Is the man in the poem Adam to the woman's Eve, or is he Satan, the serpent who, in traditional typology, is frequently represented as exercising a fatal fascination over the innocent dove?[15]

The poem gradually develops that sort of problematic question. The figure of the dove is associated with innocence, and the Holy Spirit takes the form of a dove; but the dove is also associated with the pagan Aphrodite and represents, in that figural love context, sensual beauty and pleasure. So we also come to wonder if the woman's eyes are 'downcast' in an emblematic pose of modesty or if they are 'cast down' as a sign of her unhappiness (or of her future betrayal?). In a similar way, we are brought to worry over the meaning of her fluttering pulses and what they tell us about this relationship.

Finally, one notices the pronoun 'your' in line 10. At first it seems to refer, simply, to the entire human race, whose mother Eve is. But the love context works a subtle shift in our attention as one begins to suspect that 'your' refers to women only. When that happens, the critical edge of the poem makes itself very plain, for such an idea insists upon the special insight and experience of a dependent group or class. Indeed, for the poem to address itself directly to women only, and hence to exclude men from its innermost levels of discourse, is to emphasize the alienation of women from men and their lack of true intercourse. An apparently benevolent love ideology is represented at the poem's level of immediate appearance – which is the level of stylistic 'dominance' – but the subversive insights of an estranged feminine experience reveal the deceptiveness of those appearances at more oblique levels. For people who do not normally question the 'truth' of the mischievous social structure and set of ideas represented at the dominant levels – and these may be women as well as men – the poem offers the opportunity of a new freedom via critical understanding. Christina Rossetti defines herself as an individual even as she speaks directly to others as individuals ('Your . . . and mine'), and the form of this address dramatizes a relationship radically different from what is represented in the poem's nondialectical structures (and via the poem's focusing symbol of those nondialetical structures).

Many of Rossetti's poems operate in this way: that is, they test and trouble the reader by manipulating sets of ambiguous symbols and linguistic structures. Here is another example, only in this case we are not dealing so much with ambiguous symbols as with a cunning play with language.

> I cannot tell you how it was;
> But this I know: it came to pass
> Upon a bright and breezy day
> When May was young; ah pleasant May!
> As yet the poppies were not born
> Between the blades of tender corn;
> The last eggs had not hatched as yet,
> Nor any bird foregone its mate.
>
> I cannot tell you what it was;
> But this I know: it did but pass.
> It passed away with sunny May,
> With all sweet things it passed away,
> And left me old, and cold, and grey.
>
> ('May', Rossetti 1979–90: 1.51)

Though much could be said about this fine poem, I want to concentrate on two of its elements only. First, the poem is clearly playing for variations upon the Biblical phrase 'it came to pass', which is worked to mean both 'something happened' and 'something came only in order to go away again'. This something made its appearance in May, a time traditionally associated with the renewal of life and the coming of love, but the something belied its appearance and turned spring into a spiritual winter. What is most disturbing about these events is the suggestion of purposiveness applied to the actions of the unspecified something ('it').

All of this recapitulates the 'vanitas vanitatum' theme so prevalent in Rossetti's poetry. But we observe that another ambiguous unit in the poem – the pronoun 'it' – pushes the work into a terrifying level of generality. As a pronoun, 'it' refers here both to May and to a wholly unidentified referent, something unknown and inexplicable both to speaker and reader. This mysterious referent has its invisible character reinforced by the poem's other employment of 'it': that is, as part of an expletive structure in which 'it' serves no pronominal function at all (as in 'it is raining today' or 'it seems all right to do that'). In grammars like these, 'it' stands for an entire conceptual field, but nothing in particular (not even a defined conceptual field itself), so that 'it' finally comes to stand as a sign of total conceptual and experiential possibility. From a Christian point of view, the poem thereby develops the meaning that the world is an illusion, a field of betrayal, an entire vanity; from a more secular point of view, it suggests that understanding the meaning of human events in such a world will always be impossible. Love comes and love goes, but from the point of view of the feminine speaker of this poem, love's movements are arbitrary and beyond her understanding. Her despair arises from the fact that she is purely a relative creature even in those human situations where she is most intimately and deeply involved.

As in all of Christina Rossetti's poetry, the subject matter in these two works is social and psychological. The poems are also typical in that they deal with love and the idea of beauty from a peculiarly feminine perspective: both poems not only represent the dependency relation of women to men, they associate that relation with deceptions, fears, and the inability to bring understanding and control into human affairs (for men and women alike). In the memorable words of Swinburne's Althaea: 'Love is one thing, an evil thing, and turns / Choice words and wisdom into fire and air. / And in the end shall no joy come, but grief.'

For Christina Rossetti, love appears as a serious problem when marriage reveals its problematical aspects. In *Maude*, for example, marriage is not entirely rejected, but it is represented as the least attractive possibility available to the women in this book (where only two men appear, and they only in a nominal way). The author makes perfectly clear, through the character of Mary and especially through Maude's sonnet 'Some ladies dress in muslin full and white', that marriage will seem unattractive to any woman (a) who has a sense of, and belief in, her own personal worth and integrity, and (b) who cares for something other than the things of this world, and especially its material comforts and luxuries. Well before Christina Rossetti became one of what Dora Greenwell was to call 'Our Single Women', this poet had a deeply personal view of her world and a profound sense of her own integrity. The spectacle of the Victorian marriage market appalled her. Wives, she says in 'A Triad' (Rossetti 1979–90: 1.29), are 'fattened bees' who 'Grow gross in soulless love'. In the end, as we see so frequently in her works (for example, in 'The Iniquity of the Fathers Upon the Children' [Rossetti 1979–90: 1.164]), her heroines characteristically choose to stand alone, as Agnes does in *Maude*. Those who do not – those who choose either love and marriage or love and romance – almost invariably find either disaster or unhappiness or a relationship marked by a sinister and melancholy ambiguousness.

Thus, if one were to speculate on her biography and on her several 'missed opportunities' in love and marriage, one would probably be closer to the truth to say that Christina Rossetti remained a single woman because she felt deeply ambivalent about love relations with men. One would also, probably, be closer to the truth than Packer was if one agreed that this ambivalence was both natural, explicable, and – finally – justified, both historically and, in terms of her life and career, personally.

The figure which threatens the single woman most directly in Rossetti's work is the spinster, who – in the words of 'A Triad' – 'famished died for love'. Her most important poem dealing with the fears of spinsterhood is the remarkable narrative 'The Lowest Room' (Rossetti 1979–90: 1.200), but the motif recurs throughout her work. 'A Triad' also shows that if the married woman is the spinster's opposite, her dialectical contrary is the fallen woman, who 'shamed herself in love' but substituting sensual pleasure for frustration. In Rossetti's myth, these last two figures 'took death for love and won him after strife', but all three fail – 'all short of life' – for two principal reasons: first, they are not self-conscious about the meaning of their choices, and second, none of them is truly 'single' since each one's peronality only exists in a dependency relation to something or someone else.

The figures of the spinster and the fallen woman appear throughout her poetry, often in those generic forms but more frequently in slightly altered guises. Both figures appear in various love relationships, sometimes as nuns whose beloved is Jesus (or who leave the world for the convent when they lose a mortal lover), and sometimes as the betrayed woman. Such figures appear most memorably in works like 'The Hour and the Ghost' (Rossetti 1979–90: 1.40) as the women who are wailing for their demon lovers. In this mythological territory, the fallen woman is merely another transformational form of the true love or the beloved. This mutation occurs because, in such a (symbolistic) world, love is always appearing in unreal and delusive forms. Marriage is not equivalent to love, but then neither is a romantic relationship. A fierce tension emerge when these two alternatives both reveal their deplorable, threatening aspects, as they do in 'The Hour and the Ghost'. 'The Lowest Room' increases the tension by making two sisters the spokeswomen for each position, thereby forcing the women into a dismal and wrenching conflict with each other.

Rossetti's negation of romantic love appears throughout her early poetry, especially in the many works inspired by Charles Robert Maturin and in various derivative Metastasio and Byronic scenarios. Among her most moving revelations of the daemonium of such 'love' are to be found in the poems dealing with her brother Dante Gabriel and his works. 'In an Artist's Studio' represents such a love ideology (along with its related structures of artistic expression) as a type of introverted vampirism. 'An Echo from Willow-Wood' goes on to interpret romantic love, along with her brother's great representation of its divine tragedy, *The House of Life*, as a Munch-like drama of inevitable loneliness and identity loss.

Men and women, their 'true loves', their marriages: Christina Rossetti examined these subjects in the life and art of her world and saw the piteous networks of destruction in which they were all, fatally as it were, involved. All of her work, in its secular as well as in its more directly religious forms, represents a protest against these ways of living. Her 'devotional' poems, as she called them, are an integral and important part of her protest and no merely belated form of sentimental piety: the *vanitas* and *contemptus mundi* themes are part of her resistance against her age's worldliness and luxury, along with its subtle forms of exploitation. All are weighed and found wanting. At first her impulse was to try to refuse to have anything to do with the world: thence emerge the 'thresholds' of conventual life and escapist Romanticism which appear so frequently in her work before 1860. But she would not follow either of those paths to the end, though she understood, and used, the critical power of each. Rather, she became, finally, one of nineteenth-century England's greatest 'Odd Women'.

Personal independence is, therefore, one of her central subjects, and it is memorably developed in a poem like 'Winter: My Secret' (Rossetti 1979–90: 1.47). This work's effectiveness depends upon the particularity of its experience, that is, on the fact that it is so entirely the expression of a special point of view. And not merely a special point of view: the circumstance dramatized in the poem we necessarily locate in terms of a particular person, place and period. The teasing and ironic banter is a transformed reflex of a certain type of 'feminine coyness' which social conventions developed and reinforced in women. Of course, the poem uses these conventional patterns of behaviour and usage only to subject them to an implicit critique, but the special character of this critique is that it is carried out in such a decorous and oblique fashion (contrast, for example, Lord Byron's or even Arthur Hugh Clough's handling of similar materials). Rossetti's critique is launched from the vantage, as it were, of the poet's 'secret' place. The indirectness of this subtle poem is part of its strategy for preserving the integrity of its 'secret', and hence for maintaining the very possibility of integrity and truth in speech. Independence and integrity – of which this 'secret' is the symbol – can only be secured by a diplomatic resistance. As in the similar poem 'No, Thank You, John' (Rossetti 1979–90: 1.50), the politeness of the refusal veils a differential severity which will not be compromised. In that reserve of purpose lies Christina Rossetti's power, her secret, her very self.

Consequently, her work employs the symbol of the personal secret as a sign of the presence of individuality. Independence is a function of the ability to have a secret which the sanctioned forces of society cannot invade. Maude has her locked book, and Rossetti's poetry is punctuated with a number of secret places and secret choices. That she was well aware of the importance of secrecy in her work is plain not merely from 'Winter: My Secret' but from a variety of other equally important poems (see 'Memory', for example [Rossetti 1979–90: 1.147]).

Goblin Market is Rossetti's most famous poem, and certainly one of her masterpieces. The point needs no argument, for no one has ever questioned the achievement and mastery of the work. What does need to be shown more clearly is the typicalness of *Goblin Market* in Rossetti's canon – indeed, its centrality.

Though Rossetti herself declared that the work was not symbolic or allegorical, her disclaimer has never been accepted, and interpretations of its hidden or 'secret' meaning have been made from the earliest reviews. Everyone agrees that the poem contains the story of temptation, fall and redemption, and some go so far as to say that the work is fundamentally a Christian allegory. Nor is there any question that the machinery of such an allegory is a conscious part of the work. *Goblin Market* repeatedly alludes to the story of the fall in Eden, and when Lizzie, at the climax, returns home to 'save' her sister, the poem represents the event as a Eucharistic emblem (see especially 471–2). Other, less totalizing Christian topoi and references abound. The important 'kernel stone' (138) which Laura saves from the fruit she eats, and which she later plants unavailingly (281–92), is a small symbolic item based upon the New Testament parable (see Matthew 7:15–20) about the fruit of bad trees; indeed, the entire symbology of the fruits is Biblical, just as the figures of the merchant men are developed out of texts in the book of Revelation (18:11–17).

Rossetti draws from this passage her poem's controlling ideas of the evil merchants as traffickers in corruption and of their fruits as deceptive and insubstantial. Consequently, an important key for interpreting the poem proves to be her own commentaries on the Revelation text. The commentary on verse 14 has a manifest relevance which can pass without further remark:

14. And the fruits that thy soul lusted after are departed from thee, and all things which were dainty and goodly are departed from thee, and thou shalt find them no more at all.

Or according to the Revised Version: 'And the fruits which thy soul lusted after are gone from thee, and all things that were dainty and sumptuous are perished from thee, and men shall find them no more at all': – reminding us of St. Paul's words to the Colossians: '... The rudiments of the world ... (Touch not; taste not; handle not; which all are to perish with the using).'

As regards the second clause of the doom (*in this verse*), the two Versions suggest each its own sense. The Authorized, as if those objects of desire may have been not destroyed but withdrawn whilst the craving remains insatiable. According to both texts the loss appears absolute, final, irreparable; but (collating the two) that which *departs* instead of *perishing* leaves behind it in addition to the agony of loss the hankering, corroding misery of absence.

(Rossetti 1892: 421)

Her commentaries on verses 15–17 are equally pertinent. There the sacred text speaks of the coming desolation of Babylon, the merchants' city; Rossetti says of this event that, though it has not yet come to pass, it 'must one day be seen. Meanwhile we have known preludes, rehearsals, foretastes of such as this', and the thought leads her to her 'lamentation'. In this she cries 'alas' for those traditional political symbols of corruption (Sodom or Tyre, for example), but her lament builds to an interesting climax: 'Alas England full of luxuries and thronged by stinted poor, whose merchants are princes and whose dealings crooked, whose packed storehouses stand amid bare homes, whose gorgeous array has rags for neighbours!' (Rossetti 1892: 422). Of course, Rossetti was no Christian Socialist (or even a Muscular Christian), and her chief concern here is not with the material plight of the socially exploited. Rather, she focuses on that material condition as a sign, or revelation, of an inward and spiritual corruption. Babylon, Tyre, Sodom, England – as in Tennyson and T. S. Eliot, these are all, spiritually, *one* city ('Unreal city'), the passing historical agencies of the recurrent reality of a spiritual corruption.

The Bible, both the Old and New Testaments, characteristically associates these 'Babylonian' corruptions with sensuality and sexual indulgence, and Rossetti uses this association in her poem. The goblin merchants tempt the two sisters with fruits that offer unknown pleasures, more particularly, with fruits that promise to satisfy their unfulfilled desires. The figure of Jeanie is introduced into the poem partly to make plain the specifically sexual nature of the temptation and partly to show that the issues are intimately related to the middle-class ideology of love and marriage. Jeanie's is the story of the fallen woman.

In this context, the final (married) state of the sisters might easily be seen as sanctioning the institution of marriage as the good woman's just reward. To a degree this is indeed the case; but *Goblin Market* presents the marriages of Laura and Lizzie in such an oblique and peripheral way that the ideology of the marriage-as-reward is hardly noticed and is conspicuously de-emphasized by the poem. The only men present in the story are the goblins, and Laura and Lizzie's emotional investments are positively directed toward women and children only. In fact, the poem's conclusion suggests that the sisters have made (as it were) 'marriages of convenience', only, in *Goblin Market*, that concept has been completely feminized. It is as if all men had been banished from this world so that the iniquity of the fathers might not be passed on to the children. Hence we see why the only men in the story are goblin men: the narrative means to suggest, indirectly, that the men of the world have become these merchants and are appropriately represented as goblins.

The ultimate evil of the goblin merchants is that they tempt to betray, promise but do not fulfil. Indeed, they do not merely fail in their promises, they punish the women who accept these promises as true. Yet the power of their temptations does not come from the inherent resources of the goblins; it comes from the frustration of the women, which is represented in Laura's (and Jeanie's) longings and curiosity. The goblins, therefore, tempt the women at their most vulnerable point, which turns out to be, however, the place of their greatest strength as well.

Here we approach the centre of the poem's meaning, the core of its paradoxical symbolism. The temptation of the goblins always turns to ashes and emptiness because it does not satisfy the women's fundamental desires (see Rossetti's commentary on Revelation 18:14 above). But in terms of the Christian allegory, this simply means that the goblins offer 'passing shows' to match what in the women are 'immortal longings'. Notice how tenderly Laura and Lizzie are presented together immediately after Laura's 'fall'; how she finally emerges from her experience completely unstained; how the poem turns aside, at all points, any negative moral judgement of her character; and how it does not read Laura's condition as a sign of her evil. Rather, Laura's suffering and unhappiness become, in the poem, a stimulus for feelings of sympathy (in the reader) and for acts of love (by Lizzie). These aspects of the poem show that, for Rossetti, the 'temptation and fall' do not reveal Laura's corruption but rather the nature of her ultimate commitments and desires, which are not – despite appearances, and were she herself only aware of it – truly directed toward goblin merchants and their fruits.

Laura's desires (they are 'Promethean' in the Romantic sense and tradition) are fulfilled in the poem twice. The first fulfilment is in the notorious passage at 464–74, which is as patently erotic and sensual in content as it is Eucharistic in form. The significance of this elemental tension becomes clear when we understand that the scene introduces a negative fulfilment into the work: Laura is released from the spell of erotic illusions ('That juice was wormwood to her tongue, / She loathed the feast' (494–5)) and permitted to glimpse, self-consciously, the truth which she pursued in its illusive form:

Laura started from her chair,
Flung her arms up in the air,
Clutched her hair:
'Lizzie, Lizzie, have you tasted
For my sake the fruit forbidden?
Must your light like mine he hidden,
Your young life like mine be wasted,
Undone in mine undoing
And ruined in my ruin,
Thirsty, cankered, goblin-ridden?' –
She clung about her sister,
Kissed and kissed and kissed her:
Tears once again
Refreshed her shrunken eyes,
Dropping like rain
After long sultry drouth;
Shaking with aguish fear, and pain,
She kissed and kissed her with a hungry mouth.

(475–92).

This passage anticipates the poem's conclusion – the second, positive scene of fulfilment – where Laura tells the children the story of a sisterly love and bids them follow its example: 'Then joining hands to little hands / Would bid them *cling* together, – For there is no friend like a sister' (560–2, my emphasis). For passion and erotics are substituted feeling and sympathy, and for men are substituted women and children, the 'little' ones of the earth.

Thus we see how the Christian and Biblical materials – the images and concepts – serve as the metaphoric vehicles for understanding a complex statement about certain institutionalized patterns of social destructiveness operating in nineteenth-century England. As in so many of her poems, *Goblin Market* passes a negative judgement upon the illusions of love and marriage. But the poem is unusual in Christina Rossetti's canon in that it has developed a convincing positive symbol for an alternative, uncorrupted mode of social relations – the love of sisters.

This situation requires some further explanatory comment. In the story of Laura and Lizzie, we can observe patterns of conceptualization familiar from Rossetti's other works. One notes, for example, that the goblins' power over women comes ultimately from the women's (erroneous) belief that the goblins have something which the women need, that the women are incomplete. Part of the meaning of *Goblin Market* is the importance of independence, including an independence from that erroneous belief. Lizzie's heroic adventure on her sister's behalf dramatizes her integrity, her freedom from dependency on the goblins: she is not a relative creature but is wholly herself, and capable of maintaining herself even in the face of great danger.

Nevertheless, the premium which Rossetti placed upon personal integrity was always threatened by the demon of loneliness ('And left me old, and cold, and grey'). *Goblin Market* turns this threat aside, principally via the symbol of sisterly love and the alternative socializing structures which that symbol is able to suggest and foster. An important formal aspect of the poem's resolution depends upon our awareness that Lizzie is not Laura's 'saviour', for this would simply represent a variant type of a dependency relationship. The true beneficiaries of the grace issuing from the events are 'the children', or society at large in its future tense.

So far as *Goblin Market* tells a story of 'redemption', the process is carried out in the dialectic of the acts of both Laura and Lizzie. Laura behaves rashly, of course, but without her precipitous act the women would have remained forever in a condition of childlike innocence. Lizzie's timidity is by no means condemned, but its limitations are very clear. Laura's disturbed restlessness and curiosity suggest, in relation to Lizzie, an impulse to transcend arbitrary limits. But Laura's precipitous behaviour is the sign of her (and her sister's) ignorance and, therefore, of their inability to control and direct their own actions. When Laura 'falls', then, her situation reveals, symbolically, the problem of innocence in a world which already possesses the knowledge of good and evil. Where ravening wolves prowl about in sheep's clothing, the righteous must be at once innocent as the dove and cunning as the serpent. Lizzie's function in the poem, then, is to repeat Laura's history, only at so self-conscious a level that she becomes the master of that history rather than its victim. Still, as the story makes very clear, her knowledge and mastery are a function, and reflex, of Laura's ignorance and weakness. The definitive sign of their dialectical relationship appears in the simple fact that Laura is not finally victimized. She is only a victim as Jesus is a victim; she is a suffering servant. In a very real sense, therefore, the poem represents Laura as the moral begetter of Lizzie (on the pattern of 'The child is father to the man'). Lizzie does not 'save' Laura. Both together enact a drama which displays what moral forces have to be exerted in order, not to be saved from evil, but simply to grow up.

Laura and Lizzie, then, share equally in the moral outcome of the poem's events. The fact that their names echo each other is no accident – and who has not sometimes confused the two when trying to distinguish them at some memorable distance? Still, it makes a difference if one locates the poem's principal moral centre in Lizzie alone, as readers have always done. In fact, to have read the poem this way is to have read it accurately (if also incompletely); for Christina Rossetti, as a morally self-conscious Christian writer, encouraged such a reading, as she wanted to do – and needed to do –

for both personal and polemical reasons. She encouraged it because *that* way of reading the poem supports a Christian rather than a secular interpretation of the theme of independence. All readers of the poem will recognize its polemic against the women's dependence upon the lures of the goblin men; but from a Christian viewpoint, this polemic is based upon the idea that people should not put their trust in mortal things or persons, that only God and the ways of God are true, real and dependable. Therefore, in the affairs of this world, the Christian must learn to be independent of the quotidian – translate, *contemptus mundi* – and come to trust in the eternal. So far as Lizzie seems a 'Christ figure' – a Eucharistic agent – *Goblin Market* argues for a severe Christian attitude of this sort.

But, of course, Lizzie seems something much more – and much less – than a Eucharistic emblem, as Christina Rossetti well knew: she never placed *Goblin Market* among her 'Devotional Poems'. Consequently, because Lizzie is primarily a 'friend' and a 'sister' rather than a 'saviour', the poem finally takes its stand on more secular grounds. Nevertheless, it uses the Christian material in a most subtle and effective way: to mediate for the audience the poem's primary arguments about love, marriage, sisterhood and friendship.

In much the same way does the poem use the disarming formal appearance of a children's fairy story. This choice was a stroke of real genius, for no conceivable model available to her could have represented so well a less 'serious' and 'manly' poetic mode. When her publisher Alexander Macmillan first read the poem to a group of people from the Cambridge Working Men's Society, 'they seemed at first to wonder whether I was making fun of them; by degrees they got as still as death, and when I finished there was a tremendous burst of applause.'[16] All three phases of their response were acute. *Goblin Market* cultivates the appearance of inconsequence partly to conceal its own pretensions to a consequence far greater than most of the poetry then being produced in more 'serious', customary and recognized quarters.

Lizzie triumphs over the goblins (329–463) by outplaying them at their own games, but one should notice that her victory is gained in and through her correct formal behaviour. It is the goblins who are violent, disorganized, out of control – and impolite. She addresses them as 'good folk' (362) and says 'thank you' (383) to their insidious offers. The goblins smirk and giggle at her apparent simplemindedness, yet the poem clearly represents her as enjoying an unexpressed, superior laughter at their expense. Lizzie's behaviour is the equivalent, in *Goblin Market*, of what we spoke of earlier in relation to 'Winter: My Secret' and 'No, Thank You, John.'

Lizzie's behaviour is also a stylistic metaphor standing for Rossetti's poetry, whose correct beauty judges, particularly through its modest address, all that is pretentious and illusory. The fruits, the language, the behaviour of the goblin merchants are all metaphors for what John Keats had earlier called 'careless hectorers in proud, bad verse'. The issues here are nicely suggested in a brief passage immediately following Lizzie's victory over the goblins: 'Lizzie went her way . . . / Threaded copse and dingle, / And heard her penny jingle / Bouncing in her purse, – / Its bounce was music to her ear' (448, 451–4). This is Rossetti's sign of a true poetic power – a mere penny which jingles like the surface of the verse. Nonsense (the original title of 'Winter: My Secret') and childishness – Edward Lear, Lewis Carroll, *Goblin Market* – come into a great inheritance amid the fat and arid formulas of so much High Victorian 'seriousness'.

But *Goblin Market* gains its results in the most obliging and diplomatic fashion. Christina Rossetti was a severe woman, and her ironic intelligence and quick tongue were observed, and respected, by all of her contemporaries who knew her. But so were her modest and retiring ways. She did not cultivate the weapons, or methods, of George Sand or even of Elizabeth Barrett Browning. Lizzie's behaviour with the goblins is Rossetti's poetic equivalent for her own life and work. What Lizzie does – what Christina Rossetti does in her verse generally – is not to make a frontal assault upon her enemy, but quietly to secure his defeat by bringing righteousness out of evil, beauty out of ugliness. Rossetti's model for her revisionist project appears explicitly in her Revelation commentary cited above:

> Yet on the same principle that we are bidden redeem the time because the days are evil, Christians find ways to redeem these other creatures despite their evil tendency. Gold and silver they lend unto the Lord: He will pay them again. Precious stones and pearls they dedicate to the service of His Altar. With fine linen, purple, silk, scarlet, they invest His Sanctuary; and fragrant 'thyine' wood they carve delicately for its further adornment. . . . Whoso has the spirit of Elijah, though his horse and chariot have come up out of Egypt, yet shall they receive virtue as 'of fire' to forward him on his heavenward course. And this despite a horse being but a vain thing to save a man.
>
> (1892: 420)

Out of these convictions develop, naturally, the charming catalogues of the goblins as well as their own temptation speeches; but we recognize this habit of mind most clearly in the unspeakably beautiful litanies praising the poem's loving sisters:

> Golden head by golden head,
> Like two pigeons in one nest
> Folded in each other's wings,

They lay down in their curtained bed:
Like two blossoms on one stem,
Like two flakes of new-fall'n snow,
Like two wands of ivory
Tipped with gold for awful kings.
Moon and stars gazed in at them,
Wind sang to them lullaby,
Lumbering owls forbore to fly,
Not a bat flapped to and fro
Round their rest:
Cheek to cheek and breast to breast
Locked together in one nest.

                                                          (184–98)

Thematically this passage is important because of its position in the poem.
Although the lines describe the evening rest of the sisters *after* Laura's
encounter with the goblins, the passage does not draw any moral distinctions
between Laura and Lizzie. In the perspective of Christina Rossetti's poem,
Laura remains fundamentally uncorrupted. By goblin standards, she is now a
fallen woman, but the poem intervenes to prevent the reader from accepting
such a judgement.

This moral intervention occurs at the level of poetic form and verse style.
As such, it does not merely tell us of the need for a new moral awareness, it
suggests that this new awareness cannot be an abstract idea. On the contrary,
it must operate in a concrete form appropriate to the circumstances – in this
case, within the immediate literary event of the poem itself. The poem's
general social critique (which is abstract) appears in the verse as a series of
particular stylistic events (which are concrete). In a wholly non-Keatsian
sense, then, Beauty becomes Truth: not because the beauty of art represents
a purified alternative to worldly corruptions, but because art's beauty is itself
a worldly event, an operating (and, in this case, a critical) presence which
argues that human acts will always escape, and dominate, what is corrupt.

In this sense one can and ought to say that *Goblin Market* is *about* poetry.
For the poem's critique of the symbolic goblins is itself a symbolic mode of
statement comprehending all that is suggested by, and hidden in, the
symbol; and part of what is hidden in the symbol of the goblins is the
particular corruption of the age's literature. *Goblin Market* develops its
general social indictment by passing a special judgement upon poetry. For
the corruption of the goblins operates in all quarters of society, as the poem's
generalizing form (symbolic fairy story) necessarily implies: in the infrastruc-
tural regions ('the market'), of course, but also in all of the related
superstructural institutions, including that of literature. Fundamentally the

corruption originates in the 'marketplace' where women 'have no place' and 'do not belong'. But Rossetti wittily inverts the meaning of this alienated condition by suggesting why women must not seek positions in the capitalized market if they want to preserve their integrity and, thereby, to deliver a prophetic message to the future – the need for an alternative social order. Her argument is an outrageously subtle revision of the age's notorious attitude toward women expressed, for example, in John Ruskin's 'Of Queens' Gardens'.

In this respect, Christina Rossetti's poetry takes up an ideological position which is far more radical than the middle-class feminist positions current in her epoch. The principal factor which enabled her to overleap those positions was her severe Christianity, as a close study of her religious verse would clearly show. Space does not permit me to develop that demonstration here, though I hope I have shown, in the course of this essay, how such a demonstration might be carried out. Christina Rossetti's notorious obsession with the theme of the world's vanity lies at the root of her refusal to compromise with her age or to adopt reformist positions. Like Giacomo Leopardi's pessimism,[17] Christina Rossetti's *contemptus mundi* is the basis of her critical freedom and poetic illumination.

Unlike the atheist Leopardi, however, Christina Rossetti did not set herself in open revolt against her age. Yet her conservative posture once again proved an asset to her work, for in accepting the traditional view of 'a woman's place', she uncovered a (secret) position from which to cast a clear eye upon the ways of her world. Lizzie, *Goblin Market*, and Christina Rossetti, then, all act in similar ways. All are radically critical, yet they are modest and oblique at the same time; they are independent; they preserve the idea of the importance of beauty in a dark time; and they cherish the secret of their work. *Goblin Market* specifically is a serious critique of its age and of the age's cultural institutions which supported and defined what was to be possible in love, social relations and art. When Swinburne spoke of Christina Rossetti as the Jael who led their hosts to victory, he said more than he knew, but he did not say too much.

NOTES

10   Scott is, according to Packer 1963, Rossetti's 'lost love'.

11   That Christina Rossetti understood Landon's cultural significance is plain from her poem 'L.E.L.' (Rossetti 1979–90: 1.153), which was written in response to Elizabeth Barrett Browning's earlier important poem on Landon.

12   Rossetti 1892: 195–6, 215 and 217–18. Hatton has an excellent discussion of this subject (1955: lxxxii–lxxxvii).

13 The poem offers a good instance of Christina Rossetti's method of pruning her original version; see Hatton 1955: 233.

14 For a good discussion of Christina Rossetti's characteristic treatment of the figure of Eve, see Hatton 1955: 237.

15 The woman in the poem has 'two choices', acceptance or refusal, but the poem presents a network of alternative choices which reflect and elaborate upon the elementary narrative choice.

16 Alexander Macmillan to D. G. Rossetti, 28 October 1861, quoted in Packer (ed.) 1963: 7.

17 See Timpanaro 1965: 133–82.

8

Christina Rossetti's Religious Poetry: Watching, Looking, Keeping Vigil

DOLORES ROSENBLUM

Christina Rossetti, remembered primarily for her powerful verse fable *Goblin Market*, also wrote some four hundred and fifty short religious lyrics. In a sense, of course, all Rossetti's poetry is deeply religious, concerned always with the relation of this world to the next. By religious or devotional lyrics, however, I mean specifically those poems her brother William set apart and arranged in chronological order under the heading of 'Devotional Poems' in his edition of the *Collected Poems*.[1] Each of these poems fits into one of these four categories: presentation of the speaker in colloquy with her Lord; direct speculation about the meaning of Christ's sacrifice, the nature of death and the afterlife, and the proper human stance toward all of these; celebration of a particular holiday; or elaboration on a particular Biblical text. Eleven of these live on in Protestant hymnals; several Hopkins-like soul-agonies and the visionary 'Amor Mundi' and 'The Convent Threshold' are routinely anthologized; the rest are read – if at all – as documentation of Victorian religiosity and repressed sexuality.[2]

Apparently self-effacing, these poems can seem self-indulgent in their aesthetic impoverishment, as though Rossetti, released from the exigencies of literary originality, wrote without much attention to craft.[3] The course of a Rossetti religious lyric does, indeed, seem predictable and circular, as the speaker-self, repeating the same desperate argument, invokes a familiar and schematic iconography. The same fatal ground is gone over, the same spectacle passed in review: Earth vanishes; the apocalypse arrives or pends; the New Jerusalem looms into view; souls stream upward into the splendours of a crystalline heaven. The lyric speaker watches, weeps and prays, always wakeful and longing for rest. Since time is always passing, this speaker must find a way to pass time, which amounts to biding her time until the end, when there will be an abrupt reversal, and all losses will be made good. In the meantime, she will endure, keeping vigil, like the angels of the poem 'Easter Even', 'Wondering, on watch, alone'.[4] Yet the stylized topography and the inflexibility of the speaker's stance reflect something more than literary destitution; rather, these are the components of a personal myth of loss, stoic endurance and restitution.

This personal myth is derived from a mode that is deeply conventional, however. In his recent study of Tractarian poetry, G. B. Tennyson has shown how Rossetti is influenced by Tractarian aesthetics, sharing topics and formal strategies with the poets of the Oxford Movement. Shaped by an aesthetic which includes the doctrine of 'Reserve', Rossetti's religious poetry shows affinities with the intense yet restrained utterances of poets like Newman and Isaac Williams.[5] The restraint that aligns her with these particular poets marks her off from other religious poets of the period: with the exceptions of 'From House to Home', 'Amor Mundi' and 'The Convent Threshold', her religious verse has little of the Romantic intensity that characterizes Richard Watson Dixon's dream visions, for instance, and little of the metaphorical variety and range of subject found even in Keble's poetry. This same restraint saves Rossetti from the sentimental excesses of some of her female contemporaries and predecessors: Felicia Hemans, for instance, who sets her vision of paradise within the bathetic frame of a child questioning its mother about the precise location of 'the better land'; or Dora Greenwell, who invents a 'Life Tapestry' for the view of Him who sees the 'fairer side' of warp and woof; or Adelaide Procter, who sends a 'Message' to a dead friend in heaven, and, lacking an angel messenger, tries out variously a 'Cloudlet's fleecy breast', a Lark, a Rose, a Censer, and finally 'Music's outspread wings'.[6] Among the models available to her, then, Rossetti chooses one that is characterized by a restricted lexicon, by extensive Biblical quotation,[7] by repetitive formulations and by limited metaphorical invention.

Paradoxically, this self-effacing mode affords Rossetti the means to compose a distinctive self as woman and poet. As Sandra Gilbert has pointed out, Rossetti belongs to a company of woman poets who, from Anne Finch's day on, have cultivated an 'aesthetic of renunciation', substituting suffering and self-abnegation for the 'self-assertion lyric poetry traditionally demands'.[8] Gilbert emphasizes the deep asceticism that influenced Rossetti's choices in life and art; in this she differes crucially from her two great contemporaries, Elizabeth Barrett Browning and Emily Dickinson. Barrett Browning eventually substitutes an 'aesthetic of service' for an 'aesthetic of pain', her heroine Aurora Leigh achieving a 'reasonable compromise between assertion and submission'.[9] Dickinson, though living reclusively as a nun, in her poetry becomes 'greedy, angry, secretly or openly self-assertive'.[10] Rossetti, however, remains true to the aesthetic of pain and destitution. From beginning to end she writes of broken vows and futile hopes, premature decay and barren growth, her lyric personae and her narrative subjects waiting out their lives in 'the lowest place' (237), holding a stoic pose against the return of vain and unquenched desire. If lyric self-assertion is indeed impossible for the nineteenth-century woman poet, then Rossetti paradoxically creates a self by abdicating the self, and, especially in the religious poetry, invents a language by piecing together fragments of a ready-made language. By stylizing certain literary and scriptural conventions, and by exaggerating the renunciatory pose, Rossetti expresses at once her extreme alienation and her self-possession. She has given up everything because nothing in this world is 'enough'; she is stripped down to the essential self who can endure untiringly until the end when she shall see and be seen 'face to Face'; she offers an ever-watchful self to an all-seeing God who recognizes her, even now, in time, as she is: 'I am not what I have nor what I do; / But what I was I am, I am even I' (263).

As the previous sentence suggests, the language of the Bible provides Rossetti with a crucial metaphor for her personal myth, the visual metaphor whereby 'seeing' stands for knowing, loving and having. For although Rossetti is not what we would call a visual poet, her poetry is pervaded with references to faces, masks, eyes, spectacles and displays, and to the acts of seeing, looking, staring, gazing and watching. In her appropriation of the visual metaphor, and in particular the Pauline text, Rossetti belongs to the line of religious poets stretching from Donne, who in 'Good Friday, 1613. Riding Westward' plays upon the permutations of 'seeing' and Christ's passion, to such contemporaries as Elizabeth Barrett Browning, for instance, who struggles to bear 'This everlasting face to face with God', and John Keble, who exhorts the 'sons of Israel' to 'Turn to Him whose eyes are here, / Open, watching day and night, / Beaming unapproached light!'[11] While most nineteenth-century poets are drawn to the visual metaphor, and especially the image of the face-to-face encounter,[12] Rossetti is unique in her pervasive use and stylization of this imagery. Although there are other image patterns in her religious poetry, such as the opposition between dearth and sufficiency,[13] the visual metaphor is central to her conception of self as woman and poet, woman and Christian.

In religious poetry the issue of gender – who 'sees' and who is 'seen' – is in a sense obviated: the lyric speaker who contemplates God's suffering or transfiguration while offering up an unworthy self is necessarily passive, a consciousness that denies or denigrates its own powers, at times an unmoved 'stone', as Rossetti declares in 'Good Friday' (234), at times, if anything, a 'female' consciousness awaiting God's will. But the metaphor of sight, particularly as it involves gazing upon a face, belongs also to the secular tradition, where it has acquired specific and fixed gender assignments: from Sidney through Keats and Shelley to Dante Gabriel Rossetti, the poet writes as a male 'seer' who gazes upon a beloved – or calm and cold, even terrifying – female face. This face answers his look, or does not; mirrors his soul, or does not; in any case, it is always an *object* of vision. As a woman poet, then, Rossetti must deal with the fragmentation of her poetic consciousness into an observer and an observed. Characteristically, she takes on both roles, becoming the observer seeing herself observed, the witness of the reification of self, very often precisely as a visual object.[14]

As a Victorian woman, moreover, and as a woman in that particular family, Rossetti was especially susceptible to the kind of selflessness and paralysis suggested by the image of woman as a visual icon. Not only was lyric assertion problematic, not only was it impossible for her to range intellectually and imaginatively, but also in actuality she was expected to occupy, indeed 'chose' to occupy, a fixed place, following the narrow and delimited route from home to church and home again. This life situation was literally realized, even parodied, by the demands of her brother's aesthetic. Like him she was a poet; when he turned to his painting, however, she assumed the traditional role of model, becoming one of the first avatars of his pensive ideal beloved. Even when she relinquished this role, as he discovered his 'stunners', she was surrounded by women holding fixed poses and transfixed in his art. The actual conditions of modelling underline the symbolic meanings of the act: not only do the women in his paintings appear cataleptic; the models in actuality had to hold rigid positions for long periods of time. In their biography of Dante Gabriel Rossetti, Brian and Judy Dobbs point out that in their pursuit of casual and natural poses the pre-Raphaelite painters often required their models to assume acutely uncomfortable poses, not realizing the 'anatomical and muscular differences between someone moving *through* a particular point in an action, and asking the model to, as it were, *freeze* at that point.'[15] In 1879, when Dante Gabriel, in desperate need of his favourite model to pose for new copies of the Proserpina, writes to beg Jane Morris, by now chronically ailing, to pose once more 'in an easy position and by short stages', her reply makes clear the sheer physical difficulty of the undertaking.[16] The combination, then, of Dante Gabriel's aesthetic and his actual technique produces an image of woman that stresses not only her mysterious iconic powers, but also her social powerlessness, the kind of confinement that Katherine Lochnan sees imaged in those pre-Raphaelite paintings which represent their subjects as 'imprisoned in a tower, cramped by a frame, or confined within a two-dimensional space'.[17] Thus in adopting the meditative pose as an emblem of the woman seeing herself observed, in both her life and her art, Rossetti must have been aware of the ambivalences in the image, the ways in which it was authentic and falsifying, the ways in which it defended and betrayed her.

The ambivalence was compounded by certain problematic aspects in the actual face Rossetti presented to the world. In his 'Memoir' in the *Collected Works*, her brother William lists forty-five portraits, scrutinizing each item with a view to arbitrating between two questions: whether the work is an accurate likeness, and whether it shows Christina to be truly beautiful. Her nineteenth-century biographer, Mackenzie Bell, comments on the 'heavy and even unemotional', 'comparatively unattractive' quality of her face in repose, contrasting this mask with the animation that came over her features when she spoke.[18] And certainly Dante Gabriel's 1877 portraits of her, which no doubt reveal the morbidity of his vision at that time as much as the melancholy of his subject, show a face that is sombre, even forbidding. Whatever the source of Rossetti's impassive expression, however – and it is important to remember that in middle age she contracted the exophthalmic bronchocele that coarsened her features and darkened her skin – she must always have felt that her looks were disturbing, even unpicturable. Expected to pose so that her likeness could be captured, she assumed a mask, whether forbidding, or simply blank, unobtrusive. And out of this essentially limiting and alienating situation of posing, combined with the role-limitations inherent in the visual metaphor, Rossetti constructed a poetic myth of the enduring model woman, not only a visual icon, but also a display of stereotypical qualities: Christian – and female – forbearance, humility, renunciation and stoic endurance.

In the religious lyrics Rossetti was able to transcend these limitations by transforming the model into a more powerful figure, perhaps inherent in all religious writing: the witness who testifies not only to present loss but to future restitution. Further, by discovering the power of compassionate 'looking' Rossetti was able to modify the isolation of the witness by the more participatory act of vigil-keeping. Since, however, the experience of posing and the image of the model remain central throughout all her writing,[19] I want to consider now, as a key to the religious lyrics, a crucial secular poem that provides the clearest instance of the relation between model and witness, watched and watcher.

In a poem that pays tribute to the pathos of Elizabeth Siddal's life, 'In an Artist's Studio', one woman is the model, or, in this case, the pictured woman, and another is the watcher. The relation between them, however, can be taken to stand for the relation between aspects of a single self. Looking at the portraits, the speaker is struck by their reductive sameness:

> One face looks out from all his canvases,
> One selfsame figure sits or walks or leans:
>
> . . . every canvas means
> The same one meaning, neither more nor less.

Unlike the artist, whose vision is single, indeed monomaniacal, the speaker witnesses the discrepancy between the artist's frail illusion and the woman's unpicturable reality, and testifies to the pathos of both:

> He feeds upon her face by day and night,
>   And she with true kind eyes looks back on him,
> Fair as the moon and joyful as the light:
>   Not wan with waiting, not with sorrow dim:
> Not as she is, but was when hope shone bright:
>   Not as she is, but as she fills his dream.
>
> (330, 24 December 1856)

The woman vampirized by art, in life more dead than alive, in art endowed with ghostly life, suggests the kind of depersonalization that woman-as-model experiences. The watcher commemorates her symbolic death.

Paradoxically, however, woman-as-model can be converted into an emblem of self-possession and untiring endurance. Again Rossetti stylizes, even caricatures a given convention, here an inescapable way of seeing. Although the woman who, transfixed in art or immobilized by social roles, *cannot* move may appear feeble, more dead than alive, the woman who *will not* move is persevering, even obstinate. The fixed position, like the fixed language, gives her a vantage point from which she can look out for the source of her deliverance. The model and the watcher can thus combine as witness: the woman who presents herself as testimony both of her suffering and her survival, offering this spectacle as a guarantee of eventual restitution. Such a figure is the heroine of Rossetti's 'A Soul', who, out of her powerlessness, makes herself into a statue:

> She stands as pale as Parian statues stand:
>   Like Cleopatra when she turned at bay,
>
> . . . .
>
> Indomitable in her feebleness,
> Her face and will athirst against the light.
>
> (311, 7, February 1854)

The thirsty face turned toward the light, blank and iconic, is one of a range of watcher's faces in Rossetti's devotional poems. Another watcher's face, and not so different, is the 'set' face (derived from Jeremiah and Isaiah), as in 'Yea, therefore as a flint I set my face' ('From House to Home', 25, 19 November 1858), 'Our face is set to reach Jerusalem' (122, *c.* 1877), and 'Set faces full against the light' (145, before 1886). Indeed, the watcher's face may be both obscured and unseeing: 'Therefore to Thee I lift my darkened face; / Upward I look with eyes that fail to see, / Athirst for future light and present grace' (227, before 1886). What signifies, then, is not the quality of the vision, but the act of self-display. Whether the observer is God or His creation, this female persona is at once spectacle and witness: the watcher watching herself being watched.

As self-displaying watcher the speaker of the devotional poems enacts the expectancy of unsatisfied desire for the transcendent union, 'face to Face'. Throughout her career Rossetti focuses on the divine face as the watcher's fulfilment, for 'Who looks on Thee looks full on his desire' (269, before 1893). At the apocalyptic end, when all spectacles have passed away, those who are not 'cast down, in want,' will see 'in the eternal noon / Thy Face' (128, *c.*1877). This face may be distant or averted, for it takes agonized wrestling to 'make Thy face of mercy shine again'; the wrestler beseeches the Lord for strength to 'hold Thee fast until we see Thy face, / Full fountain of all rapture and all grace' (247, before 1875). Distant or present, it is to this viewer that the speaker of the devotional poems offers herself as spectacle and witness, a figure carved in stone, 'Thy Mercy's all-amazing monument' (266, before 1893).

So far my emphasis has been on the pose and the 'blind', transfixed look. As generated by the watcher's pose, the religious poetry would seem to be poetry of alienation, the self conscious only of its division and its separation from a distant God. In the pattern of Christ's life and death, Rossetti finds the perfect analogue for the self isolated as object of vision. 'None with Him' (238, 14 June 1864) represents Christ's extreme loneliness in life as a consequence of a human failure of vision:

> My God, to live; how didst Thou bear to live,
> . . . Few men prepared to know
> Thy Face, to see the truth Thou cam'st to show.

The loneliness of His death is similarly intensified by a visual failure, as Christ becomes a grotesque spectacle: 'A curse and an astonishment, past by, / Pointed at, mocked again'. Rossetti concludes that by comparison her own suffering is inconsequential, her response cowardly. But the analogy works the other way as well: because she experiences the isolation of self as spectacle, whether derided, or misunderstood, or merely appraised, she can comprehend Christ's isolation. Christ's isolation thus becomes the adequate symbol for Rossetti's own predicament. Similarly, she can write of the martyr's ordeal as primarily the ordeal of a woman seeing herself stared at unfeelingly: 'a gazing-stock' for 'Pitiless eyes' ('A Martyr: The Vigil of the Feast', 259, before 1882). The self as 'gazing-stock' is the opposite, but complementary, pole of self as 'all-amazing monument'. Both situations are equally desperate, and equally isolated.

Although Rossetti's primary impulse may be to 'freeze' in a submissive yet self-displaying pose while awaiting an apocalyptic dissolution of roles, many of her religious poems render a more integrative experience of self. In another group of poems Rossetti explores the more integrative variant of the visual metaphor, compassionate 'looking'. In over twenty of the devotional poems the speaker asks Christ to look on or upon, look down, look back: that is, to respond actively to the sinner in her need. On the one hand, then, the persona of the religious poems 'sets' her face both to withstand hostile or falsifying stares and to keep watch for the transcendent union 'face to Face'; on the other, she achieves now, in her imperfect mortal state, an intimate and reciprocal relation:

> Yea, Lord, be mindful how out of the dust
> I look to Thee while Thou dost look on me,
> Thou Face to face with me and Eye to eye.
> (267, before 1893)

The divine face that participates in this type of encounter is not the beatified countenance, but the disfigured face of the crucified Christ. In 'The Descent from the Cross' Rossetti discovers the face that requires her to look with compassion:

> Is this the Face that thrills with awe
>   Seraphs who veil their face above?
> Is this the Face without a flaw,
>   The Face that is the Face of Love?
> Yea, this defaced, a lifeless clod,
>   Hath all creation's love of God,
>   Hath satisfied the love of God,
> This Face the Face of Jesus Christ.
> (254, before 1882)

Although the face that awes seraphs is in no way a false abstraction, like the idealized portraits of Elizabeth Siddal, there are structural parallels between this poem and 'In an Artist's Studio'. 'The Descent from the Cross' can, in fact, be read as an inversion of the secular poem. While in 'In an Artist's Studio' it is the idealized face that replaces the living, suffering face, in 'The Descent from the Cross' it is the idealized face that is absent, displaced by the reality of the dead Christ's disfigured face. Although the change in Christ's face is perceived as shocking 'defacement', it is also a change through which transcendent value persists: this face is still 'the face of Love'. The speaker recognizes this face, just as she recognizes Elizabeth

Siddal's marred face, because it is the face that is most like her own: the face of suffering and mortal change.

Looking upon this face of suffering can become a means of rescuing a relation and thus a self. For although the woman fixed in art appears to look back at the artist-spectator, she is not present in a relation. Her image reflects 'his' need, but 'she', as Christina Rossetti makes clear, is elsewhere. In the religious poems, however, if the watcher looks steadfastly upon Christ's suffering, there is a chance that looks will really go both ways, that Christ will respond to the spectacle of the watcher's suffering. Christ's suffering face is thus a proper revision of the fair face of the ideal beloved: it mirrors human suffering; it looks back with 'true kind eyes'.

Although Rossetti can imagine Christ actively looking for her 'Elsewhere and nearer Me' (221, before 1893), His look may be averted, and the speaker's utterance aimed at 'turning' that look: 'Lord, wilt Thou turn and look upon me then' (228, 30 September 1863); 'Turn, look upon me, let me hear Thee speak' (230, before 1886); 'Turn, as once turning / Thou didst behold Thy Saint' (231, before 1893). The speaker seems to beseech Christ as if He were a fixed and silent icon, projecting upon Him that fatal stillness which she experiences as part of her persona. But Christ's answering look, when the speaker does succeed in evoking it, breaks down her own iconicity. By His look Christ calls forth the speaker's integrated self. When, for instance, she asks the Lord to 'look' and 'see' what she has to offer, Christ answers that He looks not so much for flawed attributes – a 'marred' will, a heart 'crushed and hard' – as for a whole self: 'I crave not thine, but thee' (220, before 1886). Because her whole self, even marred and suffering, finds acceptance in Christ's expectant look, the speaker can imagine a relation of intense mutuality, represented as an exchange of looks:

> Lord, does Thou *look on* me, and will not I
>   Launch out my heart to Heaven to *look on* Thee?
>   Here if one loved me I should *turn to see*,
> And often think on him and often sigh.
>
>   (229, before 1893, my italics)

The analogy with lovers' looks is compelling not because it demonstrates Rossetti's thwarted erotic impulses, but because it so clearly demonstrates in what ways a relation is adequate. What Rossetti expects from God is no more than what she expects from a human relation. In her secular poetry, however, the human relation appears most often as failed:

> He looked at her with a smile,
>   She looked at him with a sigh,

Both paused to look awhile:
Then he passed by –
('Under Willows,' 368, 27 July 1864)

But while earthly lovers pass by, put off by what they see, and the would-be beloved remains 'silent and still', transfixed again in the watcher's pose, Christ looks persistently and stirs the speaker out of her immobility. Christ's look calls forth not only a whole self but an active one. Thus in a brief poem for the Vigil of St Peter, Rossetti, while retaining the visual metaphor, links it with movement:

O Jesu, gone so far apart
Only my heart can follow Thee,
That look which pierced St. Peter's heart
Turn now on me.

Thou who dost search me thro' and thro'
And mark the crooked ways I went,
Look on me, Lord, and make me too
Thy penitent.

(175, before 1893)

As a prayer, the poem assumes that words can have effect, that both the one who speaks and the one who is spoken to can be moved from fixed positions. If words bridge the distance between the speaker and Jesu, the speaker will attempt to establish a relation by working through a series of verbal definitions. Jesu's defining characteristic is His removal to a distance – 'gone so far apart'. Although both as lyric speaker and as watcher the suppliant maintains a fixed position, she moves synechdochically: her 'heart' follows the spatial route as far as it extends. But at this limit, like the heart, the poem itself has to turn back, and so it does, through the historical moment of Peter's denial and Christ's reproach to the present 'turn now on me'. As readers, we are expected to know the exact nature of St. Peter's sin, but not in what particular way his 'heart' was 'pierced' – whether with shame, remorse, sorrow, love, or all of these. All we know is that the speaker means to bring that piercing look into the present, purely as an act of attention.

The second stanza establishes a present context for the relation by extending the visual figure. Jesu has already looked piercingly at the speaker and judged her past goings, the 'crooked ways' as opposed to the heart following. Now the speaker asks Him to supersede those seeing acts with the look that not only judges, but also binds the one looked at in a relation to the one who looks. Jesu's attentive look will transform the speaker from a distant spectacle of sin and guilt into a self who is intimately related to God as 'Thy penitent'. God's penitent 'moves' inwardly: she changes position within a relation; she knows and is known, loves and is loved.

In the 'look' that registers compassion and compels a relation, Rossetti finds a way out of both her usual predicament and her usual defence against the pain of her predicament, as expressed in the figure who is both spectacle and watcher. Earlier I suggested that 'witness' was a useful term for the compounded watched-watcher. The witness testifies to her predicament by displaying a self in isolated immobility; she also testifies to the resolution of that predicament by describing what she sees: both God's glories and His sufferings, both woman's iconic mask and her changing, marred face. *One day*, then, not now, all distinctions will be subsumed in light, and we shall see and be seen 'face to Face'. Although the witness takes a stand, she or he still has the status of on-looker, distanced from the spectacle – whether of self or another – even in the act of representing it. But Rossetti discovers that the spectacle of suffering requires her to abandon the solipsism of the watcher-witness, and to commemorate other sufferers by 'looking' compassionately. 'Looking' can thus transform the act of witnessing into 'keeping vigil'. The vigil-keeper, as in 'The Vigil of St. Peter', looks back as well as forward. By commemorating the dead, the vigil-keeper establishes a community of suffering that links the living with the dead and constitutes a meaningful present.

Thus in the poem that begins 'Our Mothers, lovely women pitiful; / Our Sisters, gracious in their life and death' (214, before 1893), Rossetti keeps vigil for the dead while they, perhaps, watch over her. Like Tennyson, who speculates about Hallam's continuing participation in the concerns of the living, Rossetti cannot be sure that the dead women remain aware of their living sisters and daughters. But 'if they see us in our painful day, / How looking back to earth from Paradise / Do tears not gather in those loving eyes?' In the community of sufferers, even paradisal women cannot look at the spectacle of other women's pain without feeling identity. The poem ends with the consolation: 'Ah happy eyes! whose tears are wiped away / Whether or not you bear to look on me.' Rossetti can endure the possibility that looks do not go both ways, that she keeps vigil in isolation, by postulating heavenly consolation: eventually, too, her tears will be wiped away.

In poems like 'Our Mothers', vigil takes the form of valediction, the mode that both acknowledges and overcomes loss. In 1858, when she was twenty-eight, Rossetti wrote 'A Burden', a valediction for 'her' dead. Lying 'at rest asleep and dead', the dead in 'A Burden' exert a strong pull on the living. While the dead are fulfilled, the living still 'hope and love with throbbing breast', and long for the 'nest of love beneath / The sod'. A coherent pattern breaks through these effusions: the dead are both present and absent; they forget and remember; and, as the speaker extols them, 'They watch across the parting wall' (204–5).

Some time 'before 1886' Rossetti refined 'A Burden' to a twelve-line lyric, much less speculative and melodramatic than the earlier poem. In the later poem Rossetti wisely refrains from ruminations about the vanity of human wishes and simply celebrates the dead as irrevocably absent and firmly unforgotten:

> They lie at rest, our blessed dead:
> The dews drop cool above their head,
> They know not when fleet summer fled.
>
> Together all, yet each alone:
> Each laid at rest beneath his own
> Smooth turf or white allotted stone.
>
> When shall our slumber sink so deep,
> And eyes that wept and eyes that weep
> Weep not in the sufficient sleep?
>
> God be with you, our great and small,
> Our loves, our best beloved of all.
> Our own beyond the salt sea-wall.
>
> (127)

Although these dead do not look back, the speaker does not suffer in isolation; she takes her place as vigil-keeper within the community in which all are 'together' and yet 'alone'.

For despite her reclusive ways, her retreats into invalidism as well as art, Rossetti was not a private person. She was sister, daughter, friend and member of the larger community of the Christian church. She wanted to know who would be her society in the life to come; she wondered how the dead fared now, during the waiting time ('Have dead men long to wait? – ' (215, September 1858), and how they looked upon the living. Like many Victorian women, she kept vigil at a number of deathbeds – father, sister, brother, mother, aunts. In her poetry, she took on the responsibility of keeping the dead 'unforgotten'.

In doing so, she both commemorated the pain of her own history and transcended that pain by imagining it absorbed within a communal history. Thus she could write movingly of the separation between Paul and Barnabas: 'For saints in life-long exile yearn to touch / Warm human hands, and commune face to face; / But these we know not ever met again' (174, *c*.1877).

As a spinster she might have felt exiled from the country of love; as a Victorian woman poet she was in some sense exiled from the country of poetry; as 'saint', however, she could choose her exile. Significantly, saints do not give up their yearnings. What Rossetti always wanted was the kind of mutuality in which no one is object or other; thus the final resurrection is imaged as the most complete reintegration: each soul will return 'Bone to his bone', 'Each with his own not with another's face'. 'O faces unforgotten!' she says, 'if to part / Wrung sore, what will it be to re-embrace?' (215, before 1893). Only the final reintegration makes the present separation – self from self, self from other – endurable.

Thus Rossetti always comes full circle. By keeping vigil she testifies to the final outcome, but only the final restitution gives meaning to the vigil. Within this circle, however, she discovers a range of poetic stances. By marking the points at which her personal experience as 'model' woman, as painful spectacle, and as patient watcher converges with a systematic and pervasive metaphor – the visual metaphor for our cognitive and affective experience – we can see how the poetry reflects a coherent myth of self and how that myth informs the poetry.

In her handling of literary and Biblical traditions, Rossetti is both unique and the quintessential Victorian woman poet. To begin with, as a woman weighed down by certain monolithic cultural projections – woman as virgin bride, or dutiful helpmeet, or barren spinster, as ideal beloved or fatal temptress – she is even more susceptible, perhaps, than her male contemporaries to self-doubt and even more committed to assertions of certitude. Her actual powerlessness requires both stoic resignation and the confident belief that this, too, shall pass. The question remains: to what extent does her poetry transcend the cultural and literary stereotypes of her time? To what extent does the austere self-abnegation of her verse reflect a severely limiting aesthetic?

Undoubtedly she shares with other nineteenth-century women poets a tendency to exaggerate those conventions that represent life as brief and sorrowful and the poet-speaker as gratified only by the stigmata of her deprivation. The popular poet of the previous generation, Letitia Landon (L.E.L.), writing in 1829, describes her poetic programme thus: 'Aware that to elevate I must first soften, and that if I wished to purify I must first touch, I have ever endeavoured to bring forward grief, disappointment, the fallen leaf, the faded flower, the broken heart, the early grave.'[20] Although Landon's poetry is greatly inferior to Rossetti's, she exhibits the same concerns and the same 'aesthetic of pain' that Gilbert describes as characteristic of Rossetti. In Landon's tribute to Felicia Hemans this aesthetic is stated explicitly:

> Yet what is mind in woman, but revealing
>   In sweet clear light the hidden world below.
>
> . . . .
>
> The fable of Prometheus and the vulture
>   reveals the poet's and the woman's heart.[21]

Landon's stance here is clearly Romantic, shadowed by Shelley's Prometheus and Byron's heroic outcasts. But in the poetry of Christina Rossetti, as well as other Victorian poets, the myth of suffering for art's sake – Promethean, egoistic, male – is overlaid by the myth of suffering for its own sake – Christian, selfless, female. Further, that self-consuming suffering is often symbolized by a particular female type, the paralysed woman who is fatal only to herself, the sequestered maiden or the betrayed bride who yearns endlessly and endures forever unsought-for: Tennyson's Mariana, his Lady of Shalott, his Elaine; Arnold's Iseult of Brittany, who gazes 'Listlessly through the window-bars / . . . / From her lonely shore-built tower';[22] the female subjects of Rossetti's own 'Repining' and *The Prince's Progress*.

For this repining watcher, who experiences death-in-life, the only resolution is death itself.[23] And, in fact, the woman laid out in death or buried in the earth is an obsessive subject in Rossetti's early poems,[24] she passes 'out of sight of friend and of lover' only in what is presumed to be Rossetti's last poem, 'Sleeping at Last', (417, *c.*1893). Sometimes still a conscious watcher, as in 'After Death' (292, 1849), Rossetti's dead woman testifies both to the transcendence of desire and to the persistence of desire: she is dead because life is not *enough* – and because the aesthetic of renunciation requires this ultimate gesture.

It is important to remember, however, that the 'broken heart' and the 'early grave' are not solely female preoccupations. The dead or dying woman is a compelling image for nineteenth-century male poets as well, ranging from the tired-hearted subject of Arnold's 'Requiescat' (1849–53), who now 'In quiet . . . reposes', to the 'young and fair' subject of Wilde's 'Requiescat' (1881), who 'hardly knew / She was a woman', and now lies semi-sentient 'Under the snow', hearing 'The daisies grow'.[25] This kind of fatal woman – not the devouring Venus but the deathly still Proserpina – is, of course, one of Swinburne's obsessive subjects. The enigmatic 'she' of his 'A Leave-Taking'[26] is the apotheosis of the cruel beloved, as indifferent as death. The speaker takes his leave of her because no matter what apocalyptic transformations he might evoke, even 'all heaven in flower above', she would not 'hear', 'weep', 'love', 'care', or 'see'. The last stanza of this poem suggests why Swinburne finds this monolithic figure so fascinating. Even though it is the poet and his companions ('we') who leave, it is 'she' who negates *their* reality:

> Let us go hence, go hence; she will not see.
>   . . . but we,
> We are hence, we are gone, *as though we had not been there.*
> Nay, and though all men seeing had pity on me,
>   She would not see.

(my italics)

This sphinx-like figure, so like Rossetti's deathbed heroines and earth-blind watcher, embodies the ambiguity of female iconicity, for what looks like scornful indifference from the male perspective may be stoic indifference from the female perspective, the only way a female consciousness can deal with its own negation.

For the male poet, then, the figure of the dead woman can serve as a symbol of ultimate enigmas: the still perfection of art, the indifference of nature. For the female poet, however, the dead woman can represent only the perfection of her reification in life: the face composed in death is an extension of the smiling mask in life, as in Rossetti's 'Dead before Death' (313, 1854); the dissolution of the grave is both a reflection of her 'selflessness' and a resolution of her fragmentation. Living or dead, as a representative *object*, as sign, her real presence is negated: 'they' look, but do not see 'her', only her iconic power. In Rossetti's case, the contrast with Elizabeth Barrett Browning proves instructive. Barrett Browning, who also felt the constrictions of the smiling mask,[27] was ultimately able to break down the stoic pose that culminates in the pose of death, to reclaim the beautiful, open face as woman's own, and to exchange the power of silent iconicity for the power of living speech. In *Aurora Leigh* the heroine confronts and triumphs over a series of falsifying masks in order to discover in Marian Erle's resurrection from living 'death' a 'true' face and an authentication of her new poetics. For Rossetti, however, woman's 'true' face remains sorrowful and changeful, as well as ultimately unpicturable, absent from art. The smiling, composed face, or 'set' face blindly turned toward the light remain necessary (if falsifying) masks, and the renunciatory pose her only defence against the pain of falsification.

In her religious poetry, however, Rossetti transcends both the 'aesthetic of pain' and its trivialization in lesser poets by adopting a timeless background and a ritualized pattern for self-abnegation. By becoming 'witness' as well as 'model', the vigil-keeper as well as the dead person, Rossetti overcomes the despair inherent in the renunciatory pose. Ultimately, by exploring the possibilities of compassionate 'looking', Rossetti transforms the witness's isolated gazing into a collective act: the vigil — and valediction — for the dead. In a body of religious poetry as firmly incised as a witness-stone she not only registers her alienation, but also achieves, by 'looking', integration and community.

NOTES

1 Most of these were originally published by the Society for Promoting Christian Knowledge in three volumes of prose: *Called to be Saints* (1883), *Time Flies* (1885) and *The Face of the Deep* (1892). In 1893 the SPCK published *Verses*, collecting the poems previously published in the prose works. As David Kent (1979) has pointed out, the poems in *Verses* were arranged in eight sections reflecting Rossetti's own sense of a particular sequence. In the *Poetical Works* (1904) William arranged the selections from *Verses* in chronological order, thus disrupting the original order. Kent's argument that the sequential order takes precedence over the chronological order confirms my sense that chronological development is not an important criterion in assessing Rossetti's work, and that certain themes and strategies recur repeatedly as Rossetti elaborates upon a closed structure analogous to the cycle of the liturgical year.

2 Germaine Greer, for instance, faults Rossetti's religious poetry for not being 'metaphysical', and sees it as the product of sexual hysteria. She claims that as a typical Victorian woman poet Rossetti 'used the aspirations of piety as a metaphor for her own frustrated sexuality' (1975: x).

3 Hoxie Neale Fairchild sees her as a mechanical, uncritical writer who 'wrote an immense amount of rubbish'. Fairchild is somewhat wiser and more humane than Greer, however: 'It will not do to say that whenever she voices a longing for Jesus what she really wants is union with a man' (1957: 302, 307).

4 *Poetical Works*, ed. W. M. Rossetti, 1904: 167. Subsequent quotations are from this edition, hereafter cited in the text. Since only the first volume of R. W. Crump's *Complete Poems* is available at this writing, this edition could not be cited.

5 G. B. Tennyson 1981: 202.

6 The quotations in this paragraph are taken from Hemans, *Songs of the Affections*, ed. Reiman 1979: 225; Miles (ed.) 1891: 1967: VIII, 358; Procter 1914: 204–5.

7 The extent of Rossetti's allusions to scripture is well documented by Jiménez 1979.

8 Gilbert and Gubar 1979: 564.

9 Ibid., 575.

10 Ibid., 564.

11 Barrett Browning 1900; 1973: II, 236. Keble 1869: 19.

12 In an important and wide-ranging essay (1980), W. David Shaw analyses the range of optical models available to Victorian writers and asserts the centrality of what he calls the 'optical' metaphor to Victorian poetics.

13 'Eye hath not seen, nor ear hath heard, / Nor heart conceived that full "enough"', which sums up the insufficiency of earthly satisfactions, is a crucial tag for a number of poems. See Jiménez 1979: 128.

14 Rossetti's sense of self reflects the experience of self as object and other described by Simone de Beauvoir (1952). This alienated experience of self can be

considered as intensified by the actual experience of being looked at. The art
critic John Berger, echoing de Beauvoir, describes woman as split between the
surveyor and the surveyed; the surveyor part watches the surveyed in order to
exemplify how the whole self is to be treated. In so exemplifying herself, woman
'turns herself into an object – and most particularly an object of vision: a sight'
(1977: 46–7).

15   Dobbs 1977: 79.
16   D. G. Rossetti 1976: 99–100.
17   Lochnan 1978: 1.
18   Bell 1898: 53.
19   For a fuller treatment of Rossetti's adaptation of the model's pose in the body of
     her work, see Rosenblum 1979.
20   Landon 1855: I, xiv.
21   Miles (ed.) 1891–7; 1967: VIII, 110.
22   Arnold 1965: 199.
23   Citing Welsh (1971) and Douglas (1977), Gilbert and Gubar suggest that the
     self-abnegating Victorian woman is indeed death-like. She represents the
     'mystical otherness of death', as well as the 'secret striving for power by the
     powerless'. Deprived of power in worldly spheres, she rules over the kingdom of
     the dead, and can even be seen as the bearer of death (1979: 24–7).
24   These include 'A Portrait', 'After Death', 'Rest', 'Life Hidden', 'Sound Sleep',
     'Two Thoughts of Death', 'Song', 'A Dirge', 'A Pause', 'Buried', 'The Last Look',
     'Gone Before'.
25   Arnold 1965: 346; Wilde 1908; 1969: 57.
26   Swinburne 1925: I, 185–6.
27   See Barrett Browning's 'The Mask' in 1900; 1973: III, 190.

9

'Men sell not such in any town': Exchange in *Goblin Market*

Terrence Holt

Goblin Market has been read as a nursery tale, as a portrait of a divided self, as a fantasy about sexuality, and, most recently, as a parable about sisterhood.[1] The emphasis in all of these readings has been on the goblins, and the issues of gender and sexuality they seem to represent, while the 'market' of the title has received little attention. A reading of the poem's economics, however, helps to resolve some of the issues that have troubled readings focusing on gender. Seen in terms of the economic, sexual and linguistic exchange incorporated in it, the poem becomes a parable not only about gender relations, but about power relations as well.[2] *Goblin Market* attempts to imagine a position for women outside systems of power, but its language, which cannot escape from gender, undoes the attempt: the autonomy is an illusion.

In *The Madwoman in the Attic*, Sandra Gilbert and Susan Gubar observe that Christina Rossetti's *Goblin Market* has become a 'textual crux for feminist critics' (566). Gilbert and Gubar themselves see in it a bitter renunciation of literature − of an art, they argue, that is (and perhaps can only be) male.[3] More recently, Dorothy Mermin has described *Goblin Market* as an assertion of women's literary power. The two readings seem impossibly opposed, suggesting that another, unacknowledged, force is at work within the text, a force that neither reading sees whole.

One such force within *Goblin Market* is economic. Economic language and metaphors, terms of finance and commerce ('buy', 'offer', 'merchant', 'stock', 'money', 'golden', 'precious', 'sell', 'fee', 'hawking', 'coin', 'rich', etc.) permeate the poem, which opens with an extended invitation to the market: 'Morning and evening / Maids heard the goblins cry: / "Come buy our orchard fruits, / Come buy, come buy."'[4] The phrase 'come buy' echoes throughout the poem, its iteration stressed by the description of it as the goblins' 'shrill repeated cry' (l.89), their 'customary cry, / "Come buy, come buy," / With its iterated jingle / Of sugar-baited words' (II. 231–4). Economic metaphors inhabit apparently innocent words: the cry is 'customary' because it solicits the custom of Lizzie and Laura; the words 'jingle' not only because of their iteration,[5] but because they evoke the jingle of coin (cf. 11. 452–3). That the goblins are costermongers, economic creatures as well as sexual ones, suggests that sexual and economic systems of relation may intersect in other ways as well.[6]

Despite the pervasiveness of the goblins' cry, however, the ostensible function of this discourse of the marketplace is to stress the difference between maidens and goblins. Exchange, *Goblin Market* claims, is the province of goblins, not of girls. Indeed, Lizzie and Laura seem to know instinctively that 'We must not look at goblin men, / We must not buy their fruits' (11. 42–3). The market is dangerous to maids, who belong safely at home. This emphasis on difference is of course partly a matter of sexual difference. But this is not so much an interest in the prurient possibilities of difference as an attempt at keeping the sexes apart. A separation between maidens and goblins must be preserved, the poem warns, because commerce with goblins is dangerous to maids. The goblins' glen is 'haunted' (l. 552), and has caused the death already of one maid (ll. 147–61). Lizzie's virtuous horror of the place (ll. 242–52) alludes to a nameless threat, but her delicate evasion only pretends to conceal the obvious: the threat is the proverbial fate worse than death.

The sexual threat in the glen touches as well on another concern in *Goblin Market*, the place of women in the literary world. The glen echoes with a literary tradition that has used women as sexual scapegoats. The 'bowers' (l. 151) from which these fruits are plucked parody a similar snare in Spenser, the Bower of Bliss; Laura's reaction to this low, swampy place (ll. 226–7) suggests its affinity with the Slough of Despond in *The Pilgrim's Progress*.[7] A woman who enters the glen, especially a woman writer, places herself in a historical context that assigns her a negative value on the literary exchange.

A difference between maidens and goblins must be preserved, furthermore, because commerce with the goblins is also potentially infectious: the threat in the goblins' glen is not only that one may be attacked by them, but that one may become like them. Their victims become as 'restless' (l. 53) as the brook that whispers there, a restlessness like the 'Helter skelter, hurry skurry' (l. 344) activity that typifies the goblins. Lizzie, counselling her sister to keep away, assumes that separation can enforce difference, an assumption echoed in the two passages that introduce us to the sisters' home.

Home in *Goblin Market* seems the opposite of the goblins' glen, isolated from the world of commerce. The first scene in the home (ll. 184–98) stresses the sisters' isolation, in implicit contrast to the goblins' prolific trade. The home is also a scene of busy industry, wherein the sisters produce healthful foods independently of the marketplace, foods that differ pointedly from the goblins' exotic fruits:

> Early in the morning
> When the first cock crowed his warning,
> Neat like bees, as sweet and busy,
> Laura rose with Lizzie:
> Fetched in honey, milked the cows,
> Aired and set to rights the house,
> Kneaded cakes of whitest wheat,
> Cakes for dainty mouths to eat,
> Next churned butter, whipped up cream,
> Fed their poultry, sat and sewed;
> Talked as modest maidens should:
> Lizzie with an open heart,
> Laura in an absent dream,
> One content, one sick in part;
> One warbling for the mere bright day's delight,
> One longing for the night
>
> (ll. 199–214)

The sisters produce foods for their own consumption, enacting on an economic level the hermeticism of their domestic scene. The description of the sisters as they set to work compares them to bees, and the simile is peculiarly apt: they are bee-like not only in the quiet hum of their industry, but especially in their self-sufficiency, producing with their own labour the food that sustains them.

The sisters themselves glean from nature the raw materials of food they produce at home, and have no need to resort to the market to trade for someone else's wares. By contrast, the goblins' wares may not even have been, originally, their own. Lizzie's question about their fruit – 'Who knows upon what soil they fed / Their hungry thirsty roots?' (ll. 44–5) – questions the root-origins of those fruits; the goblins have the look of middlemen, and their fruits, coming from a tropic distance, seem far from their native soil. This goblin capital is thus doubly alienated, an alienation that makes the sisters' apparently uncomplicated and direct nourishment by the land yet another sign of their difference from the commercial goblins.

The repeated journeyings back and forth between market and home make this difference literal, defining a physical distance between them. The two are separated by an extensive waste (l. 325), a steep bank (l. 227), and a gate

(l. 141). The goblins themselves stress the difference between the two places in their conversation with Lizzie, who wants to take some of their fruit back to succour her dying sister: 'Such fruits as these / No man can carry; / Half their bloom would fly' (ll. 375–7), they tell her. Indeed, the failure of the 'kernel-stone' to grow goblin-fruit at the sisters' home (ll. 281–5) reinforces their message. The two places belong to different biological (and moral) orders, a difference that, despite Laura's despair, is ultimately consoling: if that kernel had grown, what havoc might its fruit have wrought in the sisters' domestic haven?

But the repeated distinctions between the glen and the home, which seem intended to assert the sisters' independence from goblin economics, are not as absolute as they seem. The home is inescapably involved in economics – as the word's Greek root, *oikonomia* ('management of a household'), suggests. The domestic is historically a scene of economic exploitation, prison and workhouse as much as haven.[8] *Goblin Market* expresses the potential involvement of the home in exchange in part by the very strength of its attempt to evade such involvement.[9]

The insistence on the separation between the two realms cannot conceal the home's contamination by exchange. Even in our first view of it, Laura already keeps house in an 'absent dream', 'sick in part' and 'longing for the night' (ll. 211–14). She only seems like a modest maiden; inside, the goblin's poison is working in her veins. The honey they gather is tainted: it has appeared already in the poem, literally in a goblin's mouth. 'In tones as smooth as honey' (l. 108), the goblins hawk their wares to the sisters. The honey not only sustains the home but is at the same time an inducement to go outside it, to partake in the system of exchange that invades and undoes that world.

Another sign of that undoing is one of the more peculiar rhetorical features of the poem, the use of parenthesis.[10] The parenthetical phrase '(Men sell not such in any town)' is, like the goblins' 'come buy', a characteristic iteration, characteristic not of the goblins, but of the poem itself. As a figure, parenthesis tropes the attempt of the poem to bracket off the sisters from the surrounding world of exchange. But this parenthesis seems to exempt 'men' from the goblins' world of exchange. The apparent oddness of this claim reminds us that parenthesis, rather than existing outside of the discourse it interrupts, speaks (as in the dramatic convention of the aside[11]) to the heart of the matter. The bracketing off of a parenthetical phrase does not exclude it, so much as clear for it a privileged space. The rhetorical form of parenthesis, even as it figures the bracketing off of the sisters from the dangers of the marketplace, also points to the paradox undermining that strategy: we know that in terms of rhetoric what we seem to set aside is actually not separate from, but centrally involved in, the discourse it interrupts.

The content of this particular parenthesis, '(Men sell not such in any town)', by exempting men while neglecting the women we would expect to find exempted, suggests another problem. The claim that 'men sell not' seems to distract us from the possibility that women might be involved in exchange. The phrase appears twice: first when the poetic speaker describes the goblins in the act of laying out their wares (ll. 97–104), and second when Laura repeats the description to her children (ll. 552–6). Each time, the speaker and Laura lay great stress on the allure of the fruit, enticing their audiences – Lizzie or us – to come and participate either (as buyer) in the goblins' market or (as reader) in *Goblin Market*.[12] The poem raises its seemingly irrelevant question as to what men do or do not sell at just those moments when the sisters' separation from the world of marketing threatens to collapse.

Human (not goblin) men are invoked here, introducing ad hoc a 'real' set of distinctions between men and women, because the fantastic structure of domestic maiden and merchant goblin threatens to break down. But instead of obfuscating the question of who is involved in the market and who is not, the introduction of 'men' only reveals the goblins as scapegoats for the sisters' involvement in exchange. The mention of human men reminds us that the opposition between maidens and goblins is an artificial one, that the goblins are literary constructs, and it begs the question of their function: either to stand for men in a transparent allegory, or to stand for someone else. But 'men sell not', and the only someone else remaining is the sisters themselves. This brings us to a recognition of the specular relationship between community and scapegoat, projector and projection, sister and 'queer brother'.

Strategies of exclusion elsewhere in the poem tend to follow this same self-defeating logic, by which excluded material returns to the domestic fold in the inevitable return of the repressed. Laura's fall and redemption is paradigmatic: intended to assert the sisters' essential difference from the goblins, it leads instead to a collapse of distinction. Although Laura wants what the goblins have to sell, she cannot buy it, precisely because of her difference from them. The sisters' domestic retreat is distinguished from the goblins' world of exchange by the reiterated fact that their retreat has no money. Laura tells the goblins:

> 'Good folk, I have no coin;
> To take were to purloin:
> I have no copper in my purse,

> I have no silver either,
> And all my gold is on the furze
> That shakes in windy weather.'

(ll. 116–20)

Laura's paradise of unalienated labour has no need for money, and no means of getting it. But her attraction to the world of exchange, her powerlessness within it, and most of all the nature of the exchange she makes there suggest that her lack of a coin stands for fears that what a woman really lacks is a privileged term of gender.

The goblins' response puts this essentialist logic into motion, equating her body with her value within a gendered system of exchange. Laura does have gold to exchange: '"You have much gold upon your head,' / They answered all together: / 'Buy from us with a golden curl"' (ll. 123–5). The clipping of her lock, the crucial act in the drama of exchange in the poem, is sexually problematic. As the allusion to Pope hints,[13] and what follows seems to confirm, the scene is in many ways a rape. But any attempt to read it in this way must take into account Laura's complicity: Laura enters into this exchange with her eyes literally wide open (ll. 50–4). The similarity of the goblin feast to a rape disguises something worse. Especially in its erotically charged context, the shearing of something long from a woman's body is powerfully suggestive of castration.[14]

Such a reading is complicated, however, by an equally crucial paradox. Although Laura seems to castrate herself as the condition of entering into intercourse with the goblins, this act only confirms her in a condition already hers. She has already told them that she has 'no coin', that her 'purse' is empty (ll. 116, 118). Moreover, she has been described from her first appearance in terms of her desire for the goblins' fruit, her felt lack of what those 'fruit globes fair or red' (l. 128) represent. The goblins' bargain is a cheat, requiring that she give up precisely what she desires. Worse, in figuring women as castrated men, the gesture denies the essential difference between maidens and men. Worst of all, in shearing her own lock, Laura collaborates in this construction of her within a male order.

The implications of the sisters' construction within a phallocentric conception of gender are fended off by projecting those implications on to the goblins. As half-animal, half-human monsters, the goblins displace the burden of anatomical deformity. Each 'merchant man' possesses an animal attribute – cat's face, tail, rat's pace, snail's foot (ll. 71–6). In differing so strangely from their essential, human form, they seem to possess no integrity of body or of character. Varying not only from each other, but from themselves – 'Leering at each other, / Brother with queer brother; / Signalling each other, / Brother with sly brother' (ll. 93–6) – the goblins are marked off from themselves. The iterated 'brothers' are estranged by the intervening modifiers, and the modifiers themselves, 'queer' and 'sly', add to the goblins' duplicity. The sisters suffer no such self-division: their sameness is emphasized both by the description of them (ll. 184–190), and by the contrast to the goblins' unruly variety.

But this attempt to reverse the traditional hierarchies of sexual privilege also fails. The sisters' saving sameness is characterized in figures that culminate in 'wands of ivory . . . for awful kings' (ll. 190–1). The sisters, too, differ from their essential qualities of femininity and sameness. The 'wands' are not only phallic, but also 'tipped with gold': value and the phallic coincide, repeating the pervasive assumption that whatever the goblins have is worth having. Worse, these wands are *'for* awful kings'. The sisters, even in the heart of their sanctuary, are figuratively in service of a male system of power. Rather than reversing traditional hierarchies, the figurative language restates them.

There are other attempts to reverse traditional valuations of male and female in other ways as well, most notably by figuring the goblins as parasitical users of language, associated with mimicry, mockery and theft.[15] 'One parrot-voiced and jolly / Cried "Pretty Goblin" still for "Pretty Polly"' (ll. 112–13): the substitution of 'Goblin' for 'Polly' is typical, as a goblin displaces a woman as the one whose speech is supplementary to an original voice. 'Chuckling, clapping, crowing, / Clucking and gobbling' (ll. 334–5), the goblins approach Lizzie 'Chattering like magpies' (l. 345), thieves not only of shiny objects (such as a maiden's penny) but of speech itself.[16] Their theft of speech is not only parasitic but deficient: their stolen speech is merely animal noise, 'Barking, mewing, hissing, mocking' (l. 402), meaningless parody that in its half-animal departure from sense echoes the goblins' bodily difference from the sisters' physical integrity.

But this attempt to ascribe to the goblins the deficiency traditionally associated both with women's bodies and with women's writing succumbs to the same internal contradictions that thwart other such attempts in the poem. Through their mockeries, the goblins succeed in compromising the very bodily integrity the sisters must preserve. At the climax of their violence against Lizzie, they 'Scratched her, pinched her black as ink, / Kicked and knocked her, / Mauled and mocked her, / Lizzie uttered not a word' (ll. 427–30). The lines associate goblin sexual violence with writing, and although it attempts to render that writing deficient, claiming that the goblins fail in their assault on her virginity, the imagery of ink contradicts the claim: Lizzie leaves the market marked by goblin pens. Lizzie's stained, dishevelled appearance as she leaves the market confirms what the poem has already told us when the goblins 'Twitched her hair out by the roots' (l. 404).

As if to dispel the implications of this loss, the raucous goblins disappear 'without a sound' (l. 445), taking on the obdurate silence that has been Lizzie's only defence. Here, again, the poem differs with itself: if Lizzie's silence is her strength, to silence the goblins strengthens them; and if unspotted virtue is what such silence is supposed to buy, Lizzie's traffic with the goblins has hardly been the sharp trading the poem goes on to declare it.

The malign influence of the goblins' fruit follows the same vexed logic of projection. 'In an absent dream . . . sick in part', and 'longing', Laura shows all the symptoms of the disease of sexuality that the poem has attempted to make the goblins' problem. Blaming it on the goblins makes Laura's problem something external, not (as one might fear) something essentially and inescapably female: this is only *a* curse, not *the* curse. But such essentialist fears about gender resist repression in *Goblin Market*: Laura's illness goes deep, and its effect is pervasive. 'Gone deaf and blind' (l. 259), she sinks farther from any proficiency with language, becoming capable only of watching 'in vain / In sullen silence of exceeding pain' (ll. 270–1). Unlike Lizzie's heroic silence in the face of the goblins' assault, Laura's silence signifies her weakness: 'Her tree of life drooped from the root: / She said not one word in her heart's sore ache' (ll. 260–1). She 'dwindles' (l. 278) into a comparison with the waning moon, another emblem of changefulness traditionally associated with women.

As the similarity of Lizzie's tactics of silence to Laura's symptom of silence suggests, and the identity of the means of Laura's fall and of her deliverance reveals, the magic used to counter the goblins is the same as the goblin magic itself.[17] Magic is traditionally a practice of fetishism, and the magic in *Goblin Market*, with its stress on deracinated fruits and uprooted hair, is no different.[18] The most important fetish that the sisters enlist in their commerce with the goblins is the penny that Lizzie takes to purchase Laura's salvation. Arming Lizzie with a coin is for the poem an act of apotropaeia, but the attempt is foredoomed because the coin, once used to supplement an assumed deficiency, represents a tacit acceptance of that assumption.[19]

Lizzie needs the coin to fill the void that might otherwise ordain the sisters' powerlessness, but her possession of that coin transgresses the economic logic that divides the world of *Goblin Market* into goblin and maiden, have and have-not. Unlike Laura, Lizzie is not penniless. She 'put[s] a silver penny in her purse' (l. 324) and goes off to save Laura. In light of Laura's poverty, Lizzie's access to cash here is so unproblematic that it begs the question of how she came by the coin. Their only gold, we know, is 'furze' (l. 120) (which the *OED* tells us is of no economic value), and everything else we have learned about them confirms them in their innocence of exchange, not only their pennilessness but their complete lack of anything (beside their bodies) that they might convert to coin. The very self-sufficiency of their *oikonomia* makes that penny a wildly unlikely object for Lizzie to produce at this moment.

So has Lizzie, too, sold herself in the market? Of course she has: by figuring the sisters' only exchangeable goods as their bodies, the poem makes that penny nothing but a sign of sexual experience. The kind of freedom from exchange that the poem has attempted to imagine for these sisters is impossible, whether we look to the historical context within which *Goblin Market* was composed, or within the poem itself, where so many disturbing traces of goblin activity appear in the heart of its ostensibly excluded zones. The penny appears in Lizzie's hands as yet another sign of an inescapable taint, an original guilt as well as an originary lack. Moreover, that it can only magically supply her with a penny confirms that she cannot really have one, and tacitly accepts and asserts the goblins' valorization (which is actually a disvaluation) of women's bodies, a valorization predicated on women's lack of these arbitrary symbols of power.

Another issue vexing Lizzie's use of the penny is that exchange also functions in *Goblin Market* as a kind of scription, in which attempts at fixing distinctions, at determining meaning or value, unleash instead a runaway, inflationary spiral of desire.[20] As Laura eats, more and more fruit does not satisfy. 'She sucked and sucked and sucked the more' (l. 134), but her hunger only sharpens. As her disease grows, it fixes on no object of desire; the signifying elements of her exchange do not arrive at any final referent: they only iterate, and Laura is left with 'emptied rinds' (l. 137), dreaming

> of melons, as a traveller sees
> False waves in desert drouth
> With shade of leaf-crowned trees,
> And burns the thirstier in the sandful breeze.
>
> (ll. 289–92)

The iteration of empty signs strikes no root into the real, and leaves Laura finally a victim of mirages, seeing only 'false waves' repeating the iterative structure of signification. These lines seem to represent the dead end of Laura's descent: from here on until her miraculous cure, she appears only in terms of what she does not, will not, or can not do (ll. 293–8, 309, 320–1). No wonder the thing she wants will not cloy with use: it uses her more than she uses it; her inscription within desire seems to render her incapable of activity in the world of things, and a victim – not the master – of the world of signs.

Implicit in Laura's deficiency is a belief that men – goblin or human – are empowered; just as that assumption of deficiency disvalues women's bodies, it values men's. The central figure for value in *Goblin Market* is actually not the penny, but what it buys – the goblins' fruit, the object of Laura's desire. The fruit is not only the goblins' property, it is the prop of their power within exchange, the sign of their construction as male, putative possessors of both the phallus and power. The identification between power and the phallic goes beyond the goblins' mastery over Laura, or Lizzie's problematic possession of that penny. As Lizzie resists the goblin onslaught, she appears

> Like a beacon left alone
> In a hoary roaring sea
> Sending up a golden fire, –
> Like a fruit-crowned orange-tree
> Sore beset by wasp and bee, –
> Like a royal virgin town
> Topped with gilded dome and spire
> Close beleaguered by a fleet
> Mad to tug her standard down
>
> (ll. 412–21)

Laura, too, as the cure works in her, is described as a 'watch-tower', a 'mast', a 'tree', even a 'foam-topped waterspout'. When the sisters achieve power, these figures for triumph retain their goblin trait, calling into question their function as figures of a total victory for women. The fantasy collapses, as if under its own weight: the watch-tower is shattered by an earthquake (ll. 513–15), the mast struck by lightning (l. 516), the tree uprooted (l. 517), and the waterspout 'cast down headlong' (l. 520). And to the extent that these images repeat the heroic images of Lizzie's resistance, Laura's fall is the collapse of Lizzie's power as well.

Mastery of language and literature seems to compensate the women for their powerlessness in other realms. After Lizzie's triumph, as she runs back to her sister, she 'heard her penny jingle / Bouncing in her purse, / Its bounce was music to her ear' (ll. 452–4). She gets back her penny, compensating her loss of all that penny stands for. Its jingle is similarly consoling: it appropriates the 'iterated jingle' of the goblins' cry. As the poem moves toward its conclusion, music, song, and poetry burst forth from Lizzie and Laura. Laura in particular is compensated for her former powerlessness within language: her 'sullen silence of exceeding pain' (l. 271) is redeemed as she becomes the chief user of language in the closing lines of the poem. The ending of the poem, in which Laura appears as a story-teller, confirms this reassuring control. Just as the goblins call the sisters at the beginning of the poem, Laura in its closing lines calls another audience to come to *Goblin Market*:

Laura would call the little ones
And tell them of her early prime,
Those pleasant days long gone
Of not-returning time:
Would talk about the haunted glen,
The wicked, quaint fruit-merchant men,
Their fruits like honey to the throat
But poison in the blood;
(Men sell not such in any town:)

(ll. 548–56)

Within her retelling of the tale she must repeat the goblins' fruit-cry: thus Laura expropriates the goblins' mercantile cry, seeming to recapture the honey they have expropriated. But more than taking over the goblins' marketing words, Laura takes over the words of *Goblin Market* itself: the tale she tells is, presumably, the tale we have been reading. Incorporating the text into her tale, Laura seems to bring the entire system of exchange – the goblin market, and the poem disseminating it – with all its disquieting iterations, under her control.

But the containment this gesture at closure seems to establish is, like other such attempts at enclosure within the poem, of mixed success. As closure, this ending only signals the start of yet another telling of the story. The evident nostalgia of Laura's retelling of her adventures,[21] the enjoyment and complicity implicit in her assumption of the goblins' role of caller or crier, story-teller or -seller, leave us with a world not purged of goblin marketing, but bound together by incitements to exchange. The poem ends with an assertion of women's power over that world, but to the extent that such a claim only contradicts doubts raised elsewhere in the poem, the claim leaves the issue of women's power unresolved. The question left open might be, 'Can women actually profit in a market so dominated by goblins?' Or, to put it in literary terms, 'Can women find poetic voices in a world where the structures of representation are male?' The enduring value of *Goblin Market*, finally, is that it does not offer a simple resolution to an insoluble dilemma. It does not evidence any despair of answering the question affirmatively, as Gilbert and Gubar claim, nor does it really represent a wishful utopian fantasy of success. Rather, it ends not with the resolution of the question, but with the definition of a long, uphill struggle.

Goblin Market does not end in despair of the possibilities of a woman's literature. That its closing lines portray a woman as an effective story-teller says as much. But couching such a proclamation in a fairy-tale context (Laura literally becomes a teller of fairy [of goblin] tales, a marginal purveyor of old

wives' romances rather than a modern, realist poet such as Elizabeth Barrett
Browning envisions in *Aurora Leigh*) also expresses a fear that women may
not achieve such power so readily in the real world. The poem ultimately, if
indirectly, brings us to recognize that utopian fantasies of a separate women's
culture are just that: fantasies of an impossible utopia.

Although Lizzie returns in triumph to her sister, her joy is not alone the
full story. The complete passage reads:

> She heard her penny jingle
> Bouncing in her purse,
> Its bounce was music to her ear.
> She ran and ran
> As if she feared some goblin man
> Dogged her with some gibe or curse
> Or something worse:
> But not one goblin skurried after
> Nor was she pricked by fear.

(ll. 452–60)

The fear that dogs Lizzie's footsteps as she runs home to her sister qualifies
her triumph. The passage concludes with an unconvincing claim that she
runs only because her 'kind heart made her windy-paced' (l. 461). But the
'gibe or curse' that Lizzie fears – the words that might 'prick' her – still
echoes with 'something worse', something that the lines do not name, and
whose effects the poem as a whole denies. Certainly Lizzie's explanation
makes sense: she runs to aid her dying sister. But it is just as certainly only
half the story: if there is no fear (and we have seen much demonstrating that
there is something to fear), why mention it?

The unnameable threat is the very power to name. Such a power is, in the
world of *Goblin Market*, essentially goblin. In the goblins' and sisters'
struggle to construct each other as essentially deficient, a goblin gibe has the
power of a curse because language itself favours the goblins. Throughout the
poem, although the sisters are implicated in goblin speech, the goblins
appear as the more powerful users of language, able to determine the terms
of a bargain or of a discourse of gender. The central element in Laura's
enslavement, in fact, is her acceptance of the goblins' use of figural language.
Troping the gold she lacks with the gold on her head, the goblins lead her
to accept their construction of her within their gendered system of exchange:
she bargains on their terms. This is the 'gibe or curse' that dogs Lizzie's
steps, the 'something worse' that cannot be named: the power of the goblins
to determine her significance, to name her price within their system. The
goblins' systems of exchange, including language, are constructed in terms

of what the sisters lack – it surfaces as the 'prick' even within these lines[22] – and in those terms the sisters will always be found at a loss for words.

Both the fear of goblin pricking and the sisterly denial define the logic of the closing scenes of the poem, as one stratagem after another is deployed to conceal the fear that would, if acknowledged, render the sisters as mute in their home as in the company of the goblins. Laura's recovery, bringing 'Life out of death' (l. 524), demands impossible reversals, just as the establishment of their women's utopia requires impossible dispensations from the laws of exchange. Chief among these exceptions and reversals, of course, is that mysterious penny and its return, but others obtrude here as well: the disappearance of grey from Laura's hair (l. 540), and especially the recovery of her 'innocent old way' (l. 538). If, as the poem so broadly hints, Laura's transgression was sexual, such a recovery is physically impossible: time, as we read a few lines later, is 'not-returning' (l. 551). Grey hairs do not turn gold; sexually experienced women do not become virgins; death comes after life: a bargain is a bargain.

'Life out of death' is a familiar Christian paradox. In such terms, it marks a crux, both a turning point for Laura and the sign of her redemption through Lizzie's Christ-like passion. This redeeming turn is structurally apocalyptic, offering a discontinuous transition from the conditions of life or history into a realm where the ills of the world are healed by effacing that world, its laws, and all its material concerns. In one set of terms from current critical theory, such a redemption offers a consoling fantasy of the subject's escape from power relations – an impossible exemption, in other words, from the very forces that give the subject existence.[23] The consolation of what follows in *Goblin Market* is plain, but the wishful, fantastic nature of this consolation – its historical discontinuousness and the impossibility of its realization in Rossetti's world – are equally apparent, as repressed threats return in the closing passages of the poem.

The most important repression to return is implicit in the families that the sisters raise, 'Afterwards, when both were wives' (l. 544). 'Wives' suggest husbands, bringing up once again the question raised elsewhere by the parenthetical mention of men and their role in the world of exchange – where are the men? Such questions arise inevitably in an androcentric world, and coming up at the conclusion of *Goblin Market* direct our attention away from the sisters to the inescapable male subject. In *Goblin Market*, 'sisters' become 'wives' – become defined not in relation to other women but in relation to men. The outcome of the sisters' tale seems to assume this change, as if such were the only natural, the inevitable event. Well it might: the change in nomenclature once more concedes on the linguistic level the androcentrism the sisters have fought so hard against and points to the reason for their ultimate defeat in that struggle. The verbal ground they fight on – the language literally constructing them – is already lost. Although 'wife', the *OED* tells us, is ultimately 'of obscure origin', it defines the term unhesitatingly: 'A woman', merely confirms what the derivation of 'woman' from the Old English *wif-man* already tells us: her origins obscure, woman takes her definition in relation to 'man' (a term the *OED* defines by the etymologically tautological 'A human being'). The control that the mercantile goblins exert in this poem, the extension of their law throughout the world of *Goblin Market*, simply gives mercantile expression to an underlying verbal law.

The answer to the implied question about the husbands is obvious: the goblins are the husbands, of course,[24] and in that relation to these 'wives' they overcome the sisters' attempt to escape them. Through their progeny, the goblins supply the audience for the literary creations of the women. Laura, appearing at the end of the poem as the story-teller in the centre of the children's circle, takes up once more the position she occupied earlier in the poem, where she appears surrounded by goblins (ll. 91–6), the object of their gaze.[25] This reminder of that earlier scene calls into question her command of the situation at the end. To be in the middle of an audience is not necessarily a position of authority: perhaps, the ending suggests, to achieve a voice as a woman is no escape from the gendering of representation. And the goblins do not merely surround, they occupy these literary creations as well, displacing the sisters from their own story: this is *Goblin Market*, not 'Laura and Lizzie', or whatever name that unwritten, other poem might have had.

The networks of power binding *Goblin Market* more than occupy the scene of poetic exchange that closes the poem: they overrun the confines of the poem, including us as well in a final dissemination that asserts the pervasiveness of such relations. We, as readers, become goblins too: as audience, in answering Laura's call to come hear the story of *Goblin Market* we share the place of the goblin children. Our stance throughout the poem as voyeurs of sexual exchange recalls that earlier, 'leering' circle of goblins. Ending with its own beginning, the poem describes an endless cycle of iterations in which, by reading the poem, we readers have become embroiled. But our involvement actually aligns us with both sides of the binary structure of the poem in yet another collapse of such distinctions. Doubling the audience within the poem, we become part of the subject of the story. Caught up in its repetition-compulsions, we are held in a situation of compelled audition not unlike Laura's addiction to the goblin fruit: once we have gone to 'Goblin Market', our independence is also in doubt.

The poem brings us to question our own exemption from the systems of power it has revealed. Here, finally, is how Rossetti does not escape but redefines the glass coffin that Gilbert and Gubar see as one fate of women's writing. By refusing to allow the reader to remain complacently on the outside of the poem, by insisting on our implication in systems of power to which we are also subject, Rossetti transforms *Goblin Market* from a fairy tale to a cautionary parable about the difficulty of achieving freedom. This glass coffin is not, finally, only a woman's problem: we are all interred within our separate ideologies, whether of gender, politics, or literature, blind to the very assumptions that seem so transparently true – and thus imprison us.

In imagining women as castrated and in that castration different from men, the reader of *Goblin Market* encounters the full implications of a male strategy that denies male fears by projecting them on to women. Perhaps this is why *Goblin Market* can be read, as Gilbert and Gubar do, as a renunciation of the literary tradition. The androcentric construction of gender seems to have had enormous implications for Rossetti in her own career. If that construction influenced Rossetti's perception of her own literary liabilities, she could well have concluded that the only position she could occupy in the literary world was on the margins: an attitude of abject self-denial; the stance adopted, in fact, in the bulk of her work, the religious poems which in their self-denial and barely tempered despair deny *Goblin Market*'s song of triumph.

Whatever Rossetti's own beliefs, conscious or unconscious, about her own abilities, if we as readers also arrive at such a conclusion about *Goblin Market*, we do her an injustice, and risk relegating the bulk of her work to the same dusty shelf it has occupied for so many years. The flaw in such a conclusion, of course, is that there is a volume – not an inconsiderable one – on that shelf in the first place. Writing is never self-denial. Although unflinching in its assessment of the difficulty of life, especially the life of a single woman, a woman not the 'correlative of a husband', Rossetti's verse yet celebrates endurance, uphill struggle even though the road may be uphill until its end. And so *Goblin Market*, far from rejecting women's literature, as Gilbert and Gubar conclude, makes our desire for such a literature, even while we recognize that wish as utopic, all the more important in the ways it forces us to acknowledge – and even to try to open up – our inscription within oppressively gendered systems of relation. Perhaps this is why the poem ends as it does, emphasizing not triumph achieved and strength attained, but unending struggle. For men and women both, struggling to free themselves from misprisions of the self, there is indeed 'no friend like a sister . . . To strengthen whilst one stands' (ll. 562–7).

NOTES

1 Contemporary study of *Goblin Market* begins with Weathers 1968. See also Stevenson 1972: 105–7; Greer 1975; vii–xxxvi; Golub 1975; Moers 1976:

100–7; Gilbert and Gubar 1979: 564–75; Sagan 1980; McGann 1980; Battiscombe 1981: 102–13; Connor 1984; and Mermin 1985.

2   For the theory of power relations, see Foucault 1979 and 1982; Martin 1982.

3   Gilbert and Gubar 1979: 575. For phallogocentrism, see Lacan 1977: 281–91; Gallop 1985: 133–56; Irigaray 1985: 13–129; Felman 1975 and 1981; and Jacobus 1986: 83–196, esp. 110–36.

4   Rossetti, *Goblin Market*, in *Complete Poems* ed. R. W. Crump, 1979–90: I, 11–26, ll. 1–4. All further quotations from this edition appear parenthetically by line number within the text.

5   For the role of iterability in linguistic circulation, see Culler 1982: 102.

6   See Gallagher 1983: 55–7, for discussion of costermongers as emblems of eighteenth- and nineteenth-century anxieties about economic and gender roles.

7   Spenser's villainesses typify the monstrous-feminine as defined in Kristeva 1982: 1–31; the rhetoric of scum, filth and blood in Bunyan's description of Christian's family as well as the Slough draws heavily on the religious vocabulary Kristeva also identifies (56–89) with the 'holy abject'.

8   Gilbert and Gubar 1979: 579; see also 122–6, 134–7, 171–80, 289–91, 381–2, 545, 558–9, and Poovey 1984: 3–47.

9   For discussion of the futility of such evasions, see Freud 1953–74: XVII, 219–52; Derrida 1980: 202–32; and Foucault 1980: I, 1–50.

10 Parenthesis, we may recall, is a figure in formal rhetoric. The *OED* defines it as 'a grammatical or rhetorical figure', a 'word, clause or sentence inserted into a passage with which it has not necessarily any grammatical connection.' The term has been recognized in English rhetoric since 1577 at least, when Henry Peacham's *The Garden of Eloquence* (1971) defined parenthesis specifically in terms of its supplementary relation to the grammar of the sentence (a relation Derrida explores in depth in *Of Grammatology*, 1976.

11 The function of the aside, for instance, is 'to allow the inner feelings of the character to be made known to the audience' (Holman 1972: 46).

12 Although in both instances the speakers are ostensibly quoting the goblins, recent theoretical discussion argues that distinctions between citation and use are not so distinct as we would like to believe. See Culler 1982: 110–25.

13 Gilbert and Gubar note this allusion in passing (1979: 566).

14 Locks of hair are, as Freud points out, a common phallic symbol. See 'Medusa's Head,' 1953–74: XVIII, 273–4.

15 For the standard critique of such strategies, see Derrida 1976: 141–64.

16 Connor also notes the 'furious variegation' of the goblins' speech as characteristic, reading it as part of their function as tempters into the 'verbal promiscuity' of language (1984: 444).

17 For the identity and futility of the strategies of resistance available to the subject constructed in terms of the phallus (strategies strikingly similar to the responses of Lizzie and Laura) see Kristeva 1980: 191.

18 For fetishism and its relation to castration, see Freud, 'Fetishism,' 1953–74: XXII, 152–7.

19 The self-defeating logic of the apotropaic gesture is also described by Freud in 'Medusa's Head'.

20 'Scription' is Kristeva's term for language that aspires to root itself in the world of things. For discussion, see Kristeva 1980: 115–21.

21 A quality Mermin also notes (1985: 117).

22 The *OED* finds this sense of 'prick' current as early as 1592.

23 The terms are, of course, Foucault's and find their fullest exposition in his *Discipline and Punish* and 'The Subject and Power'.

24 As Mermin observes, the mystery of paternity in *Goblin Market* is no mystery. The poem 'is clear and simple in its essential structure: two girls live alone; they encounter goblin men; they have children' (1985: 113–14).

25 For discussion of the male identification of the audience and its relation to the gaze, see the references in note 3 above, Mulvey 1975, and Lacan 1981: 67–119. Whether that structure is actually in Rossetti's text and our culture or whether it is merely projection of my own is a question I am not, for a variety of structural reasons, in a position to settle. The charges of essentialism levelled at Lacanian theory may be answered, however, by a reminder that gender – those qualities and expectations we attach to biology – is a matter of convention, not of anatomy. But the tendency in some contemporary theory, especially that influenced by Foucault, to move from a proclamation of the inescapability of a (male) system of power to an attempt to subsume feminism is disturbing and gives this writer pause; for discussion of this (probably intractable) question, see Langbauer 1989.

10

The Tiresian Poet: Michael Field

Chris White

Between 1870 and 1913 Katherine Bradley and Edith Cooper lived together, converted to Catholicism together, and together developed the joint poetic persona of Michael Field. In their roles of aunt and niece, as adoptive mother and adopted child (Leighton 1992: 208), their love was socially structured and sanctioned. At the same time, as Catholics and classicists they developed a language of love between women. As 'Michael' and 'Henry' their life together is recorded in the surviving manuscript journals. And as Michael Field they presented themselves to the world as a single Poet. The capitalization, and the sense of the importance of this activity, are theirs. Bradley and Cooper's primary concern was always with Michael Field the Poet, and the name itself reveals to a large extent how they conceived of their practice as poets. Before the adoption of the joint persona they used the pseudonyms Arran and Isla Leigh, and the assumption that they were either a married couple or a brother and sister brought them more favourable reviews than they ever had as Michael Field. Although Bradley and Cooper used metaphors of marriage to describe their love, it would be surprising if they had wanted to be publicly portrayed as a heterosexual couple. With the invention of 'Michael Field', they were believed by their reviewers to be a man, as can be seen in a review from *Harper's New Monthly Magazine*, which stated that 'Mr Field has a voice of his own, whatever his sins of literary omission or commission' (Field 1884: iv).

'Michael Field' cannot be regarded as a true pseudonym. In comparing themselves to Elizabeth Barrett Browning and Robert Browning, Michael Field asserted *'we are closer married'* (Sturgeon 1922: 47). Following Edith's death, Katherine invoked the words of the marriage service when approaching the *Athenaeum* to 'write a brief appreciation of my dead Fellow-Poet, not separating what God has joined, yet dwelling for her friends' delight on her peculiar & most rare gifts'.[1] To Havelock Ellis, responding to his attempts to discover who wrote which piece, they asserted, 'As to our work, let no man think he can put asunder what God has joined' (Sturgeon 1922: 47).

The name 'Michael Field' therefore contains a compelling contradiction: the writers deploy the authority of male authorship, and yet react against such camouflage. Michael Field is not a disguise. Nor is it a pretence at being a man, whatever the assumptions of the critics. Even though their attempts to develop a framework in which to talk about their love and desires in part depended upon a screening from the world, this effort did not rest wholly upon the use of a male pen-name. Rather, the poetic persona Michael Field gave them another role in which to play out their understanding of their relationship. The persona is distinct from Bradley and Cooper, and separate from their pet names Michael and Henry, which were in common currency among friends. Michael Field the Poet is always presented as the highest point of their work.

Three principal figures are used in their poetry to provide a framework in which the woman poet can be creative in her own right: Sappho, the Virgin Mary and Tiresias. The first is a not unexpected precedent for the woman poet. The Virgin Mary makes a late appearance in Field's work, and serves as an ambiguous representation of female creativity and power. Tiresias, a mystic, is mediated for Field through Sappho's writing, and functions as a model of ambiguous gender identity and the power of women. These three will be discussed in the course of this essay through their relationship to the development and practice of the Poet Michael Field.

In their treatment of their role as Michael Field and of their love for each other, Bradley and Cooper construct a position of opposition, reliant upon their alliance with one another, against the misapprehensions and prejudices of the world. This is the impulse behind their declaration of 1893, in 'Prologue', a poem whose title indicates that it is to be read as preceding all others:

> It was deep April, and the morn
>   Shakespeare was born;
> The world was on us, pressing sore;
> My love and I took hands and swore,
>   Against the world, to be
> Poets and lovers evermore,
> To laugh and dream on Lethe's shore,
> To sing to Charon in his boat,
> Heartening the timid souls afloat;
> Of judgement never to take heed,

> But to those fast-locked souls to speed,
> Who never from Apollo fled,
> Who spent no hour among the dead;
> Continually
> With them to dwell,
> Indifferent to heaven and hell.
>
> (Field 1893: 79)

This poem works simultaneously with several sources of authority to justify the women's creative intimacy. Alongside the poem's opening evocation of Shakespeare and an embedded reference to Wordsworth's 'The world is too much with us' (Wordsworth 1994: 132–3), the vow to be 'poets and lovers evermore' has a classical resonance, where the Poet is set above ordinary mortals, singing reassurance to all 'timid souls' on their way to Hades – a destination which places the poetry wholly outside the Christian context of heaven and hell. Classicism and poetry are set against the world 'pressing sore' upon them, and are productive of a physical and erotic bond between the two poets.

'Prologue' also implicitly figures a political understanding of the position of women as lovers, rather than evoking a private and personal retreat from the world into romantic friendship.[2] Michael Field is writing here what would today be called 'lesbian' verse, an exploration further developed in 'To E. C.' (Leigh 1875: 2). But that is not to say that their texts' frequent uses of the words 'Sapphic', 'Beloved', 'Lover', and 'Lesbian' necessarily indicate a same-sex sexual relationship.

Bradley and Cooper wrote at a time when treatments of Sappho's verse were numerous and diverse. There are instances of deliberate suppression of the female pronouns, as in T. W. Higginson's translation published in 1871. A standard work on Greek culture describes Sappho as 'a woman of generous disposition, affectionate heart, and independent spirit . . . [with] her own particular refinement of taste, exclusive of every approach to low excess or profligacy'.[3] Another academic author declared that there was 'no good early evidence to show that the Lesbian standard was low',[4] that is, sexual. In other versions, she was portrayed as a woman who, having fallen in love with the fisherman Phaon, committed suicide when that love was unreciprocated (Mahaffy 1874: 100–1). Where some writers attempted to recuperate at all costs the great poet from accusations of lewdness, Michael Field holds her up as a paragon among women, and puts the passion back into the poet's community of women.

It is in this context that the significance of Michael Field's 1889 volume *Long Ago* can be appreciated. It consists of a series of poems based on and completing Sappho's fragments, deploying Sappho and her words as a well-spring of authority. *Long Ago* explores both the heterosexual version of Sappho

and passion between women. The latter is exemplified clearly in poem
XXXV:

> Come, Gorgo, put the rug in place,
>   And passionate recline;
> I love to see thee in thy grace,
>   Dark, virulent, divine.

(Field 1889: 56)

If this female-female eroticism, a celebration of dangerous beauty and
sensuality, is one version of Sappho, there are at least two other Sapphos in
Long Ago. The second Sappho is the heterosexual lover of Phaon:

> If I could win him from the sea,
> Then subtly I would draw him down
> 'Mid the bright vetches; in a crown
> My art should teach him to entwine
> Their thievish rings and keep him mine.

(Field 1889: 8)

This is a posssessive heterosexual desire, springing from a manipulative battle
to win a male lover in a destructive competition with his fisherman's work at
sea.

   Long Ago is also inhabited by a third Sappho, a woman at the centre of a
loving community of women that she must keep safe from the intrusions of
men. In poem LIV, 'Adown the Lesbian Vales', for instance, Sappho is in
possession of a 'passionate unsated sense' which her maids seek to satisfy. The
relationship between Sappho and her maids is premised upon a need to keep
the women away from marriage: 'No girls let fall / Their maiden zone / At
Hymen's call' (Field 1889: 96). This poet or Poet is a virginal figure, a
connection also broached in *The New Minnesinger and Other Poems*, published
by Bradley in 1875 under the pseudonym Arran Leigh. The title poem of
that book discusses the craft of the woman-poet, 'she whose life doth lie / In
virgin haunts of poesie' (Leigh 1875: 2), and argues that the virgin woman
poet, by virtue of her freedom from men, be 'lifted to a free / and fellow-life
with man' (12). Heterosexuality is a form of bondage. If this is replaced by
the 'fellow-life' of equal comradeship, then bondage is at an end. But
whatever 'realm' a woman endeavours to enclose, she must 'ever keep / All
things subservient to the good / Of pure free-growing womanhood' (13).
This version of femininity offers an ambiguous challenge to the terms of
patriarchal culture. It exists apart from patriarchal dictates, but includes
fellowship and equality with men. It embraces the productiveness of

womanhood and an all-woman community, but concedes the reality of attraction to men, destructive as that is. But virginity is not sterile in this formulation: it is simultaneously pure and productive.

In *Long Ago*, the possession of virginity is the sole source of female power, freedom and joy. Its loss means an effective expulsion from the group of virgin women, or the separation of two women who have loved one another. For example, poem LVI tells the story of Leto and Niobe, who 'were friends full dear', until Niobe, the mother of seven sons and seven daughters, boasted that she was superior to Leto, who had only two children, Apollo and Artemis, fathered by Zeus. Artemis killed Niobe's daughters and Apollo killed her sons, and Niobe was transformed into a rock by the gods:

> Leto and Niobe were friends full dear:
> > Then they were foes
> > As only those
> Can be who once were near
> Each to the other's heart,
> Who could not breathe apart,
> Nor shed a lonely tear.

> Leto and Niobe were virgins then,
> > Nor knew the strange,
> > Deep-severing change
> That comes to women when
> Elected, raised above
> All else, they thrill with love,
> The love of gods or men.

(Field 1889: 99, ll. 1–14)

Heterosexuality kills friendship between women, where that friendship is dependent upon their both being virgins. This poem is not interested in the drama of gods, war and vengeance that is the substance of the original myth, but in the effect of marriage and motherhood on women's love for each other.

The significance of virginity is further explored in poem XVII: 'The moon rose full, the women stood'. Sappho calls to her virginity, her 'only good', to come back, having been lost to Phaon. The inviolate state is 'that most blessèd, secret state / That makes the tenderest maiden great'. Sappho's loss of virginity effectively puts an end to her poetic gift:

> And when
> By maiden-arms to be enwound,
> Ashore the fisher flings,

> Oh, then my heart turns cold, and then
> I drop my wings.

(Field 1889: 33)

Michael Field's Sappho, therefore, is not the denizen of a lesbian or Lesbian idyll. Rather, she is the subject of a contradiction which emerges from those versions described above. The Lesbian community of women is more than a society of friendship. But it is also a site of poetic production and, moreover, the production of the Poet identity. Both are threatened by men and heterosexuality.

In the Preface to *Long Ago* there is an ambiguous appeal to 'the one woman' who has dared to speak unfalteringly of the fearful mastery of love. In this invocation, Sappho the Poet, Aphrodite and Michael Field are placed in an imaginary alliance. The multiple identity of the 'one woman' implicitly acknowledges that in order to speak 'unfalteringly' of woman's love for woman, it is necessary for Michael Field to work in alliance with other women and other women's formulations of such love. This construction in the preface is thus both strategic and passionate. The identity of the Poet Michael Field allows Bradley and Cooper to place themselves on a level with Sappho-as-Poet, and in the preface to the volume the collective 'I' of Michael Field writes:

> When, more than a year ago, I wrote to a literary friend of my attempt to express in English verse the passionate pleasure Dr. Wharton's book had brought me, he replied: 'That is a delightfully audacious thought – the extension of Sappho's fragments into lyrics. I can scarcely conceive anything more audacious.'
>
> In simple truth all worship that is not idolatry must be audacious; for it involves the blissful apprehension of an ideal; it means in the very phrase of Sappho –
>
> Ἔγων δ' ἐμαύτα
> τοῦτο σύνοιδα

That Greek phrase is of paramount importance to the volume as a whole and means 'and in myself I know this well'. It conveys a sense of being one person who is a poet, and, in a modern theoretical sense, of being someone who knows a subject in a field of knowledge. Identity, as poet and subject, is central to Michael Field's production of Sappho, and of themselves as akin to Sappho. The Preface continues:

> Devoutly as the fiery-bosomed Greek turned in her anguish to Aphrodite, praying her to accomplish her heart's desires, I have turned

to the one woman who has dared to speak unfalteringly of the fearful mastery of love, and again and again the dumb prayer has risen from my heart —

σὺ δ' αὕτα
σύμμαχος ἔσσο
[you will be my ally]

Faith and vocation meet in the relationship between Sappho and women, or between these two women. That second Greek phrase contains the notion of allegiance and of greater strength derived from women combining together. Bradley and Cooper combine to form Michael Field. Sappho calls upon the allegiance of Aphrodite to give authority to her poetry and her love.

A number of the poems in *Long Ago* document the trials and tribulations of being a woman-poet. The establishment of the Poet identity means either trying to write like a man in man's language with a man's voice, or inventing a new language, a new voice that expresses in public terms the truth the woman-poet wishes to speak. In XXXIV, Michael Field portray a Sappho trying to be heard:

> 'Sing to us, Sappho!' cried the crowd . . .
> I did not think of who would hear;
> I knew not there were men who jeer . . .
> I heard a hostile sound
> And looked, oh, scornfuller than those
> 'Mong men I ne'er have found.
>
> (Field 1889: 54–5, ll. 1–6)

The silence that is restored at the end of *Long Ago*, when Sappho throws herself from the Leucadian rock, is the final success of the jeering men. In poem L there emerges a complicated negotiation of the relationship between gender and art. Sappho appeals to the Muse to make her poetry more like that of the male poet Terpander, who was crowned the winner of the poetry competition at the Pythian games four times. Terpander has power and authority in the world, and can sway the tyrant. Sappho cannot even be heard above the jeering.

> A listener at thy knees I would remain,
> So thou rehearse
> To me that strain
> Sung by the poet-sage,
> Manful, and crisp, and free,

Of so undaunted style,
It can command
And move to clemency
The tyrant.

                                             (Field 1889: 83, ll. 3–11)

Here is not a 'woman-poet', but a poet who has a style and a voice which has
a powerful impact upon the world. Terpander's poetry is said to have a 'sweet
refrain / Of sunny truth' (Field 1889: 84, ll. 24–5), while Sappho has a
'tossed bosom' (l. 23). She is not calm, but is subject to her femininity, a
feature marked in this poem by the word 'bosom' which is used to represent
feminine beauty and desirability, the weakness of the role of the woman-poet
and the aspiration to be just 'poet'. The public voice of the woman-poet is
hard-won and never straightforward.

One of the most fascinating poems in *Long Ago* uses the figure of Tiresias
– a character who appears nowhere in Sappho's work – to suggest that life as
a woman is superior to life as a man. The Greek epigram at the head of poem
LII precisely echoes that in the Preface, 'and in myself I know this well',
marking this poem as the crux of the volume. Tiresias, in his youth, is said
to have found two serpents; when he struck them with a stick to separate
them, he was suddenly changed into a woman. Seven years later she/he was
restored to manhood by a repeat of the incident with the snakes. When he
was a woman, Jupiter and Juno consulted him on a dispute about which of
the sexes received greater pleasure from marriage. Tiresias decided in Jupiter's
favour, that women derived greater pleasure, and Juno punished Tiresias for
this judgement by blinding him. Jupiter tried to make some amends by
giving him second sight. This story is reproduced in detail in Michael Field's
poem, but their interpretation of the myth is significantly different from the
received version of a story about women's deceitfulness and vindictiveness.
Michael Field turns this myth, that is more than a little disparaging about
men's enthusiasm for marriage, into a positive valuing of women. Women
are not only more sensitive, more feeling (the usual attributes of femininity);
they are also more capable than men of experiencing pleasure. The choice of
the figure of Tiresias allows the presence of both sexes together simul-
taneously. At the moment of transition from female to male, Tiresias has a
masculine consciousness and a feminine memory, and is an emotional
hermaphrodite. While the feminine is better, the moment of transition is
one of fullness, with both genders working together. Tiresias is a representa-
tion of the absence of any clear split between male and female in Michael
Field's utopian vision.

For Michael Field this is a narrative about the knowledge and power that
come from living as a woman:

He trembled at the quickening change,
He trembled at his vision's range,
His finer sense of bliss and dole,
His receptivity of soul;
But when love came, and, loving back,
He learnt the pleasure men must lack,
It seemed that he had broken free
Almost from his mortality.

(Field 1889: 89–90, ll. 13–20)

Tiresias not only experiences greater pleasure, but possesses emotional depth, sensitivity and perceptiveness, that men, by virtue of being men, wholly lack. Where in the received version of the myth, Tiresias has unique knowledge because he has lived as both man and woman, for Michael Field he has special and great knowledge because he is a man who has lived as a woman: he has had woman's knowledge and experience added to his masculinity, which is portrayed here as an experience of lack or absence. Womanhood, with the addition of a base of masculinity, is the complete gender identity.

The reversal of the hierarchy of gender roles is pursued through new and inverted perspectives on other Greek myths.

Tiresias, ere the goddess smite,
Look on me with unblinded sight,
That I may learn if thou hast part
In womanhood's secluded heart:
Medea's penetrative charm
Own'st thou to succour and disarm,
Hast thou her passion inly great
Heroes to mould and subjugate?
Can'st thou divine how sweet to bring
Apollo to thy blossoming
As Daphne?

(Field 1889: 91, ll. 50–60)

The poetry works through a series of inversions and paradoxes. Medea is penetrative and succouring, father and mother simultaneously. In the original version, Medea was overcome by love for Jason (he of the Argonauts fame), and abandoned her family and her home to go with him. Daphne fled from Apollo and his attempts to rape her, and had her prayers answered to be delivered from him when her father transformed her into a laurel tree, which Apollo subsequently made into the laurel crown of the winner of poetry competitions. Michael Field, however, make Jason the passive, conquered one, the victim of Medea's power, and Daphne as the active, whose blossoming, a flourish of self-hood, attracts Apollo, rather than being a retreat from his passion.

Language, the difficulty and effort of speaking from the poetic and sensual self, is both often the subject of Michael Field's work, and also reflected or represented in the syntax and style of the poetry. *Long Ago* charts the process of the struggle to poetic speech and the means by which it will be destroyed.

The development of a female-female language to describe a particular sensuality elsewhere produces a set of fruitful metaphors derived from flowers and fruit. Women are (like) roses. Women's bodies are rose-like. The rose is active and has its own motion, it is not merely a receptacle. In poem LVIII of *Long Ago*, a woman's flesh is rendered in rose metaphors:

> And just about
> The elbows' pout
> The warm flesh glows
> Into a flower, incomparable rose.
> Such fluctuating stealth
> Of light doth interfuse
> Their virgin health,
> In its soft buoyance, as indues
> You, O ye roses, with your heavenly hues.
>
> > (Field 1889: 105, ll. 7–15)

This poem represents an active, original and exploratory use of metaphor, not using one thing to stand in for one or more other things, but as a new order of thinking that cannot fully be rendered in analytic prose, but which requires many successive sentences to describe the plural meanings and shifts that happen in a very few lines of verse. I offer the following rendering of poem LVIII:

> Flesh becomes rose, but that rose is invested with qualities of stealth(y)/light, which is equated in turn with virginity. The association of stealth-secrecy-dark is broken, making stealth a quality of light. The organic growth of the translation from flesh to flower is gradual, secret, and a light is cast upon the object of desire: the beloved's elbow. The organic growth is translated/misplaced into light, 'glow' replacing the more expected 'grow', the coming of the light standing in for plant growth, plant growth becoming light. Two types of light are collapsed into another and held alongside one another, light as luminescence and light as weightlessness. These become two of the defining qualities of

rose-flesh. Virginity/lesbianism is a condition without weight, imply-
ing heterosexuality as a heavy, dark condition. The secrecy of lesbian-
ism, its stealthy progress, becomes a positive condition, in contrast to
the heavy, dark, public face of heterosexuality. Sappho's desire for the
Graces (they of the elbows) translates fleshliness to flowers, secrecy into
light. In this way the metaphor of the innocent and natural is used to
change the status of lesbian desire and to remove the taint of the
unnatural.

The poem 'Your Rose is Dead' produces an image of sensual pleasure that
is dependent upon an appreciation of refined morbidity in the decay of the
rose. Again the scenario is one of walking through a cultivated garden,
examining the flowers, but the apparently literal roses are female, sensual and
the object of love:

> Your *rose* is *dead*.
> They said
> *The Grand Mogul* – for so her splendour
> Exceeded, masterful, it seemed her due
> By dominant male titles to commend her.
>
> (Symons 1928: 55, ll. 1–5)

The opening of the poem combines a degree of Orientalism, an erotic power
derived from exoticism, with the mixed gender identity that is shared by the
name of Michael Field. The assertion of finality produced by others is refuted
by the speaker of the poem, who declaims that the dead rose 'was woman to
the rage of my desire' (l. 8). The speaker is ungendered, so this poem is not
straightforwardly or simply readable as a lesbian poem, but the text pursues
a celebration of a woman who has been loved for a very long time, and whose
aged appearance has made no difference to the love, even when compared to
younger, more perfect, more alive blooms:

> My rose was dead? She lay
> Against the sulphur, lemon and blush-gray
> Of younger blooms, transformed, morose.
>
> (Symons 1928: 55, ll. 9–11)

The very agedness and decline of the loved rose augments the desire of the
speaker for 'Her shrivelling petals' (l. 12), which 'gave her texture and her
colour' (l. 17) and made her 'Majestic in recession / From flesh to mould' (ll.
19–20). The rose becomes the body of the woman, in a rapid shift from flesh
to decay, physicality to morbidity. Where the others walk away from the

dying rose that is the private possession of the speaker, the speaker remains with her, faithful and loving:

> And they pass on to pluck another;
> While I, drawn on to vague, prodigious pleasure,
> Fondle my treasure.
>
> (Symons 1928: 56, ll. 22–4)

The pleasure is described in terms that are amorphous (unnameable) and huge (overwhelming), and the pleasure originates in the very imperfections of the rose, which bespeak the length of time that their love has lasted. The poem ends with these lines:

> I feel fresh rhythms quicken,
> Fresh music follows you. Corrupt, grow old,
> Drop inwardly to ashes, smother
> Your burning spices, and entoil
> My senses till you sink a clod of fragrant soil!
>
> (ll. 28–32)

Sensuality is expressed in terms of poetic production, of rhythmic language and verbal music, a new art inspired by an old love(r). To sight, touch and smell has been added the sense of hearing, as the sensate life of the speaker's body is increasingly incorporated into the celebration of the female body. The possessive 'My rose' is succeeded here by the speaker's desire to be ensnared by the rose-lover, and the hierarchy of power is broken down in a gesture of mutual possession.

This ambiguous rendering of the body as positive-negative is almost entirely missing from poems devoted to religious subjects, but the connection between the Sapphic/poetic domain and the Catholic sphere is not wholly broken. One fragment of Sappho's work that does not appear in *Long Ago* seems to have been recast for *Mystic Trees*, a volume written primarily by Cooper following their conversion to Catholicism. The version from the volume of Sappho's work used by Michael Field reads:

> As a sweet-apple rosy, O Maid, art thou,
> At the uttermost tip of the uttermost bough,
> Unseen in the autumn by gatherer's eyes –
> Nay seen, but only to tantalize.[5]

'She is One' appears thus in its entirety:

> High, lone above all creatures thou does stand,
> Mary, as apple on the topmost bough,

The gatherers overlooked, somehow –
    And yet not so:
Man could not reach thee, thou so high dost grow
Warm, gold for God's own Hand.

(Field 1907: 51)

Mary is simultaneously overlooked (unseen) by the gatherers, whilst she over looks (looks over) them. That paradox, the gaze/non-gaze which travels in both directions at the same time, connects to or is like that position of the Poet Michael Field, simultaneously overlooked and undervalued, while looking down from the great height of the Poet identity. This invests their position in metaphorical terms with superior status and ability. Being unreachable by man (unappreciated by the poetry-reading public) puts the Poet Michael Field closer to God, to warmth, to become 'gold'. Being out of the centre of literary fame means being on the margins, which is translated into being at the top of the tree, a transformation of the usual metaphor of positioning.

The virginity/poetry equation made throughout *Long Ago* is remade here, the unquestionable status (the high position) transposed from poetry to a proximity to heaven. The rose has been augmented by the mystic tree, which comes much nearer to heaven, but which still has its roots in the earth. Mary emerges as superior to Sappho, whose experience and representation of heterosexuality is negative and corrosive. Where Mary can give birth without sex, Sappho ceases to be creative with heterosexual desire.

In 1913, autumn arrived in the garden of pleasure and desire. Included in *The Wattlefold* is the following poem, presumably written by Bradley, who kept her own cancer a secret from Cooper and who died only a few months after Cooper:

Lo, my loved is dying, and the call
Is come that I may die,
All the leaves are dying, all
Dying, drifting by.
Every leaf is lonely in its fall,
Every flower has its speck and stain;
The birds from hedge to tree
Lisp mournfully,
And the great reconciliation of this pain
Lies in the full, soft rain.

(Field 1930: 195)

Separation has arrived, finally, in death. The individual women have become individual leaves, instead of a complete plant. The flowers that represented sensual pleasure are corrupted, and the strong poetic voice has been replaced by lisping birds. Michael Field, where the sum is greater than the individual parts of Bradley and Cooper, are broken in two, and the capacity of Michael Field to speak strongly and loudly as a Poet is reduced to Bradley's ability to find only a lisping voice. Two women, writing under/through a man's name, operate as a Tiresian poet, whose strength derives from femaleness and whose authority derives from the masculine Poet identity which can change the world. Individually they, and the sensual world they celebrated, could only lisp mournfully, until another 'reconciliation' in the next world.

NOTES

With thanks as ever to Elaine.

1 Michael Field, 'Works & Days', MS journals, British Library MS. Add. Ms. 46803, f101ᵛ. The published journals appeared as *Works and Days*, ed. T. and D. C. Sturge Moore, 1933.

2 This assertion differentiates my reading from that of Faderman 1985.

3 William Mure, *Critical History of the Language and Literature of Ancient Greece* (1850–7), cited in Jenkyns 1982: 2.

4 Gilbert Murray, *Ancient Greek Literature* (1897), cited in Jenkyns 1982: 2.

5 Bergk, fragment 93: Haines, fragment 133, p. 158. Michael Field used the edition of Sappho in Wilhelm Theodor Bergk, *Poetae Lyrici Graeci*, Lipsiae, 1854. I have used C. R. Haines 1946, a text which uses Bergk and his translations as one source of authority on Sappho's fragments.

11

'Fair Hymen holdeth hid a world of woes': Myth and Marriage in Poems by 'Graham R. Tomson' (Rosamund Marriott Watson)

LINDA K. HUGHES

In 1879, at the age of nineteen, the beautiful Rosamund Ball married George Francis Armytage, a wealthy young gentleman who had attended Cambridge and rowed in the University Boat. The couple 'lived happily' for five years,[1] and in 1884 the young woman, who was also a gifted poet, anonymously published her first volume, *Tares*. This collection of terse, melancholy lyrics won praise from the 21 March, 1885 *Academy*: 'Condensed, forcible, even vigorous, exact, and often masterful is the handling of words in this little book ... If this is the book of a young writer, we have no hesitation in saying that it is work of the greatest promise' (203). The review closed by quoting 'Nirvana', which surveyed the prospect of a Christian afterlife only to repudiate it: 'Give us darkness for anguished eyes, stillness for weary feet, / Silence, and sleep; but no heaven of glittering, loud unrest.'

Perhaps not coincidentally, the same year Rosamund Armytage's poems were published her husband 'had reason to complain of her conduct, and quarrels ensued between them' ('Armitage'). The couple legally separated in January 1885. In October 1886 Rosamund left the house George Armytage had allotted her and, with painter Arthur Graham Tomson, 'took lodgings at a farmhouse in Cornwall, where they lived together as man and wife' ('Armitage'). She was quickly divorced by Armytage, and the court awarded custody of their two young daughters to the husband.[2] She bore another child, a son named Graham, in October 1887, a month after she and Arthur married.

Renaming herself Graham R. Tomson, Rosamund now began a quick and sparkling ascent in the literary world, tantalizing London artistic circles with her finely crafted poems, her personal grace and charm, and the faint aura of scandal that surrounded her. Andrew Lang announced the arrival of a 'new' poet in the pages of *Longman's Magazine*; Oscar Wilde frequently attended Graham R. and Arthur Tomson's Sunday afternoons[3] and called her 'one of our most artistic workers in poetry [who] treats language as a fine material.'[4] She attracted the notice of Thomas Hardy, and, following letters, social calls, and a discreet flirtation, appears to have inspired the character of Mrs Pine-Avon in *The Pursuit of the Well-Beloved*.[5]

The poet also won the friendship of women poets and writers. She and Elizabeth Pennell saw each other almost daily at the height of their friendship.[6] Mona Caird, who wrote famous essays on marriage in the *Westminster Review*, came to her Sunday afternoons, as did Amy Levy and Violet Hunt (Waltman 384, 391–2, 456). After Graham Tomson published two more volumes of poetry and contributed poems and essays to a number of leading periodicals, she edited *Sylvia's Journal* in 1893 and 1894, shaping this woman's magazine along the lines of Oscar Wilde's *Woman's World*. Violet Hunt, Jane Barlow, and E. Nesbit contributed short stories, Katharine Tynan poems, a one-act play, and a series of articles on male poets' heroines. By the middle of the decade Graham Tomson published poems in *The Yellow Book* and prose in the 'Autolycus' column, entirely written by women, in the *Pall Mall Gazette*.[7] She dedicated her fourth volume of poetry, issued by the Bodley Head in 1895, to Alice Meynell 'In Sincere Admiration and Friendship.'

But 1895 was a cataclysmic year for Graham R. Tomson. After nearly seven years of marriage with Arthur Tomson, she had become involved with H. B. Marriott Watson, a member of the Henley 'regatta' who had collaborated with J. M. Barrie on a play and contributed short stories to *The Yellow Book* and a volume of essays to John Lane's 'Keynotes' series. By February, at the age of thirty-four, she was pregnant with Watson's child. She again chose to leave a husband for another man and was served with divorce papers, losing custody of yet another child. She paid a literary price for her defiance of convention as well. Having won a reputation as Graham R. Tomson, she now surrendered the name, and the reputation, for her third life as a poet under the name Rosamund Marriott Watson. The Watson affair, unlikely to shock on the grounds of adultery alone, divided literary circles who had met repeatedly at the Tomson home in St John's Wood. The Henley crowd sided with H.B. and Rosamund, the Pennells and others with Arthur Tomson, and Rosamund was banished from her close friend[8] and previous circles of influence. She and H.B. removed themselves first to Chiswick, then to the Surrey village of Shere, where Henley, Barrie, and others had gathered, often observed by Rosamund and Elizabeth Pennell, to play cricket (Pennell, *Nights* 213–14).

Rosamund still had future accomplishments ahead of her: she served as poetry reviewer for the *Athenaeum* from 1904 to 1911, succeeding Augusta

Webster and E. Nesbit,[9] and at the turn of the century William Archer selected her, along with Meynell, Henry Newbolt, Kipling, Yeats, Arthur Symons and others, for profiling in *Poets of the Younger Generation*.[10] But she gradually disappeared from sight, her last two volumes of poetry disappointing successors to the work she had produced through 1895. When she died prematurely, at 51, the *Athenaeum* affirmed that 'her place in English poetry should be secure', based on her 'gifts of technique' and the 'haunting quality' of her verse; and the writer reminded readers that 'some years ago she was recognized in these columns as one of three women poets who remained to us after the death of Christina Rossetti' (6 January 1912, 11).The obituary in the London *Times* more accurately set the tone of later reception, agreeing that her poems 'entitle her to rank highly among the numerous "minor poets". . . of the last two decades', but giving her scant space and absorbing her into her husband's identity, terming her 'the wife of Mr. H. B. Marriott Watson, the well-known novelist' (2 January 1912, 9).

This marital and poetic history indicates a principal reason for Graham Tomson's nearly entire erasure from literary history, and her cultural significance. Her connections in the literary and art worlds, as well as the merits of her poetry, entitle her to a place in histories of the 1890s; the details of her unconventional life, and the implicit inscription of that unconventional life in her poems, illuminate the history of women's lives and expressive strategies. More specifically, her poems exploring marriage as problem as some of the few poems by nineteenth-century British women to do so. As well, Graham Tomson's adaptation of myth to explore this volatile subject matter not only typifies her own reticence in poetry but also aligns her with a characteristic twentieth-century strategy Jan Montefiore, Alicia Ostriker and others have identified: women's rewriting of myth in order to appropriate poetic authority while expressing deeply personal emotion and/ or oppositional discourse.[11] Finally, her poems help extend the debate about the legitimate grounds for reading women's poetry, especially the role of biographical detail. Because this woman's exercise of sexual freedom led to silence about her actions in her day and our own, I have deliberately opened this essay by reinscribing what I know of her life into the historical record. The example of this poet raises the larger question of how much awareness of biographical detail can alter or construct readers' sense of literary merit.

Although a number of women used essays and fiction to offer searching critiques of marriage in the 1890s – Mona Caird's *The Morality of Marriage* and George Egerton's *Keynotes* come to mind – marriage as problem figured rarely in poetry of the time.[12] Nineteenth-century British women poets tended to avoid the subject altogether. If Elizabeth Barrett Browning's 'Lord Walter's Wife', as Leighton argues (1992: 85–7), indicts the status of women as property in marriage, nevertheless her most famous works celebrate marriage and maternity. Christina Rossetti's quizzing, sceptical lyrics about courtship and betrothal are among her most memorable, but her work does not present similarly searching meditations on marriage.

Four poems published by Graham R. Tomson in 1889 and 1890, however, explore marriage as problem. 'Ballad of the Bird-Bride' and 'A Ballad of the Were-Wolf' rework northern mythology and folklore, while two long narrative poems rewrite classical myth. 'Procris' refashions the story of Cephalus and Procris from Ovid's *Metamorphoses*, 'The Story of Marpessa' an episode from Book 9 of the *Iliad*. In all four works Tomson appropriates the indirection and authority of myth to explore scenarios of distrust, discord, betrayal, jealousy and aggression in marriage. Three of the four directly involve violence, with the wife (or her kindred) wounded, killed, or maimed by the husband, and the wife, in a single case, poised to recoil violently in turn. 'Marpessa' involves scant violence but most directly expresses doubt about the efficacy and endurance of marriage.

That Graham R. Tomson's readers, at least among her literary circles, would have read these four poems in light of her own marital history is evident from the comments of two contemporaries. A chance remark in Arthur Symons's letters suggests the degree to which the scandal of her first divorce could inform perception of her appearance in public: 'Graham Tomson was there [at William Sharp's] too, in an antique peplum of red, looking very handsome, but I was only introduced to her husband (he is No. 2 and they both look about three and twenty) – not a fascinating person, which makes Bunand anticipate the chance of some day offering himself as "*le troisième*"!'[13] William Archer's more subdued remark in *Poets of the Younger Generation* also indicates that informed readers detected personal undercurrents in her poems: 'The personal note in her poetry is exceedingly discreet. The heart-throb is always there, but it is not obtruded upon us. She hits the happy mean between absolute impersonality and tactless self-exposure'(470).[14] If Archer perceives her poems as expressive strategies, however, he also praises her for sparing readers discomfiting confrontation with the experiences toward which the poems gesture.

The ballad has often been perceived as women poets' particular medium.[15] Graham R. Tomson's most evocative ballads are set in a fey, otherworldly realm of fairy lore or myth. The displacement of action to an apparently nonreferential plane not only tapped her most powerful imaginative gifts – the articulation of liminal states poised between the familiar and alien – but also freed many of the emotional restraints she customarily imposed on her poetry. The result is an often arresting exploration of such issues as scandalous sexual involvement ('The Ballad of the Willow Pool'), women's power for revenge ('The Quern of the Giants'), and, in 'Ballad of the Bird-Bride' and 'Ballad of the Were-Wolf', troubled marriage.

'Ballad of the Bird-Bride' was first published in the January 1889 issue of *Harper's* in America, then reissued as the title-poem of her 1889 Longman's volume. The ballad represents male force in taking a wife, the wife's enduring ties to a world larger than the home she shares with her husband, and the sundering of home and separation of parent and child when the husband breaks his promise to his wife and murders one of her doubles. An Eskimo hunter sees wild grey gulls settle on an ice-floe and transform themselves into beautiful women. He captures the fairest, brings her home as his bride, and sees the wildness in her eyes fade when their first child is born. When he and his wife begin hunting together, she makes him swear never again to hunt gulls for food or clothing. They live happily until famine threatens the family and – forgetting his promise – he shoots three arrows one day and kills four gulls.

Suddenly the landscape, once colourless, is suffused by the red of a setting sun and bloodstains on the snow. The wife announces that the hour is come, summons the children, clothes all in the feathers of the gull, and they depart. The ballad ends with the husband announcing his claim to wife and children amidst the whistling of a cold, wild wind and bleak grey skies.

This tale is clearly a variant of the swan-maiden story common to European and Arabic tradition. Intertexuality, so often crucial to uncovering oppositional discourse in Victorian women writers, clarifies the significance of Graham Tomson's 'Bird-Bride'. The poem has been cited as a possible source of Tess's vision of 'weird Arctic birds' in *Tess of the D'Urbervilles*,[16] but Tomson's shaping of the poem is more productively viewed within the context of William Morris's 'Land East of the Sun and West of the Moon' from *The Earthly Paradise*, as well as the probable source of both Morris's and Tomson's poems, Sabine Baring-Gould's *Curious Myths of the Middle Ages*.[17] Both the Morris and Tomson poems correspond to a recurrent structure identified by Baring-Gould: '1. A man falls in love with a woman of supernatural race. 2. She consents to live with him, subject to one condition. 3. He breaks the condition and loses her. 4. He seeks her, and – a) recovers her; b) never recovers her.'[18] The emphasis in Morris's telling falls on the power of heterosexual desire. The swan-maiden is at first captured by force, when John seizes her plumage and prevents her from flying away with her sisters. But he is so dazzled by her beauty that he falls in love immediately and demonstrates his devotion so convincingly that he inspires returning love and desire in the swan-maiden, who takes him to her otherworldly realm where they live in bliss for some years. Their sundering comes only when, lonely for earth, John returns to his native land on the condition that he never utter his desire for his beloved; if he does, she will appear but they will thereafter be forever separated. One evening, wracked by desire to see her, he cries this need aloud and invokes the penalty. Yet eventually, by overcoming his earlier failure to endure silent waiting and unfulfilled desire, John miraculously finds the land east of the sun and west of the moon, and he and his beloved live forever after in paradisal bliss.

The emphasis in Graham Tomson's poem is on violence and the fragility of vows and relationships. Against the backdrop of Morris's poem, the forcing of the female into marriage in Tomson's ballad becomes more pronounced:

> Swift I sprang from my hiding-place
> And held the fairest fast;
> I held her fast, the sweet, strange thing:
> Her comrades skirled, but they all took wing,
> And smote me as they passed.[19]

Moreover, instead of reciprocating the man's love and focusing only on her bond with him, this bird-maiden retains her native wildness within the confines of domestic walls:

> I bore her safe to my warm snow house;
> Full sweetly there she smiled;
> And yet, whenever the shrill winds blew,
> She would beat her long white arms anew,
> And her eyes glanced quick and wild.
>
> (2)

Even after the birth of her first child, when 'her wandering glances sank to rest' and 'she loved' her husband 'dear and leal', her tie to her sister birds and the wild skies prompts her to forbid her husband to slay grey gulls again.

In contrast to Morris's poem, where the broken vow is itself an expression of love and desire, the broken promise in Tomson's ballad, like the capture of the bride, turns on male aggression: 'My bow twanged thrice with a swift, straight shot, / And slew me sea-gulls four' (3; cf. *The Rime of the Ancient Mariner*). That the husband shoots only three arrows but kills four birds suggests that in killing her sister gulls he also attacks his wife. The sudden change in the register of landscape against a sky inscribed as female signals the outpouring of bloody anger:

> The sun hung red on the sky's dull breast,
> The snow was wet and red;
> Her voice shrilled out in a woful cry,
> She beat her long white arms on high,
> 'The hour is here,' she said.
>
> (3)

A Samoyed version of the swan-maiden myth retold by Baring-Gould also sets the story in a forbidding northern (probably Siberian) climate and turns on a series of violent acts (*Curious Myths*, 564–7. And the variants Baring-Gould identifies (*Curious Myths*, 563, 575–6), unlike Morris's poem but like Graham Tomson's, emphasize the constant threat that the bird-bride will fly away at the first opportunity. But neither Morris nor Baring-Gould makes mention of children, whose crucial role in the sundering of the home is Graham Tomson's particular contribution.[20] The children figure not only in the moment of separation ('"Fetch me the feathers, my children three . . . Babes of mine, of the wild wind's kin"'[4]) but also in the husband's continuing desolation after all are gone. Indeed, the poem situated in the husband's point of view hovers interestingly between sympathy for his anguished loneliness – he had, after all, shot the gulls only when famine threatened his family – and exposure of his aggression and possessiveness of family members as forms of property. Thus the poem closes, on one hand, with his cry for continuing domestic ties, and, on the other, with his repeated claim of possession set at naught by the cold winds and empty skies, which turn his attempts to capture presences through the act of naming into mere noise and blankness:

> O winged white wife, and our children three,
> Of the wild wind's kin though ye surely be,
>   Are ye not of my kin too?
>
> Ay, ye once were mine, and, till I forget,
>   Ye are mine forever and aye,
> Mine, wherever your wild wings go,
> While shrill winds whistle across the snow
>   And the skies are blear and grey.
>
>   (5)

The implicit exposure of violence and the ownership on which bourgeois marriage is predicated, as well as the wresting away of children in 'Ballad of the Bird-Bride', are extended in one of Graham R. Tomson's most powerful poems, 'A Ballad of the Were-Wolf'. The 'Were-Wolf' likewise represents woman's wildness that can underlie a tame domestic exterior. In this poem a rough farmer returns home to gloat to his wife that 'I hae scotched yon great grey wolf / That took our bairnies twa', cutting off the creature's right fore-paw: "twas ae sharp stroke o' my bonny knife / That gar'd her haud awa'.'[21] He orders the wife, who has remained silent against the chimney nook, glowering at the farmer with a red light in her eye, to hang the paw as a trophy on the wall. The farmer then declares that either he or the wolf will die next time they meet, and tosses the paw to his wife. When it lands in her lap, it is a bloody human hand. She then stands up, 'Wi' the red licht in her e'e,' and 'stripped the claiths frae her lang richt arm'. The first of these is white, the last one 'red / And the fresh bluid dreeped adown.' She silently stretches out her long right arm, 'An' cauld as the deid stude he. / The flames louped bricht i' the gloamin' licht – / There was nae hand there to see!' (73).

Here a violent power struggle characterizes the marriage. The female may be a compliant wife by day, but at night she escapes the confines of the hearth and marauds the farm, wrestles with her husband, and steals away the children, whose fate is undisclosed. If mutilated by her husband, the wife appropriates violent aggression and revenge to herself in turn. Rather than fleeing, this wife stays on the domestic scene, poised to rend her husband apart or die trying. Nor is the husband awarded any show of sympathy, as in the 'Eskimo' legend. If seen as one who unaccountably finds himself on intimate terms with a monster, he is a shocked victim who finds that the one he considered his enemy, and the one he considered his domestic support, are one and the same. If seen as a husband whose actions in the poem typify his domestic role (he alone speaks and orders his wife about while she sits silent by the hearth), he is himself a brute, insensitive, tyrannical, boastful of his manly prowess.

The wife's 'lang richt arm' connects her to the bird-bride, whose long arms beat when the wind blows. These arms destroy the illusion of perfect proportion, mumble the hint of hunkering beast, and reach further and grasp more than feminine 'limbs' do. In a popular book of myth lore, John Fiske explicitly identified swan-maidens with werewolves, since both relied on donning an outer skin to effect their transformations from human to beast. Even more surprising, Fiske linked these amalgams of human and beast to the figure of the angel; because, as Fiske argues, the figure of the werewolf originated in the howling night wind, the werewolf is a 'leader of departed souls . . . The swan-maiden has also been supposed to summon the dying to her home . . . Even for the angels – women with large wings, who are seen in popular pictures bearing mortals on high towards heaven – we can hardly claim a different kinship.'[22] Graham Tomson likewise links the bird-bride and the female werewolf to the angel – the angel of the house.

This link of violent wolf to wife occurs in the probable source of Tomson's poem, Howard Williams's *Superstitions of Witchcraft*, first published by Longmans in 1865:

A gentleman while hunting was suddenly attacked by a savage wolf of monstrous size. Impenetrable by his shot, the beast made a spring upon the helpless huntsman, who in the struggle luckily, or unluckily for the unfortunate lady, contrived to cut off one of its fore-paws. This trophy he placed in his pocket, and made the best of his way homewards in safety. On the road he met a friend, to whom he exhibited a bleeding paw, or rather (as it now appeared) a woman's hand, upon which was a wedding-ring. His wife's ring was at once recognized by the other. His suspicions aroused, he immediately went in search of his wife, who was found sitting by the fire in the kitchen, her arm hidden beneath her apron, when the husband, seizing her by the arm, found his terrible suspicions verified. The bleeding stump was there, evidently just fresh from the wound. She was given into custody, and in the event was burned at Riom, in presence of thousands of spectators. (Quoted in Fiske, 139).

In Tomson's work the husband must confront the woman unaided, and she rises to meet him rather than being seized, imprisoned and burnt. Her violence is represented not simply as transgression, an unprovoked attack on male innocence, but also as reaction to male violence. Tomson's treatment of the werewolf legend thus exposes violent undercurrents in domesticity often glossed over in Victorian verse. Her ballad might be seen as a fierce woman's counterpart to the scenario of Robert Browning's 'Pompilia'.

Such an insistence on female ferocity was rare in British women's poetry, if rather more familiar in fiction. Laura Hansson argued in 1896 that George Egerton's stories in *Discords* presented 'not the well-known domestic animal which we call woman', but 'a wild creature belonging to a wild race, untamed and untamable, with the yellow gleam of a wild animal in its eyes . . . Her best stories are those where the wild instinct breaks loose.'[23] I suggest that Graham Tomson's two ballads based on northern mythology also let loose the wild instinct of women, and do so in response to wounds received – in marriage. Marriage in these poems is not so much a site of fulfilment or sorrow, as a scene of contending wills, sundered homes, violence and flight.

In the two long narrative poems based on classical legend, 'Procris' and 'The Story of Marpessa', some violence remains, but by comparison to the ballads the violence here is subdued and subordinated to a more restrained, formal exploration of emotional difficulties in marriage, particularly jealousy, distrust, changing attachments and fading passion. The formality is perhaps attendant upon Graham Tomson's deliberate engagement with the most authoritative tradition in western poetry, the classical. By 1889 Tomson has ample female precedent in such an undertaking: Elizabeth Barrett Browning's precocious translation of Aeschylus, Augusta Webster's 1866 translation of *Prometheus Bound* and *Medea* (Leighton 1992: 165), and women's access to formal education in the classics after Cambridge and Oxford were opened to women and degrees granted to them at the University of London.

Her two narrative poems were most likely prompted by *Selections from the*

Greek Anthology, a collection of English translations she edited and published in 1889. I cannot establish whether Tomson formally studied Latin and Greek, though accounts by Molly Hughes and others[24] suggest that some middle-class girls were able to study classical languages in the home. In any case, the most notable feature of Graham Tomson's substantial introduction to the *Greek Anthology* is its tone of assured authority as she surveys extant anthologies from Meleager's in 100 BC to Frederick Jacobs's monumental edition of 1813, provides concise accounts of authors whose works comprise the anthology, and pronounces on the merits and appeal of each poet. Tomson takes care to inscribe women in the classical tradition. Her selection includes one poem each by Sappho and Erinna, and in the introduction Tomson laments, 'How many perfect blossoms plucked from the gardens of Sappho and Stesichorus have disappeared [with the loss of Meleager's anthology], and by what weeds have they been replaced!' (*Selections* xx). She herself contributed no translations, but she features prominently among her list of distinguished contributors – Dr Richard Garnett (Superintendent of the British Library's Reading Room), Andrew Lang, Edmund Gosse, John Addington Symonds – a woman, Alma Strettell, whose translation of Agathias opens the volume, and whose name is one of five mentioned on the title page.[25]

The intersection of classical learning and female perspectives informs 'Procris' and 'Marpessa' as well. The story of Procris and Cephalus occurs rarely in English literature, perhaps because it involves a female goddess's kidnap of a mortal male against his wishes, rather than the usual inverse scenario. Thus the major reference point for treatment of the myth is Ovid, who emphasizes the gods' interference in mortal lives. In the *Metamorphoses*, Cephalus unfolds his tale when he is asked about the marvellous javelin he carries. Abducted by Aurora, Cephalus had implored to be returned to Procris, his new wife. This Aurora eventually granted in disgust, warning Cephalus that he would have cause to regret his choice.

Suspicious, he decided to test his wife's loyalty and, aided by Aurora, transformed his appearance. He returned to the grieving Procris and opened a campaign of seduction. She steadily refused until he offered great wealth rather than mere love. Finally she succumbed. He instantly doffed his disguise and rebuked her; she fled the house, hating all men, and devoted herself to Diana, becoming a huntress. Only when Cephalus confessed his wrong, admitting he would have succumbed to comparable temptation, and when Procris had sufficiently vented her anger, did she return to Cephalus, and the poem then celebrates the mutual joy and love of their early years of marriage. Procris gave Cephalus the gifts she had received from Diana, a javelin that, when thrown, unerringly flew to the heart of its prey, and a hound that could not be outrun by game. After the passage of idyllic years, she was horrified by news that Cephalus called out to a nymph named Aura whenever he hunted. She investigated, hiding in the underbrush to observe her husband. When he called on 'Aura', she rustled in the grass and moaned; thinking it to be a quarry, he threw the javelin and gave her her deathwound. Dying, she asked that he not marry Aura, only to be told this was his playful name for the breeze that cooled him after exertions at hunting. She died, and he remained a grief-stricken husband – though, curiously, not surrendering the javelin that killed his wife.

In Ovid the major emphasis is on the tragedy of a loving husband who, through Aurora's interventions and sheer mischance, kills his beloved wife. Here jealousy is unwarranted, unfaithfulness an illusion. In Graham R. Tomson's 'Procris', which appeared in two illustrated instalments in the May and June *Universal Review* in 1890, jealousy is central. As Procris announces in rising to tell her tale to Persephone:

> the greatest woe, I ween,
> Is Love's sweet surety lost in doubting pain,
> Is Love and Life by Folly forfeited,
> Is Happiness death-smitten by Distrust.
> For when Blind Love by pallid Fear is led
> His vines turn serpents, and his apples dust.[26]

At first, however, Procris is an idealized, loving wife. Of Procris's actions during the abrupt and lengthy absence of her husband when he is kidnapped by Aurora, Ovid says nothing. He shows interest in the domestic interior only when Cephalus returns home. In Tomson, Procris first slips into a state of emotional numbness after her husband disappears, then rebounds into frantic action:

> I fled forth, alone, upon the waste,
> Bearing aloft in my uplifted hands,
> Through the thick night, a glimmering golden lamp;
> All dread of thieves or evil beasts forgot,
> And on my hair and raiment fell the damp,
> Dull dew, Night's sluggish tears, but mine flowed not.
>
> Next morn I wakened in my carven bed
> From a long swoon, and heard the grievous sound
> Of all my women weeping me as dead;
> For, seeking his lost flock, a shepherd found
> My lifeless form stretched stark upon the earth,
> So on his shoulders, for compassion's sake,

He lifted me – a burden little worth! –
And bore me homeward through the tangled brake.

(85)

Through the plot device of Procris's search for her husband, Tomson not only invests the character with more plausible reactions to her husband's disappearance but also skilfully structures her poem. This first time Procris searches for her husband in the woods, driven by love and fidelity, the search almost kills her. Late in the poem, when Procris searches for her husband a second time, now motivated by distrust and jealousy, she dies.

Marriage is also threatened in the poem by the vagaries of desire. During her husband's absence, Procris endures frantic grief at night ('I would clench my hands and beat my head / Upon the moon-kissed marble of the floor' [86]), numb housewifery by day. But when a strange, attractive merchant unexpectedly appears, his voice awakens her desire once again. The poem decorously implies that Procris responds to an unchanging essence of love that underlies her husband's changing appearance; but the narrative also represents the appeal of a handsome new face to a lonely woman bereft of her accustomed mate, and the sweetness of giving in to desire:

A stranger, fair of presence, sought my gates –
. . . .
With stately mien and godlike through the halls
He paced, and in my presence bending low,
He spoke – even as forgotten music falls,
His greeting sank into my soul, – and so
I hearkened, sitting in mine ivory chair.
. . . .
Still, as he spoke, I looked into his eyes
And seemed to read some old sweet spell therein,
Almost remembered – almost now defined,
Though still a mist-veil, luminous and thin,
Held memory half asleep and prescience blind,
And as his hands and lips sought mine, I sighed,
'Thy prayer is heard, I will be thine, ah me,
The gods have whelmed me in a sweeping tide
That bears my whole soul's being on to thee.'

(88, 90)

As in Ovid, Cephalus immediately denounces his wife as a harlot whose insufficient fidelity contrasts tellingly with his own immovable love when

tempted by a goddess. Procris takes to the wilds a second time, this time
intending to kill herself out of horrified shame, although saved by Artemis,
who gives the javelin to Procris so that the woman will never again be
destitute of power:

> 'Dear child', she said, 'this safeguard give I thee,
> That speeds, unerring, to its victim's heart;
> Whate'er the cast, whate'er the quarry be,
> 'Twill flee as deadly from a young child's hand
> As from a hero's strong in warlike skill –
> No more again defenceless shalt thou stand,
> But hold the power to spare or slay at will.'
>
> (227)

Procris is later reconciled to Cephalus and again reverts to a life of
domesticity: 'now the distaff and the cradle-song / Were mine, and by
the hearth my wonted place' (228). But conventional domesticity cannot
withstand the threat of jealousy and suspicion, and when Procris hears
rumours of Cephalus's dallyings with a nymph, she takes to the woods a last
time.

Immediately the narrative aligns her with the prey Cephalus hunts. As she
hides, she sees how beautiful are the deer who wander past, with 'Their deep
wild eyes and slender antlers' (230). The herd flees when Cephalus enters,
calling on the nymph Aura, and she herself becomes the lovely animal
slaughtered in sport:

> As a poor fawn sinks helpless in the snow
> Benumbed, scarce feeling how the grey wolves tear
> Her quivering flesh, yet sees the red blood flow,
> So sank I, moaning, in my leafy lair;
> And, as I fell, a spear, unerring, flew
> To find its welcome in my breaking heart.
>
> (231)

As Cephalus declares, 'I deemed thy form this leafy screen within, / Clothed
in fair vesture, for a milk-white doe' (233).

Yet again one of Graham Tomson's marriage poems ends in bloodshed,
here in the killing of the wife. As well, Tomson again adds to her mythic
sources the plight of children when mother and father are sundered. As she
lies dying, Tomson's Procris, unlike Ovid's, fears for the fate of her children
if Cephalus mates with a goddess:

> Yet give not to the Goddess of the Dawn
> (For once-loved Procris' sake) thy marriage-vows,
> And all thy wealth of love from me withdrawn.
> But let some mortal woman rule thy house,
> Aye, and the little children – thine and mine –
> And pray that she entreat them tenderly.

                                                    (233–4)

The poem ends with her narrating, from the vantage point of Hades, her own death and anguish over her inability to trust her husband: 'thus mine own mad folly laid me low, / . . . mine own hand, distrustful, frayed the cord, / The silver strand that bound my life to his' (236).

'Procris' in many respects offers a more conservative treatment of marriage than do the ballads. Rather than power asymmetries within marriage, the poem imputes the impossibility of lasting marital happiness to personal defects. This emphasis is clear from one of Tomson's revisions of Ovid. In the Latin poem, Procris becomes the lover of the strange merchant for material gain – a motive that might have furthered a nineteenth-century critique of economic systems underlying bourgeois marriage. Tomson suppresses the materialist motive, merely noting the exquisite gifts the merchant lays before Procris, and emphasizes instead the shifting tides of desire. Procris's repeated expression of guilt, her anguish over her inability to remain steadfast in love and trust, also support a conservative reading of the poem's marriage theme.

Yet, as in the ballads, it is the wife who is speared or wounded by the husband; her blood flows amidst the sundering of the marriage tie. There is even a muted continuation of the theme of woman's wildness, when Procris lives in the forest and follows the hunt with Artemis, or when she becomes the dying leopard or milk-white doe hunted down by Cephalus. And it is possible that she uses the story to explore adultery – a forbidden subject if underwritten by a woman poet's own experience. In the version of the legend related by Apollodorus, Procris is an adulteress who uses Cephalus's absence to pursue a love affair, and Cephalus's killing of her is at least partly intentional.[27] Within this framework, Tomson's treatment of the legend stretches the limits of the sayable in Victorian women's poetry, given her depiction of Procris's wavering allegiance to her husband; and the issues of guilt, regret and suspicion may be highly charged personal explorations kept safely under control through the distancing agency of myth. Perhaps it was the potentially explosive allusiveness that led her to exclude this work from her published volumes. As well, the work's sheer length, or her sense that it lacked a coherent perspective on marriage, could account for the suppression. The poem is also uneven, ending on an unstressed syllable and lapsing into

cloyed or conventional diction in some passages. Still, it is strongly plotted
and offers a fresh treatment, from a female vantage point, of a legend that
turns on the instabilities and troubles of marriage. 'Procris' suggests that not
even a love that persists in the face of a goddess's temptations is enough to
secure unwavering trust and perfect fidelity in a wife, and that the vagaries
of desire and jealousy render the marriage tie always vulnerable, if not
transient.

'The Story of Marpessa', which inspired the title of my essay, appeared in
the September 1889 *Universal Review. The Iliad* (9.556–64) records Marpes-
sa's preference of the mortal Ides over the god Apollo (a complement to
Cephalus's preference of Procris over Aurora). To Stephen Phillips in his
1897 poem, 'Marpessa', the legend suggested the triumph of human love.
From Graham R. Tomson the legend evoked a narrative of patriarchal
conspiracy masquerading as courtship. The poem's fluent cadences build to
an abrupt termination, a formal dissonance that extends the narrative's
suggestion that the ideals of courtship and happy marriage are delusive
snares.

Like Procris, Marpessa speaks from Hades, telling her story to the shade of
an apparently male poet. The opening stanza announces the poem's focus on
the illusion of happy marriage:

> Alone I strayed along the dusky mead
> Musing on divers things beyond recall,
> On love and constancy; and if indeed
> This were reward of that, or if at all
> To seize and hold Love's rolling golden ball
> Were possible to folk of mortal clay –
> And, as I raised mine eyes, I saw a tall
> Fair woman move to meet me on the way.[28]

The woman, of course, is Marpessa. At first she is trivialized by the male
poet, who mocks her interest in fashion and gossip. The tone changes quickly
when the poet asks Marpessa for her story and she replies with a critique of
the men, both human and divine, who have figured in her life.

Homer mentions only that Marpessa's father is named Euenos. Tomson
invents a tyrannical father (along the lines of Elizabeth Barrett's) who, in this
pre-Freudian text, plays out the family romance by forbidding his favourite
daughter to marry:

> still my loving father's chiefest pride
> Was I. But time drew on and lovers tried
> To win me, and my sire Euenos cried

> That no man born should win me for his wife,
> But by his footstool ever must I bide.

(100)

Prince Ides, the most comely of her suitors, offers 'Most lordly bride gifts
... in vain', for her father still maintains, '"My lamb remains within my
fold"' (100–1). Ides rebels against the father's law, but as Marpessa notes, he
does so without every consulting her own wishes. The result is as much a
kidnap as the seizing of the bird-bride in Tomson's ballad:

> One morn to hear a beggar's plaint I rose,
> And singing ran adown the shining stair
> And through the court into the orchard-close
> Abloom; no suppliant I ween was there,
> But Ides clasped my knees with many a prayer,
> Yet never tarried for my yea or nay –
> In his strong arms he lifted me and bare
> Swift to his chariot, and so sped away.

(101)

Another intervention occurs when Apollo flashes down before the chariot in
a burst of light that, if blinding, also forms a kind of mesh or net, yet
another trap for Marpessa:

> Then on mine eyes a flaming fire there beat,
> And all around me floated, fold on fold,
> Close-binding every limb from face to feet,
> A cloud – a wondrous mesh of misty gold.
>
> And then a little way along the air,
> Borne by the softest wind that woos the Spring,
> I floated onward in the Sun-god's snare.

(102)

She represents herself in the familiar image of the 'caged bird', dumbly
resisting Apollo's overtures in a show of 'ruffled plumes and clouded eye'
because she cannot forget the 'fowler's nets' that have brought her to his
realm.

One day, however, Ides appears and defies the god and his power. Apollo
then offers to let Marpessa choose whichever lover she prefers, tempting her
to choose him through offers of divine ecstasies and his own extraordinary
beauty:

> He leaned towards me in his loveliness
> And from his forehead fell his yellow hair.
>
> Then all my soul within my breast was stirred;
> Meseemed the longing for my parents slept,
> And I forgot great Ides' spoken word,
> And all the tears my captive eyes had wept;
> So like some fawn a snake doth charm I stept
> Towards Apollo's arms a little space,
> While strange bewilderment my senses kept,
> Nor aught beheld I but his wondrous face.
>
> (104)

The spell snaps not because of Ides, but because Marpessa suddenly hears the voices and sees the shadows of women seduced and betrayed by Apollo:

> Thin voices, shrill and sorrow-stricken, spoke
> That seemed the sound of some out-worn Despair;
> Pale phantoms flitted through the golden air
> (As withered rose-leaves drift upon the wind),
> And low the ghostly voices wailed, 'Forbear!
> Or fade, like us, forgotten out of mind.'
>
> . . . .
>
> And each one's speech, in passing, murmured low,
> Was, 'Once – ah, once – Apollo loved me well.'
>
> (104–5)

The radiant Ides now awaits her choice of 'earthly life' with 'all the cares of wife and motherhood'; she embraces this choice, but not without passing doubts about its efficacy: '"The gods love lightly, nor for long – may be / That men are sometimes of a constant mood – / Take me, oh Ides, and be true to me!"' (105). As in any poem celebrating courtship and marriage, this culminating scene is figured as a moment of great release and joy. But the image of fleeing Apollo's nets is uneasily answered by the bonds in which Ides holds his new-won bride:

> Then, through the net-like haze of golden light,
> Even as a snared heron, freed at last,
> Doth seek her own grey marsh-lands with delight,
> Nor fears the chilly skies nor winter blast,
> So, gladly, from the Sun-god's thrall I passed,
> Mine eyes with too much radiance dazed and dim;

> But goodly Ides seized and held me fast,
> And all my heart's hid love went out to him.

(105)

The narrative uses the language of courtship, but Ides' grasp recalls the seizing of the bird-bride in the ballad, an act of entrapment rather than union.

The entire poem, in fact, seems to build to a climax of romantic fulfilment and sweetness, and Marpessa's narration ends with the usual conclusion of romance: 'Thereafter soon my love and I were wed.' Suddenly the stanza breaks, for the only time in the poem, as the poet insists on a question. What had seemed a conventional courtship poem abruptly unravels as Marpessa's narrative is pried open and left suspended on a question that cannot be answered:

> 'And was thy mortal lover true to thee?'
> I asked – but silently the phantom fled,
> Nor any answer more vouchsafed to me.

(105)

If there is an answer it lies with Marpessa's nurse, mentioned early in the poem, where she seems to function as a conventional blocking agent in a courtship plot.[29] The nurse, however, like Artemis with Procris, is a tutelary figure who dispenses counsel:

> And mine old nurse would say, 'Nay, never weep,
> Unthinking Haste the seed of Sorrow sows
> Full oft, for grey Experience to reap;
> Though now to thee a smiling face he shows,
> Fair Hymen holdeth hid a world of woes;
> He waits to lure thy feet through thorny ways,
> (For men are aye a fickle folk, God knows!)
> So live a maid unwedded all thy days.'

(101)

Just as the poem weaves a common pattern of tyranny among male figures, it also interrelates the female figures. Marpessa's mother, a type of Demeter longing for Persephone, refuses to uphold bourgeois domestic pieties when grief-stricken at her beloved daughter's kidnapping: 'Unceasing still thy lady-mother grieves, / Nor more takes thought for wise housewifery, / Nor with her maids the purple web she weaves' (103; cf. Tennyson's grieving Demeter, who, in the absence of the abducted Persephone, fails to send life through the earth). Significantly, it is to her mother's arms that Marpessa speeds when Ides takes her home; her tyrannical father goes unmentioned. Though, unlike the other poems discussed here, 'Marpessa' says nothing of a wedded couple's children, Marpessa is herself both wife and a daughter torn from her mother's love through paternal control and heterosexual desire. What becomes of mother or daughter, or any child of Marpessa's, remains untold because the outcome of marriage itself is so problematic it cannot be narrated.

'The Story of Marpessa' is a strong poem that merits wider knowledge. As with 'Procris', Graham Tomson did not include it in any of her published volumes, but H. B. Marriott Watson retrieved the poem and drew attention to its inclusion in his brief preface to the posthumous, collected poems of Rosamund Marriott Watson. Perhaps he acted on her own awareness of the poem's merits, or her wishes that it be better known. This work, like the other three poems, interrogates marriage as a lifelong arrangement or occupation for a woman, calls attention to changing attachments, and suggests that marriage too often functions as a trap for women who retain some trace of wildness or desire for cultural power. 'Marpessa', moreover, presents this critique in finely crafted narrative verse that limpidly unfolds until the narrative abruptly subverts and cracks open the courtship structure it has seemed to endorse. Formally as well as ideologically suggestive, 'The Story of Marpessa' again demonstrates the resources that myth offered to this poet for exploring and expressing volatile personal and social issues.

This group of four poems may slight materialist conditions underlying marital institutions or what would today be called the construction of gender. But the poems are significant in suggesting the fragility and even undesirability of marriage, the violent emotional and physical currents that can underlie marital discord or dissolution, the pain of broken families, and the asymmetries of domestic and public power. Graham Tomson herself never gave up on companionship with men and was involved continuously in relationships from the age of 19 until her death at 51. But she did give up on the institution of marriage, choosing to remain with H. B. Marriott Watson and their child Richard without the sanction of legal matrimony.[30] Her unconventional life, the theme of marital discord, and her appropriation of myth to represent subject matter usually excluded from nineteenth-century women's poetry all entitle the woman known variously as Rosamund Armytage, Graham R. Tomson, and Rosamund Marriott Watson to a place in literary history. Graham Tomson's poems also give added force to an issue frequently addressed in the study of Victorian poetry, most recently by Angela Leighton. Leighton concludes that biographical details are crucial to the study of Victorian women poets, since these figure so largely in the production and reception of their work, yet also argues that biographical backgrounds do not 'cause' poems nor carry sufficient weight where aesthetic matters are concerned (4). I would like to suggest that biographical details, when admitted as part of a reading strategy, can at times construct the perception – hence the operation – of greater aesthetic richness and complexity in a poem. For male poets whose lives are lavishly documented, biographical details figure significantly in formalist and psychoanalytical or psychosexual readings. For example, a great deal of attention has been accorded Tennyson's handling of myth in 'Morte d'Arthur' in relation to Arthur Hallam's death; knowledge of this background permits perception of multivalent meaning, although some of Tennyson's contemporary readers would have been oblivious to these significations. A similiar enrichment of a woman's poems can occur when her biography is factored into the reading. The following poem was first published in the January 1897 *Yellow Book* (volume 12) under the name Rosamund Marriott Watson. It displays all the characteristics of a skilful minor poet of the era – evocative diction and sound effects, faultless technique, a delight in the evanescent and liminal:

Children of the Mist

The cold airs from the river creep
  About the murky town,
The spectral willows, half-asleep,
  Trail their long tresses down
Where the dim tide goes wandering slow,
Sad with perpetual ebb and flow.

The great blind river, cold and wide,
  Goes groping by the shore,
And still where water and land divide
  He murmurs evermore
The overword of an old song,
The echo of an ancient wrong.

There is no sound 'twixt the stream and sky,
  But, white mists walk the strand,
Waifs of the night that wander by,
  Wraiths from the river-land –
While here, beneath the dripping trees,
Stray other souls more lost than these.

Voiceless and visionless they fare,
  Known all too well to me –

> Ghosts of the years that never were,
> The years that could not be –
> And still, beneath the eternal skies
> The old blind river gropes and sighs.

(281–2)

If read as a conventional nature poem and lament for passing time the poem is pleasant, even touching, but not particularly memorable. If, instead, it is read as the poem of a woman who had lost three children (the eldest sixteen when the poem appeared) because she was twice divorced before custody of her own children was a realistic possibility, the poem is a very different work indeed. Suddenly it can be read as an achingly moving poem, one characterized by astonishing control over image and emotion. The old, cold and blind river becomes the stream of consciousness itself, at once deeply yearning yet steeled not to feel more than is strictly permissible.

The same intensification of aesthetic power occurs if we come back to 'Ballad of the Were-Wolf' and read it, too, in the context of the poet's experience of failed marriage and divorce. The poem is a fierce rendition of rage and violence, and I have generally preferred to read it as a story about power, discord, and defiance of the 'feminine' body. But the reference to the couple's 'bairnies twa' suggests, when connected to Baring-Gould's commentaries on female were-wolves who slew children,[31] a possible expression of guilt. That is, if the female were-wolf suggests female wildness and the power to shift shapes in order to revolt and exact retribution for wounds and wrongs received, it can also suggest the self-projection of a mother as monster who drives children away from the hearth where she sits. Neither interpretive possibility eliminates the other; rather, including both intensifies the poem's richness, generating a central image that refuses to settle but itself endlessly shifts shapes of signification. A good poem is suddenly even better.[32]

NOTES

1 'Armitage [*sic*] v. Armitage and Tomson,' 'Probate, Divorce, and Admiralty Division' column, London *Times*, 1 February, 1887, p.3. Subsequent citations ('Armitage') are given in the text.

2 In 1885, when Rosamund and George Armytage separated, the husband had full rights to children unless convicted of aggravated assault. An 1886 act allowed women's wishes to be considered, but women still had no legal rights in the matter. Any woman who had committed adultery, as Rosamund had, was automatically excluded from custody of children. See Caird 1897: 55; McGregor 1957: 23; Savage 1983: 106; and Levine 1990: 89.

3   See Waltman 1976: 391, and Hind, Introduction, *Christ in Hades*, by Stephen Phillips (1917: 19). Subsequent references to Waltman are given in the text.

4   Wilde in *Woman's World* 2 (1889), quoted in Krishnamurti (ed.) 1991: 86.

5   Millgate 1971: 297–8, 329, 332. Millgate's biographical note, 'Thomas Hardy and Rosamund Tomson' (1973) was a crucial starting place for my own work.

6   Pennell 1916: 157–8. Subsequent references are cited in the text.

7   Pennell quotes Tomson's bit of doggerel about the 'Autolycus' column 'O, there's Mrs. Meynell and Mrs. Pennell, / There's Violet Hunt and me!' (1916: 158). Katharine Tynan writes of the prestige of the 'Autolycus' columns to women writers (1916: 112, 117), and of her joy when, in 1896, 'I reached the summit of my hopes in those days. I got an "Autolycus" column in the *Pall Mall*' (149).

8   See Pennell 1929: 1, 280–1, and Mix 1960: 129–30. As Dubois and Gordon, among others, note, sexual freedom and divorce were sometimes repudiated by feminists, whose resistance to sexual double standards and sexual exploitation of women took the form of demanding sexual purity for all, including men (1983: 7–25). Rosamund's banishment from a former woman friend should be seen in this context.

9   I wish to thank Marysa Demoor, who is indexing and writing a study of women reviewers for the *Athenaeum*, for this information.

10 Archer 1902; 1970: 469–80. In 1911 W. G. Blaikie Murdoch still treated Marriott Watson as a poet worthy of serious consideration (1911; 1970: 49–50), as did Harold H. Williams a few years later ('In poetry the most notable contributors to the *Yellow Book* were Mr. Arthur Symons, John Davidson, Ernest Dowson, Lionel Johnson, Laurence Binyon, Mr. W. B. Yeats and Mrs. Marriott Watson; (1918: xviii; see also 142, 148–9). As late as 1960 Mix cited her as the best woman poet who contributed to *The Yellow Book* (1960: 129).

11 Montefiore, 1987: 39–40, 95; and Ostriker 1982: 72ff. Of course, Victorian women poets prior to Graham Tomson used myth, particularly Christina Rossetti. Angela Leighton also notes the example of Augusta Webster's 'Circe', situated in the woman's point of view and hinting that men are brutes even without the aid of potions (1992: 193–6); subsequent references are given in the text. Tomson is distinctive in using myth to explore discordant marriage.

12 Augusta Webster's *Mother and Daughter* sonnets, published posthumously in 1895, were a notable exception, as was Amy Levy's 'Xantippe'. See Leighton 1992: 193, and Hickok 1984: 50, 65, 71–2. Hickok notes the general exclusion of the 'New Woman' among representations of women by female poets (9, 164).

13 15 June 1889 letter to James Dykes Campbell, in Beckson and Munro (eds.) 1989: 50. Antonin Bunand, according to Beckson and Munro, was a 'French critic, author of *Petits lundis: notes de critique* (Paris, 1890)' (51, n.2).

14 Archer identifies 'an astonishing correctness of style and perfection of technique' as her most striking quality (1902; 1970: 469). Graham Tomson herself, in the introduction to *Selections from the Greek Anthology*, expressed the desire to suppress

scandalous biographical information in poets' histories: 'Fortunate poets! There is no one who can tell us of the youthful indiscretions of Meleager ... no dishonourable ghoul to "howk up" and reprint some old, forgotten love-letters of "pure Simonides", proving him thereby not pure, in very sooth, but most unworthy – a weak and garrulous sensualist' (1889: xxi). Lest I be thought a 'ghoul' myself, I should add that in the same introduction she laments the anonymity of poets in the Greek Anthology who, being unknown, have lost the immortality they might claim by virtue of their poetry (xxxv). Subsequent references to *Selections* will be cited in the text.

15 See Ruthven 1984: 117.

16 Gittings 1978: 64–5.

17 Boos 1991: 502. I wish to thank Florence Boos for suggesting Baring-Gould in relation to Tomson.

18 Baring-Gould 1866; 1914: 485. Baring-Gould offers this narrative structure in relation to Lohengrin, not swan-maidens, but implies that it is a recurrent pattern. Subsequent citations of this work are given in the text.

19 Graham R. Tomson, *The Bird-Bride: A Volume of Ballads and Sonnets* (1889: 2). All other citations of the poem will be given in the text.

20 Matthew Arnold, of course, had depicted an abandoned spouse and children in 'The Forsaken Merman' when Margaret returns to the human, Christian realm and the merman and his mer-children are left alone; here the wife returns to the wild, not to the realm of duty, and she takes her children with her.

21 Graham R. Tomson, *A Summer Night and Other Poems* (1891: 71). Subsequent references to the poem are given in the text.

22 My quote is from an early article by John Fiske, 'Werewolves and Swan-Maidens' (1871: 144). Fiske's writings were gathered into a volume that continued to be reprinted into the 1880s and 1890s.

23 Hansson 1896: 88–9.

24 Hughes, *A London Child of the Seventies* (1934: 44); see also Levine 1990: 142–3. Graham R. Tomson filled out a query form for the third edition of *Directory of Writers for the Literary Press*, compiled and published by W. M. Griswold in 1890. On the form she indicated that she had never been an instructor in college and that she held no college degree. This information does not preclude education at a women's college that granted no degree. My information derives from a 26 October 1992 letter from the Boston College Library Reference Librarian.

25 Strettell, sister of Mrs Comyns Carr, published a number of translations during her lifetime, from Italian, German, French, Spanish and other languages. Tomson's work on the Anthology garnered praise from *Woman's World*: '[It] has been admirably carried out ... Mrs. Tomson has performed her task with unusual judgment and good sense ... Mrs. Tomson herself supplies an introductory essay, which contrives to convey a good deal of information in a picturesque shape' (Review of *Selections from the Greek Anthology*, ed. Graham R. Tomson, *Woman's World* 3 [December 1889]: 105). Thomas Hardy offered a milder compliment: 'The preparation of [your preface] must have cost you an

immense labour & research, & I trust that your taste in its production will be recognised' (1978: 199).

26   *Universal Review* 7 (1890): 80. Subsequent references to the poem will be given in the text.

27   Tomson could have read a summary of Apollodorus's version, in English, in Antoine Banier's work published in the eighteenth century: 'As [Cephalus] had a passionate Love for the Chace, and rose up early every Morning to that Exercise, hence he was said to be enamour'd with *Aurora*. *Procris* his Wife, who was in love with *Ptelean*, as we learn from *Apollodorus*, no doubt propagated this Report, in order to hide or justify her Intrigue.' Cephalus returns, Procris flees to Crete and becomes the lover of Minos II, and Minos gives her the famous hunting dog. 'Cephalus at last was reconciled with his Wife, but having killed her in hunting, tho' by Mischance, it was presumed to be from some Remains of Resentment he still retained against her' (Banier, 1739–40; 1976: iv, 378–9).

28   Marriott Watson, *The Poems of Rosamund Marriott Watson* (1912: 99). Subsequent citations of the poem will be given in the text.

29   For discussion of courtship and marriage plots, see Boone 1984: 65–81; and 1989.

30   A search of marriage records at St Catharine's House in London revealed no record of a marriage ceremony. Dr G. Krishnamurti, in a personal communication, confirmed this finding based on his own investigation.

31   Sabine Baring-Gould 1865; 1973: 66–7. Baring-Gould records the case of a late-sixteenth-century woman who, suffering 'a fit of lycanthropic madness', is smitten with lust for blood when she sees two young children, and attempts to kill them (78).

32   Research for this essay was supported in part by TCU RF/Research Grant 5–23645. Anyone wishing a typescript of the Tomson poems discussed in this essay may write to me and enclose a check of $2.00 payable to 'English Department, TCU.'

12

The Restless Wanderer at the Gates: Hosts, Guests and Ghosts in the Poetry of Mary E. Coleridge

KATHARINE MCGOWRAN

'I have no fairy godmother ... but lay claim to a fairy great-great-uncle, which is perhaps the reason that I am condemned to wander restlessly around the Gates of Fairyland, although I have never yet passed them' (Coleridge 1910: 11). Mary Coleridge's description of her own 'anxiety of influence' not only displaces the very concept into a more fantastic realm, subject to different laws, but also reads as a metaphor of exclusion. She positions herself outside the gates and undertakes the role of the wanderer, becoming a kind of Ancient Mariner figure, in search not only of a listener but, it seems, of poetry itself. The situation of these ideas in the realm of fairy-tale also suggests a capricious side; as if Mary is haunted by the witches and demons of Samuel Taylor's texts. Poetic inspiration (if that is what is contained within the 'Gates of Fairyland') takes on the unreliable quality of enchantment, as if it too is somehow 'fey'. J. Hillis Miller's comment that a literary text is 'inhabited ... by a long chain of allusions, guests, ghosts of previous texts' (1977: 446) suddenly seems more literal when the ghosts are blood relations.

Mary's vision of herself as 'condemned to wander restlessly' is also suggestive of a process in which she internalizes the role of a figure within a poem. Rachel Blau du Plessis's comment that 'Women as figures in poems and women as writers of poems are in a complex and sometimes contradictory relationship' (1988: 86) goes some way to describing the complicated process which occurs in Mary Coleridge's poem of 1892, 'The Witch'. In it she takes up the voice of Geraldine from Samuel Taylor's 'Christabel' – a figure who is at once 'damsel in distress, witch, sorceress, lamia-snake, nature goddess, daemonic spirit ...' (Holmes 1990: 288). In 'The Witch', the Geraldine figure enters the poem as 'damsel in distress'.

I have walked a great while over the snow,
And I am not tall nor strong.
My clothes are wet, and my teeth are set,
And the way was hard and long.
I have wandered over the fruitful earth,
But I never came here before.
Oh, lift me over the threshold, and let me in at the door!

The cutting wind is a cruel foe.
I dare not stand in the blast.
My hands are stone, and my voice a groan
And the worst of death is past.
I am but a little maiden still,
My little white feet are sore.
Oh, lift me over the threshold, and let me in at the door!

(M. Coleridge 1954: 145)

The discrepancy between the title of the poem and the frail figure who emerges is marked. Her very lack of power is stressed. The threatening 'richly-clad' 'damsel bright' of Christabel gives way to a figure who is more plaintive, more child-like. The nature of 'The Witch' is never fully revealed. Mary adopts the fairy-tale strategy of metamorphosis in her poem, turning a 'lamia figure', a 'sorceress', into a little white maiden, managing to make a gesture in the direction of 'things not being quite what they seem', without losing the possibility of duplicity from the witch.

Perhaps the most curious feature of the poem is the confusion effected by a slippery, shape-shifting 'I' which masks and swaps the identities of the two figures in the poem.[1] While the teller of the tale in fairy-tales often affirms his or her own identity, Coleridge seems to lose hers. The swapping of identities takes place at the threshold, the site of crossing over, a liminal phase which Bronfen has described as: 'Betwixt-and-between . . . an in-between state of life-in-death . . . the site of the double, the ghost' (Bronfen, 1992: 192). Coleridge uses the fact that the pronoun 'I' has no independent meaning to blur and confuse the relationship between the figures in the poem. In an early diary entry she describes the source of her pseudonym 'Anodos', the wanderer of George MacDonald's *Phantastes*, in terms which imply a distrust of the personal pronoun, as if it were easier to write in the third person: 'lest this *I* should grow troublesome and importunate, I will christen myself over again, make George MacDonald my godfather, and name myself after my favourite hero, Anodos in *Phantastes*' (Coleridge 1910: 23). In 'The Witch' the 'I' proves similarly restless, shifting between the two figures in the poem.

Furthermore, while the gender of the witch is at least fixed as feminine, the gender of that other 'I' is unspecified.

> Her voice was the voice that women have,
> Who plead for their heart's desire.
> She came – she came – and the quivering flame
> Sank and died in the fire.
> It never was lit again on my hearth
> Since I hurried across the floor,
> To lift her over the threshold, and let her in at the door.

(145)

If the 'I' is female, then the poem locates a commonality between the two: 'Her voice was the voice that women have,' confusing the issue of the 'unspeakable' mark revealed to Christabel which separates the women in Samuel Taylor's poem. Instead, this poem seems to locate the point at which self starts to turn into its other, its double, where distinctions become blurred. The two 'worlds' of the poem, the 'inside' of hearth and home, and the 'outside' of snow and 'cutting wind' seem to merge as the witch is carried over the threshold. The fire in the hearth is put out, quenched perhaps by the snow, never to be lit again. The eroticism hinted at in this stanza also suggests the threshold as a threshold of experience, of awakening sexuality. However, whether this union is between two women, or a man and a woman is never revealed. If this other 'I' is, instead, male, then the poem takes on a different aspect. The 'voice that women have / Who plead for their heart's desire' stresses not commonality but difference. The phrase 'that women have' excludes the speaker, suggesting that this unspecified 'desire' may be one that is recognized by men, but is not one which they share. Furthermore, what this woman's voice pleads is:

> 'Oh, lift me over the threshold, and let me in at the door!'

The 'heart's desire' of the female 'I' is to be let in. While Samuel Taylor's Geraldine is let in from the outside by Christabel, the witch is let in by somebody already inside. It is as if Mary herself is speaking from the gates of her own imaginary landscape, pleading admittance perhaps to the 'Fairyland' of her great-great-uncle's poem. The threshold is both the focus of her own poem, and the point of its intersection with his. The poet must be lifted over the threshold, given admittance to a place which is the domain of someone else. While this is, as critics have argued, the position of every writer to an extent, in Coleridge's case the situation is exacerbated both by her sex and by the fact that her precursor is a blood relation. Her choice of the witch, the

Geraldine figure, seems likewise laden with implication. In Mary's poem the Romantic opposition of self and other is confused by the shifting 'I' which can 'speak' for both. This blurring of distinctions implies a world in which the categories of good and evil are not so finely distinct. The threshold in this poem is more fluid, more unstable as a boundary than the rigid one at the castle in 'Christabel':

> They crossed the moat, and Christabel
> Took the key that fitted well;
> A little door she opened straight,
> All in the middle of the gate;
> The gate that was ironed within and without,
> Where an army in battle array had marched out.
>
> (S. T. Coleridge 1964: 220)

Yet the crossing of the threshold in 'The Witch', which is described in terms which convey urgency as well as desire, is qualified by the hint of some sort of sacrifice:

> She came – she came – and the quivering flame
> Sank and died in the fire.
> It never was lit again on my hearth
> Since I hurried across the floor,
> To lift her over the threshold, and let her in at the door.

The 'quivering' flame sinks and dies and is never lit again. This further adds to the ambiguity of the poem. The 'desire' somehow 'sinks and dies' with the quivering flame, the hearth remains cold and empty, unwelcoming. While the host unlocks the door willingly, something dies upon the witch's entry. The 'quivering' flame can never be rekindled, and this suggests an awareness of limitation, as though the 'heart's desire' of the woman poet can never be achieved without loss. The strangely resigned note on which the poem ends is similar to the tone of Mary's description of her own dilemma. She is 'condemned' to be always at the gates; something remains out of reach. While her 'exclusion' is from an imaginary, figurative 'fairy' landscape, it is expressed in this poem in strongly physical terms: the 'restless wanderer' is one who is condemned to roam both mental and physical territories. In taking up the voice of the witch she may enter, but her presence there seems to demand some kind of sacrifice. The movement into the poem is qualified by a lingering sense of loss.

Mary's poem 'The Witches' Wood' again suggests a territory which belongs to someone else. Indeed her use of fantasy seems dogged by this

sense of unbelonging and a fascination with an area which is somehow not
subject to rules, or which is unstable, beyond control. While fantasy provides
a place in which the poet is autonomous, it is also the territory of someone
or something else. She describes the pull of fantasy in an article entitled
'More Worlds Than One' which appeared in *The Reflector* in March 1888:
'Unreality attracts certain minds, as money attracts the miser'. Reality is, she
says, 'quite without the strange power of pleasing which is the property of
things and people that never were.' There are, she states, 'three whole worlds
at our disposal: the world that is, of which we know something; the world
that will be, of which we know nothing; and the world that never was and
never will be, about which we know everything' (1910: 174). Coleridge's
imaginary worlds and people, therefore, lie between the 'something' and
'nothing' of the 'real', and the heaven or hell of the 'world that will be'.

This unreal world is itself an 'in-between' place, a threshold between life
and afterlife. Marina Warner has stated that: 'the wonders that create the
atmosphere of fairy-tale disrupt the apprehensible world in order to open
spaces for dreaming alternatives' (1994: xvi). While these 'dreaming alterna-
tives' can be used for political ends, as they are in works by contemporary
women writers like Rosamund Marriott Watson and Dora Sigerson,[2] Coler-
idge seems to explore these 'open spaces' more perversely, revelling in their
non-referentiality. However, there still remains a sense of the outsider in
these poems which locate themselves in a fairy world. While the 'restless
wanderer' may prove a figure of disruption, Coleridge somehow always
remains outside, or under the rule of someone else. The great-great-uncle is
both someone who leads her in the direction of this 'other' world yet also
someone who has been there before. He is the host and she is the guest, her
identity is confused by the sense of being a visitor in someone else's poem.
And while this is more obvious in 'The Witch', because of its explicit relation
to Samuel Taylor's poetry, her other 'fairy' poems contain many similiar
ambiguities and confusions.

The poem 'The Witches' Wood' plays with the idea of metamorphosis,
creating an unsettling atmosphere in which the use of metaphor is constantly
pushing towards a metonymic substitution. There is a third person narrator
in the poem, but no wanderer, no 'knight-at-arms' to somehow intercede
between the reader and the strange landscape. Coleridge employs the device
used by Keats in 'La Belle Dame Sans Merci' of referring to the absence of
the recognizable natural world.

> There was a wood, a witches' wood,
>   All the trees therein were pale.
> They bore no branches green and good,
>   But as it were a gray nun's veil.

This is repeated in the fourth stanza;

> There never did a sweet bird sing
>   For happy love about his nest.
> The clustered bats on evil wing
>   Each hollow trunk and bough possessed.

                                                    (174)

The poem constantly reminds the reader what should be, forcing the nastier and weirder reality to be viewed alongside the natural. There is also a sense of the cautionary tale about this poem:

> They talked and chattered in the wind
>   From morning dawn to set of sun,
> Like men and women that have sinned,
>   Whose thousand evil tongues are one.
>
> Their roots were like the hands of men,
>   Grown hard and brown with clutching gold.
> Their foliage women's tresses when
>   The hair is withered, thin, and old.

The trees of the wood both are and are not men and women. Only the world 'like' seems to stand between an actual transformation. The suggestion of a Dantesque metamorphosis as punishment for human sin adds to the idea of magic and fairy-tale. The metaphor of roots as 'men's hands / Grown hard and brown with clutching gold' is curiously similar to Mary's own metaphor of the mind which covets unreality; 'Unreality attracts certain minds, as money attracts the miser'. This idea suggests unreality as a kind of fairy currency. The miser further points to the fate of those who covet this fairy 'gold', suggesting a simultaneous gain and loss. These roots grow under the ground, hidden from view, suggesting the secret hoarding of the miser, and the foliage of thin 'withered' women's hair which covers the branches adds to the sense of sterility. The gap between seeming and being, what 'is' and what 'is like' is never closed but remains a vague threat. What drives the poem are the witches, who do not appear, but manifest themselves in this shifting ground between the familiar, the homely, and its transmuted, unhomely other. The absence of any human figure is mirrored by the absence of the poet herself. Unlike 'The Witch', there is no 'I', but the poem ends with a strange image of eternal night:

> And in the midst a pool there lay
>   Of water white, as though a scare
> Had frightened off the eye of day
> And kept the Moon reflected there.

The surface of the pool literally 'captures' the image it reflects. The 'scare' which frightened off 'the eye of day' remains unspecific, yet the 'water white' pool and the captive moon which remain in a kind of stalemate reflection suggest a kind of ghostly femininity which is trapped. The possessive 'kept' adds to a vague sense of desire, as if the covetousness of the hands which clutch after gold is somehow echoed at the end by a desire for the more insubstantial silver of the moon.

Like 'The Witches' Wood', 'The White Women' is located in the 'other' realm:

> Where dwell the lovely, wild white women folk,
>   Mortal to man?
> They never bowed their necks beneath the yoke,
> They dwelt alone when the first morning broke
>   And Time began.

                                                          (212)

The question which opens the poem places the poet outside, while the enclosed nature of this place is reinforced by constant metaphors of defence and inaccessibility:

> The deadly shafts their nervous hands let fly
>   Are stronger than our strongest – in their form
> Larger, more beauteous, carved amazingly,
> And when they fight, the wild white women cry
>   The war-cry of the storm.

> Their words are not as ours. If man might go
>   Among the waves of Ocean when they break
> And hear them – hear the language of the snow
> Falling on torrents – he might also know
>   The tongue they speak.

> Pure are they as the light; they never sinned,
>   But when the rays of the eternal fire

> Kindle the West, their tresses they unbind
> And fling their girdles to the Western wind,
>> Swept by desire.

The idea of another, incomprehensible language pushes the poet even further away from her own text. The white women speak 'the language of the snow / Falling on torrents', a language which effaces and conceals, which seems to cover its own tracks. The snow which falls upon the torrents is also suggestive of the 'water white' of 'The Witches' Wood', a metaphor which seems to deny interpretation yet which replaces the transparency of water with a colourless colour; one which seems both innocent and blank, but may also conceal the traces of something else.

> Dreams are not – in the glory of the morn,
> Seen through the gates of ivory and horn –
>> More fair than these.

The sense here that this 'dreaming alternative' is somehow better than any dream, places the women not only outside sight and language, but also beyond poetic dreams themselves. The idea of exclusion is reinforced by the image of the gates (through which the poet has seen dreams before), and the poem remains at arm's length, as something unmediated, a tale not spoiled by the intrusive 'I'.

This lack of intrusion, of the 'I' which 'crosses over', highlights the confusion effected in those other poems in which the self as 'I' enters the poem. 'Wilderspin' is another tale concerned with inside and outside:

> In the little red house by the river
>> When the short night fell,
> Beside his web sat the weaver,
>> Weaving a twisted spell.
> Mary and the Saints deliver
>> My soul from the nethermost Hell!
>
> In the little red house by the rushes
>> It grew not dark at all,
> For day dawned over the bushes
>> Before night could fall.
> Where now a torrent rushes,
>> The brook ran thin and small.

(200)

The poem remains curiously unspecific – the evil suggested by the fervent prayer of the first stanza: 'Mary and the Saints deliver / My soul from the nethermost Hell!' seems to come (contradictorily) from the innocuous-sounding 'little red house'. The weaver is also a 'fairy weaver' who weaves not cloth but 'twisted spells'. The time in the poem is also confusing and the narrative voice which relates the events adds to this. The narrator seems to speak from beyond the events, afterwards (hence the past tense), yet the prayer / incantation is spoken from the present as if the speaker is still under some kind of curse. The 'short night' of the first stanza gives way to a midsummer time where day dawns 'before night could fall'. This second stanza suggests impediments, night is stopped from falling, the power of the torrent is reduced to a thin brook (and is only restored in the present of the narrator – 'Where now a torrent rushes'.) This general blocking is echoed by the shortened metre. Control is located elsewhere in this poem, and the sense of this is reinforced by the weaver figure who sits 'beside *his* web' (my emphasis). In this case the possessive pronoun implicitly refers both to the web and to the poem; as if the twistedness of his spell somehow wreaks havoc on the internal logic of the poem itself. Meaning is also impeded, the poem bewilders, treading a fine line between 'sense' and a perverse, twisted 'non-sense'.

The weaver in the house is not the welcoming host of 'The Witch', but someone more autonomous and more obstructive. It is as if the 'fairy great-great-uncle' here proves a more complex figure in Mary's imagination. The weaver in this poem is a Rumpelstiltskin figure, a version of the 'Elfin Knight' who 'would snatch [the heroine] . . . away to the underworld as his bride' (Warner, 1994: 134). This threat of the underworld is suggested by the refrain which calls upon the orthodoxy of the church to provide salvation from the fairy spells of poetry. However, the wish for protection expressed in this refrain is offset by a sense of longing. The feeling of enticement, of invitation which is powerfully evoked by the 'chamber' in the house is matched by a responding desire to enter, to be 'snatched away'.

> In the little red house a chamber
>   Was set with jewels fair;
> There did a vine clamber
>   Along the clambering stair,
> And grapes that shone like amber
>   Hung at the windows there.

A 'guest' is expected, and the desire for the delights of this chamber is echoed by the movement of the vine which 'clambers' along the stair. The awkwardness suggested by 'clamber' strikes a creeping, sinister note. The grapes at the window signal to the outsider the delights within, tempting like a goblin feast of fruit. There is also a sense of what is within, of 'jewels fair', as if the 'little red house' contained within it what the poet reaches after – the temptation of 'fairy gold' which somehow buys inspiration but also demands its price. The fruit and currency recall Rossetti's *Goblin Market* where a fairy economy calls a similarly twisted tune.

Here again, the poem works by shifting its pronouns. The narrator possesses the ability to 'shape-shift' so that the fourth stanza speaks not only from inside the house, but also perhaps with another voice:

> Will the loom not cease whirring?
> Will the house never be still?
> Is never a horseman stirring
> Out and about on the hill?
> Was it the cat purring?
> Did someone knock at the sill?

This shift in tense takes the narrator back in time to the 'present' of the poem. As in 'The Witch' it is as if the figure within the poem and the figure without speak with the same voice. The urgent questioning of the stanza also creates a listener, demands a reply – as if the whirring of the loom requires the intervention of the horseman to silence or perhaps even answer it. Yet whatever finally takes place in the 'little red house' remains hidden.

The voice inside is eager for the guest (like the host in 'The Witch'). Yet this time the suggestion of evil comes not from the 'witch' outside but the wizard-weaver within:

> To the little red house a rider
> Was bound to come that night.
> A cup of sheeny cider
> Stood ready for his delight.
> And like a great black spider,
> The weaver watched on the right.

> To the little red house by the river
> I came when the short night fell.
> I broke the web for ever.
> I broke my heart as well.
> Michael and the Saints deliver
> My soul from the nethermost Hell!

The rider is both an expected 'guest' and also the victim of a lure. While the 'cup of sheeny cider' promises hospitality, the presence of the weaver / spider suggests the unspecified danger which awaits. The web seems to represent not only the 'work' of someone else which must be broken (recalling the Oedipal struggle of Bloom's battling 'father' and 'son' poets), but also a figure of entanglement. The rider is 'bound' to come, suggesting both the inevitability of the 'knight-at-arms' rescuer of fairy-tale and also the idea of a magical draw, the irresistible pull of the weaver, the desire to enter. The 'fruits' of the house, signalling in fairy-tale fashion the delights waiting inside, also hint at the danger of this temptation. When the web is broken, the heart is broken too. The 'I' again proves 'troublesome', an unknown quantity, changing each time it is articulated. This 'I' speaks for weaver, rider and poet who are all drawn into this web of poetry and influence – a web which can never be unravelled and whose secrets can never be spelled out. 'Wilderspin' itself proves similarly impenetrable, the reader becoming trapped inside the entangling art of the poem.

Coleridge seems trapped herself within this network of poetry and influence. She is caught somewhere between destruction and desire, like a female version of the Bloomian poet 'condemned to learn his profoundest yearnings through an awareness of other selves. The poem is within him, yet he experiences the shame and splendour of being found by poems outside hime' (1973: 26). The 'I' in these poems becomes a figure itself for change and inconstancy, for the gain and loss in the process of asserting poetic identity. And while its shifts and transformations result partly from the 'crossing over' into the 'witches' woods' of Mary's imagination, the pleading of the witch and the broken heart of the rider suggest that there is something more behind this unstable pronoun. The 'I' itself is, like the woman poet, interstitial, 'betwixt-and-between' on the threshold of a house of poetry which is already inhabited. The threshold is the place where guest meets host in Mary Coleridge's imagination, a place of reciprocal desire, yet also of loss. The curious relation between the two figures: poet and precursor, great-great-uncle and niece, weaver and rider, is one which expresses both a desire for union and a desire for difference. The threshold is the place of making and destroying, between the new poem and the entangling web of the old which weaves the spell of inspiration. While the spell of the old must be broken by crossing the gates, this act involves the loss of enchantment, of the host / uncle who both provides inspiration and also blocks it. Coleridge's answer to this contradiction of her art is to go on being a 'restless wanderer at the gates'.

NOTES

1 Angela Leighton, 'Writing in White: A Woman Poet of the Nineties' in a collection of essays, forthcoming, University of Ghent, 1996.
2 Marriott Watson's 'Ballad of the Bird-Bride' and 'A Ballad of the Were-Wolf', depict violence and oppression within marriage, while Sigerson's nationalism is implicit, both in her choice of Irish myth and legend as subjects, and in the poems themselves. Her political sympathies are evident in works like 'The Wind in the Hills' and 'False Dearbhorghil' and 'All Soul's Night'.

13

The Damsel, the Knight, and the Victorian Woman Poet

DOROTHY MERMIN

Looking back at her childhood from the vantage point of fourteen years old, Elizabeth Barrett wrote that at four and a half, 'my great delight was poring over fairy phenomenons and the actions of necromancers – & the seven champions of Christendom ... beguiled many a weary hour. At five I supposed myself a heroine and in my day dreams of bliss I constantly imaged to myself a forlorn damsel in distress rescued by some noble knight.'[1] Which was she in these daydreams: the forlorn damsel, or the noble knight? 'I supposed myself a heroine', but 'I imaged *to* myself a damsel rescued ...' The knight is more distant – 'some noble knight' – and the fact that the daydreams arose as an escape from weary hours suggests an unwilling identification with the damsel. But from an early age Elizabeth Barrett despised sentimental young women and wanted to dress as a boy and run away to be, perhaps, 'poor Lord Byron's PAGE': a daydream that tries to defer gender identification by deferring adult sexuality, but cannot defer it indefinitely.[2] In her earliest literary imaginings, then, we find her hovering between two mutually exclusive and equally unsuitable literary roles – one precluded by the need for activity and self-assertion, the other precluded by gender. This is the predicament in which the two best Victorian women poets, Elizabeth Barrett Browning and Christina Rossetti, found themselves when they looked for a place where a woman could situate herself without self-contradiction and in which she could not just daydream, but speak.

A study of their encounters with this problem can help us answer the question that puzzles and teases the feminist critic of Victorian poetry: why were there so few good women poets in nineteenth-century England when there were so many excellent women novelists? Victorian critics thought it was probably because the female imagination cannot go beyond the personal and superficial. Now, of course, we find a different kind of explanation. Most women lacked the classical education that served as the rite of initiation into high culture. Traditional conceptions of the poet's role – as priest, for instance – were inherently masculine. Publication seemed like unwomanly self-display, or even sexual self-exposure, and could be justified more easily if one wrote novels to make money rather than poems just for glory. With less prestige than poetry, and a less formidably male tradition, novel writing was more accessible, as new occupations often are, to women. It is sometimes said, too, that women could not summon up the sense of self and the self-assertiveness that poetry requires, and that they were too repressed to write strong lyrics.[3] Of course, many of the hindrances to women poets also hindered men. Fear of self-exposure and the felt lack of a central, stable self with an existence independent of its relations to others were problems for male Victorian poets too. Sexuality and rage do not seem to be significantly more repressed in Barrett Browning's or Rossetti's works than in Matthew Arnold's or even Tennyson's. Nor did the men of a self-consciously prosaic and doubting age find bardic or priestly robes more comfortable than women did. But for women, cultural and psychological barriers were reinforced by the difficulty of situating themselves within the inherited structures of English poetry.

Barrett Browning records in two narrative poems her early realization that as a woman poet she would have to play two opposing roles at one time – both knight and damsel, both subject and object – and that because she can't do this she is excluded from the worlds her imagination has discovered. The speaker in 'The Deserted Garden' had as a child loved to read and dream in an abandoned garden, a secret and magical place that she entered with 'Adventurous joy' and where as she read her 'likeness grew' 'To "gentle hermit of the dale,"' / And Angelina too.'[4] But as if in consequence of this impossibly doubled identification with figures of romance, she 'shut the book', she grew up, and the garden was again deserted. A later and longer work, 'The Lost Bower', tells how as a child the speaker once made her way through thickets and brambles to a lovely bower but never could find it again. Discovering the bower is even more of an adventure than penetrating the deserted garden: it is a heroic exploit, an accomplished quest; but the traditional plot that the child is enacting requires the bower to contain a female figure, and there is no one to be that figure except herself. So she says, 'Henceforth, *I* will be the fairy / Of this bower ... the dream-hall I have won' (241–2, 245). That is, she will be both the quester and the object of the quest. It's an awkward arrangement, and it doesn't work. When she looks for the bower again, she can't find it, because, as she realizes, she is now being the prince in the story of the Sleeping Beauty, and there is no Beauty in the bower to draw the prince on with the light of her dreaming spirit. She can't be two people at once, both the questing prince and dreaming princess, both a poet and his fairy inspiration, and so she never arrives. This was the 'first of all my losses' (300), the speaker says, and it prefigured many more. It is the loss of a poetic world and a poetic subject, lost because she can't fill both roles that the story requires. The speaker describes herself at the poem's end as weary and waiting, just as four-year-old Elizabeth Barrett was when she 'beguiled many a weary hour' with daydreams of romance, and as Rossetti's speakers typically are: this is the state which for both women, apparently, induces poetry. But she has found that there is no place for herself in her daydreams. Barrett Browning said that the incident described in 'The Lost Bower' had really happened, and her poems testify that, metaphorically at any rate, it really had.[5]

The same patterns appear in crucial places in Rossetti's poetic career. The necessary pairing or doubling of damsel and knight is the subject of the two enigmatic lines of her first recorded verse, composed before she could write: 'Cecilia never went to school / Without her gladiator.' And in 'The Dead City', which opened her first collection of poetry, the speaker moves like a questing prince into the heart of imaginative experience and is balked just when it is time to find and rescue the Sleeping Beauty. Like the speakers of 'The Deserted Garden' and 'The Lost Bower', she (or perhaps he) wanders boldly through the woods alone 'with a careless hardihood'; she eventually finds within an empty city a palace decked for feasting that anticipates in its particular luxuries the world of pre-Raphaelite sensuousness and art that Rossetti was later to describe in *Goblin Market*. Everyone at the feast has been turned to stone, but she cannot revive them with a kiss: all the young people are paired off already and their gaze is strange and unwelcoming. She averts her eyes in fear, the palace vanishes, and the poem ends with the assertion that this imaginative quest was not for her: 'What was I that I should see / So much hidden mystery?'[6]

The problem is not only or even primarily one of narrative, although it is articulated most clearly in terms of plot. The Victorian woman poet has to be two things at once, or in two places, whenever she tries to locate herself within the poetic world. Her problem may be said to begin, oddly enough, with the fact that for the Victorians writing poetry seemed like woman's work, even though only men were supposed to do it. Critics liked simple, homely poetic subjects and language and sincere, spontaneous expressions of feeling – the artless spontaneity, in short, which is still assumed by critics who should know better to be characteristic of women. The enormous popularity of Tennyson's *In Memoriam* owed a geat deal to the scenes of domestic pathos – widows, widowers, grieving mothers and the like – that belong in women's sphere. Male Victorian poets worried that they might in effect be feminizing themselves by withdrawing into a private world. Arnold tried to exorcise this fear in *Sohrab and Rustum*. Bulwer-Lytton enraged Tennyson by jeering at him with the epithet, 'School-Miss Alfred'. But Tennyson's most potent figures for the artist are female; the poor mill girl in Browning's *Pippa Passes* is a Shelleyan poet; and Shelley himself in Arnold's memorable formulation becomes a 'beautiful and ineffectual angel' – just like a woman.[7]

For association of poetry and femininity, however, excluded women poets. For the female figures on to whom the men projected their artistic selves – Tennyson's Mariana and Lady of Shalott, Browning's Pippa and Balaustion, Arnold's Iseult of Brittany – represent an intensification of only a part of the poet, not his full consciousness: a part, furthermore, which is defined as separate from and ignorant of the public world and the great range of human experience in society. Such figures could not write their own poems; the male poet, who stands outside the private world of art, has to do that for them. The Lady of Shalott could not imagine someone complex and experienced enough to imagine the world beyond range of her windows, or to imagine *her*. A woman poet who identified herself with such a stock figure of intense and isolated art would hardly be able to write at all. Or, like the Lady of Shalott preparing her death-ship, she could write only her own name, only herself. For a man, writing poetry meant an apparent withdrawal from the public sphere (although honour and fame might in time return him to it), but for a woman it meant just the opposite: a move toward public engagement and self-assertion in the masculine world. She could not just reverse the roles in her poetry and create a comparable male self-projection, since the male in this set of opposites is defined as experienced, complexly self-conscious, and part of the public world and therefore could not serve as a figure for the poet. (When Elizabeth Bishop makes the reversal in 'The Gentleman of Shalott' the result is a very un-Victorian sort of comedy.) We can formulate the problem like this: a man's poem which contains a female self-projection shows two distinctly different figures, poet and projection; in a woman's poem on the same model, the two would blur into one.

Furthermore, it's not really *poets* that are women, for the Victorians: *poems* are women. The cliché that the style is the man arises more readily and with much greater literalness and force when the stylist is a woman and it is often charged with erotic intensity. The young lovers in Gilbert and Sullivan's *Iolanthe* describe their perfect love by singing that he is the sculptor and she the clay, he the singer and she the song. Ladislaw in *Middlemarch* tells Dorothea that she needn't write poems because she *is* a poem. Edgar Allan Poe remarks in a review of Barrett Browning's works that 'a woman and her book are identical'. In her love letters Barrett Browning herself worried about the problem of her identity – was she her poems, were they she, which was Browning in love with? 'I love your verses with all my heart, dear Miss

Barrett,' he had written disconcertingly in his first letter, '. . . and I love you
too.' When Aurora Leigh crowns herself with an ivy wreath in secret
anticipation of poetic fame, she looks to the admiring Romney like a work of
art, not the artist she means to become (see *Aurora Leigh*, 2, 59–64). Dante
Gabriel Rossetti describes a woman and a sonnet as interchangeably self-
enclosed and self-admiring: the woman is 'subtly of herself contemplative';
the sonnet is 'of its own arduous fulness reverent.'[8] How does one tell them
apart? Christina Rossetti was an artist's model as well as an artist, and she
says in a sad little poem called 'A Wish': 'I wish I were a song once heard /
But often pondered o'er' (3–4). As we can see in Tennyson's *The Princess*, the
lyric in particular seemed female to the Victorians – private, nonlogical,
purely emotional – and it is surely no accident that large numbers of English
and American women began to publish poetry in the nineteenth century,
when the lyric established its dominance. Victorian poems like Victorian
women were expected to be morally and spiritually uplifting, to stay mostly
in the private sphere, and to provide emotional stimulus and release for
overtasked men of affairs.[9] All this may have encouraged women to write
poetry, but at the same time it made writing peculiarly difficult because it
reinforced the aspects of conventional Victorian femininity – narcissism,
passivity, submission, silence – most inimical to creative activity. Since
women already *are* the objects they try to create, why should they write?

Where male writers have two figures in poems, for women it often happens
either that one of the two disappears and ruins the economy of the poem,
like the Sleeping Beauty in 'The Lost Bower' and 'The Dead City', or else
that the two collapse into one. A simple example of the collapsing of subject
and object is women's use of flowers, which traditionally represent female
objects of male desire. Women poets tend to identify with the flower. Barrett
Browning flatly equates a fading rose with a failed poet in 'A Lay of the Early
Rose' and sympathizes equally with both. Rossetti's 'The Solitary Rose'
congratulates a flower that is fortunate enough to be unseen and therefore
unplucked; the rose is like Wordsworth's violet by a mossy stone considered
from the violet's point of view, and the poem is a literal presentation of what
Rossetti's great *carpe diem* poem, *The Prince's Progress*, later presents figura-
tively – a 'gather ye rosebuds' from the point of view of an ungathered rose.
On a larger scale, however, as Margaret Homans has shown, nineteenth-
century women writers fear and resist identification with nature: nature for
women is not the maternal other, in relation to whom the Romantic poet
defined his poetic identity, but – as the mother – always a possible self.[10]
But nature doesn't write, just as mothers don't write (in the world as Rossetti
and the young Elizabeth Barrett experienced it), and poems don't write, and
the forlorn damsel can't rescue herself. In 'Winter: My Secret' Rossetti

identifies with the teasing incommunicativeness of the season: like winter, her speaker won't speak.

When the woman poet looks for something that can stand in the same relation of significant difference to her within a poem that a female figure stands in to a man, the equation often reads: a male poet is to a woman as a female poet is to a child or an animal. Tennyson in *In Memoriam* compares his loss to that of a girl whose lover has died, and calls the girl a 'meek, unconscious dove'.[11] Barrett Browning, in contrast, writes about real doves ('My Doves'), which like Tennyson's young woman are less intellectual and closer to God and nature than the poet is. When her cocker spaniel, Flush, appears in her poems he behaves like a woman, spending long days indoors, filled with love and sympathy, watching tenderly and patiently by a bedside, a 'low' creature who 'leads to heights of love' ('Flush or Faunus'). Rossetti's animals are generally male, like Flush, but like the women portrayed by pre-Raphaelite men they are compellingly attractive and yet somewhat repulsive, mysterious, and inhuman: the lover whom Rossetti affectionately compares to a blind buzzard and a mole in 'A Sketch', the sexy, self-satisfied crocodile in 'My Dream', and the goblins in *Goblin Market*. Animal poems have helped to confine Barrett Browning and Rossetti to the women's and children's section of the literary world. But the animals don't come just from emotional hunger, or sexual repression, or cultural pressure toward certain acceptable female subjects: they are generated by the need in certain kinds of poems for someone or something to take the woman's role in relation to the speaker.

Barrett Browning and Rossetti both wrote long poems in which they make the poet a questing male figure and then take the side of the passive female object against the ostensible protagonist. In Barrett Browning's *The Poet's Vow*, a woman deserted by a male poet posthumously denounces him, and in Rossetti's *The Prince's Progress* our sympathies are directed toward the waiting princess who dies before the dilatory, self-indulgent prince arrives. But such a strongly gendered identification with imagination's object, in direct antagonism to the questing figure or the poet who imagines, takes it for granted that poets and questers are male. Recent women poets have taken a more radically revisionist approach to traditional stories of this sort, making poems precisely out of the act of revising – from a woman's point of view – the male versions of the stories;[12] but Barrett Browning and Rossetti don't do this. In their revisionary stories the crucial shift in point of view is incomplete and usually concealed, and Victorian readers apparently never saw it.

In *Lady Geraldine's Courtship* Barrett Browning makes an interesting attempt to split her identification between a male poet and a female object, but as a result the poem loses the articulation and psychological tension that is generated by difference. She tries to equalize the two figures and participate equally in both. The poet is poor and lowly born, but male and a poet, and he is the speaker. Lady Geraldine is rich and noble and the active agent of the plot, but she is the object of desire and represents the subjects (nature, beauty and the like) about which poems are written. She *owns* a garden of art. In the centre of that garden, moreover, there is a statue of a sleeping woman, representing Silence, but Lady Geraldine argues that the statue represents the power of meaning to '"exceed the special symbol"' (121) embodying it: that is, a silent work of art in female form says more than speech does. Lady Geraldine herself is both a singer and a song: 'Oh, to see or hear her singing', says the enamoured poet-narrator, 'For her looks sing too' (173–4). This is the only one of Barrett Browning's ballad-narratives with a happy ending: the lady takes the initiative, the lovers marry, the two roles merge. This may be the ultimate narcissistic fantasy of the nineteenth-century woman poet, in which she imagines herself enacting both roles perfectly at the same time rather than, as in 'The Lost Bower', failing in both. That the poem represents a fantasy of wish fulfilment is suggested by the fact that it was written very easily, much of it in a last-minute rush to meet a printer's deadline, and perhaps too by its enormous popularity.[13]

It is in Barrett Browning's and Rossetti's amatory sonnet sequences, however, that we find speakers who most clearly locate themselves in two opposite parts of the poems at once. Here the woman poet-speaker plays both roles whose opposition had traditionally generated such sonnets: the self-asserting speaker and the silent object of his desire. The speaker in Barrett Browning's *Sonnets from the Portuguese* speaks and desires like a male sonneteer, but she is also responding as a woman to male voices – not just her lover's but those of a long poetic tradition. This relation to tradition is even clearer in Rossetti's *Monna Innominata*, since each poem is preceded by a quotation from the sonnets of Dante and Petrarch. In both sequences the roles often jarringly conflict: as object of love, the woman should be beautiful, distant and unquestionably desirable, and she disturbs and embarrasses the reader when she presents herself as subject as well as object of desire and when her sense of her inadequacy as an object of love is expressed in the self-denigrating humility that traditionally belongs to the male lover-speaker.[14] Elsewhere, Rossetti suggests that it is a transgression for a woman to speak her love. 'But this once hear me speak', a woman says to her lover, although she knows that 'a woman's words are weak; / You should speak, not I' ('Twice', 7–8). Instead of listening, however, the lover looks – he looks at her heart and breaks it.

A similar but usually less problematic merging of roles appears when the speaker's voice comes from in or beyond the grave to which men's poetry so often relegates women. The poet is necessarily doubling roles whenever she speaks from the place where only silence should be – the place of poetry's object, not that of the speaking subject – but these poems, unlike the amatory sonnet sequences, are constructed more fully in response to male poems than in imitation of them. Barrett Browning gives a narrative context to such a situation in *The Poet's Vow*, where the woman whom a male poet abandoned because he loved nature more writes out an accusation and has it sent to him with her corpse.

> I left thee last, a child at heart,
>   A woman scarce in years.
> I come to thee, a solemn corpse
>   Which neither feels nor fears.
> I have no breath to use in sighs;
> They laid the dead-weights on mine eyes
>   To seal them safe from tears.
>
> (416–22)

She is responding, of course, to Wordsworth:

> A slumber did my spirit seal;
>   I had no human fears:
> She seemed a thing that could not feel
>   The touch of earthly years.
>
> No motion has she now, no force;
>   She neither hears nor sees;
> Rolled round in earth's diurnal course,
>   With rocks, and stones, and trees.[15]

She appropriates Wordsworth's speaker's power of language and applies to herself his descriptions both of the woman (she does not feel or see or move) and of himself (she does not fear, her eyes are sealed as his spirit was). But she is dead.

Like the woman in *The Poet's Vow*, Rossetti's speakers are often situated at or beyond the border between waking and sleeping, life and death: a place where the female object of desire can become, for a long transitional moment, subject and speaker. A paradigm of this appears in the first issue of the pre-Raphaelite magazine, *The Germ*, which contains two poems on facing pages: Dante Gabriel Rossetti's 'My Sister's Sleep', which tells how the speaker's sister died in her sleep, and his own sister's 'Dream Land' – about a woman who has travelled to a deathlike land of dreams in a progression like that which is described with unctuous delectation in 'My Sister's Sleep'.[16]

And in what may be Rossetti's most famous lyric, 'Song: When I am Dead, My Dearest', the speaker thinks about what would happen if she were to die and becomes a legitimate object of song:

> When I am dead, my dearest,
>   Sing no sad songs for me;
> Plant thou no roses at my head,
>   Nor shady cypress tree.
>
> (1–4)

She won't hear the songs or see the flowers; and she won't care. The strangeness of the poem comes from the fact that it centres not on the mourning lover's consciousness but on that of the dead beloved, in which the memory of the lover will have ceased to matter and might even disappear.

> And dreaming through the twilight
>   That doth not rise nor set,
> Haply I may remember,
>   And haply may forget.
>
> (13–16)

We miss the full resonance of this lyric unless we recognize it not just as self-pity or self-abnegation, but as a response to the long tradition of songs in celebration of women who are dead and silent. Rossetti in tacit reciprocity writes about the indifference of corpses, the grievances of ghosts, and women whose sleep of death will end in a happy resurrection beyond all earthly loves. The speaker in 'Remember' will not mind – 'if the darkness and corruption leave / A vestige of the thoughts that once I had' (11–12) – that her lover forgets her; 'At Home' is the lament of a ghost shut out from the home that has forgotten her; in 'After Death' the speaker recalls with pleasure that a man who had not loved her during her life pitied her when she died; the eponymous ghost in 'The Poor Ghost' is drawn back by her lover's tears only to discover that his grief has abated and he would prefer her to stay in her grave; and 'Sleeping at Last' finds solace in the thought of being 'out of sight of friend and of lover' in the grave. Many of Rossetti's most interesting and successful poems merge the traditionally opposite roles of the poetic speaker and the silent object in this way, and they may seem self-enclosed and solipsistic – as if the speaker were speaking only to herself, as in a sense she is – unless we reinstate the silent other who is present only by implication: the male poet who spoke first.

One might expect women to be more comfortable in devotional poetry, where gender would seem not to matter and where male speakers often take an essentially feminine role. But the difficulty arises here in a different form: religious poetry reinforced the impulses toward self-effacement and self-suppression that threatened women's very existence as writers. For Barrett Browning and Rossetti, Christ can be a maternal as well as a masculine figure, and their submission to God the Father places them in the childish position from which Victorian women artists had to struggle to escape if they were to write at all. This throws their poems badly off balance, in comparison to poetry by men. For George Herbert, for instance, to recognize that he is God's child does not make him childlike in other ways – that he is normally adult and self-dependent is in fact what gives meaning and dramatic force to the recognition. But for Victorian women there is no such clear disjunction between their religious and their social roles. In the writings of both Rossetti and Barrett Browning, religion sanctions the life-weariness, the acceptance of inactivity, and the willing subsidence toward death which often appears in poems by male Victorian poets too, but which the men present with a countering element of resistance that is expressed either tonally or through a dramatic frame – in 'Tithonus' and 'Tears, Idle Tears', for instance, 'Andrea del Sarto', or *Empedocles on Etna*. Here again, where men's poetry has two aspects, women's has only one. (It's no accident that Rossetti's most successful religious poem is 'Up-Hill', which is composed entirely of a dialogue between speakers of no apparent gender.) Oppositions are more drastic in the women's religious poetry, choices more absolute. When they conceive of the world that stands in opposition to God as female, it appeals to them not as a sexual opposite, a possible object of desire, but as an unacceptable potential self; Rossetti describes the world as a beautiful woman who is revealed at night to be a hideous fiend and wants to make the speaker equally hideous: 'Till my feet, cloven too, take hold on hell' ('The World', 14). Like the male Victorian poets, speakers in Rossetti's religious poems lament their emotional aridity; unlike their male contemporaries, however, they lament their speechlessness too: 'I have no wit, no words, no tears' ('A Better Resurrection', 1); 'What would I give for words, if only words would come!' ('What Would I Give!' 4). If she could, she would speak her own sinfulness, but 'if I should begin / To tell it all, the day would be too small / To tell it in' ('Ash Wednesday "My God, my God, have mercy on my sin"', 2–4) – and so she does not tell it.

It is perhaps surprising that neither of these women poets made much radical use of the dramatic monologue, the primary generic innovation of the Victorian period, which exploits the problematic nature of the speaking subject and would therefore seem to offer an opportunity either to escape or to explore problems of gender. But the women's dramatic monologues are different from the men's. The women seem usually to sympathize with their protagonists, and neither frame them with irony as Browning does nor

distance and at least partly objectify them like Tennyson by using characters
with an independent literary existence. The women did not find figures in
literature or mythology or history through whom they could express in an
apparently dramatic and impersonal manner feelings that they did not wish
directly to avow. Nor do they show off their own virtuosity the way
Browning does in 'My Last Duchess', for instance: we are not made aware of
the poet signalling to us from behind the speaker's back. Once again, that is,
we find that where men's poems have two sharply differentiated figures – in
dramatic monologues, the poet and the dramatized speaker – in women's
poems the two blur together. Browning's dramatic monologues usually create
a collusion between poet and reader that presupposes shared values and
responses which enable the reader to spy out the poet signalling from behind
the mask; women could not expect to evoke such collusion and seldom tried.
In fact, unless a woman poet's mask was male, or exceedingly bizarre (Barrett
Browning's infanticidal black American slave, for instance, in 'The Runaway
Slave at Pilgrim's Point'), she might not be perceived as wearing a mask at
all. How could she be, if women are poems, not poets, and speak
spontaneously and sincerely? When Rossetti assumed a dramatic mask of her
own invention to complain about woman's lot in 'The Lowest Room' and 'A
Royal Princess', her brother Dante Gabriel objected because the voice in the
poems was not the voice that he was accustomed to think of as her own, and
he didn't like it – 'falsetto muscularity', he called it, and said that it derived
from Mrs Browning;[17] and yet he didn't think of the poems as dramatic either.
He didn't want his sister to speak in any voice except the one he chose to
consider her own. Like their other works, the women's dramatic monologues
were expected to be, and were almost always perceived as being, univocal.

Emily Brontë, whose poetry was almost unknown in the nineteenth century
and seems in most respects totally detached from the Victorian context in
which Barrett Browning's and Rossetti's is so thoroughly embedded, none
the less presents the woman poet's situation in similar ways. The speaker in
'I saw thee, child, one summer's day', for instance, is a vision-bestowing
spirit; and while many of Brontë's poems appear to be dramatic lyrics spoken
by characters in the Gondal saga, the context is available to us, if at all, only
through scholarly reconstruction, and the poems generally offer even fewer
indications of authorial distance than Barrett Browning's or Rossetti's. The
story of the damsel and the knight, Sleeping Beauty and the questing Prince,
provides much of the basic structure of the Gondal world of Byronic exile,
wandering, captivity and ambiguous rescue. And although the same roles can
be taken by both men and women and the gender of speakers is often unclear,
two of the latest, longest and best poems describe the rescue or awakening of
a woman as an imposition of male imaginative dominance. In 'Ah! why,

because the dazzling sun', the speaker's visionary experience is dispelled when the stars that have looked into her eyes in a happy mutuality are driven away by the sun's violent intrusion into her bedroom: 'Blood-red he rose, and arrow-straight / His fierce beams struck my brow.'[18] She hides her closed eyes in the pillow, but

> It would not be – the pillow glowed
> And glowed both roof and floor,
> And birds sang loudly in the wood,
> And fresh winds shook the door.
>
> (33–6)

She is forced to become the centre of Nature's awakening by the 'hostile' and 'blinding' light of an alien imagination which destroys her own.

Essentially the same story is told and retold six months later as a Gondal episode in 'Silent is the House – all are laid asleep', which begins with a brief, mysterious struggle for the position of central consciousness. The first stanza introduces in the third person the speaker of the second and third stanzas: a woman, apparently, who waits at her window every night for 'the Wanderer' (8) and speaks defiance of those who may scorn and spy but will never know about the 'angel'(12) who nightly visits her. Her defiance appears to be vain, however, since she is immediately displaced as speaker by a man named Julian who tells how he found in his dungeons a beautiful prisoner, A. G. Rochelle, whom at first he cruelly scorned. Julian reports Rochelle's account of the '"messenger of Hope"' (67) who has come to her every night, like the Wanderer-angel to the speaker of the opening stanzas, bringing visions of '"the Invisible, the Unseen"' (81); but then he takes over as narrator again to tell how he 'watched her' (93) like the spies defiantly imagined by the earlier speaker, fell in love, overcame the temptation to keep her imprisoned, and finally freed her and won her love – and (although he doesn't mention this) ended her visions. As in 'Ah! why, because the dazzling sun', the woman's visionary power disappears under the gaze of an intruder-rescuer – is it rescue or rape? – that objectifies and transforms her. For Brontë, the story of the damsel and the knight is the story of the female subject's displacement into the position of the erotic object of male imagination, and she makes poems out of the struggle between them.

In America the same situation produced different results. The contradiction in the double role of the woman poet appears in Emily Dickinson's work less as a difficulty to be evaded or overcome than as an essential organizing principle; Dickinson read Barrett Browning's work with great attention, and perhaps it taught her how to go beyond itself. Even more than Rossetti, Dickinson likes to situate her speakers in or beyond the grave, and they

characteristically identify with flowers, children, smallness, powerlessness and
silence; but at the same time they implicitly or ironically assert their power
in revolt against the patriarchal universe, and the tension between these
opposing attitudes is essential both to the poems' meaning and to their form
– the smallness and apparent childishness of the verses (and the fact that
Dickinson did not publish them) in conjunction with their explosive force.
Furthermore, Dickinson went far beyond her British counterparts in explor-
ing subject and object; her explorations suggest that the result would be a
horrifying stalemate and may help us to understand why Barrett Browning
and Rossetti (who psychologically and poetically were much more conven-
tional than Dickinson) and even Brontë never dropped the essential point of
difference that is created in poetry by gender.

> Like Eyes that looked on Wastes –
> Incredulous of Ought
> But Blank – and steady Wilderness –
> Diversified by Night –
>
> Just Infinites of Nought –
> As far as it could see –
> So looked the face I looked upon –
> So looked itself – on Me –
>
> I offered it no Help –
> Because the Cause was Mine –
> The Misery a Compact –
> As hopeless – as divine –
>
> Neither – would be absolved –
> Neither would be a Queen
> Without the Other – Therefore
> We perish – tho' We reign – [19]

Since both are the damsel waiting for rescue as well as potential knights,
neither can rescue the other and they remain frozen in an intensified and
more terrible version of the changeless, eventless condition in which Barrett
Browning daydreamed and Rossetti's speakers wait for God. In 'I would not
paint – a picture' Dickinson considers the problematic position of the woman
poet in her own art: is she artist, or audience, or instrument, or the work
itself? She would like to be everything at once – the situation that Barrett
Browning and Rossetti found both inevitable and impossible for most kinds
of lyric poetry. Dickinson imagines this situation as highly precarious,

offering the possibility of an exhilarating self-sufficiency that ends in self-destruction.

> Nor would I be a Poet —
> It's finer — own the Ear —
> Enamored — impotent — content —
> The License to revere,
> A privilege so awful
> What would the Dower be,
> Had I the Art to stun myself
> With Bolts of Melody![20]

Being both poet and audience, both subject and object, would mean turning eroticism and aggression inward: both to marry ('dower') and to 'stun' oneself, to be 'impotent' and yet to wield the tools ('bolts') of violence — and to wield them against oneself.

Recent American women poets have found other ways both to use and to evade the problematic situation of the woman poet as the Victorians experienced it. Subjects and emotions new to serious poetry and new ways of experiencing such familiar ones as love, exclusion, enclosure and longing provide escape from patterns of relationship embedded in the structure of traditional English poetry. Sylvia Plath expresses rebellion and rage of a kind that Barrett Browning and Rossetti either turn inward against themselves, producing depression that sometimes comes close to despair, or else express indirectly in narrative and political poetry. Anne Sexton and others have done explicitly, aggressively and forthrightly what Rossetti and Barrett Browning more timidly and unobtrusively tried to do, reinterpreting old stories from a woman's point of view. Elizabeth Bishop transforms the passivity and the sense of enclosure, exclusion, frustration and impotence that debilitated so much of the work of nineteenth-century women poets into images of exile and travel in which the poet becomes an endlessly questing spirit; and exotic animals and peasants serve the function in Bishop's poetry that animals and children do in Barrett Browning's and Rossetti's, standing in the relation to the woman poet that women have stood in to men. And in writing about love between women it may be possible to escape the shadow cast by the traditional relations between subject and object in amatory poetry.

Rossetti and Barrett Browning, however, were hindered and often debilitated by a situation which Dickinson and later poets were able to exploit or transcend. They sometimes tried to use the problematic nature of woman as speaking subject in an attempt to explore and to protest against women's roles both in poems and in society, but since the surface of their poetry — diction, subject matter and (at least apparently) tone — did not contradict what Victorian women were expected to say, their shifts in point of view and revisions of old stories generally went unobserved and unencouraged. Rossetti stopped trying to rebel: in her devotional writings she finds an appropriate place for a conventional Victorian woman's voice. Barrett Browning, on the other hand, turned after *Sonnets from the Portuguese* away from the old poetic situations – that is, from the lyric tradition – to narrative form and highly topical contemporary subjects and made her revisionary view of the world defiantly, if incompletely and intermittently, explicit. In *Aurora Leigh* she works the problem through in terms of plot. At the beginning of the poem Aurora is the forlorn damsel, a dispossessed orphan in a rigidly patriarchal world, but by the end she has become a poet and a knight. First she rescues Marian Erle, a damsel in distress, and then she rescues – by marriage, as knights and princes used to do – Romney Leigh, the man who had tried at various times to rescue both Marian Erle and Aurora herself, and had been rebuffed by both of them. But the humiliation, blinding and subjugation of Romney that makes the happy ending possible is not a solution to the woman poet's difficulties; it is her fantasy of revenge. It suggests that for women to speak, men must be forcibly silenced; for women to be heard rather than looked at – to be artists rather than works of art – men must be blinded. Similarly, in Rossetti's *Goblin Market* a girl ventures forth and rescues her sister from the thraldom of goblin sexuality, and later the two sisters with their daughters set up a society that apparently excludes men. Neither of the two major Victorian women poets developed any better solution than this punitive reversal of roles or rejection of men on the one hand, enacted in narrative rather than lyric, or the retreat into feminine submissiveness and self-suppression represented by Rossetti's devotional poetry on the other. They could imagine an androgynous ideal – Barrett Browning celebrated George Sand in two bold sonnets as a mixture of male and female qualities, and Rossetti wrote movingly of the one escape from the restrictions of gender ordained by Christianity: 'in Christ there is neither male nor female, for we are all one'[21] – and they sometimes blurred the gender of their poetic speakers. In narrative and political poetry they could thematize and redefine the terms in which the speaking subject located herself within a poem. But despite the substantial although flawed success of *Sonnets from the Portuguese* and *Monna Innominata*, and the many excellent lyrics in which Rossetti implicitly responds to the male tradition, neither Barrett Browning nor Rossetti fully solved within their lyric poetry the problem of the damsel and the knight.

NOTES

1   Barrett Browning, 'Glimpses into My Own Life and Literary Character,' in Browning 1974: 123.

2   Barrett Browning to Mary Russell Mitford, 22 July 1842, in Browning 1983: II, 7.

3   Gilbert and Gubar offer most of these suggestions (1979: 545–9). The distinguished Victorian critic R. H. Hutton answers the question with the assertion that women's imaginations cannot abstract themselves as men's can from 'the visible surface and form of human existence' (1858: 467).

4   Barrett Browning, 'The Deserted Garden' (1990 ed. Porter and Clarke) ll.17, 69–72; all further references to poems in this edition, identified by line number, will be included in the text. The ballad of Edwin and Angelina appears in Oliver Goldsmith's *The Vicar of Wakefield*, Ch. 8.

5   Barrett Browning to H. S. Boyd, 4 October 1844, in Browning 1898: I, 201.

6   Christina Rossetti, 'The Dead City', in Christina Rossetti 1911: 11. 2, 273–4; all further references to poems in this edition, identified by line number, will be included in the text. The verse about Cecilia is given in William's introductory memoir, p. xlix. 'The Dead City' first appeared in *Verses*, printed by Rossetti's grandfather, G. Polidori (London, 1847).

7   Hair notes the critical enthusiasm for *In Memoriam*'s domestic themes and images (1981: 7–10). Bulwer-Lytton jeered at Tennyson in 'The New Timon', and Tennyson responded with similar insults in 'The New Timon, and the Poets'. Matthew Arnold's phrase about the angel first appeared in his essay 'Byron' (1960–77: IX, 237). As Moers points out, 'The spontaneous, the instinctive, the natural, the informal, the anticlassical and the artless: all these terms of art have been associated with the woman's voice in literature from the beginning of time. They are also applied to the start of modern literature that we call Romanticism, and that cannot be separated from the raising of the woman's voice in letters' (1976: 163).

8   See Gilbert and Sullivan, *Iolanthe* (n.d.: 19–20; see George Eliot, *Middlemarch* (1956: 166); Poe, 'The Drama of Exile, and Other Poems' (1902: XII, 1); Robert Browning to Elizabeth Barrett Barrett, 10 January 1845 (1969: I, 3); Dante Gabriel Rossetti, 'Body's Beauty', 'Introduction', in 'The House of Life' (1911).

There are many similar examples. Eric S. Robertson coveted a fine copy of Katherine Philips's poems: 'I indulged myself with another peep at the "matchless Orinda", still longing to possess and love what so many reverent hands had fondled' (1883: 2). An unidentified earlier critic wrote: 'Beauty is to a woman what poetry is to a language, and their similarity accounts for their conjunction; for there never yet existed a female possessed of personal loveliness who was not only poetical in herself but the cause of poetry in others' (*Fraser's Magazine*, 7 (1883), 601); that the latter part of this sentence says the opposite of what it apparently intends reflects the silliness of the thought.

Gubar discusses the conception of women as works of art in '"The Blank Page"'(1981).

9   Woolford points this out in 'EBB: Woman and Poet' (1979: 4).

10 Homans 1980. For brief discussions of women poets' use of flowers, see Kaplan 1975: 20–4, and Ostriker 1980: 256–7.

11 Tennyson, *In Memoriam* (1969: 6, 1. 25).

12 Ostriker discusses the remaking of old myths by twentieth-century women poets in 'The Thieves of Language' (1982: 68–90). She notes that 'feminist revisionism differs from Romantic revisionism' in that 'it accentuates its argument, in order to make clear that there *is* an argument' (87) – which is just what Barrett Browning and Rossetti do not do.

13 To make the two volumes of *Poems* (1844) of equal length, 'there was nothing for it but to finish a ballad poem called 'Lady Geraldine's Courtship', which was lying by me, and I did so by writing, i.e. composing, *one hundred and forty lines last Saturday*! I seemed to be in a dream all day! Long lines too – with fifteen syllables in each' (Barrett Browning to H. S. Boyd, 1 August 1844; 1983: I, 177). On the poem's popularity, see Hayter 1962: 85–6.

14 See Mermin 1981: 351–67; Homans 1985: 569–93; and Moers's discussion of nineteenth-century women's love poetry (1976: 162–72).

15 Wordsworth, 'A Slumber Did My Spirit Seal' (1952: II, 216).

16 See *The Germ: Thoughts towards Nature in Poetry, Literature and Art*, no. I (Jan. 1850; Portland, Maine, 1898), pp. 20, 21. McGann attributes Rossetti's idea of the sleep that follows death to the millenarian doctrine of 'Soul Sleep' (1983: 133–41).

17 Dante Gabriel Rossetti to Christina Georgina Rossetti, 3 December 1875, in D. G. Rossetti 1967: III, 1380.

18 Emily Brontë, 'Ah! why, because the dazzling sun' (1941: 11. 21–2); all further references to poems in this work will be included in the text. Homans gives a somewhat different analysis of Brontë's poems about visionary visitants (1980: 110–22).

19 Emily Dickinson, 'Like Eyes that looked on Wastes' (1955: no. 458).

20 Emily Dickinson, 'I would not paint – a picture' (1955: no. 505).

21 Christina Rossetti 1879: 32.

14

'Because men made the laws':
The Fallen Woman and the
Woman Poet

Angela Leighton

In 1851, from her vantage point in Florence at the windows of Casa Guidi, Elizabeth Barrett Browning looked towards an England that was confident and powerful; an 'Imperial England' (*Casa Guidi Windows*, 2. 578),[1] that had come through the Hungry Forties, and was embarking on the new decade with a Great Exhibition. Instead of rejoicing, however, she issued accusations:

> no light
> Of teaching, liberal nations, for the poor
> Who sit in darkness when it is not night?
> No cure for wicked children? Christ, — no cure!
> No help for women sobbing out of sight
> Because men made the laws?
>
> (2. 634–9)

Quick to take up the cause of the downtrodden – the poor, children and women – she points accusingly to the dark underside of economic expansion, an underside of ignorance, crime and prostitution. The glittering facade of commercial prosperity only hides the need for 'God's justice to be done' (2. 655).

Barrett Browning's message is neither new nor unusual. The Victorians were the first to acknowledge their double vision, as well as their double standards. The age which so thoroughly explored the underlying reaches of the individual subconscious was also one haunted by the social underworld of class. Doubleness was of its very nature. In some ways, Barrett Browning sounds a note of characteristically middle-class concern. She is conscience-stricken at the plight of the poor, and uses them to castigate the materialism of the age. Yet the last two lines mark a sharpening of her attitude. Her social criticism turns into a specific grievance over the condition of women in England's cities: 'No help for women sobbing out of sight / Because men made the laws?' The figure of the fallen woman elicits from the woman poet her most pointed accusation.

Yet, prostitution at this time was not associated with specific laws. It was not a criminal offence, unless it entailed disorderly behaviour. The age of consent was twelve, until in 1875 it went up to thirteen. Only in 1885, partly as a result of W. T. Stead's sensational exposure of the white slave trade in the pages of the *Pall Mall Gazette*, did it become sixteen. Spooner's Bill, introduced in 1847 to suppress trading in seduction and prostitution, was itself quickly suppressed in the House of Commons, when the names of 'some of the highest and noblest in the land'[2] were in danger of being made public in it. The Contagious Diseases Acts, by which suspect prostitutes were subjected to forced medical examinations, and against which Josephine Butler waged her fierce campaign of repeal, were not passed until the 1860s. In general, as historians have often pointed out, 'prostitution does not seem to have threatened any fundamental principle of the state,'[3] and on the whole the law tended to let it alone, if only for the reason that 'some of the highest and noblest in the land' had an interest in it.

When the French romantic socialist, Flora Tristan, visited England in 1839, she was astonished at the numbers of prostitutes to be seen 'everywhere at any time of day.'[4] In her *London Journal* she describes how they collected round the taverns and gin palaces – the 'finishes', as they were called – and she recounts in some detail the lurid sport that was enjoyed at their expense. The Englishman, she notes with disgust, is a sober prude by day and a drunken lecher by night (87). She herself showed none of the shrinking horror of the middle-class Englishwoman in her investigations. She availed herself of some stout protectors, and went to the 'finishes' to have a look.

Tristan is passionate in her denunciations of two aspects of English life, which she blames for the prevalence of prostitution: the inequality of wealth between the classes, and the social and legal inequality between the sexes. She is full of indignation, above all, at the legal dependence of the married Englishwoman, who, at this time, had no right to sue for a divorce, to own property, to make a will, to keep her earnings, to refuse her conjugal services, to leave the conjugal home, or to have custody of her children if separated. Such overwhelming legal dispossession leads Tristan to a quite surprising conclusion in her defence of woman as a class: 'As long as she remains the slave of man and the victim of prejudice, as long as she is refused training in a profession, as long as she is deprived of her civil rights, there can be no moral law for her' (82).

However, it is precisely in the area of the 'moral law' that the Victorian woman holds power. Deprived of 'civil rights' by the law of the land, hers are the compensatory rights of morality. She is the chief upholder and representer of morality, and also its most satisfying symbol. Thus, angel or demon, virgin or whore, Mary or Magdalen, woman is the stage on which the age enacts its own enduring morality play. The struggle between good and evil, virtue and vice, takes up its old story on the scene of the woman's sexual body. The 'moral law', as a result, has a glamorous simplicity as well as a fascinating secretiveness. Its simplicity is mythic, and its secrets sexual.

Yet this 'moral law' of woman's sexuality also relies on a hard core of technical fact. The woman's virginity on which, as Engels points out,[5] the whole social and familial system depends, is not a spiritual virtue, which can be constantly reclaimed, but a physical virtue, subject to proof. If, on the one hand, woman represents a last remaining absolute good in a world of threatening expediency and enterprise, she also, on the other hand, represents a perishable good, the misuse of which diminishes her value. The 'moral law' is not only feminized, but economized, and thus comes very close to the law of commodity.

The broad implications of this 'economizing' of sexuality are brought out in a notorious passage from William Lecky's *History of European Morals*, published in 1869: 'That unhappy being whose very name is a shame to speak ... appears in every age as the perpetual symbol of degradation and sinfulness of man. Herself the supreme type of vice, she is ultimately the most efficient guardian of virtue.'[6] It is in the interests of the very principle of morality to keep the 'type of vice' separate from the type of 'virtue.' The moral stakes of Lecky's opposition are high. The individual 'type' carries the burden of a whole system. Unsurprisingly then, for the Victorians, the fallen woman is a type which ranges from the successful courtesan to the passionate adulteress, from the destitute streetwalker to the seduced innocent, from the unscrupulous procuress to the raped child. To fall, for woman, is simply to fall short.

The logic of Lecky's statement is manifestly not moral; it is economic. The unspoken fact which makes women either types of 'vice' or types of 'virtue' is the unquestioned fact of male sexual need. Such a need justifies the supply and demand, by which the 'type of vice' offers what the type of 'virtue' necessarily abhors. Thus the 'moral law' erects its mythology of good and bad on a laissez-faire economics of male sexuality, which relies on a social apartheid between woman. 'No cure for women sobbing out of sight / Because men made the laws?'

More than any other poet, Barrett Browning probes the notion of the moral law as the mythologized superstructure of social inequality. In *Aurora Leigh*, the sexual fall of Marian Erle constantly entails a quarrel with that law. At times Marian's innocence seems too white to be true. However, the purpose of that innocence is not to indulge the squeamishness of the reader, but to deflect moral judgement from the personal to the social. The idea of the law, recurring throughout the poem, provides the connection between those two separate spheres.

Thus, for instance, in book 3, Barrett Browning describes the birth of Marian, in a mud shack, liable, 'Like any other anthill' (3. 836),[7] to be levelled by a ruthless landlord. The defiant mixture of physical detail and political reproach is typical:

> No place for her,
> By man's law! born an outlaw was this babe;
> Her first cry in our strange and strangling air,
> When cast in spasms out by the shuddering womb,
> Was wrong against the social code, – forced wrong: –
> What business had the baby to cry there?
>
> (3. 841–6)

Here, 'man's law' is unequivocally the law of property rights, land ownership and class difference. This law casts out, from the start, the girl child born in poverty. The poor have no business to be giving birth to girls on other people's land. The 'social code' of wealth, class and, by implication, sex, makes Marian's life a kind of 'wrong' from the beginning.

The story of Marian Erle charts, every step of the way, the complicity between 'man's law' and moral law. For instance, the description of the mother's attempt to prostitute her daughter to that same 'squire' who also owns the land, is a continued indictment of 'the social code', as well as a rare reference in nineteenth-century literature to the scandal publicized in the *Pall Mall Gazette*. The trade in children for prostitution, both at home and abroad, was a thriving one, and one which had a singular appeal to the male customer afraid of catching venereal disease and willing to pay extra for virginity. As Flora Tristan noted: 'The demand for children is . . . enormous' (97). Yet, noticeably, even while Barrett Browning blames the mother, she traces her motives back to yet another kind of violence: 'Her mother had been badly beat, and felt / The bruises sore about her wretched soul' (3. 1041–2). The temptation to 'Make offal of [our] daughters' (7. 866) finds its originating cause in all men's violence: squires' or fathers'. Only because Marian Erle is 'poor and of the people' (4. 845) is she more readily tradable than her wealthier sisters.

Marian's rape in a French brothel thus only continues a theme begun early. If Barrett Browning's account of the rape seems sensational, this is not because it is improbable. The trade in girls to Continental brothels may have been exaggerated by Stead in 1885, but it was none the less a fact, and he witnessed the use of chloroform. Marian's unconsciousness is not a pretext to prove her innocent, but a truth to prove the guilt of the system. Barrett Browning constantly emphasizes the culpability of the system, and particularly, of course, the class system, involving 'some of the highest and noblest in the land'. Although she finally exonerates Lady Waldemar, her possible responsibility for Marian's fate lurks behind the story till the end.

Barrett Browning's deflection of moral responsibility from the personal to the social is then made clear in the dramatic encounter between Aurora and Marian in Paris. Accused by Aurora of being corrupt, Marian snatches up her child, and fiercely repudiates the morality by which she has been judged:

> 'Mine, mine,' she said. 'I have as sure a right
> As any glad proud mother in the world,
> Who sets her darling down to cut his teeth
> Upon her church-ring. If she talks of law,
> I talk of law! I claim my mother-dues
> By law, – the law which now is paramount, –
> The common law, by which the poor and weak
> Are trodden underfoot by vicious men,
> And loathed for ever after by the good.'
>
> (6. 661–9)

Marian's self-defence consists in making a radical connection between the church law of marriage and the common law of oppression, between legalization of motherhood in a 'church-ring' and legalization of poverty by an accepted system. As law thus comes to seem less of a moral absolute, and more of a social commodity affordable by the rich, the very nature of virtue and vice becomes uncertain. Furthermore, there is an explicit gender shift to parallel the shift from sexual to social. The 'types of vice', here, are those 'vicious men' who tread the poor 'underfoot'. Thus the terms of Marian's own rape, 'being beaten down / By hoofs of maddened oxen into a ditch' (6. 676-7), subtly echo the language of a more general beating down of a whole class of 'poor and weak'.

Against this continuing social protest one must read the end of *Aurora Leigh*, when Marian rejects Romney's offer of marriage, his '"gift"' (9. 255) of law to her, as Aurora puts it, ironically echoing that earlier '"gift"' (2. 1085) of money to herself, when Romney had tried to trap her in marriage, and make her family inheritance 'Inviolable with law' (2. 1111). Both women repudiate the male gift that comes not as love but law. Against it, Aurora asserts her right to work. Now Marian asserts her right to live by a morality free of any Christian or social legitimacy: 'Here's a hand shall keep / For ever clean without a marriage-ring' (9. 431–2). For all her adulation of Romney, she denies the law which he can confer, and rejects the fathering he offers. Her own child, she once asserted, is '"Not much worse off in being fatherless / Than I was, fathered"' (6. 646–7). The law of the father is associated in her memory with the law of violence. Conveniently for Aurora, Marian has good reason to do without.

Once again, Barrett Browning is drawing general conclusions. The legalism of inheritance, property and blood is present in the best-minded of men. Even Romney, Marian declares, in marrying her, would be haunted by the law of birthright. The children on his knee would never be equal. '"He is ours, the child"' (9. 409), she insists with passion, meaning mother's and God's. Fathers, even the best of them, will always have a taint of the other system, a system which excludes women: 'Because men made the laws'. It is interesting to remember that, at this time, by Victorian law, the fallen woman had automatic custody of her children; the legitimate wife did not. '"He is ours, the child"' gains added determination from the fact.

However, it is the actual encounter between Aurora and Marian which represents Barrett Browning's most obvious flouting of the moral law. The 'type of vice' and the type of 'virtue' meet and go together, in a liaison which is stressed at various levels in the text. Simply in terms of narrative, Aurora and Marian defy the conventions of class difference, sexual rivalry and moral discrimination which should separate them. This social alignment is then doubled by an alignment of voice, by which the virtuous poet and her vicious subject share a first-person narrative which is intimately gendered from the start. The speech of *Aurora Leigh* passes from woman to woman – from Barrett Browning to Aurora to Marian to Lady Waldemar. Each interrupts, and sometimes disproves, the authority of the others. This strategy of shared and relativized speech leaves little room for moral mediations, for charity, or disapprobation. The first person of this dramatic monologue secures her identity, not in opposition to, but in association with, the other women whose speech becomes closely allied to her own.

Thus *Aurora Leigh* asserts an identity of social and aesthetic purpose against the laws of difference between women. To say '"my sister" to the lowest drab' (5. 789), as Lady Waldemar must in Romney's phalanstery, is a greeting repeated throughout this text. By the end, Aurora has sistered Marian: '"Come with me, sweetest sister"' (7. 117), and even Lady Waldemar is begging to be recognized, as not so bad a sister as she has been judged. The class divisions which Romney so notably fails to bridge are bridged by this implicit sisterhood of women who, although they are rivals for the same man, are drawn to each other from a common bond of sexual powerlessness.

As Sally Mitchell has pointed out, upper- and middle-class women in the nineteenth century had more in common with working-class women than with the men from their own class (101). The trio of heroines in *Aurora Leigh*, though separated by class, share the common vulnerability of their sex.

The idea of sisterhood as a social liaison between women was given an impetus during the 1850s from a somewhat unexpected quarter. At this time, amid considerable controversy and opposition, the first Anglican Sisterhoods were established. Among those prominent in their support were Mrs Jameson and Florence Nightingale. Often the argument in favour of religious Sisterhoods in fact turns on the question of women's rights to education and to work, an argument which became all the more urgent as, from the middle of the century, the numbers of women rapidly outgrew the numbers of men. Mrs Jameson's lecture on *Sisters of Charity*, given in 1855, is a barely disguised advocacy of some 'well-organised system of work for women.'[8] Florence Nightingale, who gave her support to the new nursing Sisterhoods, roundly answered criticism of convent rules by declaring them preferable to 'the petty grinding tyranny of a good English family.'[9] The first issue of Emily Faithful's *Victoria Magazine*, which was set up as an enterprise run entirely by women, carried an article unequivocally in favour of Sisterhoods.[10]

Conservative opposition pointed not only to the Popish connotations of convents, but also to the risk of moral contamination in those Houses which undertook social work among the poor, the sick, or the fallen. An early article on 'Female Penitentiaries' in *The Quarterly Review* of 1848 gives a foretaste of the arguments to come. In general the reviewer lends his support to penitentiaries, but he balks at the idea of middle-class women undertaking any practical running of them. At this point his language becomes alluringly pious: 'We may express a doubt whether it is advisable for pure-minded women to put themselves in the way of such knowledge of evil as must be learnt in dealing with the fallen members of their sex.'[11] If the 'type of vice' meets the type of 'virtue', moral chaos might be loosed upon the world. The much more likely, and more injurious, contact between 'pure-minded women' and their rather less pure-minded husbands, fathers, brothers or sons, is a reality which never affects the myth. The scandal lies in the myth, in imagining the pure and the impure, nuns and prostitutes, living together. Such proximity seems a moral contradiction in terms.

'And whilst it may truly be urged that unless white could be black and Heaven Hell my experience (thank God) precludes me from hers, I yet don't see why "the Poet mind" should be less able to construct her from its own inner consciousness than a hundred other unknown quantities,' wrote

Christina Rossetti to Dante Gabriel, who had cautioned his sister against the inclusion of a particular poem in her new volume.[12] 'Under the Rose' is about an unmarried mother and her illegitimate child, a subject which, according to Dante Gabriel, might not be suitable for a woman. Licentious as he was in his own life, his moral protectiveness is roused by the possible impropriety of such a subject for a woman poet. Moral contamination, contrary to all the facts, is transmitted only from woman to woman, even when one of them is an imaginary creation. Christina insisted with due circumlocution on keeping the poem in her volume, and in later editions changed the title, perhaps pointedly, to 'The Iniquity of the Fathers Upon the Children'. Her reply at the time, however, clearly acknowledges the source of Dante Gabriel's anxiety: 'Unless white could be black and Heaven Hell'. Between herself and the unmarried mother of her poem there is a gulf as wide as heaven and hell. Yet the very extremity of these moral terms only throws into relief the nature of the task facing '"the Poet mind"'. In one place the bleak opposition between 'white' and 'black,' 'Heaven' and 'Hell' might be overcome: '"The Poet mind" should be … able to construct her from its own inner consciousness.' The 'inner consciousness' of a woman poet, as Dante Gabriel might have suspected, will be especially apt for the task.

Not only Christina's work in the refuge run by the Sisterhood of All Saints during the 1850s brought her into contact with the other sort of woman; her own imagination was unruly enough to throw into doubt and confusion the moral certainties of her own religious temperament. The clash in Rossetti's work between the fixed moral reference of heaven and hell and the derangement of that reference by an imaginative identification so strong it is anarchic, is the hallmark of her greatness as a poet. All her best poems have the intensity of a contradiction between the believer's knowledge and the imagination's desires:

> There's blood between us, love, my love,
> There's father's blood, there's brother's blood;
> And blood's a bar I cannot pass:
> I choose the stairs that mount above,
> Stair after golden skyward stair,
> To city and to sea of glass.
> My lily feet are soiled with mud,
> With scarlet mud which tells a tale
> Of hope that was, of guilt that was,
> Of love that shall not yet avail;
> Alas, my heart, if I could bare
> My heart, this selfsame stain is there.
>
>   (1–12)[13]

Christina Rossetti wrote 'The Convent Threshold' in 1858. Like so many poems about the fallen woman by women poets, it is a dramatic monologue, in which the single speaking voice is both the self's and the other's, both the poet's and the character's. The 'inner consciousness' of the text is a shared one. Such an identification, however, entails, for Rossetti, a larger, terrifying loss of bearings. Her poem sensationally blurs the distinctions, not only between nun and lover, poet and fallen woman, but also, in the end, between heaven and hell. Alice Meynell caught something of the emotional paradox of the work when she called it 'a song of penitence for love that yet praises love more fervently than would a chorus hymeneal.'[14] But it is not only love which is at stake in this poem. On the threshold of the convent, torn between sin and grace, world and refuge, earth and heaven, passion and renunciation, the woman stands on a fine line between moral opposites she can barely keep apart.

Such a border placing becomes radically displacing. This is the threshold, not only of a convent, but of consciousness; it is a consciousness tormented by white and black, heaven and hell, the 'skyward stair' and the 'scarlet mud'. Whatever brought Rossetti's imagination to this pass, 'The Convent Threshold' suggests that to cross from earth to sky, mud to stair, love to grace, lover to nun, is to risk a passage into confusion and hallucination, in which the 'inner consciousness' is wrecked by difference. This poem is rife with a sensuality more lovely, but also more damnable, than anything in Dante Gabriel. Rossetti's female imagination must always bear the cost of its Romantic desires. To 'construct' the other is to yield the 'inner consciousness' to the moral opposite which that other represents.

Thus, although 'The Convent Threshold' seems to offer a choice between going in or staying out, that choice is soon lost in a disturbingly surreal narrative of visions and dreams, past and future, death and life. The threshold is not a single step, but a shifting subliminal line; it is not a place, but a boundary. This poem is full of thresholds, and consequently full of 'faults' of level and register. To cross into the convent is not, for Rossetti, a step into safety, but a nightmare plunge into vague, unconnected territories of the mind.

The penultimate section of the poem, which is spoken from within the convent, luridly contradicts the religious aspiration of the work. Having chosen the 'skyward stair', the nun dreams of being dragged down in mud. Having chosen eternal life, she hallucinates endless death. Having chosen renunciation, she enters a nightmare of lost love. Yet, the language of this section, contrary to all the moral purpose of the poem, sounds like a true homing of Rossetti's imagination:

> I tell you what I dreamed last night:
> It was not dark, it was not light,

> Cold dews had drenched my plenteous hair
> Thro' clay; you came to seek me there.
> And 'Do you dream of me?' you said.
> My heart was dust that used to leap
> To you; I answered half asleep:
> 'My pillow is damp, my sheets are red,
> There's a leaden tester to my bed:
> Find you a warmer playfellow,
> A warmer pillow for your head,
> A kinder love to love than mine.'
> You wrung your hands; while I, like lead
> Crushed downwards thro' the sodden earth:
> You smote your hands but not in mirth,
> And reeled but were not drunk with wine.
>
> (110–25)

'The Convent Threshold' seems to stage a sinner's progress on the way to grace; but in effect the poem founders in a hellish fantasy of decay and death. Distorted time and deranged dreams torment this latter-day Héloïse.

Yet Rossetti's sense of the macabre has a playful shiftiness about it. The thresholds of dream and waking, death and life, are unnervingly unstable in this poem. 'The Convent Threshold' opens up a strange hall of mirrors in which, by some bewildering logic, the living woman dreams of being dead and of dreaming none the less of him who asks: '"Do you dream?"' Instead of leading up to heaven, the poem leads downwards and inwards, to that typically Rossettian state of semi-consciousness, which is both heartless and fixated, both capricious and afraid. Certainly some deep and terrible doubt underlies this poem of religious penitence. Its passionate hallucinations seem closer to the imagination of an Emily Brontë than to that of the 'over-scrupulous'[15] Anglican, who, in her later years, would pick up pieces of paper in the street in case the name of God was written on them.[16] 'The "Poet mind" should be . . . able to construct her from its own inner consciousness.' The evidence of 'The Convent Threshold' is that the 'inner consciousness' suffers as a result from some profound and brilliant incoherence.

The scene of encounter between fallen and unfallen woman, which 'The Convent Threshold' telescopes into the single figure of the lover-nun, recurs like an obsession in women's poetry. Its most obvious purpose is to forge a forbidden social liaison across the divisions of moral law and sexual myth. In a poem by Dora Greenwell called 'Christina',[17] the fallen speaker remembers her childhood friend Christina, with whom she still feels a sympathetic kinship: 'Across the world-wide gulf betwixt us set / My soul stretched out a bridge.'[18] The poem tells of a chance meeting between two women over the grave of Christina's dead child. In an interesting substitution of identities, Christina urges her fallen friend to come home, and take the place of her child: 'I call thee not my Sister, as of old' [but] 'Daughter' (13). However, the 'world-wide gulf' proves too wide to cross, and the unnamed Penitent returns to die in a refuge.

The religious sentimentality of Greenwell's poem keeps it from being anything more than a failed gesture of philanthropy. However, for other poets, the encounter between fallen and unfallen achieves the intensity of a recognition scene. The political sister is the psychic double, the social underworld into which the fallen disappear becoming associated with the subconscious in which the fallen re-emerge as the other self.

In a strange poem by Adelaide Procter, *A Legend of Provence*, a young nun runs off with a soldier, who then betrays and abandons her. After many years she returns to her convent, only to meet her double at the door:

> She raised her head; she saw – she seemed to know –
> A face that came from long, long years ago:
> Herself.[19]

This is not a spectre from the past, but a real, other self, who has been living, all the while, in an unfallen state personated by the Virgin Mary. At the convent door, the two halves come together. Once again, the threshold of the convent seems to be a threshold of the self, marking a split of consciousness which echoes the moral divisions of the age. If the place of the Romantic imagination is that of a border-line between the known and the unknown, the border-line of the Victorian female imagination is the same, but fraught with social and sexual anxieties.

In *Aurora Leigh* the meeting between Aurora and Marian, as critics have noted,[20] has all the emotional urgency and narrative doubling of a recognition scene:

> What face is that?
> What a face, what a look, what a likeness! Full on mine
> The sudden blow of it came down, till all
> My blood swam, my eyes dazzled.

(6. 231–4)

Marian returns like the dead, but also like the repressed. When the two women finally meet, their uncanny doubling movements suggest a twinning of purpose beyond all the charities of social aid. First Aurora leads, and Marian 'followed closely where I went, / As if I led her by a narrow plank / Across devouring waters' (6. 481–3). But a few lines later, as the moral authority is transferred to Marian 'she led / The way, and I, as by a narrow plank / Across devouring waters, followed her' (6. 500–2). These 'devouring waters' are another 'world-wide gulf'. Unlike Greenwell, however, Barrett Browning goes across. That it is a crossing both ways emphasizes the egalitarian nature of the relationship. This is not rescue work. It is self-recognition.

Such doubling effects are taken a stage further in Rossetti's *Goblin Market*. Not only are the two sisters, Lizzie and Laura, hard to distinguish; they also enact the same drama though with different intentions. Laura pays for goblin fruit with a curl of her hair, and pines away. Lizzie gets fruit without paying, and so revives her sister. 'The moral is hardly intelligible', Alice Meynell complained.[21] Rossetti herself, it seems, did not intend a moral.[22] Certainly, as Jerome McGann has argued, a 'middle-class ideology of love and marriage' underlies the story,[23] and the cautionary figure of the fallen woman, Jeanie, 'who for joys brides hope to have / Fell sick and died' (314–15), casts a realistic shadow across the fairy-tale.[24] None the less, *Goblin Market* singularly fails to press home the moral of Jeanie. Laura knows she should not loiter and look, but she does. Lizzie knows she should not take without paying, but she does. The only rule pertaining at the end is that sisters should stick together. Only together will they be a match for the goblins. Jeanie died, not because she ate the fruit, but because she had no sister to rescue her.

If *Goblin Market* is a feminized myth of Christian redemption, it is redemption through a willed confusion of fallen and unfallen. 'Undone in mine undoing / And ruined in my ruin', Laura wails (482–3). Yet, it is precisely through this shared fall, this transgression of the rule of difference, that sisterhood becomes a match for brotherhood, and the goblins are beaten at their own tricks. 'We may express a doubt whether it is advisable for pure-minded women to put themselves in the way of such knowledge of evil as must be learnt in dealing with the fallen members of their sex,' wrote the *Quarterly* reviewer. Such 'knowledge of evil', for Christina Rossetti, is not only advisable, but also awakening and saving. Lizzie, the rescuing sister, goes 'At twilight, halted by the brook: / And for the first time in her life / Began to listen and look' (326–8). The two girls desire, loiter and look, in a gesture that combines a Romantic hovering on the threshold of strange knowledge with the purposeful delay of the streetwalker.

In the end, it seems that Rossetti brilliantly displaces the message of this poem on to the two terms of the title. *Goblin Market* is the place of magic and marketing. Far from being representers of the moral seriousness of the Fall, these mischievous and childish creatures play by the rules of magic and money. They thus uncannily echo the commodity morality of nineteenth-century myths of sexuality. Moral downfall is linked to market exchange. By not paying, Lizzie tricks the market and resists not so much the fruit as the law by which fruit turns to poison because, Rossetti seems to say, goblins made the laws. There is a sense in which *Goblin Market* hoodwinks the moralizers as well.

'After much hesitation and many misgivings, we have undertaken to speak of so dismal and delicate a matter', writes W. R. Greg.[25] He begins his 1850 article on 'Prostitution' with elaborate cautions and apologies. Even William Lecky slips at times into coy circumlocutions: 'That unhappy being whose very name is a shame to speak'. When it comes to speaking, 'shame' is a constant obstruction. When it comes to women speaking, a whole complicated magic of sin and contamination comes into play. 'I am grateful to you as a woman for having so treated such a subject', wrote Barrett Browning to Elizabeth Gaskell, on the publication of *Ruth*, as if she were speaking as one of the fallen herself.[26] Certainly, the connection between writing and sinning is a close and involved one. The doubling of sisters in these texts hints at the way in which the poet is verbally implicated in the fall. Writing and sexuality double each other. 'There has always been a vague connection', writes Simone de Beauvoir, 'between prostitution and art.'[27] Such a connection is both more probable and more inadmissible when the artist is a woman. A sign of the sheer inhibitory power of the taboo imposed on women is that, as late as 1929, Virginia Woolf, in *A Room of One's Own*, looks forward to a time when the woman writer will be able to meet 'the courtesan' and 'the harlot' without 'that self-consciousness in the presence of "sin" which is the legacy of our sexual barbarity.'[28] Woolf looks forward, but she might also have looked back.

One voice from the nineteenth century which speaks out with brave shamelessness on the subject of the fallen is a voice which has been unaccountably lost to the poetic canon. 'By-the-by', wrote Christina Rossetti to a friend, 'did not Mr. Gladstone omit from his list of poetesses the one name which *I* incline to feel as by far the most formidable of those known to me.'[29] The name she gave was that of Augusta Webster.

Webster's poem *A Castaway* was published in 1870, in her volume *Portraits*, and was almost certainly known to Rossetti. A long dramatic monologue, spoken by a relatively high-class courtesan who muses on the strange course of her life, the poem becomes a magnificent and panoramic indictment of contemporary society. Webster makes the connection between the moral and the mercantile overtly and persistently, so that all trades are levelled to the same kind of value: that of profit and loss. In a narrative that is strikingly free of myths and metaphors, the Castaway judges the ways of the world. Hers is a stark and literal language, a language of the market without any goblins:

　　　　　　　　　　　　And, for me,
I say let no one be above her trade;
I own my kindredship with any drab
Who sells herself as I, although she crouch
In fetid garrets and I have a home
All velvet and marqueterie and pastilles,
Although she hide her skeleton in rags
And I set fashions and wear cobweb lace:
The difference lies but in my choicer ware,
That I sell beauty and she ugliness;
Our traffic's one – I'm no sweet slaver-tongue
To gloze upon it and explain myself
A sort of fractious angel misconceived –
Our traffic's one: I own it. And what then?
I know of worse that are called honourable.
Our lawyers, who with noble eloquence
And virtuous outbursts lie to hang a man,
Or lie to save him, which way goes the fee:
Our preachers, gloating on your future hell
For not believing what they doubt themselves:
Our doctors, who sort poisons out by chance
And wonder how they'll answer, and grow rich:
Our journalists, whose business is to fib
And juggle truths and falsehoods to and fro:
Our tradesmen, who must keep unspotted names
And cheat the least like stealing that they can:
Our – all of them, the virtuous worthy men
Who feed on the world's follies, vices, wants,
And do their businesses of lies and shams
Honestly, reputably, while the world
Claps hands and cries 'good luck', which of their trades,
Their honourable trades, barefaced like mine,
All secrets brazened out, would shew more white?[30]

A Castaway presents the fact of prostitution bare of any myth or magic. Its
causes are unremittingly social, and so are its effects – penury, poor education,
an imbalance of the numbers of women against those of men, and a shortage
of work for both sexes. Webster, who was a lifelong campaigner for women's
suffrage (though she failed to convert Christina Rossetti to her cause) as well
as for women's education, issues a moving reminder in this poem of how the
education of girls is stinted to pay for the training of their luckier brothers:

'The lesson girls with brothers all must learn, / To do without' (56). Never having been fitted for anything except marriage, what can girls do to keep alive except carry out that trade which so darkly resembles marriage, and yet is its moral opposite.

Most of the fallen women who play any prominent role in nineteenth-century literature are only variations on the real theme. Seduced, raped, betrayed, or simply fickle, they are either innocent girls led astray, or sensational adulteresses. Their actions thus remain largely within the parameters of romance. They are motivated by feeling, not by economic exigency. But Augusta Webster gives us the professional. As a result, she can point to the real unmentionable of Victorian prostitution: the male client. The endlessly elaborated discourse on the tantalizing secret of female sexuality, like any other taboo, in fact serves to disguise another, more deep-seated taboo which creates the silence on the other side of all this speech. Sexuality is not just, as Michel Foucault claims, the well-exploited 'secret' of the modern age;[31] woman's sexuality provides a gratifying decoy from the thing that is no secret at all and yet remains curiously unspoken. Gladstone, who was himself, like Dickens, a keen rescuer of fallen women, inclined to take them home to talk with his wife, confessed in his diary that his motives were suspect: he feared in himself some '"dangerous curiosity & filthiness of spirit"'.[32] By writing about the professional courtesan, Webster dares to mention the men who in reality provide the rationale of prostitution. These are not the figures of literary romance, dark seducers or passionate rakes. These are, quite simply, other women's husbands, for whom the illicit is routine:

> And whom do I hurt more than they? as much?
> The wives? Poor fools, what do I take from them
> Worth crying for or keeping? If they knew
> What their fine husbands look like seen by eyes
> That may perceive there are more men than one!
> But, if they can, let them just take the pains
> To keep them: 'tis not such a mighty task
> To pin an idiot to your apron-strings,
> And wives have an advantage over us,
> (The good and blind ones have) the smile or pout
> Leaves them no secret nausea at odd times.
> Oh, they could keep their husbands if they cared,
> But 'tis an easier life to let them go,
> And whimper at it for morality.

(39–40)

Webster exposes, with scornful simplicity, the other hidden and forbidden topic which lies behind the Victorians' obsession with fallen women. If men are the arbiters of virtue and vice, they are also the go-betweens. For them the passage from one to the other is a secret passage between separate spheres. But for women the difference is not so certain. The passage which divides the 'type of virtue' from the type of 'vice' can turn into a mirror, to reflect the self. The very nature of womanhood is split by a mirror stage, mandated by man's law. Thus, the doubleness of the social order serves to match a doubleness within. The very nature of female subjectivity is founded and wrecked on this law of opposites. Not only is the pure woman divided from 'the other'; the very self is split from its own history.

At one point, the Castaway remembers her girlhood:

> So long since:
> And now it seems a jest to talk of me
> As if I could be one with her, of me
> Who am . . . me.
>
> (36)

When she looks in the mirror it seems to reproduce the doubleness. Between 'me' and 'me' falls the shadow of the moral law. Against that law, however, the dramatic monologue asserts its single voice. The pronoun doubles poet and outcast, speaker and actor, in a drama which is transgressively sistering from the start. The voice of the poem is both act and consciousness, both object and subject, both 'me' and 'me'. The gender-specific nature of this poet's voice makes a common cause of the fact of womanhood.

One of the saddest poems on the fallen woman is Amy Levy's 'Magdalen'. In reality a poem of seduction, its note of bitter and sceptical despair as the girl prepares to die in a refuge is a sign of the continuing power of the myth as late as the 1880s. Like Rossetti before her, Levy finds in the event of the fall a mockery of all creeds and of all ethical systems:

> Death do I trust no more than life.
> For one thing is like one arrayed,
> And there is neither false nor true;
> But in a hideous masquerade
> All things dance on, the ages through.
> And good is evil, evil good;
> Nothing is known or understood
> Save only Pain.[33]

Levy was only twenty-seven when, five years after the publication of this poem, she killed herself in her parents' house without explanation. Her 'Magdalen' is an immature poem, and its language is too limply melancholy; it does, none the less, betray the strain of that social morality which founds its whole system of good and evil on the sexual propriety of women.

Charlotte Mew – a poet who was, in many ways, herself a last Victorian – was one of the last poets to write about the Magdalen. In 1894, Mew published a story in *The Yellow Book* called 'Passed', describing an encounter between the narrator and a destitute young girl whom she meets in a church, and whose sister has killed herself following some sexual betrayal. Behind the vivid melodrama of Mew's language, the story traces a rather interesting psychological story. The moment when the narrator takes the girl in her arms is one of extreme bewilderment and hallucination. Thinking of her home, she finds it 'desolate'; imagining a mirror, she sees no 'reflection'; opening a book, she finds the pages 'blank'.[34] All the usual signs of her sheltered identity have been erased. In this encounter with the homeless, distraught girl, she seems to have lost her own self. In terror, she cruelly throws the girl off, and makes her escape; but when, many months later, she glimpses the girl on the arm of the same man who betrayed her sister, the meaning of the encounter flashes on her mind. The last lines of the story confirm the suspicion that the girl is the speaker's lost reflection, her alter ego, forfeited to the differences of moral law and class division: 'I heard a laugh, mounting to a cry. . . . Did it proceed from some defeated angel? or the woman's mouth? or mine?' (78).

The 'woman's mouth or mine?' The sound of that confused 'laugh' or 'cry' comes from an 'inner consciousness' which is woman's, in general, not hers or mine, but both. Sexual morality and social difference have split the very nature of female subjectivity. For women in the nineteenth century, the Romantic split, 'I is another', carries the added penalty of a sexual transgression: 'I is the other'. The mirror, for women, is also a gulf. Yet to pass from one side of the gulf to the other is to undertake an act of social protest which is also an act of daring self-recovery.

By the time Mew came to write her own dramatic monologue of the fallen woman, the schizophrenia of Victorian morality had largely been overcome. 'Madeleine in Church' was published in 1916, and is, in spite of its title, an uninhibited love poem. The idea of the fall as a psycho-sexual event which splits subjectivity into 'me' and 'me' is missing in it. Instead, its rich evocation of passion affirms that the self is consistent with itself, and coherent with its history:

> We are what we are: when I was half a child I could not sit
> Watching black shadows on green lawns and red carnations burning
>   in the sun,

Without paying so heavily for it
That joy and pain, like any mother and her unborn child were
                                                      almost one.
                    I could hardly bear
        The dreams upon the eyes of white geraniums in the
                                                      dusk,
              The thick, close voice of musk,
          The jessamine music on the thin night air,
        Or, sometimes, my own hands about me anywhere –
The sight of my own face (for it was lovely then) even the scent of my
                                                      own hair,
    Oh! there was nothing, nothing that did not sweep to the high
                                                      seat
              Of laughing gods, and then blow down and beat
My soul into the highway dust, as hoofs do the dropped roses of the
                                                      street.
                    I think my body was my soul,
                    And when we are made thus
                        Who shall control
          Our hands, our eyes, the wandering passion of our feet
                                                      (23–4)

This poem, in some ways, marks the end of a tradition. By the time
women come to write openly about sexual passion, the figure of the fallen
woman ceases to haunt their imaginations. For she is the ghost of what has
been forbidden, denied, divided. She is the Victorian woman poet's familiar,
the double that returns like herself, the other that beats against the
internalized social barriers of the mind. She is the vivid emblem of a social
and sexual secrecy which is still clamorous with self-discovery.

The figure of the fallen woman is also, however, a sign for women of the
power of writing. Her wandering, outcast state seductively expresses the
poet's restlessness and desire. To summon her is not only to assert a political
purpose which breaks the moral law, but also to claim the power of writing
as necessarily free of control, of rule. The fallen woman is the muse, the
beloved – the lost sister, mother, daughter, whose self was one's own. In
poetry, above all, the social gesture of reclamation and solidarity becomes
also an imaginative gesture of integration and identity.

Barrett Browning, at the beginning of this tradition, invokes the fallen
woman, not only as her sister, but also as her muse. Only if the poet takes
the 'part' of the other, and speaks with her cries, will she find her own voice.
The political other is the poetic self. To speak from the 'inner consciousness'
of being a woman is to speak from that which has been divided, disenfran-

chised, but which, for that very reason, needs to be recovered. The 'depths of womanhood' may have been kept 'out of sight', but only from such 'depths' can the poet challenge men's laws:

> 'Therefore', the voice said, 'shalt thou write
> My curse to-night.
> Some women weep and curse, I say
> (And no one marvels), night and day.
>
> 'And thou shalt take their part to-night,
> Weep and write.
> A curse from the depths of womanhood
> Is very salt, and bitter, and good.'
>
> ('A Curse for a Nation', 41–8)[35]

NOTES

1   Barrett Browning, *Casa Guidi Windows* (1900: 3. 249–313).
2   Quoted in Mitchell 1981: 340.
3   Bullough and Bullough 1987: 197.
4   Tristan 1982: 83.
5   Engels 1972: 125–46).
6   Lecky 1955: II, 283.
7   Barrett Browning, *Aurora Leigh and Other Poems* (1978).
8   Mrs Jameson 1855: 13.
9   Quoted in Allchin 1958: 115.
10   Maurice 1863: 289–301.
11   'Female Penitentiaries', in *The Quarterly Review* 83 (1848): 375–6.
12   Troxell (ed.) 1937: 143. Letter from Christina to Dante Gabriel, 13 March 1865.
     13   Christina Rossetti, 'The Convent Threshold' (1979–90: 1. 61–5).
14   Meynell 1895: 203.
15   William Michael Rossetti, 'Memoir', in *The Poetical Works of Christina Georgina Rossetti* (1904: lxvii).
16   Tynan 1913: 161.
17   The poem was written in 1851, almost certainly before Greenwell had met Rossetti or had read any of her poems.
18   Greenwell, 'Christina', in *Poems* (1861: 4).
19   Procter, 'A Legend of Provence', in *Legends and Lyrics* (1914: 162).
20   See, for instance, Rosenblum 1983: 321–38; and Leighton 1986: ch.7.
21   Meynell, 'Christina Rossetti', in *Alice Meynell: Prose and Poetry* (1947: 147).
22   Note to *Goblin Market*, by W. M. Rossetti, in *The Poetical Works of Christina Georgina Rossetti* (1904: 459).
23   McGann 1980: 248.

24   Christina Rossetti, *Goblin Market*, in *The Complete Poems* (1979–90: 11–26).

25   Greg 1850: 448.

26   Waller (ed.) 1935: 42.

27   de Beauvoir 1972: 579.

28   Woolf 1945: 88.

29   Rossetti 1908: 175. Letter from Christina to William, 22 January 1890.

30   Augusta Webster, *A Castaway*, in *Portraits* (1893: 38–9).

31   Foucault 1981: 1. 35.

32   *The Gladstone Diaries*, ed. Foot and Matthew (1968–86: IV. 51).

33   Amy Levy, 'Magdalen', in *A Minor Poet And other Verse* (1884: 71).

34   Charlotte Mew, 'Passed', in *Charlotte Mew: Collected Poems and Prose* (1981: 71). Hereafter this edition is cited by page number in the text.

35   Barrett Browning, 'A Curse for a Nation', in *Aurora Leigh and Other Poems* (1978: 402–6).

15

'Poet's Right': Elegy and the Woman Poet

Susan Conley

Michael Field's sonnet, 'To Christina Rossetti', was published in *The Academy* a little over a year after Rossetti's death, yet as a commemorative piece it adopts a markedly ambivalent, even critical stance towards its subject. Ironically, its elegiac mood derives less from Rossetti's death than from its interpretation of her life and work; an interpretation which judges her an unfit subject for pastoral elegy and – partly in consequence – an unfit muse for future poets. The poem thus becomes a kind of pastoral elegy *manqué*.

> Lady, we would behold thee moving bright
> As Beatrice or Matilda 'mid the trees,
> Alas! thy moan was as a moan for ease
> And passage through cool shadows to the night:
> Fleeing from love, hadst thou not poet's right
> To slip into the universe? The seas
> Are fathomless to rivers drowned in these,
> And sorrow is secure in leafy light.
> Ah, had this secret touched thee, in a tomb
> Thou hadst not buried thy enchanting self,
> As happy Syrinx murmuring with the wind,
> Or Daphne thrilled through all her mystic bloom,
> From safe recess as genius or as elf,
> Thou hadst breathed joy in earth and in thy kind.[1]

In choosing to write a sonnet, Michael Field[2] selects the brief lyric form of which Rossetti was a celebrated practitioner, and thus follows the elegiac tradition of imitation and incorporation. The Rossettian sonnet is frequently 'a case of knives',[3] an ostensible love poem fractured by a set of unsettling devices, from mysterious gaps and ambiguities to irony and parody. Some-what appropriately, therefore, Michael Field's sonnet enacts its own masquer-ade, its own sleight of hand. Its critique of Rossetti is offered through an extended fantasy in which the poetic process is completely feminized: the ideal female poet becomes a writing muse, an ideal which Rossetti fails to represent. Yet the fantasy itself is fraught with problems, revealing the precarious and self-contradictory nature of the formula, 'woman poet', and the impossibility of inscribing Rossetti within a masculine poetic genealogy. For while the single masculine signature 'Michael Field' conceals the female writing partnership of Katherine Bradley and Edith Cooper, the poem describes the submerging of female identity and female voice necessary for its reappearance as the breath of inspiration for, and the matter of, a masculine-authored art. Further, the poem offers a prescription for reading Rossetti's work which presages its declining reputation in the decades to come.

Wanting to situate Rossetti within a literary-mythological matrix of the feminine, the poem appears to offer two possible positions for the woman poet. The first, introduced in the octave, is signified by the pair, 'Beatrice or Matilda', two Dantean heroines, who represent the beloved as muse.[4] The conventional courtly address with which the poem opens – 'Lady, we would behold thee' – accords Rossetti the status of beloved muse, but conditionally; a condition which, it is quickly made clear, was not fulfilled: 'Alas! thy moan was as a moan for ease / And passage through cool shadows to the night' (3–4). The description of Rossetti as '[f]leeing from love' (5) anticipates the introduction in the sestet of 'Syrinx . . . / Or Daphne', a second representative pair, whose transformations into natural objects to escape the threat of rape, make them still available for artistic if not amorous appropriation – Syrinx a bed of reeds made into pipes by Pan; Daphne a crown of laurels for her pursuer, Apollo (and thenceforth a prize for success in non-amorous pursuits; that is, a reward for sublimation). Both positions appear to reproduce the traditional relationship of woman to art: as muse, the inspiration for art (Beatrice and Matilda), or reified into art's symbolic matter (Syrinx and Daphne), rather than its subject-producers. (These pairings can also be seen as symptoms or signs of what is repressed by the cipher 'Michael Field', the concealed pair of female authors.) Yet it is not so simple; for, in a daring move, Michael Field makes the muse the poet: 'Fleeing from love, hadst thou not *poet's* right / To slip into the universe?' (5–6, my emphasis). This rhetorical claim invokes the elegiac trope of the dead poet's literal (bodily) and figurative reabsorption into nature, as in the early stages of Shelley's *Adonais*, which seems to me a key intertext for this poem. By elevating this communion with the universe from merely a woman's fate to a 'poet's right', the poem suggests a way in which the traditional conflation of woman with nature might be enabling rather than silencing for the woman poet. This is offered as a 'secret', and a life-saving secret at that: 'Ah, had this secret touched thee, in a tomb / Thou hadst not buried thy enchanting self' (9–10). It grants the woman poet the kind of immortality and authority in death normally reserved for her male counterparts. As Shelley proclaims of the dead Keats: 'He is made one with Nature: there is heard / His voice in all her music'.[5] Yet, as these lines suggest, the male poet speaks through rather than as feminine Nature: 'his voice' can be distinguished from 'her music'. By failing to similarly distinguish the voice of the female poet from Nature's music, Michael Field's poem founders as a liberating fantasy for women poets.

What is missing from their elegy is the apotheosis of the dead, the 'vertical transcendence' which, in conventional male elegy, 'lifts [the dead one] out of nature, out of the poem, and out of the successor's way.'[6] According to Celeste Schenck, the male pastoral elegy is 'from the first a gesture of aspiring careerism' (14), while female elegists tend to 'protest [against] final separation' (24), emphasizing instead continuities between living and dead: '[T]he female elegy is a poem of connectedness; women inheritors seem to achieve poetic identity in relation to ancestresses, in connection to the dead, whereas male initiates need to eliminate the competition to come into their own' (15). Michael Field's elegy jettisons both of these options. Firstly, in their pastoral elegy *manqué*, Rossetti is never granted the status that might elicit 'competition'. Secondly, in their fantasized position for Rossetti, the dead female poet is not, indeed, lifted out of nature but she is, none the less, re-routed into a masculine poetics, as object, via the muse-figures of Beatrice, Matilda, Daphne and Syrinx; she is still circumscribed within the 'essentially mythic structures' which Schenck claims the female elegist 'deconstructs' and 'replaces' (24).[7] Further, while Schenck distinguishes the masculine elegy as 'above all a vocational poem' (13) and 'a poetry of ambition' (15), it seems not inappropriate to view Michael Field's poem in precisely these terms. Ultimately, of course, their sonnet should be seen as a poem of ambition frustrated.

Let us return for a moment to the line in the poem in which the muse becomes poet. In anticipating the introduction of Syrinx and Daphne by allusion to the mythological stories associated with them, 'fleeing from love'[8] refers ambiguously to Rossetti's status as spinster, twice proposed to and once engaged but never married, while recasting this Victorian domestic tale in terms of pagan myths in which the fear of rape, of male lust out of control, forces women to sacrifice their lives, or at least, their human form; thus the references in the poem to 'safe recess', to 'sorrow . . . secure'. Yet there are different forms of haven in the poem; the form designated 'night' and 'tomb' is clearly held in disapprobation by Michael Field, figuring Rossetti's religious practice as a kind of death-in-life. The poem can then be read as an elegy not for Rossetti's death but for her life.

By contrast, the haven chosen by Syrinx and Daphne represents life-in-death, a traditional symbolism these figures have long served. The liberation of the woman poet offered by this poem rests on the success of its attempt to recuperate the fate of Daphne and Syrinx. Such recuperation involves reclaiming a woman's fate for a 'poet's right' – not just in terms of elegiac apotheosis through nature, as already noted, but also in terms of the conditions, in life, that enable a woman to write. Women who 'flee from love' – that is, who reject the role of Victorian wife and mother – are free to devote themselves to the service of art. Syrinx and Daphne can then be seen as models for the woman poet. As in Barrett Browning's version of the story of Pan and Syrinx, 'A Musical Instrument' (1860), Syrinx rather than Pan becomes a figure for the poet. Yet whereas 'A Musical Instrument' focuses on Pan and never actually names Syrinx, in Michael Field's poem it is the male players, Pan and Apollo, who go unnamed. Further, in the original stories Daphne and Syrinx suffer a double death, not just in their transformation from nymph into tree and bed of reeds, but then in their reappropriation by their male pursuants – as Barrett Browning's poem makes clear, in its graphic depiction of the reeds torn out of the river and 'hacked and hewed' into pipes.[9] Significantly, in Michael Field's poem Syrinx and Daphne undergo only the first transformation, the one they each prayed for in order to escape sexual possession; in this fantasy, Diana's nymphs do indeed find 'safe recess' in their natural forms. In Ovid's stories they are each then appropriated to signify masculine creativity, memorials to male sublimation. Yet in this poem they signify something else:

> As happy Syrinx murmuring with the wind,
> Or Daphne thrilled through all her mystic bloom,
> From safe recess as genius or as elf,
> Thou hadst breathed joy in earth and in thy kind.

> (11–14)

Again, this is where Michael Field's liberating fantasy for the woman poet becomes double-edged. Syrinx and Daphne have a voice, but it is indistinguishable from nature's voice, albeit a nature imbued with mystic powers. And while by eliding the further transformations or appropriations of Daphne and Syrinx the focus remains on the sublimation of *their* sexuality, it is in the service of an art which comes, as it were, naturally. Unlike her male colleagues, the woman artist does not speak through nature (like Pan) but as nature (like Syrinx).

For Michael Field the sacrifice/sublimation involved in spinsterhood is admirable, indeed necessary, in the service of art, but not in the service of conventional religion. Yet their poem does not construct art and religion as competing discourses but rather, art and institutional Christianity as competing *religious* discourses. Art here is inseparable from the pantheistic pagan revivalism favoured by Bradley and Cooper.[10] For them, conventional Christianity is a 'tomb' in which Rossetti buries her 'enchanting self' (9–10); it is a haven that is ultimately silencing for the poet. Yet, to 'slip into the universe' and join her voice to the voices of nature is not necessarily the 'safe recess' it seems, reinscribing as it does the ideological conflation of woman with nature. Rossetti's religious faith did not in fact silence her as a poet, and in her hundreds of religious poems she joins her voice to a tradition of Christian religious poetry from the Bible onwards. However, according to Michael Field, this kind of communion leads not to fame and immortality but to obscurity and death. Some critics have read, in the development of Rossetti's poetry, an attempt to displace a secular (specifically, Romantic) poetic with a Christian poetic,[11] a process of displacement which, it would seem, this sonnet attempts to reverse. Yet, while Rossetti did indeed choose to publish exclusively devotional works during the last decade of her life, both traditions – secular and religious – are in dialogic tension throughout much of her career. Such a dialogic relation is less the product of artistic licence stifled by religious scruples than a development of the precedent set for Rossetti by Dante.[12]

As I suggested earlier, Field's sonnet is ultimately a poem of frustrated ambition. Ostensibly, its ambition is thwarted by its subject, Rossetti, who in this poem becomes an anti-muse for later women poets. None the less, the poem proceeds to offer, within a constrained, conditional framework, a fantasy of female creativity where the woman poet combines the roles of writer and muse. Unfortunately, as I have argued, this fantasy is itself frustrated by its collusion with the ideological confounding of woman and nature, and the difficulty of extricating such figures as Beatrice, Matilda, Daphne and Syrinx from a masculine poetics. The 'connectedness' (Schenck) which Michael Field's elegy achieves is with these literary-mythological figures, rather than with the dead woman poet. Further, compared with the 'vertical transcendence' characteristic of the traditional masculine elegy, its version of elegiac apotheosis for the woman poet is markedly scaled down, not just in length. This is nowhere more apparent than in the closing lines – 'From safe recess as genius or as elf, / Thou hadst breathed joy in earth and in thy kind' (13–14) – whose elements can be found in the final stanza of Shelley's *Adonais*:

> The breath whose might I have invoked in song
> Descends on me; my spirit's bark is driven,

> Far from the shore, far from the trembling throng
> Whose sails were never to the tempest given;
> The massy earth and spherèd skies are riven!
> I am borne darkly, fearfully, afar;
> Whilst, burning through the inmost veil of Heaven,
> The soul of Adonais, like a star,
> Beacons from the abode where the Eternal are.

$$(487-95)$$

Here the process is complete whereby the dead Keats attains the lofty heights of poetic immortality, the abode of the Eternal, while Shelley inherits the role of poetic hierophant on earth. The same elements of the poet's apotheosis and the continued transmission of the 'breath' of poetic inspiration are found in Michael Field's lines, except that the abode of the Eternal is merely a 'safe recess'; the poet's star-like soul is reduced to a tutelary spirit ('genius') or worse, an unreliable sprite ('elf'), and its powers of influence and inspiration are at once more general and more vague: 'in earth and in thy kind'. The ambiguous 'thy kind' could refer to the whole of humanity or, more specifically, to fellow – or perhaps only sister – poets. None the less, this ambiguous generality fails to establish for the woman poet a poetic genealogy.

   Thus, although Michael Field's conceit is bold, their vision for Rossetti is not as ambitious as it could be. In any case, it fails to liberate this woman poet since it is used against her; it is offered only as what might have been, a chance Rossetti chose to pass up. With its claim that she 'buried [her] enchanting self' in a 'tomb', a note of reprimand is struck that will be heard again and again in commentary on the poet. The poem judges Rossetti's mode of Christianity a choice for death over life, a death-in-life, as 'a moan for ease / And passage through cool shadows to the night' (3–4). Against this the poem pits a pagan Romanticism allied with poetic immortality through life-in-death. Rossetti's failure to be perceived as a suitable role model for Bradley and Cooper, self-styled bohemians and New Women, foreshadows the perceptions of many late twentieth-century feminist critics, who echo Michael Field's sonnet with such verdicts as Sandra Gilbert's in *The Madwoman in the Attic*, that Rossetti '[buried] herself alive in a coffin of renunciation'.[13]

Like Michael Field's sonnet, Barrett Browning's 'A Musical Instrument' represents an intervention by a woman poet into male myths of creativity in order to find a place for herself. One of Barrett Browning's last poems, 'A Musical Instrument' was first published in the *Cornhill Magazine* in July 1860 and can be seen to represent, as Dorothy Mermin says, her 'final statement about the nature of poetic creativity'.[14] Drawing on the myth of

Syrinx, while never actually naming her, it describes Pan's fashioning of a pipe from a reed, a metaphor for poetic creativity which in turn describes the poet as the *object* of this primary creative act: a god, '[m]aking a poet out of a man' (39), is remodelling something of nature to serve the purposes of art. Yet a more ambivalent treatment of this theme would be hard to find. A striking feature of this poem is its portrayal of Pan as the embodiment of a crude, boisterous adolescent masculinity, prone to carefree acts of violence against nature:

> What was he doing, the great god Pan,
>   Down in the reeds by the river?
> Spreading ruin and scattering ban,
> Splashing and paddling with hoofs of a goat,
> And breaking the golden lilies afloat
>   With the dragon-fly on the river.
>
> (1–6)

The repetition of the phrase 'the great god Pan' in every verse but one becomes increasingly troubled with potential irony until the final verse admits:

> Yet half a beast is the great god Pan,
>   To laugh as he sits by the river,
> Making a poet out of a man:
> The true gods sigh for the cost and pain, –
> For the reed which grows nevermore again
>   As a reed with the reeds in the river.
>
> (37–42)

The poem thus betrays a great deal of anxiety about the poetic vocation. Pan is not a 'true god' and so the poetic calling is not wholly divine; furthermore, this process of making a poet out of a man is depicted as an act of violent appropriation, a violence which will in turn be repeated in the poet's every creative act. As noted, Syrinx is never named in the poem, yet this repressed portion of the myth reappears in the analogues to rape ('broken lilies') throughout the poem. The poem thus reproduces the process whereby woman is erased as individual and reified as nature, to become matter for art. Thus far Barrett Browning's poem seems completely at odds with Michael Field's version of Syrinx finding 'safe recess' in nature. However, both poems, in a radical strategy, make Syrinx the poet. Yet at what cost? Again in both poems, it is figured as life-in-death: 'hacked and hewed' (15) into a 'poor dry empty thing' (23) the reed is able, when played by Pan, to produce music so sweet it restores nature to itself (stanza vi), but not the reed – now pipe – to nature.

As Mermin argues, Barrett Browning's poem 'significantly revises previous English versions of the myth [of Pan and Syrinx]. English poets had made Pan, not Syrinx, their symbol of the artist' (243). This shifts the focus of the myth-as-metaphor to 'a female, or even feminist, point of view' (244), where art is created out of 'sexual pain' (243). That is, in contrast to male poets' identification with Pan as the primary artist, Barrett Browning's identification is with the reed (Syrinx). A consequence of this, I would add, is that her metaphor for poethood stresses the poet's subjection to a primary creator, for whom the poet is merely a channel; her emphasis falls on the poet as created, in the first instance, rather than creator. In this way her poem is imbued with the Christian poetic which motivated her earlier poem 'The Dead Pan',[15] even while its depiction of the creative act as essentially violent seems less consonant with Christianity. The depiction of Pan complicates the poem's sexual politics, especially the notion of Barrett Browning's identification with Syrinx. The violence which brings her own poem into being is above all signalled by its erasure of Syrinx, an act which represents her own partial identification with Pan; that is, as a woman poet her identity is split between Pan and Syrinx, creator and created.[16]

The poem's disavowal of Syrinx is furthered by gendering the poet/reed masculine. On this subject Mermin writes: 'In "A Musical Instrument" the reed is a figure for the poet, and as such pronomially [*sic*] male (Barrett Browning always refers to poets with the generic 'he', even in *Aurora Leigh*), but in the imagery, feeling and action as well as in the well-known myth the reed is female (242).' For Mermin, then, the masculine gendering of the poet is a blind for a female agenda. Yet the masculine gendering of the poet generates other meanings also. For example, the rape metaphorized in the poem could also be read as male rape. The poet/pipe is, after all, a 'man' (21, 39), while Pan is traditionally of bisexual impulses. In this reading the poem registers the contemporary crisis in poetic discourse, whereby poetry was seen as an increasingly feminized art-form, yet women could not be poets, only 'poetesses'. Barrett Browning's poem participates in this confusion, suggesting that the poetic vocation involves emasculation, even castration for men – 'He cut it short, did the great god Pan, / (How tall it stood in the river!)' (19–20) – and, since the poet is a 'man', masculinization for women. Appropriately, then, Pan as a god whose 'natural' form is decidedly unnatural – 'half a beast' and half a god – creates the unnatural poet-man, severed from humanity's common lot: 'the reed which grows nevermore again / As a reed with the reeds in the river' (41–2). Or what is even more unnatural, the woman poet who, as author of the poem, becomes, like Syrinx, the poem's absent presence.

The project of feminization in which 'A Musical Instrument' and Michael Field's 'To Christina Rossetti' engage – two poems which bracket Rossetti's public career – can be seen as a logical, if radical, extension of Victorian poetic discourse, in which the figure of woman frequently represents the marginalized male poet. Yet a constraining feature of this radicalness is the ideological construction of 'feminine' and 'masculine' which these poems reproduce: making Syrinx the poet – that is, reclaiming a woman's fate for a 'poet's right' – changes the emphasis but not the structure of this myth of poetic creativity. The yoking of woman and poet via the trope of the channel cuts both ways for the woman poet. On the one hand it gives her the right to be a poet; on the other, it uncovers the split or 'doubled identification'[17] in which she is both subject and object of her poem.

NOTES

1   *The Academy*, no. 1248 (4 April 1896): 284.
2   I retain throughout my discussion the pseudonym 'Michael Field' in full, rather than contracting it to the patronymic 'Field', in order to keep it conspicuously, significantly double-barrelled, and to highlight its problematic relation to a masculine poetic identity, masking as it does the collaborative authorship of two women, Katherine Bradley and Edith Cooper.
3   George Herbert, 'Affliction' (1974: 105).
4   Matilda is 'the lovely lady' who is the precursor of Beatrice in the *Purgatorio* 28, and, it later becomes apparent, her friend and attendant (Dante 1985).
5   *Adonais*, ll. 370–1 (Shelley 1967: 441).
6   Celeste M. Schenck 1986: 15, 22.
7   As Antony Harrison has pointed out to me, Schenck's argument also breaks down for both Barrett Browning's and Rossetti's elegies for L.E.L.. See 'L.E.L.'s Last Question' (Browning 1974: 178); and 'L.E.L.' (Rossetti 1979–90: 1. 153).
8   In Ovid's *Metamorphoses*, Daphne is described as 'fleeing the very word "lover"' (1986: 41).
9   Browning 1900; 1974: 438.
10 'I am Christian, pagan, pantheist' declared Katherine Bradley (although both she and Cooper converted to Catholicism in later life). See Mary Sturgeon (1922: 47).
11 See especially David A. Kent (1987: 250–73), and Catherine Musello Cantalupo (1987: 274–300).
12 'Ultimately', writes Antony Harrison, 'it is the Dantean contexts for Rossetti's poetry that allow us to arrive at some holistic view of her work, which seems, at the superficial level, to be divided into secular and religious categories' (1988: 159).
13 Gilbert and Gubar 1979: 575.
14 Mermin 1989: 242.

15 For a discussion which connects 'The Dead Pan' with 'A Musical Instrument'
    see Angela Leighton 1992: 112–113.
16 Of course, such a split identification is present in the work of male poets also,
    only a whole tradition of poetic language has developed in order to shore up the
    male poet's identity as creator and to repress and displace his identity as created
    on to Nature and Woman.
17 Mermin, 'Foreword', *Christina Rossetti: The Poetry of Endurance* by Dolores
    Rosenblum (Carbondale, 1986), p. xiii.

16

A Music of Thine Own: Women's Poetry – an Expressive Tradition?

Isobel Armstrong

Precursors

The altar, 'tis of death! for there are laid
The sacrifice of all youth's sweetest hopes.
It is a dreadful thing for woman's lip
To swear the heart away; yet know that heart
Annuls the vow while speaking, and shrinks back
From the dark future which it dares not face.
The service read above the open grave
Is far less terrible than that which seals
The vow that binds the victim, not the will:
For in the grave is rest.

(Letitia Landon [L.E.L])[1]

Swept into limbo is the host
   Of heavenly angels, row on row;
The Father, Son, and Holy Ghost,
   Pale and defeated, rise and go.
The great Jehovah is laid low,
   Vanished his burning bush and rod –
Say, are we doomed to deeper woe?
   Shall marriage go the way of God?

Monogamous, still at our post,
   Reluctantly we undergo
Domestic round of boiled and roast,

> Yet deem the whole proceeding slow.
> Daily the secret murmurs grow;
>   We are no more content to plod
> Along the beaten paths – and so
>   Marriage must go the way of God.
>
> Soon, before all men, each shall toast
>   The seven strings unto his bow,
> Like beacon fires along the coast,
>   The flames of love shall glance and glow.
> Nor let nor hindrance man shall know,
>   From natal bath to funeral sod;
> Perennial shall his pleasures flow
>   When marriage goes the way of God.
>
> Grant, in a million years at most,
>   Folk shall be neither pairs nor odd –
> Alas! we sha'n't be there to boast
>   'Marriage has gone the way of God!'
>
> (Amy Levy 1915)[2]

It is not difficult to find, from the beginning to the end of the nineteenth century, poems of protest such as those by Letitia Landon, writing early in the century, and Amy Levy, writing towards the end, in which an overt sexual politics addresses the institutions and customs which burden women, including, in Levy's case, the taboo against lesbianism. There is Elizabeth Barrett Browning's outburst against the trivial education which trains women for marriage in *Aurora Leigh* (1856), and which conditions them into acceptability 'As long as they keep quiet by the fire / And never say "no" when they world says "ay"', a statement which perhaps adds another kind of complexity to Robert Browning's 'By the Fire-side' (1855).[3] There is Christina Rossetti's passionate wish to be a 'man',[4] and as one moves later into the century there are, if possible, fiercer expressions of protest in the work of poets such as Augusta Webster and Mathilde Blind. And yet the poems by Landon and Levy are as interesting for their differences as for their common theme. For Landon marriage is a terminal moment which requires the language of sacrifice and victim. For Levy, the end of marriage and the 'law' of God still leaves a patriarchy intact, for it is men who benefit from promiscuity, not women, and the narrow coercions of heterosexual pairing continue. Ironically, a world without marriage still goes 'The way of God' by perpetuating His patriarchal ways informally.

Yet it is too easy to describe the work of these very different women as a women's tradition based on a full frontal attack on oppression. Though such an attack undoubtedly often existed, a concentration on moments of overt protest can extract the content of a direct polemic about women's condition in a way which retrieves the protest, but not the poem. It is sometimes tempting to extrapolate such material from the poems (because they supply it in such abundance), personalizing, psychologizing or literalizing by translating this material back into what is known or constructed as socioeconomic patriarchal history in a univocal way, so that all poems become poems about women's oppression. In this way the nature of the particular language and form of individual poems becomes obliterated by the concentration on a single theme.

Similarly, the same kind of difficulty attends the construction of a women's tradition according to a unique modality of feminine experience. For this would be to accept the distinction between two kinds of gender-based experience, male and female, and leaves uninvestigated a conventional, affective account of the feminine as a nature which occupies a distinct sphere of feeling, sensitivity and emotion quite apart from the sphere of thought and action occupied by men. This *was* a distinction frequently made by women poets themselves and by male critics in the nineteenth century, but it is necessary to be wary of it because, while it gave women's writing a very secure place in literary culture, it amounts to a kind of restrictive practice, confining the writing of women to a particular mode or genre. W. M. Rossetti, for instance, had this to say in his Preface to his edition of the poems of Felicia Hemans:

> Her sources of inspiration being genuine, and the tone of her mind being feminine in an intense degree, the product has no lack of sincerity: and yet it leaves a certain artificial impression, rather perhaps through a cloying flow of 'right-minded' perceptions of moral and material beauty than through any other defect. 'Balmy' it may be: but the atmosphere of her verse is by no means bracing. One might sum up the weak points in Mrs Hemans's poetry by saying that it is not only 'feminine' poetry (which under the circumstances can be no imputation, rather an encomium) but also 'female' poetry: besides exhibiting the fineness and charm of womanhood, it has the mono-tone of mere sex. Mrs Hemans has that love of good and horror of evil which characterize a scrupulous female mind; and which we may most rightly praise without concluding that they favour poetical robustness, or even perfection in literary form. She is a leader in that very modern phalanx of poets who persistently coordinate the impulse of sentiment with the guiding power of morals or religion. Everything must convey its 'lesson', and is indeed set forth for the sake of its

lesson: but must at the same time have the emotional gush of a
spontaneous sentiment.[5]

'Cloying', 'feminine', 'female', 'sentiment', 'lesson', 'emotional gush': not all
this vocabulary is offered in a critical spirit, though it betrays uneasiness, but
even the most cursory examination of the language here suggests the qualities
attributed to women's poetry – conventional piety, didactic feeling, emotions,
sentiment. Coventry Patmore parodies women's religious verse in *The Angel
in the House* in a way which attributes the same qualities to their work.
Honoria's pious sister entrusts a poem to the hero:

> Day after day, until today.
>   Imaged the others gone before,
> The same dull task, the weary way,
>   The weakness pardon'd o'er and o'er.
>
> The thwarted thirst, too faintly felt,
>   For joy's well nigh forgotten life,
> The restless heart, which, when I knelt,
>   Made of my worship barren strife.
>
> Ah, whence today's so sweet release,
>   This clearance light of all my care,
> This conscience free, this fertile peace,
>   These softly folded wings of prayer.
>
> This calm and more than conquering love,
>   With which nought evil dares to cope,
> This joy that lifts no glance above,
>   For faith too sure, too sweet for hope?
>
> O, happy time, too happy change,
>   It will not live, though fondly nurst!
> Full soon the sun will seem as strange
>   As now the cloud which seems dispersed.[6]

Since the hero is courting one of three sisters, this is possibly a cruel parody
of one of Anne Brontë's poems, but the conventions of women's writing were
sufficiently established for it to be a parody of the work of Letitia Landon (in
some moods), Adelaide Anne Procter or Christina Rossetti. What is
interesting about it is that it suggests that there *were* recognized conventions

established for women's verse by this time in the century (1854). Interestingly, Patmore's carefully regular quatrains pick up a *limited* assent to the sense of limit in neutrally simple religious and psychological language, a self-admonitory withdrawal from protest and a pious but none too easy recognition of the difficulties of transcending limit. His parody responds to pessimism rather than to piety, and even at the level of satire negotiates with more complex elements than the self-abnegation attributed to it by Patmore's hero.

It is probably no exaggeration to say that an account of women's writing as occupying a particular sphere of influence, and as working inside defined moral and religious conventions, helped to make women's poetry and the 'poetess' (as the Victorians termed the woman poet) respected in the nineteenth century as they never have been since. In a survey of poetry early in the century in *Blackwood's Magazine* John Wilson ('Christopher North') wrote enthusiastically of women poets, and a respectful study of British women poets appeared in 1848, *The Female Poets of Great Britain*, selected and edited by Frederic Rowton. At the end of the century Eric Robertson published his *English Poetesses* (1883). Though Robertson was less sympathetic than Rowton to women's poetry, believing that it would never equal the poetry of men, it is clear that the category of the 'poetess' was well established. Men assiduously edited women's work. Laman Blanchard edited Letitia Landon's *Life and Literary Remains* in 1841. W. M. Rossetti edited not only the work of his sister and Mrs Hemans but also Augusta Webster's *Mother and Daughter* sonnet sequence after her death (1895). Arthur Symons edited Mathilde Blind's works in 1900, with a memoir by Richard Garnett. It seems that men both enabled and controlled women's poetic production in a way that was often complex, and which requires more sustained discussion than can be given here. After a literary scandal about her association with a patron (probably William Maginn), Letitia Landon, in her early twenties, described her complete dependence on male help for the business of publication in moving terms.

> Your own literary pursuits must have taught you how little, in them, a young woman can do without assistance. Place yourself in my situation. Could you have hunted London for a publisher, endured all the alternate hot and cold water thrown on your exertions; bargained for what sum they might be pleased to give; and, after all, canvassed, examined, nay quarrelled over accounts the most intricate in the world? And again, after success had procured money, what was I to do with it? Though ignorant of business I must know I could not lock it up in a box.[7]

Like Mrs Hemans, Letitia Landon relied on her earnings for the support of her family, and so her dependence on men to gain access to the publishing world was of great importance to her.

That middle-class women were hosted by men into the literary world through editions of their work may be one explanation for our lack of knowledge of working-class women poets, who were not edited in this way. Contrary to common understanding there were working-class women poets, and they are still being discovered.[8] Those we know of tend to have survived because they supported conventional morals, such as the anonymous millgirl who wrote eloquently on the Preston lockout in 1862 but connected working-class well-being with temperance. Bamford praised Ann Hawkshaw but she seems to have been an educated poet with strong working-class connections who produced orthodox-seeming work with unusual subtexts. Her *Dionysius the Areopagite* (1842), for instance, is ostensibly about Christian conversion. Quite apart from her vision of an egalitarian heaven, the story is primarily concerned with a relationship between two women. She was an impressively strong and independent writer who wrote a series of sonnets on British history with another subtext concerned with subjugation. Her shorter poems, 'Why am I a slave?' and 'The Mother to Her Starving Child', are impressive. The slave cannot understand his exclusion from 'the white man's home': 'Who had a right to bind these limbs / And make a slave of me?' The mother is forced to wish her child dead rather than see it starve – and then to go mad with grief. The pun on the 'relief' of madness is sombre, with the ironic social meaning of 'poor relief' shadowing the psychological term.[9] Her work is exceptional. The pastoral didacticism of Louisa Horsfield, a contemporary, contrasts with it. Horsfield retrieves the natural world from the social sins of drunkenness, truancy and immorality in a more conventional way.[10] Ellen Johnston, addressing occasional poems to local bodies and factory workers, moves from awkward heroic poetry to simple ballad and cheerful dialect verse (for instance, in 'The Working Man'). Some of her love poems, particularly 'The Maniac of the Green Wood', are moving, but her work discloses the difficulties of discovering a language in which to address both a total community and a 'literary' audience.[11] Poetry by working-class women could be as didactic as that of middle-class women, if not more so.

If, then, a middle-class women's tradition is constructed by reference to the Victorian notion of what was specifically feminine in poetry, it is likely to be formed not only out of what were predominantly male categories of the female but also out of categories which were regarded as self-evident and unproblematical. This does not enable one to take the analysis of women's poetry in the nineteenth century very far. On the other hand, it is undoubtedly the case that women wrote with a sense of belonging to a particular group defined by their sexuality, and that this sense comprehends political differences and very different kinds of poetic language. Letitia Landon recognized this when she wrote, in her 'Stanzas on the Death of Mrs Hemans', that the poet had made 'A music of thine own'.[12] So it is possible, in spite of the reservations and precautionary remarks expressed above, to consider women poets in terms of a 'music' of their own.

What was the 'music' of the Victorian woman poet? It can be listened to, first, by seeing what the poetry of Letitia Landon and Mrs Hemans could have meant to later writers, for these were the poets to which a number of them looked back as precursors. Even when there seems no direct link between these earlier and later writers it does seem as if they worked within a recognizable tradition understood by them to belong to women. Secondly, this music can be listened to through the dissonances women's poetry created by making problematical the affective conventions and feelings associated with a feminine modality of experience even when, and perhaps particularly when, poets worked within these conventions. Victorian expressive theory later in the century, one of the dominant aesthetic positions of the period, created a discourse which could accommodate a poetics of the feminine. But women poets relate to it in an ambiguous way and interrogate it even while they negotiate and assent to expressive theory. It was this assimilation of an aesthetic of the feminine which enabled the woman poet to revolutionize it from within, by using it to explore the way a female subject comes into being. The doubleness of women's poetry comes from its ostensible adoption of an affective mode, often simple, often pious, often conventional. But those conventions are subjected to investigation, questioned, or used for unexpected purposes. The simpler the surface of the poem, the more likely it is that a second and more difficult poem will exist beneath it.

Letitia Landon, already a prolifically successful poet publishing in periodicals and popular album books, published her first volume of poetry in 1824, *The Improvisatrice*. It was, she wrote,

> an attempt to illustrate that species of inspiration common in Italy, where the mind is warmed from earliest childhood by all that is beautiful in Nature and glorious in Art. The character depicted is entirely Italian, a young female with all the loveliness, vivid feeling, and genius of her own impassioned land. She is supposed to relate her own history; with which are intermixed the tales and episodes which various circumstances call forth.[13]

The Troubadour: Poetical Sketches of Modern Pictures; and Historical Sketches (1825) followed, and her last volume, reiterating the Italian theme, was entitled *The Venetian Bracelet* (1829). The uncollected 'Subjects for Pictures' begins characteristically with a poem on Petrarch and Laura. The movement to Italy is taken up by Elizabeth Barrett Browning in *Aurora Leigh* (1856), and again by Christina Rossetti who in her extraordinary preface to *Monna Innominata*, as will be seen, considers the status of the Petrarchan tradition in relation to modern poetry by women. But perhaps the movement to Italy is less important in itself than the association of women's poetry with an 'impassioned land' or emotional space *outside* the definitions and circumspections of the poet's specific culture and nationality. As a child Letitia Landon invented a fantasy country located in Africa (it is the tragic irony of her career that she died there), very much as the Brontës were to do when they constructed Gondal and Angria (Angria was located in Africa), the imaginary lands from which so much of their poetry sprang. Adelaide Anne Procter's narrative poems move to Provence, Switzerland and Belgium. George Eliot's *The Spanish Gypsy* (1868) sends the heroine of the poem from the conflict between Moors and Spaniards to consolidate a Gipsy race in Africa. This need to move beyond cultural boundaries manifests itself in the work of the earlier poets as a form of historical and cultural syncretism which both juxtaposes different cultures and reshapes relationships between them. *The Improvisatrice* unfolds narratives within itself of Moorish and Christian conflict, and of Hindu suttee, for instance, which are juxtaposed. Felicia Hemans brings together British, French, Indian, German, American and Greek narratives from different historical periods in her *Records of Woman* (1828), which ends, in startling contrast to the historicized records, with an elegy on a recently dead poetess, Mary Tighe, taken as a point of reference by Landon in her elegy for Mrs Hemans. The dedication is made in a footnote, however, and the very possibility of a 'record' of woman is thus questioned.

This insistent figuring of movement across and between cultural boundaries, with its emphasis on travel, could be seen as a search for the exotic, an escape from restrictions into the 'other' of bourgeois society. Allied, as it so frequently is, with a metaphor of the prison, or of slavery, it could be seen as an attempt to transcend restrictions in fantasy, or an effort to discover a universal womanhood which transcends cultural differences. But it is rather to be associated with an attempt to discover ways of testing out the account of the feminine experienced in western culture by going outside its prescriptions. The flight across the boundary is often associated with the examination of extreme situations – of imprisonment, suffering, or captivity and slavery – and with an overdetermined emphasis on race and national culture, as if an inquiry is being conducted into the ways in which the feminine can be constituted. Mrs Hemans's elegy appears to emancipate its subject from cultural and historical determinations, but it suggests that we can only think of the poetess in this way when she is dead, and even that is problematical. The elegy has an uncanny aspect of contextlessness which makes it oddly surprising after the very specific 'records' which have preceded it.

The emphasis on the woman as traveller through the imagination can be associated with another aspect of Letitia Landon's account of the *Improvisatrice*. The poem is supposedly the utterance of a persona: it is a mask, a role-playing, a dramatic monologue; it is not to be identified with herself or her own feminine subjectivity. The simplest explanation for this is that, given the difficulties of acceptance experienced by women writers, the dramatic form is used as a disguise, a protection against self-exposure and the exposure of feminine subjectivity. But, given the insistence on speaking in another *woman*'s voice, from Mrs Hemans to Augusta Webster and Amy Levy (these last two wrote consciously as dramatic monologuists), it is worth considering further as a phenomenon. The frequent adoption of a dramatized voice by male poets in the Victorian period is, of course, to be connected with dramatic theories of poetry. But Landon's and Hemans's work predates these theories (though not, admittedly, the work of Walter Savage Landor, who might be said to have initiated the dramatic monologue if we are content to think of this as a tradition established by male writers), and it seems that such a mask is peculiarly necessary for women writers. The adoption of the mask appears to involve a displacement of feminine subjectivity, almost a travestying of femininity, in order that it can be made an object of investigation. It is interesting, for instance, that one of Charlotte Brontë's earliest known poems is a monologue by the wife of Pontius Pilate, and that Augusta Webster also wrote a miniature drama between Pilate and his wife, in which the woman's role and moral position is sharply distinguished from association with the husband, as if both are testing out the extent to which it is the woman's function to identify unquestioningly with the husband (and, of course, with orthodox Christianity).[14] A number of poems by women testifying to a refusal to be regarded as an object have been described by feminist critics, but by using a mask a woman writer is in control of her objectification and at the same time anticipates the strategy of objectifying women by being beforehand with it and circumventing masculine represen-tations.[15] This is the theme of Christina Rossetti's poem about masking, 'Winter: My Secret'. It should come as no surprise, then, that it was the women poets who 'invented' the dramatic monologue.

The projection of self into roles is not, as will be seen, really opposed to the axioms of expressive theory which assumes the projection of feeling and emotion on to or into an object, and thus it is not strange to find Letitia Landon speaking of the search for an 'impassioned land', a space for the expression of emotion. Brought up on Hume, she was fascinated by the nature of sensation (often isolating moments of sensation in a narrative), and with the pulsation of sympathy. She uses a metaphor of the responsively vibrating string or chord of feeling which became so common that it could perhaps hardly be said to originate with Hume, but she would certainly have found it in his work, and it recurs in her poetry with an unusual intensity. Allowing as it does of subliminal sexual meaning, it is a thoroughly feminized metaphor for her. In her elegy on Mrs Hemans, for instance, she wrote, 'Wound to a pitch too exquisite, / The soul's fine chords are wrung; / With misery and melody / They are too highly strung'. Such intense vibrations, of course, can kill, as the 'chord' becomes the result of a 'cord' or tightened string which ends sound or strangles even while it produces it. This metaphor was to resonate in women's poetry. Closely allied with it and partly deriving from it is another characteristic figure, the air. An air is a song and by association it is that which is breathed out, exhaled or expressed as breath, an expiration; and by further association it can be that which is breathed in, literally an 'influence', a flowing in, the air of the environment which sustains life; inspiration, a breathing in. All these meanings are present in the elegy, as perfume, breezes, breath or sighs, where they are figured as a responsive, finely organized feminine creativity, receptive to external influence, returning back to the world as music that has flowed in, an exhalation or breath of sound. It is the breath of the body and the breath as spirit. 'So pure, so sweet thy life has been, / So filling earth and air / with odours and with loveliness . . . And yet thy song is sorrowful, / Its beauty is not bloom; / The hopes of which it breathes, are hopes / That look beyond the tomb'.[16] Breath can dissipate, a fear peculiarly close to the Victorian woman poet. Expressive theory, as will be seen, tended to endorse and consolidate this figure. The body imprisons breath but involuntarily releases it: this is an apt figure for the release of feeling which cannot find external form.

Letitia Landon and Felicia Hemans each explore the multiplicity of roles and projections which they make available to themselves in different ways, and each takes the affective moment in different directions. A marked feature of Landon's work is the use of tenses in narrative, particularly the historic past, and the present tense used in a succession of discrete phrases to denote successive actions in the past. It is used in such a way that an action is registered, not *as* it happens but when it is either just over or just about to happen. Effects often precede causes. Seen in this way the agent is oddly detached from actions in the slight hiatus when actions are seen but not the agent's acting of them. Such a procedure makes uncertain how far the woman is in responsible control of cause and effect – she seems to *suffer* rather than to act. The woman herself seems to be displaced from action into the psychic experience existing in the gap between actions, and the whole weight of these lyrical narratives is thrown on the temporal space of the affective moment, the emotional space occurring just before or just after something has happened. In 'The Indian Bride', for instance, the girl's prenuptial journey alone on the Ganges is presented in moments which are either over or which precede their causes: 'She has lighted her lamp . . . The maiden is weeping. Her lamp has decayed'.[17] The reunion with the lover follows the same syntactic pattern: 'Hark to the ring of the cymeter! . . . The warfare is over, the battle is won . . . And Zaide hath forgotten in Azim's arms / All her so false lamp's falser alarms'. But the lamp is and is not 'false'. The bridegroom dies and she goes deterministically to her death: 'A prayer is muttered, a blessing said, – / Her torch is raised! – she is by the dead. / She has fired the pile'.[18] The tenses both obliterate and sharply question, through this strategy of detachment, by whose agency the girl goes to her death, her own, or the mores of cultural ritual. Before this the narrator has analysed the moment of acute superstitious fear when the girl is on the Ganges without light in tenses which blur the distinction between what does happen and what will happen: 'How the pulses will beat, and the cheek will be dy'd'.[19] This becomes not only a description of the girl's immediate emotional present but also a *prediction* of the future. The affective moment is in the right and the wrong place, describing the girl's immediate fears, proleptically describing the emotions of her death. But the ambiguous status of the tenses proffering the moment of feeling suggests that the girl, or the lamp, was right after all. The irrational affective moment could be trusted, and retrospectively it expands to include her death. The tenses here foreground and investigate a world of intense sensation and emotion and implicitly ask what its place in experience is.

Landon wrote many poems which pictured pictures, freezing women in a static but intense moment just before or just after an event (usually an event of communal significance) has occurred. They become objects whose life is in suspension, waiting for a critical event to occur either through their own or someone else's agency, or else waiting choicelessly. But whether dependent or independent, it is as if emotion and sensation rush in to fill the vacuum of subjectivity. Whether feeling is precipitated by action or whether action is precipitated by feeling seems to be the question such poems raise. Whether consciousness is determined by feeling or action, and what it is when there is no action to be taken at all, and where choice is limited by cultural prescription, is at issue. 'Subjects for Pictures', for instance, considers the woman as subject, often subordinate to men, in innumerable variations on the theme of choice, alternating enclosed environments with open landscapes, moving from history to history, culture to culture, ritual to ritual, myth to myth, marriage, death, murder, revival. These are all studies in the dislocation between consciousness and action, where the subject is placed remorselessly in fixed locations, immobilized by ritual or vigil. In what way the moment of feeling relates to or is determined by the rituals of a culture is a problem which fascinates Landon.

Whether Letitia Landon's figures belong to cultural rituals or place themselves in a transgressive relation to them they are almost always at the mercy of passion. Accused of an excessive preoccupation with love, Landon defended herself by arguing for what is effectively a politics of the affective state: 'A highly cultivated state of society must ever have for concomitant evils, that selfishness, the result of indolent indulgence, and that heartlessness attendant on refinement, which too often hardens while it polishes'.[20] The choice of love as a theme can 'soften' and 'touch' and 'elevate'. 'I can only say, that for a woman, whose influence and whose sphere must be in the affections, what subject can be more fitting than one which it is her peculiar province to refine, to spiritualise, and exalt? . . . making an almost religion of its truth . . . woman, actuated by an attachment as intense as it is true, as pure as it is deep', is more 'admirable' as a heroine. For as she is in art, so she is 'in actual life'.[21] If Landon appears to be completely accepting the sentimental terms in which women were seen, she is turning them to moral and social account and arguing that women's discourse can soften what would now be called the phallocentric hardness and imaginative deficiencies of an overcivilized culture. It is as if she has taken over the melting softness of Burke's category of the 'beautiful', which he saw as an overrefined and 'feminine' principle in contradistinction to the strenuous labour of the 'sublime', and reappropriated it as a moral category which can dissolve overcivilized hardness. Burke associated beauty with nostalgia for a condition which we have 'irretrievably lost'.[22] In particular its nature is questioned and explored when it hovers over that last situation occasioning the last rituals of a culture, death.

Her own early death, which seems to have been the result of an accidental overdose of poison, self-administered to cure a palsy, occasioning scandal and suspicion as her life had done, made her the Keats (or perhaps the Sylvia Plath) of women's poetry. Witty, exuberant and unconventional, and like Mrs Hemans a vigorous and energetic intellectual (just before she died she wrote to ask her brother to send to Africa '"Thiers's History of the Revolution", in French, and all George Sand's works . . . send me also Lamb's works'),[23] she was seen as a seminal figure by later writers.

Rather than exploring what cultural ritual does to the feminine subject, Mrs Hemans figures the flight beyond it, and the condition of extremity and disintegration which occurs when constraints press upon consciousness. Her method is inward and psychological where Landon's is external and classical, but it is just as analytical, turning the expressive moment towards investigation and critique. The heroic rebel and the conformist stand in dialectical relationship to one another in her work, each in dialogue with the other as each is pushed to extremity. The archetypes of her work are represented in the first section of *Records of Woman*, 'Arabella Stuart', and 'Casabianca', a short poem about an episode occurring in the battle of the Nile. 'Arabella Stuart' is a monologue spoken in imprisonment by a woman whose disintegrating mind struggles, and fails, to make the past coherent. The meaning of her history collapses. It is this, as much as the endurance of immediate confinement, which dissolves her reason (though an implicit question here is what 'reason' means). Hers was a political imprisonment (she died in captivity), made at the instigation of James I after a secret marriage and an attempted flight to France. Arabella does not know what has happened to her husband, or whether he has deserted her. The monologue opens with a memory.

> 'Twas but a dream! I saw the stag leap free,
>   Under the boughs where early birds were singing;
> I stood o'ershadowed by the greenwood tree,
>   And heard, it seemed, a sudden bugle ringing
> Far through a royal forest. Then the fawn
> Shot, like a gleam of light, from grassy lawn
> To secret covert; and the smooth turf shook,
> And lilies quivered by the glade's lone brook,
> And young leaves trembled, as, in fleet career,
> A princely band, with horn, and hound, and spear,
> Like a rich masque swept forth. I saw the dance
> Of their white plumes, that bore a silvery glance
> Into the deep wood's heart; and all passed by
> Save one – I met the smile of *one* clear eye,
> Flashing out joy to mine. Yes, *thou* wert there,
> Seymour![24]

A superficial glance at this text will immediately register what appears to be a slightly mannered Keatsian diction followed by the faintly absurd address to Seymour. 'Yes, *thou* wert there'. But women's poetry deliberately risked absurdity, as Christina Rossetti was later to see. In the extremity of the memory it is precisely important that the lover was *there*, as he is *not* in the present moment of the voice speaking from prison. The diction is used to render the vestigial, uncertain and discontinuous retrieval by memory of an event which even then may have been a dream and 'seemed' (there is a double 'seeming', the event and the memory of it) like a masque. The movement of the eye and of light is uncertain, the gaze fleeting, as the mere insignia of the helmet plumes 'glance' into the wood, with a superficial lightness whose pun on glance/gaze casts doubt on the clear eye which gazes at the woman. And if Seymour was not 'there', it is not clear 'where' the woman is either, as her gaze is constantly displaced from stag to fawn to quivering lilies (aroused *and* fearful sexuality), to huntsmen, plumes and lover. Though stag and fawn stand as conventionalized proleptic figures of the hunted woman's condition later in her story (the syntax allows that both stag and woman are 'Under the boughs'), she is not quite identified with either, or symbolically split between both, as they escape to different hiding places. This split condition is a function of her imprisoned consciousness, but it appears to be just as much a condition of her freedom: she stood isolated, 'o'ershadowed' by the tree, subject and metaphorically imprisoned even when her isolation seemed to make possible the rebellious independence of the secret love affair and marriage. These are the bitter insights disclosed by a fracturing consciousness whose mind and history disintegrate simultaneously. The bitterness, indeed, rests precisely on an awareness that the rebellion was in fact in conformity with a romantic paradigm which failed to work.

Like the woman in 'Arabella Stuart' who 'stood' transfixed under the greenwood tree, the boy in 'Casabianca' 'stood' on the burning deck, and in both cases the word seems to denote positioning outside the control of the character. The boy is subject to commands, standing ground and withstanding the assault of battle in absolute obedience to the father's orders, responding unquestioningly to the law of the father. Ostensibly this is a tale of the heroism of simple obedience of son to father. But in the oedipal fiasco the heroism of absolute obedience is misplaced, for the dead father, beneath the deck, like the unconscious, is 'Unconscious of his son', and 'His voice no longer heard'. Consummately, Hemans transposes the terror of a condition of not knowing and hearing to the father, marking the tragic irony of the son's situation, for it is he who rather 'no longer heard' his father's voice, but continues to obey that voice from the past when it no longer sounds in the present. But at a deeper level, the law of the father is founded on its imperviousness to the son's voice, begging for a relaxation of its commands. In the culminating destruction we are enjoined to 'Ask of the winds' (like the boy to his father) which 'strewed the sea' with 'fragments', what became of the son, who is burned and blown to pieces through the act of blind obedience. The voice of the 'natural' elements may, or may not, perhaps, operate with analogous laws as fierce as those of patriarchal imperatives (the voices of the father and the wind are set questioningly against one another), but the natural certainly wreaks as much havoc as the human law, whether they can be differentiated from one another or not. For a frightening moment the 'fragments' seem parts of the boy's body, resolve themselves into mast, helm and pennon 'That well had borne their part', in the final stanza, and then as frighteningly, with all the referential hazardousness of metaphor, become metonymic hints of fragmented phallic parts. The absoluteness of the patriarchal imperative is absolutely ravaging in its violence. There is a kind of exultation in this violent elegy about the way phallic law destroys itself: at the same time the boy's 'heart', both his courage and the centre of his being, the identity bound up with the patriarchal imperatives of heroism, has 'perished'. The remorselessness which separates out 'part' and 'heart' and rhymes them to suggest the way masculine identity is founded, also recognizes that this is a law to the death, killing a child on a burning deck. The unmentioned element in this masculine tragedy is the mother, but, with its constant reminder that this is the death of a child (he was 13), victim of the crucial Napoleonic battle of the Nile, the voice of the poem is gendered as female and thus brings war and sexual politics together. It is at once a deeply affective lament and a strangely Medaean lyric of castigation — and castration — which takes its revenge on war even as it sees that war takes revenge on itself.

Casabianca

The boy stood on the burning deck
    Whence all but he had fled;
The flame that lit the battle's wreck
    Shone round him o'er the dead.

Yet beautiful and bright he stood,
    As born to rule the storm —
A creature of heroic blood,
    A proud, though child-like form.

The flames rolled on — he would not go
    Without his Father's word;
That Father, faint in death below,
    His voice no longer heard.

He called aloud: — 'Say, Father, say
    If yet my task is done!'
He knew not that the chieftain lay
    Unconscious of his son.

'Speak, Father!' once again he cried,
    'If I may yet be gone!'
And but the booming shots replied,
    And fast the flames rolled on.

Upon his brow he felt their breath,
    And in his waving hair,
And looked from that lone post of death
    In still yet brave despair;

And shouted but once more aloud,
    'My Father! must I stay?'
While o'er him fast, through sail and shroud,
    The wreathing fires made way.

They wrapt the ship in splendour wild,
    They caught the flag on high,
And streamed above the gallant child
    Like banners in the sky.

There came a burst of thunder sound —
    The boy — oh! where was he?
Ask of the winds that far around
    With fragments strewed the sea! —

With mast, and helm, and pennon fair,
    That well had borne their part;
But the noblest thing which perished there
    Was that young faithful heart![25]

The Poetics of Expression

Hemans wrote overtly of politics, of Greece, emigration, the Pilgrim Fathers
(the first 'trade unionists'), and declared a Byronic response to liberty. But
the politics of women's poetry in this century cannot necessarily be associated
with the uncovering of particular political positions but rather with a set of
strategies or negotiations with conventions and constraints. It is remarkable
how resourcefully the three Brontës, each of them highly individual writers
(though Anne and Charlotte at least, politically conservative), follow Mrs
Hemans in exploring consciousness under duress, imprisoned within limit,
or how Anne Adelaide Procter (to be associated with radical thinking in the
mid-century) follows Letitia Landon in exploring the alien rituals of another
culture in her tales, and the demands of either moral or affective conventions
in her shorter lyrics. It is not necessary to assume a direct relationship
between these poets, though in some cases that can be ascertained, to see that
they share common strategies. They also share a capacity to produce a poem

with a simple moral or emotional surface which actually probes more complex questions than its simplicity suggests. Three poems by the Brontës and a group of poems by Adelaide Anne Procter indicate how Victorian women poets could exploit the legacy left by late Romantic writers such as Letitia Landon and Felicia Hemans, in particular the poem of the affective moment and its relation to moral convention and religious and cultural constraint. This will suggest the basis on which a women's tradition can be constructed – necessarily briefly in a chapter of this length – and provide an introduction to the way in which expressive theory could be allied with a feminine poetics.

Anne Brontë, a poet of great subtlety and far wider range than is often thought, negotiated the sobriety of the religious and didactic lyric to suggest precisely where its conventions are most painful and intransigent by *not* breaking these conventions, but by simply following through their logic. In this way a poem on the inevitability of suffering can end with a challenge to God either to provide the strength to endure or to release the sufferer through death ('If this be all'). 'Song' ('We know where deepest lies the snow'), a poem on the inevitability of oppression even when master and slave, hunters and hunted, reverse their positions and displace one another, chooses the trembling life of the hare rather than the cruelty of the hounds, and ends almost triumphantly by asserting the knowledge that only oppression can bring. Intransigently, it refuses the knowledge brought by power. But it is in a more overtly conventional poem such as 'The Arbour' that her gift for turning an orthodox position can be seen. It is a pastoral poem both of the affective moment and the moral lesson. It depends on the discovery of a deceptive perceptual and psychological experience which is withheld from the understanding of the reader in the same way that the discovery of the writer's mistake is delayed until it is recognized. The security, protection and fecundity of an arbour, with its 'thickly clustering' trees, 'green and glossy leaves', sunshine and blue sky, prompts a moment of release into emotion and reverie, in which the past becomes imbued with autumnal pleasure and the future invested with the fulfilment of summer: memory and desire are devoid of pain. But a perceptual trick or misprision has occurred; what has seemed 'summer's very breath' occurs when 'snow is on the ground'; 'How can I think of scenes like these?'

> 'Tis but the *frost* that clears the air,
> And gives the sky that lovely blue;
> They're smiling in a *winter's* sun,
> Those evergreens of sombre hue.
>
> And winter's chill is on my heart –
> How can I dream of future bliss?

How can my spirit soar away
Confined by such a chain as this?[26]

The conclusion reproaches the speaker for factitious sentiment, which attaches feeling to conventional metaphors of the seasons and provides an escape into fantasy from the demands of the chill winter present. Nevertheless it is an interrogative conclusion: 'How can. . . . How can . . .' not only implies the reproach, how could I?, but also asks the question, how is it possible?; it may well be that it is the moral reproach which is profoundly conventional and narrow, refusing the possibility of imaginative transformation and accepting the orthodox symbolism of winter as constraint, restriction and dearth too facilely. For the frost and the winter's sun *were* transforming. Shifting slightly the context of the feminine metaphor of breath and breathing, Anne Brontë allows that the 'whispering' of boughs 'through the air' (8) may not have been 'summer's very breath' (17), but they nevertheless nourished the body and soul, enabling the ear to 'drink[s] in' sound, and the soul to 'fly away', a statement repeated and modulated in the last stanza when the 'spirit', another form of breath, can 'soar away'. The confinement of the frosty arbour – 'Confined by such a chain as this' – is seen in two ways by the end of the poem. The wintry enclosure is a material imprisonment, holding the soul in thrall. On the other hand it is a paradoxical context of rebirth, in which the soul can soar precisely because it is chained to the material world whose wintry 'evergreens' may be more reliable auguries than the transient leaves of summer. In this context the words 'confined' and 'chain' strangely dislodge the connotation of imprisonment and take on the generative implications of the womb and the birth cord in another feminine pun on the cord which tethers and the chord from which the breath or air of life and of music is created. This seemingly docile poem is a sustained pun on the sense of confinement as imprisonment and confinement as gestation in the womb, one sterile, the other creative.

Confinement is the structural figure in both Charlotte Brontë's 'The Lonely Lady' and in Emily Brontë's 'Enough of Thought, Philosopher', though they work respectively through psychologized experience and symbol. Charlotte Brontë's poem is ostensibly a study in 'Mariana'-like hysteria and unreciprocated sexual desire. Confined and alone, insomniac, weary with the women's tasks of lace-making and music-making, the tension of the lady's feeling is expressed through the 'quivering strings' of the harp she abandons. The intensity of her emotion meets no recognition, and, in a brilliant verbal displacement, this condition is externalized in the sounds of the clock which mechanically records time and listens to itself doing so, and to the *cessation* of its own responses which vibrate – the characteristic feminine metaphor appears again – to nothing: 'the clock with silver chime did say / The number of the hour, and all in peace / Listened to hear its own vibration cease' (6–8).[27] The setting sun casts a lurid, blood-red crimson blush on the lady's face, and until the last stanza this appears to be the psychological counterpart of violent feeling which can only return upon itself. In the last stanza an army in battle, too, 'leagues away' (40), sees the sunset. 'The last ray tinged with blood' (45), and the way in which the light gives all the features of the landscape the semblance of gore, just as it had to the features of the lady's face. But the sunset is no longer simply the extension of hysterical feminine sexuality. The syntax of the last stanza affirms that the literal burning of the battle is the cause of the bloody light. The lady's hysteria is accounted for by her anxiety and ignorance as to the state of the battle. And yet there is no simple distinction here between feminine emotion and masculine violence. Feminine sexuality becomes horribly dependent upon and implicated in male aggression and warfare. It is the battle, certainly, which makes the sunset not a symbolic but a literal portent of disaster, and it is the raging battle which has caused the lady's isolation: yet she is committed to a vicarious experience of it in which hysteria and warfare have an uncanny affinity. The metaphor gives them a blood relationship.

Emily Brontë's poem rages too, but again simple opposition is deceptive, and a poem which appears to be caught in a familiar dilemma, a 'cruel strife' between 'vanquished Good' and 'victorious ill', actually breaks the restrictions of this confining oppositional and binary terminology altogether. 'The Philosopher' is a monologue which includes a dialogue within itself, and this makes problematic the 'identity' which the poem longs to lose.[28] 'O for the time when I shall sleep / Without identity' (stanza 2). Identity means both that which is in unity with itself and without difference and that which is uniquely different and the founder of difference. The Philosopher who speaks these lines is an aspect of the speaker's self, and the 'I' which resounds through the poem splits and fragments into separate experiences and definitions. The Philosopher describes a vision of a 'Spirit' in contradistinction to the listening 'man' or speaker, and the 'man' or speaker replies by addressing the Philosopher as 'seer', assimilating him to spirit and juxtaposing the two terms — 'And even for that spirit, seer, / I've watched and sought my lifetime long' (stanza 5). 'Man' appears to comprehend seer, philosopher and spirit just as philosopher comprehends seer, spirit, man. Thus the speaker's earlier statement (stanza 3) that 'Three gods, within this little frame, / Are warring, night and day' becomes easier to understand. And similarly, the second stanza's fierce assertion that the stark Manichean opposition between heaven and hell are categories whose simple dualism cannot contain the energies of desire or will is related to this. But the identity is violently at war, it seems, precisely because a universe founded on rigid categories of binary difference constantly excludes the third term. The narrator him or herself is also committed to the epistemology of opposition, so habitual is it, seeking the 'spirit', or breath, in 'heaven, hell, earth and air', and thus, not surprisingly, 'always wrong' (stanza 5). In the same way the narrator has earlier brought 'spirit' and 'man' into relationship but excluded 'woman', the unmentioned term of the poem. The vision of the spirit, on the contrary, offers a revelation of another universe, a world of 'three rivers' 'Of equal depth, and equal flow'. The rigid antitheses are broken. These are rivers of gold, blood and sapphire, retaining prismatic difference but transformed from their black confluence to the unifying whiteness of light by the spirit's agency. The specific symbolism of these rivers, reaching back to *Revelation*, matters less, perhaps, than their triple nature, their capacity to include the third term. Gold, sapphire and blood could signify Father, Son and ungendered Holy Ghost, or spirit, matter and the human, or divine, satanic and human, or androgyne, male and female. What matters is that the violence of a universe constituted through rigid categories of difference, whether spiritual, moral or sexual, needs to be 'lost'. The spirit, which is also comprehended in 'this living breath' (stanza 5) of the narrator and by the 'air' of earth is otherwise murderous and destructive. There seems to be an attempt to remove the 'spirit' and 'this living breath' from the categories of gender and a refusal to consent to the 'feminine' associations of this figure. On the other hand, the powerful energies of Emily Brontë's poetry, which push the hymn-like form of her stanzas towards violence, tend to reaffirm terrible alternatives despite the move to the third term — heaven or hell, spirit or man, male or female, a gendered or an ungendered world: the negations sound with the force of affirmation, and the affirmations with the force of negations.

Adelaide Anne Procter, writing between the mid-1840s and the 1860s, takes up the figures and forms associated with the thematizing of feminine issues and virtually typifies the woman poet's interests at this time. Like Mrs Hemans before her and like her contemporaries, Dora Greenwell and Elizabeth Barrett Browning, she wrote of political matters, particularly on the oppression and the suffering of the poor (for instance, 'The Cradle Song of the Poor', 'The Homeless Poor') and on the complexities of the master-slave relationship (for instance 'King and Slave'). She also wrote some magnificently humane lyrics on the Crimean war, refusing superficial heroism and narrow patriotism ('The Lesson of the War', 'The Two Spirits'). Like Letitia Landon, she worked with the external narrative poem and with the didactic lyric. Her narrative poems, dealing with the movement beyond the boundary, with escape, with ex-patriotism and return, are deeply preoccupied with displacement, and through this with the woman's 'place' or displacement in a culture. As so often with women writers, the more conventional the didactic lyric, the more accepting of its conventions the writer is, the more it can be used as a way of looking at conformity from within. Writing with a boldly simple directness and immediacy, Adelaide Anne Procter developed increasing strength here. A series of lyrics redefines the emotional space of sexual love arrestingly, by a conventional refusal of the role of exclusively sexual passion in a love relationship with a man in a way which outflanks conventionality. Neither 'A Parting' nor 'A Woman's Answer' retreats to celibacy or virginity as an alternative to marriage. 'Parting' thanks the man who has rejected the woman's passion and, half ironically, half seriously, expresses gratefulness for a 'terrible awaking'. The poem conventionally redirects desire towards divine love; but that desire is explicitly affirmed as the intense power of sexual love, 'all too great to live except above'.[29] It is neither sublimated nor repressed. 'A Woman's Answer' professes to promiscuity by redefining love as intense libidinal passion in many spheres – for knowledge, the natural world, art, books (*Aurora Leigh* in particular) – and not simply the sphere of sexual love. 'Envy', a terse, abruptly economical lyric, is another poem which expresses a conventional moral position, but dramatically turns the commonplace. The speaker is envious of envy, always losing to him: 'He was the first always: Fortune / Shone bright in his face. / I fought for years; with no effort / He conquered the place'. Envy wins the competition every time, and even dies first: 'God help me! / While he is at rest, / I am cursed still to live; – even / Death loved him best'.[30] The startling combat with envy comes about because it is both a traditional Christian allegorical combat *against* envy, an attempt to defeat a moral and psychological condition, and a representation of envy itself, a jealous fight *with* envy for possession of all that we envy – success, mastery, recognition – on envy's own terms. This constantly reproduces jealousy even when it is seemingly 'conquered'. Even the death of jealousy is something to be jealous of. Envy, the successful combatant, is gendered as 'him'; the speaker is a shadowy other, the bleeding subject of loss, the one 'without', even to the extent of being without a coffin. Ironically Envy engenders envy, and the *speaker* is actually forced to become the personification of envy. The submerged phallic symbolism here testifies savagely to the dominance of male power and to the *anger* of loss.

Adelaide Anne Procter began her writing career by publishing in *Household Words* and *All the Year Round*, journals which were associated with popular radicalism, and was converted to Roman Catholicism in 1851. Tractarian or Anglo-Catholic aesthetics, enunciated through Keble in particular, paid special attention to developing an expressive theory of poetry as the vehicle of hidden emotion, and that may be why Procter's poetry takes up the feminized expressive figures of the musical vibration as the epitome of feeling, and breath or breathing, air and spirit, as the representation of the imprisoned life of emotion needing to escape or to take form. Her poems of displacement, and the exploration of the 'place' of women in several senses, particularly 'A Tomb in Ghent', provide a context for the exploration of expressive feeling and its relation to the feminine and lead to a fuller consideration of the importance of expressive aesthetics to women's poetry. This is required especially for the work of Dora Greenwell, Christina Rossetti and Jean Ingelow, who seem to have been consciously aware of this theory as a problematic model of the feminine.

The longer narrative poems frequently use travel and change of place to examine the degree to which institutions are capable of flexibility. In 'Homeward Bound', a long-lost sailor, anticipating Tennyson's *Enoch Arden* (1864) returns to find his wife with another man and his child and refuses to claim her back rather than endanger her happiness or reputation. A mother transposed from one environment to another sacrifices her child to a second marriage in 'The Sailor Boy', a motif of the second marriage also explored in 'A New Mother'. In 'A Legend of Provence', a novice elopes with a wounded knight but returns to her place when marriage fails. An exiled Tyrolean girl returns to her country from Switzerland to warn of the Swiss intention to attack Austria in 'A Legend of Bregenz'. The return to roots, the testing out of the limits of the shaping and determining agencies in a culture, these seem to be at the heart of the narrative poems.

'A Tomb in Ghent' charts the commitment to a new culture by a skilled mechanic who has emigrated to Belgium, and an enforced withdrawal from it by his granddaughter, who returns to England when her father dies, attempting to find a place, to be assimilated into what is now an alien culture. This unsolved dilemma forms the frame to the story of her parents who achieve, it seems, a kind of self-expression, communication and mutuality unknown either to their parents or their children. The tale is prefaced by the legend of the dragon given to Bruges but stolen by Ghent. The story goes that the dragon will one day spread its wings and return to Palestine, where the Crusaders stole it. The legend within the legend achieves a number of purposes: exactly where the dragon belongs, and to whom, is problematical; it is displaced, like the characters, and implicitly questions the idea of the nation and the boundary. Its status as military trophy also questions the martial values and gender-bound rituals of war. The exiled son abrogates conventional roles and releases his own being through music, eventually playing the organ in the great cathedral. Music in this poem replaces the flight of the dragon and its aggression with the feminized flight of sound, analogy for the language of the spirit, a flight parallel but antithetical to that of the totem of war. Waves of sound break 'at heaven's door' bearing 'the great desire' of spiritual feeling on 'eagle wings'.[31] The expressive figuring of the feminine is associated with a male experience, but in fact this expression is enabled or inspired by the statue at the 'White

Maiden's Tomb'. The player can make the organ 'answer' and 'thrill with master-power the breathless throng' — give the congregation breath or inspiration — because he in turn is handed passion through the 'expectant' statue who 'holds her breath' with parted lips, and through the wife who is an image of the statue. Again the figure is many-sided in its implications.[32] There is a frank assimilation of mystical and musical experience to sexuality: on the one hand male creativity emerges out of female silence and becomes its gift; on the other hand the gift is returned to the woman as song, and the daughter is endowed with the power of expressive singing. Music, or the 'air', literally circulates in and between the group and the congregation, cancelling the fixities of gender and social division and releasing the stony categories from their rigidity. Momentarily, in an alien country and in the safe space of the cathedral, expressive song reconfigures relationships — but only in a place of safety untouched by national boundaries rather than transcending them.

But there are a number of poems — some of her finest — in which Adelaide Anne Procter writes with anxiety about the nature of expression. 'A Lost Chord' is the perfect harmony which eludes discovery; 'Hush!' turns on the deathly silence which displaces the sounds envisaged by the internal imagination; 'Unexpressed' speaks of the failure of articulation and the ephemeral nature of language, which dissipates and recedes 'Like sighings of illimitable forests, / And waves of an unfathomable sea'.[33] In 'Words', language is so fragile — 'the rose-leaf that we tread on / Will outlive a word' — and yet so powerful that it can transform the course of a life.[34] Nevertheless words can remain imprisoned in the self, and though each has its own 'spirit' or breath it is externalized only as *echo*, as representation without substance, dissociated from its hidden originary experience, the shadow of a sound, inveterately secondary. Thus the expressive moment is by no means unprob-lematical. The figure of overflow is warily explored by contemporaries such as Greenwell and Barrett Browning and by the slightly later poets, Rossetti and Ingelow. To see how these poets negotiate the dominant poetics of expression and deal with its ambiguities it is necessary to look more closely at the expressive aesthetic. The incipient sexual implications of the recurrent figurings of feminine discourse, the receptive vibration of the musical chord in sympathy, the exhalation or release of feeling which moves ambiguously between the body and the spirit, are present in the metaphors of expressive aesthetics, but they are given both a negative or pathological and a positive or 'healthy' signification, a hysterical and a wholesome aspect, often implicitly gendered respectively as 'feminine' and 'masculine'. Expressive theory becomes morbid either when the overflow of feeling is in excess or when it is unable to flow at all, and repressed into a secret underground life. For expressive theory is above all an aesthetics of the *secret*, the hidden experience, because the feeling which is prior to language gives language a secondary status and is often written of as if it cannot take linguistic form at all. The politics of women's poetry emerges in its transactions with this orthodoxy and, strangely, the hermeneutic problem of discerning a feminine discourse in the structure and language of a poem can be approached by addressing a theory which often tries to do without an account of language. This account of the poetics of expression is illuminated by the terms of Dora Greenwell's essay, 'Our single women', where the negative aspects of expressive aesthetics belong to the language which gives an account of the feminine.[35] The essay enables one to see how Greenwell, Barrett Browning, Rossetti and Ingelow deal with the structural implications of expressive metaphors in relation to gender, and how far later poets, Mathilde Blind, Augusta Webster and Amy Levy, were able to depart from the expressive model.

Victorian expressive theory is affective and of the emotions. It is concerned with feeling. It psychologized, subjectivized and often moralized the firm epistemological base of Romantic theory, though its warrant was in Wordsworth's spontaneous *overflow* of feeling. The idea of overflow, of projection and expression, a movement of feeling out of the self, develops metaphorically from a cognitive account of consciousness, in which mediation between subject and object was the constitutive structure of mind, and the idealist implication that the subject constructs the other as a category of mind. This can be shifted to describe projection, empathy, a moving out of the self in which the barriers and limits of selfhood are broken, a liberation of feeling almost like love, and certainly like breathing, which finds or invents forms and images to which it is attached. Expansion, movement outwards, the breaking of barriers, is the essence of poetry and the essence of *healthy* poetry. To Sydney Dobell the function of poetry is to express a mind: 'To express is to carry out'; 'to express a mind is to carry out that mind *into some equivalent*'.[36] For Arthur Hallam the movement outwards into 'energetic love for the beautiful' was a moral activity because it educated the self in a liberation from the bonds of the ego. He praised, in Tennyson's work, 'his power of embodying himself in ideal characters, or rather moods of character', so that the

> circumstances of the narration seem to have a natural correspondence with the predominant feeling, and, as it were, to be evolved from it by assimilative force . . . his vivid, picturesque delineation of objects, and the peculiar skill with which he holds all of them *fused*, to borrow a metaphor from science, in a medium of strong emotion.[37]

There is a perfect chemistry here in which empathy is called forth by objects while correspondingly subjective life moves beyond the self to fuse objects in feeling. There is also a perfect reciprocity because emotion does not master objects, and neither do objects take priority over feeling. But it is not altogether clear whether feeling is simply displaced or represented and verbalized in some way, and for some critics there is an almost inevitable hiatus between the movement of feeling and the form in which it is embodied. In 1842 G. H. Lewes quoted with approval John Stuart Mill's account of poetry from the *Monthly Repository* of 1833, where Mill assumed a disjunction between emotion and its form of expression. Poetry 'is the delineation of the deeper and more secret workings of human emotions'. It is 'feeling confirming itself to itself in moments of solitude and embodying itself in symbols which are the nearest possible representations of the feeling'.[38] The assumption is that ideally there should be a perfect match between feeling and symbol but that the correspondence is necessarily impossible and imperfect. Emotion remains secret, inaccessible, hidden. There is always a barrier to its expression. Lewes more confidently seizes on those aspects of Hegel's thinking (whose work he was reviewing) which enable him to speak of the representative medium which allows those emotions 'which fill and expand the heart' to be expressed. He quotes Hegel on mourning and the need to be 'relieved' by seeing grief in 'external form'. Tears, of course, are the model of the expressive moment, the visible, literal expression of the 'oppressed heart'.[39] He reads Hegel unashamedly as an expressive theorist but he also acknowledges that expression is bound up with repression. He thinks of Greek art, for instance, with Goethe, as a volcano burning beneath a covering of ice. Once the representation of emotion fails to be adequate to it the representation itself becomes a barrier. And this is where expressive poetics moves to the pathological. Keble's sense that the secret and hidden currents of feeling resist expression to the point of driving the poet mad, even though he had theological reasons for endorsing their repression, is not an extravagant form of expressive theory. Feeling for him is always pressing for a release which cannot be granted. One might say that the poet becomes hysterical in these circumstances, like a woman.

> What must they do? They are ashamed and reluctant to speak out, yet, if silent, they can scarcely keep their mental balance; some are said even to have become insane.[40]

The problem is accentuated for Tractarian aesthetics by the theological necessity of a due 'reserve', a refusal to bring forth an excess of feeling and an assent to hidden meaning. Keble's theory of symbol speaks of the *concealing* as well as the *revealing* nature of symbol. Christian meaning should not be carelessly *exposed* to misprision (and to democratic reading).

So there are two related aspects of Victorian accounts of expressive projection. First, if the mind cannot be 'carried out' into an equivalent of itself and find a form in representation, there will be a disjunction between the secret feelings of the mind and the form of the representation. The representation then becomes the barrier feeling is designed to break. Secondly, since the representational symbol is both the *means* of expression and the *form* of its repression, *ex*pression and *re*pression, although in conflict with one another, become interdependent. They constitute one another, so that expression is predicated upon repression. The overflow of secret and hidden feeling creates the barriers which bind and limit it, while the limits enable the overflow of feeling. This is not willingly acknowledged by the writers I have mentioned, but it follows from their thinking. Indeed, it is their willingness to construct an opposition between expression and repression rather than to allow the structural interdependence their theory implies, which accounts for the uneasiness and frustration of their thought and its ambiguities. People have noticed the superficial resemblance of this theory to Freud's account of repression, but it is radically different because it assumes a consciously *known* experience which is inexpressible because the verbal forms of language are inadequate, ineffable. Freud, on the contrary, assumed that representation is part of a symbolic structure of displacement which is a manifestation of the *unknowable* unconscious. Thus he places emphasis on the importance of the material sign or symbol where Victorian expressive theory does not. Expressive theory does have something in common, however, with Julia Kristeva's account of the opposition of the semiotic and symbolic in language. Syntax operates as a symbolic law of the paternal function in exercising grammatical and social constraints, while the instinctual drives of the semiotic and the primal processes of condensation and displacement refuse to be accommodated by the symbolic and subvert and dissolve it.[41] Kristeva is worth mentioning because she provides a way of thinking of expressive theory in terms of language. On the other hand, it is the assumption of expressive theory that language fails to embody or symbolize primal feeling which precisely defines its difficulties. It cannot account for language. For Kristeva both the semiotic and the symbolic do have linguistic form.

It is interesting that in her remarkable essay on single women (first published in the *North British Review*, 1860) Dora Greenwell, who had sympathies towards Quakerism rather than to Tractarianism, adopts the language of secrecy when she is speaking of women but, in a surprising move, compares the withholding and suppression required of women in social life with the expressive openness of their art. In poetry the female subjectivity is to be defined by its capacity to create through writing a self which is commensurate with the 'secret' identity concealed in social dealings. And yet, paradoxically, this self is constituted by secrecy, and thus the poem is an expression of feminine subjectivity through its very capacity to conceal as well as to reveal: the secret is an open secret — and a closed one.

> It is surely singular that woman, bound, as she is, no less by the laws of society than by the immutable instincts of her nature, to a certain suppression of all that relates to personal feeling, should attain, in print, to the fearless, uncompromising sincerity she misses in real life; so that in the poem, above all in the novel — . . . a living soul, a living voice, should seem to greet us; a voice so sad, so truthful, so earnest, that we have felt as if some intimate secret were at once communicated and withheld — an Open Secret, free to all who could find its key — the secret of a woman's heart, with all its needs, its struggles, and its aspirations.[42]

The theological language of the open secret of the Gospel is directly, and with extraordinary boldness, related to women's experience, so that through this language women become the prime bearers of the Christian message (we shall see that in the same way Barrett Browning identifies the fallen woman with Christ). In terms reminiscent of Letitia Landon's justification of and apologia for the introduction of the affective into the hardness of phallocentric society, Dora Greenwell defends the introduction of feminine sensitivity into art and into life, but with the difference that modern life makes it increasingly difficult to give that feminine subjectivity *expression*, thwarting and obstructing it so that there is a disjunction, just as in expressive theory itself, between internal experience and external form.

> The conditions of life grow continually less and less severe, yet more and more complicated: the springs of thought, of love, lie deeper. Conscience grows more exacting, responsibilities wider. Women's whole being is more sensitive. It may now, perhaps, be harder for her than it has ever yet been to make her wishes and her fate — '*to bring her external existence into harmony with her inner life*' [my emphasis].[43]

The affective and expressive vocabulary continues throughout the essay: Dora Greenwell asks for '*a more perfect freedom and expansion* in that which is already their [women's] own' (my emphasis).[44] She quotes Mrs Jameson on the particular nature of the 'feminine and religious element' in women's identity, and argues for the superior capacities of sympathy in women, the expressive capacity to project themselves into different psychological conditions — 'In such a task, the complicated play of sympathies ever at work within her —

the dramatic faculty by means of which she so readily makes the feelings of others her own – find full expression. To her, *sympathy is power*, because to her it is knowledge'.[45]

The essay challenges Mill on the subjection of women a number of times, claiming that women accept subordination, and adopts a flagrantly essential-ist account of feminine consciousness. Women are innately passive, responsive and nurturing rather than original and creative.

> In imaginative strength she has been proved deficient; she unfolds no
> new heaven, she breaks into no new world. She discovers, invents,
> creates nothing. In her whole nature we trace a passivity, a tendency to
> work upon that which she received, to quicken, to foster, to develop.[46]

Intellect becomes as one-sided as feeling in women: no woman remains single from choice; the true oneness of men and women in love is – the sense of loss combined with the phallic language is poignant here – 'like the healing of some deep original wound'.[47] And yet neither the essentialist conformism nor the poignancy should be allowed to obliterate the boldness of this essay. Dora Greenwell certainly wanted the 'power' granted by imaginative sym-pathy for women. Though she saw that it would be necessary to appeal to the agency of men to enable women to use their energies in productive work, she attacked the conservatism and conventionality of contemporary accounts of women, and what she advocated is striking. Though she concentrated on nursing, she wanted women to be able to work together in groups, in collaborative projects (she advocated a museum of women's arts): she wanted women to be able to enter the ministry of the church with a clear and defined and officially recognized status, participating in 'aggressive' moral reform, and she believed that in undertaking unpaid work among the poor, female labour could democratize society and erase class difference; she praised the moral qualities of working-class women. A 'certain mingling of classes on one ground' could take place.[48] In working in hospitals and with fallen women, middle-class women could assuage differences because they were egalitarian in their sympathies and did not *'come down'* to the poor.[49]

The mixture of the conventional and the unconventional in this essay is surprising and often unpredictable; it consents to a passive account of women and simultaneously subverts it, seeing the expressive model of femininity as one of struggle and limit. Rather like her own double poems, the essay is both conservative and subversive. If she could assert the virtues of passivity she could also castigate and question the 'self-complacent idolatry of the safe and mediocre, in the fullness of which we once heard a lady thank Heaven that her daughters were not geniuses. True apotheosis of the commonplace!'[50] The truth is that expressive accounts of consciousness sanctioned both the 'aggressive' movement of self outwards (here made safe by being associated with the church) and the hidden, secret life of feeling, expression and repression, energizing movement and hysteria, concealment and revelation, silence and speech. Thus the woman poet's negotiation of the aesthetics of secrecy and its contradictions is highly complex, and always deeply concerned with struggle and limit, transgression and boundary, silence and language.

Christina Rossetti took up this theme directly in relation to poetry in another extraordinary documenting of the cultural dilemma of women, her Preface to a fairly late poem, *Monna Innominata*. In this brief discussion, and with characteristically 'secret' obliquity and indirection, she claimed, like Greenwell, expressive rights for the unmarried woman in poetry. She claimed, not only the freedom of the unmarried woman to express her sexuality, but also the freedom to be absurd, undignified, if feminine sexuality necessitated this.

She calls Elizabeth Barrett Browning 'the Great Poetess of our own day and nation' and yet implicitly offers a critique of her position.[51] Beatrice and Laura, she writes, dismissing a whole mythology of women, may have been immortalized by Dante and Petrarch, but they come down to us 'scant of attractiveness'. The reason is that they and the 'unnamed ladies' who preceded them were the objects of sexual love and religious feeling but could not express it themselves. They come down to us as remote and unpassionate beings. In the same breath she makes a characteristically oblique and ambitious historical statement: 'in that land and that period which gave birth to Catholics, to Albigenses, and to Troubadours', Renaissance Italy, in other words, were generated the forms of thought and feeling and the religious and sexual conflicts which have conditioned the nineteenth-century culture evolving from them. In both periods it was impossible for a lady to 'have spoken for herself'. Elizabeth Barrett Browning, the 'Great Poetess' of her period might, she continues, have achieved another kind of art than the 'Portuguese Sonnets' 'had she only been unhappy instead of happy'. The mysterious indirectness here (for 'Sonnets from the Portuguese' is hardly a happy poem) is to be understood by remembering that in Victorian terminology to be 'happy' was to be married. And when the euphemistic terms are reversed, to be 'unhappy' is to be a spinster. Spinsters are not free to write of sexual love or passion as the 'happy' married woman is. The claims are striking. Elizabeth Barrett Browning might have been a different and perhaps a greater poet if she had remained single. Correspondingly, the unmarried woman has something important (perhaps more important?) to say about sexual feeling, but is blocked by convention from saying it. No wonder such spinster poetry might be 'less dignified', if just as honourable, than that written *to* her. She would be writing of the 'barrier', implicitly both hymenal and societal in this prose, between women and men, between herself and the object of her passion, sexual or divine. The barrier 'might be one held sacred': she would be writing of taboo subjects, unfulfilled feminine desire and rejection.[52]

The 'barrier' as the topic of expressive theory is explored, necessarily indirectly, by Rossetti, Greenwell and Ingelow. These poets worked inside the religious lyric and the love lyric and radically redefined them by exploring their limits. How they do this, and how they not only metaphorize but establish the barrier as a structural principle of their poems, is perhaps more fundamental to the nature of Victorian women's poetry than any of the direct accounts of women's experience to be found in their poems.

Of course, overt polemic about women can be found in the work of these poets, but these are less fundamental than their indirections. Certainly Christina Rossetti's work yields enough, at the level of direct statement, about sexual, social and economic matters for one to be sure that she thought of herself as a 'woman' writer and indeed saw that she was marginalized as one by the very nature of her situation. She contributed to *The Germ* but her sex naturally excluded her formally from the pre-Raphaelite *Brother*hood.

The P.R.B.

The two Rossettis (brothers they)
And Holman Hunt and John Millais
With Stephens chivalrous and bland,
And Woolner in a distant land –
In these six men I awestruck see
Embodied the great P.R.B.
D. G. Rossetti offered two
Good pictures to the public view;
Unnumbered ones great John Millais,
And Holman more than I can say.
William Rossetti, calm and solemn,
Cuts up his brethren by the column.[53]

This poem, dated 19 September 1853, might have been even tarter if she had known that William was to cut up his sister by the column when he edited her poems in 1904.

Illegitimacy, fallen women, the fierce legal bond of marriage, the sexual fate of the woman who waits, while the male is given social licence to experiment, the experience of exclusion, all this is to be found particularly in Christina Rossetti's earlier work. Her poems constantly define the lyric writer as shut out, outside, at the margin. 'Shut Out' is the title of a poem which makes the condition of exclusion paradoxically that of being shut in. 'At

Home' is a poem about being not at home in this woman's place, ironizing the visiting-card title – 'When I was dead my spirit turned / To see the much frequented house'. 'The Iniquity of the Fathers upon the Children' (1866) clearly emerges from her well-known interest in fallen women: ballads about prohibition, possession, rivalry, the rigour of the law, bonds and legal forms ('Love from the North', 'Cousin Kate', 'Noble Sisters', 'Maude Clare') testify to her awareness of the social and economic circumstances of women. She is fierce about the dependency of marriage in 'Triad' for instance. There three kinds of passion are envisaged. The last, institutionalized sexuality in marriage, is enervated and passive – 'One droned in sweetness like a fattened bee'. And yet Rossetti's generalized lyric seems almost created to resist and circumvent such analyses. The seeming sourcelessness and contextlessness of lyric, its impersonal reserve, its *secrecy*, is the form Rossetti chose. On the other hand, the intransigently enigmatic, by declaring itself as such, allows itself an extraordinary openness. Reserve and intensity, constraint and exposure, belong together because, as Dora Greenwell recognized, reserve is necessarily built upon its opposite. Once you have let it be known you have a secret you allow that there is something to give away.

NOTES

1 Landon, 'The Marriage Vow', in *Life and Literary Remains* (1841: II. 277).
2 Levy, *A Ballad of Religion and Marriage* (1915).
3 Barrett Browning, *Aurora Leigh* (1978: I. 436–7).
4 'I wish, and I wish I were a man' (Rossetti 'From the Antique').
5 Hemans 1873: xxvii.
6 Patmore, *The Angel in the House*, in *Poems* (1949: I. ii. 2, 74–5).
7 Landon 1841: I. 55.
8 Swindells 1985. This study retrieves a number of unknown writers.
9 Hawkshaw, *Dionysius the Areopagite* (1842: for the egalitarian heaven, see *Dionysius* 97–9; 'The Mother to Her Starving Child' (170–2); 'Why am I a Slave?' (191–3). Subsequent volumes were *Poems for My Children* (1847); *Sonnets on Anglo-Saxon History* (1854).
10 Horsfield, *The Cottage Lyre* (1862): 'The Truant' (44–7).
11 Ellen Johnston ('The Factory Girl') 1862: 'The Working Man' (79–80); 'The Maniac of the Green Wood' (15–19).
12 Landon 1841: II. 245–8; 246.
13 Landon 1850: I. xi (Preface to *The Improvisatrice* 1824).
14 Charlotte Brontë, 'Pilate's Wife's Dream,' in *Poems* (1984: 3).
15 For a description of objectification, see Rosenblum 1979: 82–98.
16 Landon 1841: II. 246, 245–6.
17 Landon, 'The Indian Bride', in *Poetical Works* (1850: I. 28, 30).

18   Ibid., I. 31.
19   Ibid., I. 29.
20   Preface to *The Venetian Bracelet* (1829), in *Poetical Works* (1850: I. xiv).
21   Ibid.
22   Burke 1958: 51.
23   Landon 1841: I. 205.
24   Hemans, 'Arabella Stuart', in *Poetical Works* 1873: 144.
25   Hemans, 'Casabianca' (1873: 373–4).
26   Anne Brontë 1979: 110–11, 21–8.
27   Charlotte Brontë, 'The Lonely Lady', in *Poems* (1984: 202–3).
28   Emily Brontë, 'The Philosopher', in *Complete Poems* (1941: 5–6).
29   Procter 1858; 1906: 111–13.
30   Ibid., 151.
31   Procter, 'A Tomb in Ghent' (45–52, 47).
32   Ibid., 49, 48.
33   Procter, 'A Lost Chord' (159); 'Hush!' (131–2); 'Unexpressed' (137–8).
34   Procter, 'Words' (85–6).
35   Greenwell 1866: 1–68.
36   Dobell 1876: 3–65.
37   Armstrong 1972: 93.
38   *The British and Foreign Review*, XIII (1842), 1–49.
39   Ibid., 22.
40   Keble 1912: I. 120.
41   Kristeva 1984. See in particular chapter 2.
42   Greenwell 1866: 3–4.
43   Ibid., 4.
44   Ibid., 19.
45   Ibid., 45.
46   Ibid., 27.
47   Ibid., 8.
48   Ibid., 43, ('aggressive action') 33.
49   Ibid., 59.
50   Ibid., 58.
51   Rossetti 1979–90: II. 189–90.
52   Ibid., II. 86.
53   Ibid., III. 332 (pseudonymous publication).

17

'I lived for art, I lived for love': The Woman Poet Sings Sappho's Last Song

MARGARET REYNOLDS

The action stops. The music slows, fades, dwindles away. Into the silence a woman's voice is lifted and the music follows her: 'I lived for art, I lived for love'. Alone in her distress she invokes the god she serves and complains to the female deity at whose shrine she has made offerings. Distracted, abandoned, nothing exists except her pain and her song. But she is not quite alone. Someone watches her. On stage she has an audience of one, the man who tortures her. Off stage she has an audience of thousands. Thousands of thousands across time. Behind Tosca the Diva stands Sappho, the first woman poet. And so the audience knows that this is a Last Song. Soon there will be no Tosca, no Sappho. Their bodies will be flung into space and dashed to pieces on the rocks. There will be no remains. Except the song.

Puccini's *Tosca* dates from the end of the nineteenth century but it is set in 1800 and it looks back to a time which saw the beginnings of a Sappho myth that exerted a lasting influence on the popular idea of what the woman poet was and how she conceived herself. The history of Sappho's legacy is patchy, eccentric and volatile. On the one hand it is possible to trace a scholarly journey of editions, translations and commentaries, where major developments in Greek studies take place first in France, then in Germany and Britain. On the other hand there is a separate tradition of 'fictions of Sappho' where she appears as fantasized versions of love-poet, courtesan, lesbian, schoolmistress and in various other guises.[1] These fictions may, or may not, bear any relationship to specific scholarly publications or archaeological discoveries. Rather, they reflect the temper of the time. One group who worked and re-worked the image of Sappho were the women poets of the nineteenth century.

At the beginning of the century the dominant idea of Sappho was as the female embodiment of the Romantic hero: passionate, enthusiastic, intellectual, revolutionary, artistic, lonely and doomed. Best known as a poet, a freethinker and a suicide, this Sappho was unequivocally heterosexual (DeJean 1989: 201). She had to be, because the essential burden of her song was a gloomy analysis of what it meant to be a Romantic hero trapped in a woman's body, and all too conscious therefore of the dictates of contemporary constructed sexual difference. At a time when women were becoming increasingly radical in their demands for political and social freedoms at the expense of domestic claims, this fated nineteenth-century Sappho sang a song where art and love were mutually exclusive. What is very peculiar is how closely women poets identified themselves and their subjects with this fiction of Sappho. The slippage between the real historical situations of the nineteenth century and the made-up stories of Lesbos in the sixth century BC is everywhere apparent. The assumption is continually made, perhaps because there were so few literary ancestors to provide models for women poets, that the condition of the poet is always the same whatever her time and place. Of course this parallels the Victorian conviction that the condition of femininity is always the same. But the results for women poets were ambivalent. To be identified as a 'modern Sappho' was both an inspiring blessing and an inhibiting curse.

In 1796 Mary Robinson published a sonnet sequence called *Sappho and Phaon* and she also wrote several poems based on Sappho's fragments. Robinson did not specifically identify herself with Sappho for she used many names for her contributions to periodicals, including Laura, Laura-Maria, Julia, Daphne, Oberon, Louisa and Echo. But after Robinson's death a three-volume edition of her *Poetical Works* appeared which included a biographical notice and a number of 'Tributary Poems' addressed to Mrs Robinson by the notables of the day. Of these, five invoke the name of the first woman poet and give it to the 'British Sappho' (Robinson: 1806, xxi–lvi).

However, it was Madame de Staël in France who most effectively appropriated Sappho's image and re-made it in hers. Her novel *Corinne, or Italy* (1807) was the most popular and enduring of her many versions of the Sappho myth, but of her other works *Delphine* (1802) and *Sappho, drame en cinq actes* (1821) as well as the folk-song from her juvenilia 'Romance to the tune: We loved each other since childhood', all draw on the Sappho plot (DeJean 1989: 138). Corinna was the other Greek poetess of antiquity, but de Staël's heroine blends into the Sapphic model to produce the nineteenth-century archetype of the woman poet.[2] The influence of this model was immense, and Byron, of all people, related how he took de Staël to task for her bad example to impressionable young women:

I continued saying, how dangerous it was to inculcate the belief that genius, talent, acquirements, and accomplishments, such as Corinne was represented to possess, could not preserve a woman from being a victim to an unrequited passion, and that reason, absence, and female pride were unavailing.

I told her that 'Corinne' would be considered, if not cited, as an excuse for violent *passions*, by all young ladies with imaginations *exalté*, and that she had much to answer for. (Blessington 1969: 26)

And so she did. For de Staël's Corinne/Sappho, glorious in her intellectual achievements but, as a consequence, thwarted in love and condemned to melancholy self-destruction, soon became the marker for the destiny of the woman poet. Most obviously this was exactly what happened when Bentley published an English translation of *Corinne* in 1833 where the prose text was translated by Isabel Hill, but the verses and songs of Corinne were specially commissioned in English 'metrical versions' from Letitia Elizabeth Landon. It was a clever move on the part of the publisher, for did he not have here, in living flesh, the very person of the fictional poetess? L.E.L. was one of the earliest women poets to write the despairs of Corinne and Sappho in verse. Her long poem *The Improvisatrice* (1824) re-worked de Staël's *Corinne* and there her heroine's first poem is 'Sappho's Song'. In the public mind – in her own mind – L.E.L.'s life – a glittering career, a failed love-affair, a suicide – made her seem to act out the inevitable destiny inherited from Sappho.

For other women poets the indentification was not so disastrous. But it was potent. Elizabeth Barrett Browning, for instance, perhaps with L.E.L.'s example in mind, seems to have tried to avoid the comparison. True, she once described herself as '"little & black" like Sappho' (Barrett Browning 1984: VIII, 128), but in general, and surprisingly, given her training as a Greek scholar, she mentions Sappho only occasionally and seems always conscious of her threatening legacy rather than her empowering example. Others, however, often made the connection. When Sara Coleridge met Barrett Browning in 1851 she wrote of the younger poet:

She is little, hard-featured, with long dark ringlets, a pale face, and plaintive voice, something very impressive in her dark eyes and brow . . . She has more poetic genius than any other woman ever shewed before, except Sappho . . . (Coleridge 1873: II, 447).

Except Sappho. Always Sappho. She is the pinnacle of female poetic achievement to which her belated rivals can only aspire. The curious thing is that for much of the Victorian age, very little of Sappho's transcendent reputation was based on her poetry. To begin with there wasn't very much of it. For the most part only the poem generally called 'Hymn to Aphrodite' ('Ornate-throned immortal Aphrodite'), the incomplete poem recorded by Longinus in *On Sublimity* ('He seems as fortunate as the gods to me'), and a few other fragments quoted in commentaries by ancient writers were known.[3] What little there was of Sappho's poetry seemed to accord exactly with the nineteenth century's idea of what women should write and, especially as the century wore on, with what poetry itself should be. Because Sappho's remains were about love and feeling, because they were intense and (albeit the result of an accident of history) short, they seemed to epitomize women's lyric poetry. Thus is traced a progression from Mary Ann Stodart's argument that Sappho's work is the ur-text of women's poetry ('We have but few remains of the earliest and best Greek poetesses; or her who earned the high title of the Lesbian muse; but those remains "more golden than gold", are all breathings from the dearest affections of the heart' (Stodart 1842: 88), through to Swinburne's assertion that Sappho's is the finest of all poetry ('Judging even from the mutilated fragments fallen within our reach from the broken altar of her sacrifice of song. I for one have always agreed with all Grecian tradition in thinking Sappho to be beyond all question and comparison *the very greatest poet that ever lived*' (Swinburne 1914: 817–18).

Sappho is the essence of poet. Of course this says more about Swinburne and contemporary attitudes to poetry, and to women, than it can about her. But then this is part of the problem with Sappho and all the fictions of Sappho. For most of the nineteenth century the main body of daughter-texts by women poets descend not from the authentic writings of the real Sappho, but from the imposter phantoms that throng into the spaces between the fragments of her text and her story.

From the few scraps of 'Testimonia' in classical authors which gave (true or false) stories of Sappho there are a number of specific tropes which attracted her nineteenth-century successors. All of these cluster around the (true or false) moment when Sappho makes herself into the picture of living art as she improvises her farewell song to art and love, before leaping off the Leucadian rock into the sea. This moment encompasses ideas which appear again and again in Victorian women's poetry: the woman poet as art object; her artless, improvising performance; the leap into space which expresses her abandon; the nothingness and absence which follow her self-immolation; and the farewell song, the text which represents her only remains.

Sappho was a popular subject for painters and sculptors of the Romantic period and, perhaps not surprisingly, the poems on Sappho written by women early in the nineteenth century often focus not on the real woman, but on the imagined 'picture' of the woman. When Felicia Hemans published her

'Last Song of Sappho'; she introduced it with reference to a painting and thus makes clear that the voice in the poem is that of the deserted, soon-to-be-dead Sappho.[4] L.E.L.'s poem 'Sappho's Song' follows the same pattern except that it is slightly more complicated in that the picture which accompanies the poem has been painted by the Improvisatrice herself. The popular association of painting and poetry, in part promoted by the illustrated annuals, dictates the opening of *The Improvisatrice* where the poet/painter describes her early canvases which sketch out her own fate told in the poem. The first of her pictures shows Petrarch separated from Laura. Her second picture, however, blends the poet-subject and muse-object:

> My next was of a minstrel too,
> Who proved what woman's hand might do,
> When, true to the heart pulse, it woke
> The harp. Her head was bending down,
> As if in weariness, and near,
> But unworn, was the laurel crown . . .
>
> I deemed, that of lyre, life, and love
> She was a long, last farewell taking; –
> That, from her pale parched lips,
> Her latest, wildest song was breaking.

Then follows 'Sappho's Song', enacted. Caroline Norton's poem 'The Picture of Sappho' is probably, like Hemans's, based on Westmacott's picture, but in this case Norton writes herself into the poem as the viewer of the portrait and questions its likeness to life:

> Thou! whose impassion'd face
> The Painter loves to trace,
> Theme of the Sculptor's art and Poet's story –
> How many a wand'ring thought
> Thy loveliness hath brought,
> Warming the heart with its imagined glory!
>
> Yet, was it History's truth,
> That tale of wasted youth,
> Of endless grief, and Love forsaken pining? . . .

The American poet Elizabeth J. Eames took up a similar position in her 'On the Picture of a Departed Poetess' which begins: 'This still, clear radiant face! doth it resemble / In each fair faultless lineament thine own?'

These poets know about representation and construction. The painter, the sculptor and the poet make and re-make the image of the woman. The woman poet herself then reproduces that image for her own purposes, but she questions its historical veracity and its authentic lifelikeness. The slide from fact to fiction and back again to measuring against fact suggests the ways in which these writers recognized the temptations of the motherless poet. When you only have one ancestor, and that ancestor is part speculation and myth, the anxiety which results makes the axis for many a Sappho poem.

Christina Rossetti, who so often takes up and refines the subjects of her contemporaries, wrote two poems specifically about Sappho,[5] as well as many where Sappho is not named, but similar themes are re-worked. 'A Study. (A Soul.)' suggests the posed image of the woman as art object: 'She stands as pale as Parian statues stand' (Rossetti 1979–90: 3. 226), and her longer poem '"Reflection"' implies, through its ambiguous title, a sophisticated version of the later woman poet who looks and questions and puzzles over the image of her own self who is at the same time her ancestor. This other woman who gazes 'through her chamber window' belongs to the speaker, is part of the speaker, 'my soul's dear soul', and yet she 'never answers' the speaker to whom she presents a mystery: 'Who can guess or read the spirit / Shrined within her eyes'. In the end the speaker allows her vision to die into an art object which still provokes her curiosity:

> I will give her stately burial,
> Tho', when she lies dead:
> For dear memory of the past time,
> Of her royal head,
> Of the much I strove and said.

> I will give her stately burial,
> Willow branches bent:
> Have her carved in alabaster,
> As she dreamed and leant
> While I wondered what she meant.

Hitherto most convincing readings of this poem place it within a courtly love tradition making the speaker male (Leighton 1992: 62). Certainly Rossetti's speaker here, like any male voyeur, kills the woman-object of her gaze into art, and it is right to place this poem in the long tradition of gaze narratives which runs from Chaucer's Book of the Duchess to Adrienne Rich: 'When to her lute Corinna sings / neither words nor music are her own; / only the long hair dipping / over her cheek, only the song / of silk against her knees / and these / adjusted in reflections of an eye'. (Rich 1963: 22–3). But there is nothing in this poem to suggest that the sex of the speaker is definitely male, and the frequency with which Victorian women wrote poems about pictures of other women poets makes it possible to read '"Reflection"' as a poem addressed to that seductive but troubling icon. That the 'gazing' is done twice over, by both the speaker who looks at the woman, and the woman herself who looks elsewhere, also implies an identification between the speaker-subject and the woman-object. 'Gazing through her chamber window / Sits my soul's dear soul' the poem starts, suggesting a self who gazes through the window which is the eye of the soul. This reiteration never lets up; the next three lines start with 'Looking' and the third stanza repeats 'Gazing gazing still'.

Then there's the title. '"Reflection"' is in inverted commas which hints, in typographical terms, at the repetitions we should perceive: the double of one woman reflecting on another; the double of the mirror image; the double of the self who analyses self; the double sets of quotation marks – so that we cannot know who speaks the poem. If the word in the title is a typical Rossetti pun, the punctuation is a pun too. That the title of the poem was 'Day-Dreams' in the first draft manuscript and in the 1896 and 1904 editions (Rossetti 1979–90: 3. 464) reinforces the suggestion that this is a poem about poetic ambition and the models available to the woman poet.

These images of the looked-at woman poet include questions about and criticisms of assumptions of sexual difference.[6] Rossetti's mysterious image may be a cool puzzle to the viewer, but the more usual Sappho picture is set at the moment of her most intense distress, at the moment when she is indeed 'abandoned' – in every sense. She is exposed, her dress slips to reveal her breast, she is ecstatic, vulnerable, about to leap into space and 'die' – also in every sense! The viewer can do what he likes with her. That's what she is there for. Scarpia certainly thinks so; Phaon does too, and Lord Nelvil in *Corinne*. As Lawrence Lipking puts it: 'The woman forgets herself, the man's attention is pricked' (Lipking 1990: 41).

But Victorian women poets are often sophisticated critics of the 'male gaze', partly because they do it so well themselves. When they picture the image of Sappho they too succumb to the lure of the gaze and admit the excitement offered by the image. But they are excited as much because this titillating picture is of themselves. It is the picture of their own image that they desire and get, with all the paradoxes and difficulties that result. This self-conscious looking at the self looking at Sappho who is and is not a self-portrait, overlaps into how the woman poet, quite literally, dressed herself, whether she acquiesced – like Caroline Norton, L.E.L. and Eliza Cook who all at times adopted the fashion for hair bound up in ribbons à la Sappho – or whether she resisted – like Christina Rossetti in Max Beerbohm's famous cartoon, refusing to don any of the 'stunning fabrics' offered her by Dante Gabriel (Beerbohm 1922: 12).

The trouble is that in the process of being made into a picture at the point of suicide, this Sappho is twice dead. She is admired at the threshold of self-extinction because she will shortly die, and then she is frozen into the necessity of that imminent death as an art object. This is the story traced in Landon's 'A History of the Lyre'. The speaker first sees the poet Eulalie among the ruins of a lost time:

> We stood beside a cypress, whose green spire
> Rose like a funeral column o'er the dead.
> Near was a fallen palace, – stain'd and gray
> The marble show'd amid the tender leaves
> Of ivy but just shooting; yet there stood
> Pillars unbroken, two or three vast halls,
> Entire enough to cast a deep black shade;
> And a few statues, beautiful but cold, –
> White shadows, pale and motionless, that seem'd
> To mock the change in which they had no part, –
> Fit images of the dead.

At the end of the poem Eulalie dies, as prophesied by this first vision, but not before she has commissioned the statue which will be her monument:

> and in the midst
> A large old cypress stood, beneath whose shade
> There was a sculptured form; the feet were placed
> Upon a finely-carved rose wreath; the arms
> Were raised to Heaven, as if to clasp the stars;
> Eulalia leant beside; 'twas hard to say
> Which was the actual marble . . .

As the poems ends even L.E.L., in the persona of her speaker, seems to perceive the problematic situation for the woman poet who is indistinguishable from the object which she has made of herself. 'Peace to the weary and the beating heart, / That fed upon itself!' are the last lines of the poem. Barrett Browning probably had Eulalie's fate in mind when she re-cast it in *Aurora Leigh*. In book 2 she exposes the sexualized assumptions of difference which the beautiful image of the performing woman poet so dangerously courts:

> I drew a wreath
> Drenched, blinding me with dew, across my brow,
> And fastening it behind so, turned faced
> .. My public! – cousin Romney – with a mouth
> Twice graver than his eyes.
> > I stood there fixed, –
> My arms up, like the caryatid, sole
> Of some abolished temple, helplessly
> Persistent in a gesture which derides
> A former purpose.
>
> > > > (2. 56–63)

Barrett Browning clearly saw that the Sappho/Corinne/Eulalie poems written by her forerunners had had a 'purpose' but that its paradoxes made it an 'abolished temple'. Like the haunting images which accrue around the picture of Aurora's mother, painted from her corpse (1. 128–63), as Sappho's image must always be made out of her corpse, Barrett Browning argues that such pictures of the dead can always provide fruitful metaphors for the imagination, but that they can never represent the living woman.[8]

And yet, to represent the living woman in process, in performance, is often the challenge and the goal in Victorian Sappho poems, for not only is Sappho just about to die; she also performs, she sings. Many of the earliest Sappho poems of the period make a point of reproducing that performance. Hemans's 'The Last Song of Sappho', Landon's 'Sappho's Song' and Rossetti's 'Sappho' all aim to give the actual words in the mouth of the ancient poet in the process of utterance. The authenticity of this expression of woman's experience is partly guaranteed by the improvised, immediate and urgent sense of the poem happening now, in process. It is a problematic strategy.[9] Certainly it gives Sappho a voice and makes her speak out, as if alive again. In Hemans's related poem 'Corinne at the Capitol' she makes a parade of the performance happening before our eyes by using the present tense throughout and by repeating 'now'; 'Now thou tread'st the ascending road'; 'Thou has gained the summit now'; 'Now afar it rolls – it dies – / And thy voice is heard to rise'; 'All the spirit of thy sky / Now hath lit thy large dark eye'; 'Now thy living wreath is won'. As if to further emphasize the living presence of Corinne in performance, Hemans contrasts her heroine with the dead things of the past around her: 'While, from tombs of heroes borne, / From the dust of empire shorn, / Flowers upon thy graceful head ...'. Hemans celebrates the demise of the old rule and projects the vivacity of the new. That Hemans ends this poem with a brief moral on the virtues of hearth and home is really irrelevant because it comes altogether too late in the wake of this glittering vision. In another Sappho-related poem 'To a Wandering Female Singer' she also conjures up the immediacy of the poet's performance, but this time makes herself the audience who listens and interprets the poet's song, reading therein her recorded distress: 'I know it by thy song!'.

If the project to re-animate Sappho by singing her song for her is a positive one of recuperation, it is also an awkward one, always threatening to dwindle into ventriloquism. This danger is one which Rossetti's two Sappho poems acknowledge. Her 'Sappho' is in part one of the 'last songs' posed on the cliff-top but, as Leighton has explained, it also prophesies and enacts a performance set beyond death, on the other side of the grave (Leighton 1992: 143). Using a technique which is typical in Rossetti, repetition evokes the blankness of death in life, and a series of negatives mark out the imagined afterlife where the dead speaker is still capable of speech. Even more explicitly, Rossetti's poem 'What Sappho Would have Said had her Leap Cured instead of Killing Her' acknowledges its task, however teasingly, of putting words into the dead woman's mouth. And what does this cured Sappho sing? A song of rest certainly. She is grateful for the pause, having been suffering and leaping for some two and a half thousand years:

> I would have quiet too in truth,
> And here will sojourn for a while.
> Lo; I have wandered many a mile,
> Till I am footsore in my youth.
> I will lie down; and quite forget
> The doubts and fears that haunt me yet.

And yet she still will not lie down. This ghost who haunts all her followers is herself haunted by the burning memory of what she has been. Being 'cured' is nothing if it means that Sappho — the sign, the ultimate icon of love-suffering — is empty and has rubbed herself out;

> Ah, would that it could reach my heart,
> And fill the void that is so dry
> And aches and aches; — but what am I
> To shrink from my self-purchased part?
> It is in vain; is all in vain;
> I must go forth and bear my pain.

Calling upon 'Love', this 'cured' and empty Sappho asks to be herself again: 'Oh come again, thou pain divine, / Fill me and make me wholly thine.'

Rossetti recognizes here that this art-object Sappho, the puppet speaker, can only be animated by the cooperative imagination of another. There is no real Sappho, there are hardly any poems, there are only a few fragments of evidence. But there are still the performances when she comes alive again under pressure of the pose, the song, the leap, the loss.

But the great days of the improvisatrice were gone by the middle of the century and Sappho passed into another related form where she could contine her performance – opera. The Viennese dramatist Franz Grillparzer was given the germ of the idea for his play *Sappho* (1818) when he met an acquaintance who suggested that she would make a good subject for an opera libretto (Grillparzer 1876: 7). He wrote a play instead, but the idea was still around, and in 1851 Gounod's opera *Sapho*, with libretto by Emile Augier, was performed in France. The succession was appropriate and acceptable. Women (and men) improvising poetry in public, once the essential sight for the tourist in Italy as de Staël herself had found (Gutwirth 1978: 173), was no longer a fashionable entertainment. Women on the stage as actresses were still in the ambivalent and sexually suspect position they had endured in the eighteenth century. But women who could sing were quite another matter. The introduction of *bel canto*, with its emphasis upon the natural singing voice (as opposed to the extravagances of the castrati), meant that if there was one place where a woman performing could be tolerated, it was on the operatic stage. Sappho and Corinne and all their like, under these circumstances, become obvious candidates for operatic treatment. And they got it. Gounod did *Sapho*, and Rossini had already done a version of Corinne in his *Il Viaggio a Reims* (1825).

The women poets of the nineteenth century seem to have recognized the succession and Sappho's displacement into opera. In the middle of the century Barrett Browning's Aurora Leigh is not a performer on the Sappho model. She improvises a poem-in-process certainly, but it is a private, written document offered for the edification of the reader and the poet-narrator herself. It is an internal drama by an author who 'will write no plays' (5. 267) but who will 'take for a worthier stage the soul itself' (5. 340). More than this, Aurora consciously refuses to perform woman, to become a collectable art-object for Lord Eglinton who would like her to adorn his home, and sends him instead to the actress, the dancer or the opera singer (5. 898–909). George Eliot picks up the same thread with *Armgart*. Her work is a verse-drama, but her heroine is an opera singer whom we never see perform. Instead her off-stage triumph is related by her teacher who, again like the man who proposes to her, wishes to possess her, to add her to his collection. We are back with the idea of the spectacle, and neither of these women poets like the view.

Barrett Browning had seen the problem in her 1844 poem 'A Vision of Poets'. Sappho is the only woman poet to appear there, and the vision of her is not unequivocally glorious:

And Sappho, with that gloriole

Of ebon hair on calmèd brows
O poet-woman! none forgoes
The leap, attaining the repose.

The 'repose' here is both the serenity which allows the woman poet to write, the confidence which allows her to perform, as well as the 're-pose', the pose of that performance which is endlessly repeated by other women. No sooner does Barrett Browning think of Sappho than she thinks also of all the other women poets who follow her – including herself. And the price for this re-posing is the leap. The leap of feeling which throws itself at life and self-expression; the leap of daring and the risk which challenges conventions of containment; the leap of desperation and despair which wipes out the self thrust into empty space.

From Lucifer to *Rebel without a Cause* via Jane Austen's *Persuasion*, the fall, the leap, the plunge, suggests a net of metaphors to do with pride, display, self-love, rebellion, punishment and dissolution. In the nineteenth century 'fallen woman' meant something quite different from fallen angel, and 'Found Drowned' became such a recognizable cliché in London and Paris that G. F. Watts's 1848 picture of that name needs no further gloss to encourage the audience to speculate on the manner of this woman's life and the probable reasons for her suicidal jump. How could the women poets not look at Sappho's leap and remember all of this? How could they not also recall that their nearest bold ancestor, Mary Wollstonecraft herself, had emulated Sappho – as well as all those anonymous women who leapt into the Thames.

Barrett Browning knew very well that Sappho's leap meant much more than a pedant's quibble over fact or fiction. Even scholarly writers of the time inadvertently betray their own censorious attitudes to Sappho and her kind. In his monumental textbook *A Critical History of the Language and Literature of Ancient Greece* (1850) William Mure devotes several pages to the story of Sappho's plunge and to the phenomenon of the 'Lover's Leap' in general, and decides, in spite of other evidence, in favour of the tale on the grounds that 'a female of her temperament and habits' suffering an unrequited passion would be highly likely to throw herself off a cliff. He goes on to list the historic reasons for the practice, whether voluntary or not: punishment, sacrifice and remedy.

The first two are obvious and fit with Victorian meanings given to the leap. The third, he explains, works by way of a transition from passion to reason: 'the revulsion of feeling and temperament consequent on the plunge, the terror, and the excitement of the whole ceremony, would be such as to banish the dominant passion from the breast, and to give place to the sway of reason or other counteracting influences' (Mure 1850: 3. 280–9). Assuming, of course, that the leaper survived.

Mure's language here, albeit coded, makes it clear that the spectacle of Sappho's leap is itself a substitute for the scene which she is denied and which Victorian sensibility would not allow to be depicted; the scene of erotic consummation. And he wasn't the only Victorian to see it this way. Writing on 'The girls who leap into space' Catherine Clément quotes a passage from Kierkegaard's *Diary of a Seducer*:

> For a girl infinity is as natural as the idea that all love must be happy. Everywhere a girl turns she finds infinity surrounding her, and she is able to jump into it; her leaping is feminine and not masculine . . . her jump is a gliding flight. And when she reaches the other side she finds that, instead of being exhausted by the effort, she is more beautiful than ever, even more full of soul. She throws a kiss to those of us who remained behind. Young, newborn, like a flower growing from mountain roots, she sways over the abyss until we are almost dizzy. (Clément 1989: 78).

Here is Sappho again, posing, performing, leaping, being watched. But Clément is impatient with Kierkegaard's pretty story and wants to call things by their names: '(she) does everything he wants. She jumps; she jumps again, keeps jumping until the final leap. Oh you do veil it with modest names. She fucks. And your hero ditches her' (Clément 1989: 79). Leaping into space is one thing. Ending up in a ditch is quite another. But is that not where the abandoned woman, the fallen woman must end? Either in a ditch or drowned – which is what happens to Sappho. And what might happen to the many daughter heroines portrayed by Victorian women poets. L.E.L.'s Sappho says 'it was love that taught me song', hinting that sexual experience and textual expression go together, both part of the erotic heterosexual display which exposes the body and recognizes desire. There is no separation here between the process of writing/singing/performing and the imperatives of self-expression written through the body.[10] Once read like this, Hemans's moral at the end of 'Corinne at the Capitol' is curiously prohibitive in its sexual implications. Her conclusion 'Happier, happier far than thou / . . . She that makes the humblest hearth / Lovely but to *one* on earth' (my emphasis) condemns the possible slide into the role of prostitute which threatens the woman poet who exposes herself, not to one, but to many. Perhaps this also explains Barrett Browning's decision as the century wore on to make her woman poet heroine resolutely blameless and virgin while letting Aurora champion the cause of the fallen woman by taking up with Marian Erle.

But Sappho's leap is not just a fall. It is also brave. When Sappho leaps, she flies, she risks herself and escapes the cage. Again the image of the bird, caged or free, runs as a metaphor for female containment or release, from Wollstonecraft's *Vindication of the Rights of Woman* (1792, 1975: 146) to Angela Carter's *Nights at the Circus* (1984). This is what Sappho does with her performance; this is what the improvisatrice does, along with the woman poet and the diva: '. . . with her own death she will make singing's most symbolic gesture. Floria Tosca hurls herself from the top of the ramparts . . . "Look look how I can fly . . ."' (Clément 1989: 38). French feminist theory proposed the connections between flying and writing, between sexual and textual expression, but the Victorian women poets anticipated the image. Hemans, for instance, puts this 'flight' into 'A Parting Song' where the speaker is a Corinne figure and '. . . one / For whom 'tis well to be fled and gone – / As of a bird from a chain unbound . . .'. And in her 'The Last Song of Sappho' she actually has her Sappho looking at the sea-birds wheeling round the cliff and following their example:

> I, with this winged nature fraught,
> These visions wildly free,
> This boundless love, this fiery thought –
> *Alone* I come – oh! give me peace dark Sea!

And after the fall, after the leap, what is left? Nothing. Silence. Empty space into which the song fades. Hemans's Sappho will have 'peace' and so shall we. L.E.L.'s Sappho will 'sleep calm', Rossetti's Sappho will be 'Unconscious' and 'Forgetful of forgetfulness'.

But then there wasn't much there in the first place. By definition a 'last song of Sappho' is only about itself and only lasts for the length of the performance. Once she is gone, it's all over. This is why Lipking calls the song of the woman poet derived from Sappho via Ovid's *Heroides* an 'anti-epic': 'No action ensues. No plot ever reaches the end. Instead one love-letter follows another, and each is full of tears . . .' (Lipking 1990: 37–8). This is why Clément describes Tatiana in Tchaikovsky's version of Pushkin's *Eugene Onegin* as a 'woman poet'. Because she writes a letter/poem which is about nothing, nothing except herself and her unfocused desire (Clément 1989: 81–2). When the voice stops, the body disappears. When she stops singing, when she makes the leap, whether shameful or glorious, Sappho kills herself.

Elisabeth Bronfen argues that the act of suicide by a woman can be read as a 'communicative act', a performance, a self-authored text where the woman takes control of her own story which is otherwise denied in her particular cultural or familial position. Clarissa composing herself in death is a case in point. Bronfen further suggests that: 'the representation of a woman killing herself in order to produce an autobiographical text can serve as a trope for the relation of the writing process to death in general' and that the 'choice of death emerges as a feminine strategy with which writing with the body is a way of getting rid of the oppression connected with the feminine body' (Bronfen 1992: 142).

In the case of Victorian women's Sappho poems the argument is persuasive. Their Sappho dies, but writes in the process. She only writes, sings a 'last song' in fact, *because* she dies. Hence the attraction of this subject for women writers at a period when their own authority as writers, their own permission to write, could not be taken for granted. By writing Sappho's autobiographical lament they are permitted to write, even if they kill her (and themselves) every time. They also reassure themselves about their own literary survival. As the woman poet died but is remembered in her song, so they too will own remains in the poem.

Bronfen quotes Michael Ryan's suggestion that death offers 'the possibility of an absolute alterity', a 'passage into otherness', which has a literary analogy where the writing process promotes this 'otherness' or alterity by splitting the self into subject-writer and object-text (Bronfen 1992: 142–3). When death is suicide there is another stage still; for this passage to otherness ambivalently makes the writer simultaneously subject and object, like her text. The suicide is poised between 'self-construction and self-destruction'. In annihilating the body in order to make the story of that body, the self is the subject-writer who creates an object-text and at the same time makes a subject-text where that self can speak out of the object-self who has been reduced to the thing looked at by the text.

When a woman poet writes an autobiographical poem for another poet the sense of 'otherness' in writing is further complicated. Paradoxically, while the woman poet doubles herself by imagining a second woman poet, she also diminishes herself by splitting her consciousness to be shared with that other. Furthermore, if the suicide triumphs by constructing a new self out of self-destruction, the woman poet who retrieves and rehearses that other simultaneously celebrates the successful self-creation of the first and original woman poet, while she destroys her own self. She hurls herself into space, makes herself a void to be filled up with Sappho's translated fragments, denies her own subjectivity and speaks words which belong to another. It is not Sappho who is the puppet now but the daughter—descendant made in her image who ventriloquizes the song Sappho throws her. There is an anxiety of self-destruction in many of these 'last songs'. Each time the woman poet takes Sappho as a subject she courts self-annihilation, and not just in the time of the poem-in-process, but for all time. When the woman poet writes Sappho's text it may be that she is being written off. The shadow of this particular precursor looms large and threatening, and yet these women poets court self-destruction by reaffirming her even though they know her resurrection means their dissolution. This is what worried Mary Robinson when she set out to impersonate Sappho in 1796. 'The merit of her compositions', she wrote, 'must have been indisputable, to have left all contemporary female writers in obscurity . . .' (Robinson 1796: 18). Every time a woman writes 'Sappho's Last Song' she risks suicide, literally deconstructing herself, allowing herself to be re-absorbed into the mother/ poet who is original and singular.

Yet in Victorian society this will-to-disappear may be as much a strategy of self-protection as self-mutilation. Putting the self on display results in exploitation, possession and objectification as art-object. Willing the self to expression in performance results in sexual exploitation and silence. When a Victorian woman poet wills herself to death by covering that authentic self with a borrowed mask she may well be choosing that textual suicide, in Bronfen's words, as a 'way of getting rid of the oppression connected with the feminine body'. It is hardly surprising that the one early Victorian woman poet who probably did commit suicide, Letitia Landon in 1838, is also the one who most consistently invokes and impersonates (and is impersonated by) the ideal of Sappho. In life, L.E.L. was punished by society for her display. John Forster broke off his engagement to her on the grounds of some sexual impropriety, she married an entirely unsuitable man and left England for good. In literature she sang songs for others not herself, for Eulalie, for the Improvisatrice and for Corinne. And when both life and writing were over her contemporaries wrote songs for her, just as they wrote them for Sappho.

Victorian women poets' 'last songs' are funerary monuments, they are suicide notes attached to the corpse of the poet, they are mourning mementoes, but they are also love songs. Like Barthes' love letters these songs are empty except for the one message 'I am thinking of you'. And that reiterated message is only necessary at all because this thinking is 'blank'. The lover is in danger of forgetting the beloved. She does forget her. And then she recalls and remembers her: 'I do not think *you*; I simply make you recur (to the very degree that I forget you)' (Barthes 1978: 157). The re-called songs of Sappho and Corinne are often farewells which include an injunction to remember or to forget. Ostensibly they may be addressed reproachfully to the lover who has injured her. But in fact the audience they address is the audience who is actually writing the poems, the women poets who inherit Sappho. Hemans's 'A Parting Song' begins with an epigraph from de Staël's *Corinne* which is taken up in the refrain of the song: 'When will ye think of me, my friends?' Apart from her named Sappho poems, L.E.L. wrote two short farewell poems, 'Song' ('Farewell: – and never think of me') and 'The Farewell'. Each of these poems literally re-members the woman poet, puts her real presence back on stage, whether it is a constructed character or the writer herself.

That these 'farewell, remember me' songs imply an interested audience is not surprising. They had one. For these women poets were writing for and to each other. This became especially apparent when L.E.L. assumed Sappho's role of poet-suicide. Elizabeth Barrett wrote a 'memory song' for L.E.L. when she took the words from the mouth of the poet ('Do you think of me, as I think of you?') and turned them into a voiced poem in 'L.E.L.'s Last Question'. Then Rossetti took one line from Barrett Browning's poem about L.E.L. ('One thirsty for a little love') and re-made it into a new line 'Whose heart was breaking for a little love' which becomes the epigraph and trigger for her poem called 'L.E.L.'.

These memory love-letter poems throw a powerful sidelight on all Rossetti's many farewell poems. Her well-known 'Song' ('When I am dead, my dearest') for instance takes on quite another significance if it is put into the tradition of the woman poet singing Sappho's 'last song'. It becomes a poem about that very tradition:

> When I am dead, my dearest,
> Sing no sad songs for me;
> Plant thou no roses at my head,
> Nor shady cypress tree:
> Be the green grass above me
> With showers and dewdrops wet;
> And if thou wilt, remember,
> And if thou wilt, forget.

With a typical swerve Rossetti utters the injunction not to sing even as she contradicts it and sings another 'sad song'. Here is the woman poet singing yet another of Sappho's 'last songs'. The cypress tree is borrowed from Eulalie's stage set, the dissolved self made into a blank ('I shall not see the shadows') is the empty space where Sappho disappears; the song which the woman poet sings is the familiar one where Sappho is associated with the nightingale, who sings 'as if in pain'; and the alternate and haphazard remembering and forgetting is done by both the audience of women poets to whom she addresses herself ('And if thou wilt, remember, / And if thou wilt, forget') and by the woman poet herself who may or may not write poems which re-member Sappho or any other woman poet ('Haply I may remember, / And haply may forget').

Whatever else happened within the tradition of Sappho poems in the nineteenth century, it is clear that Sappho, sometimes threatening, sometimes empowering, represented a powerful muse-figure for Victorian women poets – a muse-figure who was perennially interesting because she was so much about their own selves and their own projects. Even when a poet seems to resist all the persuasions of the glorious-Sappho myth, she can't help hoping that there may be a new beginning.

Armgart, for instance, loses out altogether. Punished for her ambition, cured of her pride, she loses her voice and can no longer sing. But what does she do at the end of George Eliot's poem? She retires into obscurity to teach girls (presumably girls) to sing. Like Sappho, she becomes a guide and teacher and gathers disciples around her. It is a humble end to a brilliant career. And yet it is not quite the end. Others will follow.

Nor is the end of Sappho's Victorian story. For most of the nineteenth century in Britain and in France it was the myths of Sappho which had most influence. But in Germany the scholars were at work producing new editions and translations and commentaries on the recorded works of Sappho (Robinson 1925: 150). Of these contributions the work of Volger (1810), Welcker (1816) and Neue (1827) were, for individual critical reasons significant (Wharton 1887: xii–xiii), but it was the painstaking work of Theodor Bergk in his *Anthologia Lyrica* (1854) and his *Poetae Lyrici Graeci* (1852) which collected all of the works that could be ascribed to Sappho and provided an accurate (as far as possible) and (for the time) up-to-date edition of the poems and fragments. Bergk's work encouraged the English scholar H. T. Wharton to prepare an English translation of Sappho and this appeared as *Sappho: Memoir, Text, Selected Renderings and A Literal Translation* in 1885. This edition, which took Bergk's Greek as its text for the poems, was highly influential: it dismissed the web of myths around Phaeon and the Leucadian leap; it made claims for Sappho's importance as the first lyric poet; it established a standard for English translations; it quietly reproduced Bergk's feminine pronouns thus rendering Sappho's lesbianism for the first time in English; and it persuasively argued for the resilience of her poetic model throughout English literature. And there was more to come. By the time Wharton published a second edition only two years later in 1887 his text had already changed and Sappho started to reappear.

In the 1880s and 1890s new archaeological work in Egypt began, quite literally to reconstitute the body of Sappho's work. Many very early versions of Sappho's poems had been written on papyrus, a form of paper made from reeds and much more cheaply and conveniently produced than parchment made from animal skins. But a piece of paper has many uses, and if the words were not valued, then the object which bore them was. When the new Egyptian craze began at the end of the nineteenth century, tombs were excavated and mummified bodies unearthed, many of them wrapped in scraps of paper. Scraps of paper with words written on them (Ranor 1991: 3). And among them Sappho's words, or at least versions thereof (Foster 1958: 19–20).

The women poets of the mid-nineteenth century had not been entirely excluded from Greek scholarship in spite of lack of opportunity and in spite of Eliot's Dorothea being given to understand by Casaubon that Greek accents were beyond a woman's understanding (Eliot 1871–2, 1975: 89). Elizabeth Barrett Browning managed and so did George Eliot herself. By the end of the century the aims of the younger generation, agitating for education and independent lives, almost always included classical ambitions. Among these young new women none were more directly affected by the resurgent Sappho than Katherine Bradley and Edith Cooper; 'Michael Field' to their public, 'the Fields' to their friends.

Directly out of Wharton's book Michael Field made a new Sappho in their own *Long Ago* (1889). Like all their predecessors, L.E.L., Hemans, Barrett Browning, Rossetti, they also made the book and this re-vision of the 'last song' out of their own experience as poets, as women, and as lovers. But their changed circumstances, and changes in the circumstances of time, meant that this same set of experiences was radically altered. For a start they wrote in collaboration so that there was none of the lonely Romantic hero mode which marks the early nineteenth-century idea of Sappho and the woman poet. Then they wrote, by deliberate choice (Leighton 1992: 202–3) not as women who performed to be slavered over by the male spectator, but as a man and an equal, as 'Michael Field'. And finally, though they wrote as lovers, just like L.E.L. and her kind, they certainly didn't have the same problems of heterosexual assumption because they wrote as lesbian lovers, subject and object both and both together.

In *Long Ago* Bradley and Cooper takes first lines or tiny fragments of Sappho's Greek text following Bergk and Wharton and then extrapolate their own poem out of that. In fact, they improvise:

Δεῦρο δηῦτε Μοῖσαι, χρύσιον λίποισαι.

Hither now, Muses! leaving golden seats,
Hither! Forsake the fresh, inspiring wells,
Flee the high mountain lands, the cool retreats
Where in the temperate air your influence dwells,
Leave your sweet haunts of summer sound and rest,
Hither, O maiden choir, and make me blest.

This is the first poem in Field's *Long Ago* although, strictly, it functions rather as an epigraph or invocation as it comes just after Preface and before Poem I. Like all the poems it starts with the Greek quotation which may or

may not then be translated in the first lines of the poem. In this case it is, for
Wharton's translation of the Greek fragment is: 'Hither now, muses, leaving
golden . . .' (122). The ellipses are suggestive. Into this space the Fields
insert their poem making a continuum between the ancient Greek and the
nineteenth-century English where the one slides easily into the other and the
original Sappho is revised by a disciple who mimics her phrases and her
scenes. In this case the vocabulary and the tone of the poem is borrowed from
the two pieces of the Sappho poem now known as Fragment 2 (Sappho,
1990: 56–7) which Wharton included as poems 4 and 5 in his edition
(1887: 70–3). This poem has only been available in a complete(ish) form
since 1937 when a version discovered on a potsherd was published (Sappho
1990: 56–7). In the nineteenth century only the second and fourth stanzas
were known, quoted from Hermogenes and Athenaeus (Wharton 1887: 70,
72), but none the less at the time, and since, scholars have recognized that
this prayer and invocation to Aphrodite provide the essentials of the
Sapphic scene. The natural landscape in Fragment 2 is relished in a frank and
uninhibited way by Sappho's speaker; there is nothing 'bookish' here
(Jenkyns 1982: 32). Cooper and Bradley, responding to the freshness of their
model, return to this landscape in many of the poems in *Long Ago*. Not
for them any dramatic posing on the cliff top. Instead here is a feminized
place of springs and woods and hidden places, obscurely libidinous and
seductive:

> Ἀμφὶ δὲ [ὕδωϱ] ψῦχϱον κελάδει δι' ὔσδων
> μαλίνων, αἰθυσσομένων δέ φύλλων
> κῶμα καταϱϱεῖ.

> Cool water gurgles through
> The apple-boughs, and sleep
> Falls from the flickering leaves,
> Where hoary shadows keep
> Secluded from man's view
> A little cave that cleaves
> The rock with fissure deep.

> (Field 1889: 68)

In tone and style, in its choice of location and its address to women, in the
very fact that this is the first time any actual *Greek* appears (as opposed to
numerous epigraphs in French borrowed from de Staël), Michael Field's *Long
Ago* consciously attempts an authentic 'last song' for Sappho. The book even
re-works the old 'portrait of Sappho' problem by offering as illustration, not
the abandoned *déshabillé* of the art-object, but two historical artefacts. An

'archaic head of Sappho . . . taken from a nearly contemporary vase, inscribed with her name' is reproduced on the cover of *Long Ago*, and the frontispiece is 'from a figure of Sappho, seated and reading, on a vase in the museum at Athens' (Field 1889: 130). Even the very presentation of the book itself conspires to make this Sappho 'real' for it is printed in red and black on thick handmade paper and bound with vellum.

In reconstructing their 'authentic' text, the Fields were assisted by Greek scholars, historians and other learned men. They cite Wharton, Bergk and 'Mr Murray at the British Museum', but they were also friendly with J. A. Symonds who recommended his own *Studies of the Greek Poets* (1873) to Edith Cooper (Symonds 1967–9: II, 683). And Cooper was not the only attractive young poet befriended by Symonds. When Agnes Mary Robinson published her first volume *A Handful of Honeysuckle* in 1878 Symonds wrote to congratulate her and soon began a correspondence in which all things Greek, including Sappho, were discussed (Symonds 1967–9: III 108–9). Robinson did not then, like Michael Field, go on to re-produce Sappho, but her poetry shows clear signs that she knew the work through her own studies in Greek, and that she was influenced by the tone, the brevity, the nuances, of the extant works of Sappho. This subtle influence runs throughout her work. For instance, in the poem 'Love Without Wings (Eight Songs)' we are given a series of short lyrics which work on the Sapphic themes of art, love and memory, but which also read like a selection of Sappho's fragments; for instance:

V

The fallen oak still keeps its yellow leaves
But all its growth is o'er!
So, at your name, my heart still beats and grieves
Although I love no more.

Another late Victorian woman poet clearly influenced by the scholarly reconstituting of Sappho's text rather than the myths of Sappho's life is Mary Coleridge. Like the Fields and like Robinson, she had a classical education, this time with William Cory, one time classics master at Eton whose *Ionica* (1891) was suggestively homoerotic (Leighton and Reynolds 1995: 610). Coleridge not only writes poems with Sapphic themes, 'Marriage', for instance, which celebrates Hymen while it deplores the loss of maiden freedoms, or 'Broken Friendship', but she also writes memory poems which imitate the Sapphic metre, three long lines and one short:

CCXXIV

Only a little shall we speak of thee,

> And not the thoughts we think:
>> There, where thou art – and art not – words would be
>> As stones that sink.

> We shall not see each other for thy face,
>> Nor know the silly things we talk upon.
> Only the heart says, 'She was in this place,
>> And she is gone.'

The Sappho re-created by these women poets of the late nineteenth century is one whose work is important rather than her image. Nowhere is this more apparent than in the radical change of genre and style that takes place over the hundred years from Mary Robinson to Michael Field. When Robinson wrote her *Sappho and Phaon* (1796) she used the form of a sonnet sequence and went to great lengths to claim poetic authority for her work by making it clear on her title page: 'Sappho and Phaon, in a series of Legitimate Sonnets . . .'. Robinson was anxious about Sappho as a poetic model. She was anxious particularly because all the work she knew by Sappho was in fragments, pieces, scraps. These were her only literary 'remains'. For the Romantic sensibility this might be an advantage. Certainly it guaranteed that these were the genuine article: 'They [the works of Sappho] possessed none of the artificial decorations of a feigned passion; they were the genuine effusions of a supremely enlightened soul' (Robinson 1796: 25). But the price of this naive, messy honesty is poetic authority. So Robinson tidies up her Sappho and makes her story in 'legitimate' or Petrarchan sonnets which confer poetic stature and artistic control (McGann 1995: 64–5). Through the nineteenth century the women poets who wrote on Sappho had to negotiate this problem, how to convey authenticity at the same time as maintaining control? For much of the period the 'last song' was the answer. Here was the fragment-come-suicide-note-come-self-erected-monument which was innocently 'true' – because it happened at a moment of extreme provocation – and at once artistically contrived – because it was the product of a self-conscious poet. This combination was what Laman Blanchard recognized when he published L.E.L.'s uncollected epigraphs and manuscript pieces under the title of *The Life and Literary Remains of L.E.L.* in 1841. Authentic, sacred and venerated like holy relics, L.E.L.'s 'literary remains', modelled on those of her predecessors including Sappho, endorse her womanly naivete and yet imply her artful last testament.

At the end of the century fragmentation seemed no longer problematic. On the contrary, it was encouraging, illuminating, liberating. Perhaps it was because Sappho herself was no longer static but resurgent and alive again with new discovery, that these late Victorian women poets embraced Sappho's literary remains for the freedoms she offered in her lost phrases, her ellipses and empty spaces. Instead of being posed and still, instead of the formulaic model of the repeated 'last song', writers like Field, Robinson and Coleridge experiment with a kinetic verse which is suggestive and subtle, hinting at more than what is said and leaving space for guessing. May Probyn's teasing 'Rondelets' and 'Triolets' also belong to this development, as does the delicate erotic charge in the poetry of Charlotte Mew. In this all these poets anticipate the modernists and show the way to later writers, Ezra Pound for instance, whose constructive use of Sappho's silences followed on these earliest experiments.

The new emphasis on the work of Sappho did not, however, mean that an idealized image of the woman poet disappeared altogether from their verse. Sappho's image does appear, but here is no fixed icon rigidly posed at the moment of self-display and self-destruction. Instead we are given a vision of a working poet whose song is full of nuance and possibility. Michael Field's 'Fifty Quatrains' recalls the loss of Sappho's oeuvre but it celebrates the power of 'The Woman' whose song invokes 'the bands / Of low-voiced women on a happy shore' and gives 'marvellous rich pleasure' to all her hearers. And in Mary Coleridge's 'A Day-dream' (which may refer to Rossetti's poem now called '"Reflection"') the speaker is transported to a 'land where all lay clear / Betwixt the sunshine and the shining sand':

> Three tombs of Kings, each with his corners three,
>   Shut out three spaces of the golden sky,
> Clear, flat, and bright, they hid no mystery,
>   But painted mummies, of a scarlet dye,
> That lay embalmed there many a long term,
> Safe from unkindly damp and creeping worm.

The reference to Egypt and the preservation of the mummies suggests an identity for the 'ancient crone' and the young girl the speaker finds in this landscape, for both of them are versions of Sappho:

> Deep set beneath a sibyl's wrinkled brow,
>   The ancient woman's eyes were full of song.
> They held the voice of Time; and even now
>   I mind me how the burden rolled along . . .
>
> Then did I turn me to the maiden's eyes,
>   And they were as the sea, brimming and deep.

Within them lay the secret of the skies,
The rhythmical tranquility of sleep . . .

                                        (Coleridge 1954: 176–7)

Coleridge's double Sappho is a suggestive strategy. To some extent it echoes and repeats the techniques used by all the Victorian women's Sappho poems when the ancient Sappho is impersonated by the younger living poet. But the old version of Sappho's Last Song was often a trap where the younger woman poet could only rehearse the destructive cycle of posing and singing, leaping and silencing. In these late Sappho poems, however, something quite different begins to happen, and the youthful poet re-writes Sappho's legacy.

In the Preface to *Long Ago* 'Michael Field' explains the character of their project:

> When, more than a year ago, I wrote to a literary friend of my attempt to express in English verse the passionate pleasure Dr Wharton's book had brought to me, he replied: 'That is a delightfully audacious thought – the extension of Sappho's fragments into lyrics. I can scarcely conceive anything more audacious.'
>
> In simple truth all worship that is not idolatry must be audacious; for it involves the blissful apprehension of an ideal; it means in the very phrase of Sappho –

> Ἔγων δ' ἐμαύτα
> τοῦτο ὄυνοιδα

> ['And this I feel in myself.']

> Devoutly as the fiery-bosomed Greek turned in her anguish to Aphrodite, praying her to accomplish her heart's desires, I have turned to the one woman who has dared to speak unfalteringly of the fearful mastery of love, and again and again the dumb prayer has risen from my heart –

> σὺ δ' αὔτα
> σύμμαχος ἔσσο

> ['. . . be thyself my ally.']
> (Field 1889: vii. Translations from Wharton, 1887: 77 and 48)

In one sense Field's 'audacious' new project is very similar to the old ones of Hemans, L.E.L. or Rossetti. From the start it is clear that this is yet another of the self-reflexive poems about the tradition of the woman poet who sings

Sappho's song. Poem I begins with a fragment which Wharton translates as 'But charming [maidens] plaited garlands' and which he glosses with the explanation that this fragment was quoted by a commentator on Aristophanes 'to show that the plaiting wreaths was a sign of being in love' (Wharton 1887: 114).

I

Αὐτὰρ ὁραῖαι στεφανηπλόκευν.

They plaited garlands in their time;
They knew the joy of youth's sweet prime,
    Quick breath and rapture;
Theirs was the violet-weaving bliss,
And theirs the white, wreathed brow to kiss,
    Kiss, and recapture.

They plaited garlands, even these;
They learnt Love's golden mysteries
    Of young Apollo;
The lyre unloosed their souls; they lay
Under the trembling leaves at play,
    Bright dreams to follow.

They plaited garlands – heavenly twine!
They crowned the cup, they drank the wine
    Of youth's deep pleasure.
Now, lingering for the lyreless god –
Oh yet, once in their time, they trod
    A choric measure.

(Field 1889: 3)

As the Greek grammar makes plain, this 'they' is feminine. They are the women poets, Sappho's disciples and Field's own ancestors who 'unloosed their souls' in the song to the lyre and who 'once in their time' performed the song of Sappho. These women poets are indeed, as according to Wharton's gloss, 'in love' and writing their love-letter memory songs for Sappho. But they are also poets, and the 'garlands' which they plait refer also to the laurel crown worn by the poet, the crown once presented to Corinne on the Capitol, the crown which Aurora Leigh tried out on herself.

So much for the old tradition of the woman poet re-enacting her inevitable destiny. But at the end of *Long Ago* Sappho's story is given a curious new twist in this late version. The very last poem in the volume is a form of epilogue where, certainly, Sappho leaps off the cliff yet again. But the last *numbered* poem is a hymn to Eros which imagines the continuation of Sappho's enterprise and a peculiarly appropriate punishment for Phaon's failure to return Sappho's love. Either he will find that no one remembers him any more now that Sappho's song no longer applauds and praises him, or . . .

> Or will Damophyla, the lovely-haired,
>   My music learn,
> Singing how Sappho of thy love despaired,
>   Till thou dost burn,
>   While I,
> Eros! am quenched within my urn?
>
> (Field 1889: 127)

Damophyla is Sappho's successor and she, like those later successors among the Victorian women poets, sings a song which is for and about Sappho and which is still designed to make the listener 'burn'.

The passing on of Sappho's song to her younger inheritor suggests also the concept of collaboration between women poets which is, so crucially, Michael Field's unique contribution to the poetic tradition of 'last songs'. This is what is boasted by the Preface to *Long Ago* and in this these two writers truly are 'audacious'. Field collaborates with Sappho, as Sappho collaborated with Aphrodite, as Sappho collaborates with Damophyla, as the Victorian women poets collaborate with each other, singing each other's songs. In the particular case of Michael Field, of course, this partnership is more than literary, for the Fields are both lovers and poets together and, when the pseudonymous writer of the Preface says that 'he' turned 'to the one woman who has dared to speak unfalteringly of the fearful mastery of love' we can guess that Cooper and Bradley are speaking of and to each other as much as to the ancient poet (White 1990: 201).[11]

One reason why Michael Field succeeded in breaking out of the Victorian pattern of destructive repetitions of the Sappho myth may be because the shared project of collaborative living and loving and writing meant that Bradley and Cooper could revise the old doublenessess of Sappho and her descendant in the light of their own happy experience. That they lived and wrote at a time when an authentic text for Sappho was being re-discovered, and a time when their own authentic 'Greek' sexuality was being slowly named and recognized,[12] meant that they could make, not yet another reprise of Sappho's last song, but a new kind of Sappho song which was actually a duet. A duet, a collaboration, a singing in unison which gave new freedoms and new permissions.

They weren't the only poets to make this leap from solo to duet. Agnes Robinson, for instance, does this in her poem 'Love Without Wings'. In eight short songs she tells a story which appears to be a narrative addressed to and about a lover whom she remembers and, in effect, resurrects. The sex of this 'other' is not revealed but, as in Rossetti's '"Reflection"' it is clearly a version of the self:

> I was the soul of you,
> Past love or loathing,
> Lost in the whole of you . . .
> Now, am I nothing?

The relation between the two is one which revolves around poetry and song ('I haunt you like the magic of a poet, / And charm you like a song'), so that, at the end of the poem, it is the singing together, the duet created by the poet and the poem which is recalled and celebrated:

> · But once I dreamed I sat and sang with you
> On Ida's hill.
> There, in the echoes of my life, we two
> Are singing still.

Yet it is Michael Field who most consistently and powerfully evokes the idea of a shared song in a way which was to offer a convincing model for the modernist Sapphic writings of Renee Vivien, Natalie Barney, Gertrude Stein and, especially, H.D. This two-singing-together happens throughout the many voices of *Long Ago*. Indeed it is written into the very title which not only echoes the Sappho fragment quoted on the half-title page:

> Ἠράμαν μὲν ἔγω σέθεν, Ἄτθι, πάλαι πότυ.
> 'I loved thee once, Atthis, long ago.'
> (Field 1889: I and Wharton 1887: 89)

but which also refers to Rossetti's poem entitled 'Echo', which itself refers back to Sappho:

> Come back to me in dreams, that I may give
> Pulse for pulse, breath for breath:
> Speak low, lean low,
> As long ago, my love, how long ago.

There are also duets or doublenesses suggested in Field's '"A Girl"' where the first speaker leaves the page 'half-writ' so that the object of the poem may become its subject by completing the work, or in 'A Palimpsest' where the double text, old writing under new writing, reflects their double authorship. And in 'Old Ivories' Field writes a poem about two images of woman which work together to provide an erotic 'pleasure of similitude' which implies both sexual and textual sameness.

> A window full of ancient things, and while,
> Lured by their solemn tints, I crossed the street,
> A face was there that in its tranquil style,
> Almost obscure, at once remote and sweet,
> Moved me by pleasure of similitude –
> For, flanked by golden ivories, that face,
> Her face, looked forth in even and subdued
> Deep power, while all the shining, all the grace
> Came from the passing of Time over her,
> Sorrow with Time; there was no age, no spring;
> On those smooth brows no promise was astir,
> No hope outlived: herself a perfect thing,
> She stood by that time-burnished reliquary
> Simple as Aphrodite by the sea.
>
> (Field 1908: 166)

This is quite a new 'last song' for Sappho. It does still include the picture element which suggests that Sappho is a narcissistic reflection of the woman poet herself. There may, after all, be no other young woman here for the poet to see; when the speaker arrives at the window 'A face was there' . . . perhaps it is her own face, a reflection much like Rossetti's '"Reflection"' on Sappho's song of art and love. But the sense of newness in the old 'at once remote and sweet' and the persuasion that this image of a woman, whether reflected or genuinely doubled, is a clean sheet, not yet written on, 'On those smooth brows no promise was astir, / No hope outlived . . .', makes the poem look like a revision and a promise.

And so it was. In popular circles Sappho and Sapphism fell into disrepute at the end of the nineteenth century[13] and her only acceptable representative was the lonely suffering Tosca version singing her solo before plunging to her doom. But among the women poets and writers of the early twentieth century a new Sappho's song of 'art and love' was heard. Not a 'last song' but one to be endlessly re-written, and not an introspective solo, but a duet where Sappho is not a rival, but a partner.

NOTES

1   For accounts of the various treatments of Sappho see Judith P. Hallet 1979: 447–64; Gubar 1984: 43–62; and DeJean 1989, which deals with the tradition in French. For ideas of Sappho found in nineteenth-century women's poetry see also Leighton 1992.

2   Ellen Moers (1976) was the first to draw attention to the wide-ranging influence of de Staël's writings and to the powerful presence of the 'myth of Corinne' in Victorian women's writing both in Britain and America.

3   These English translations are taken from the Loeb edition, 1990. For the most authoritative Greek text to date see *Poetarum Lesbiorum Fragmenta* edited by Edgar Lobel and Denys Page (Oxford, 1955). Recent English translations include one by Mary Barnard (Berkeley and Los Angeles, 1958), by Josephine Balmer (London, 1984) and Diane Rayor (1991).

4   Hemans's headnote for 'The Last Song of Sappho' reads: 'Suggested by a beautiful sketch, the design of the younger Westmacott. It represents Sappho sitting on a rock above the sea, with her lyre cast at her feet. There is a desolate grace about the whole figure, which seems penetrated with the feeling of utter abandonment.' Hemans's headnotes should generally be read as part of the poem. Her 'Corinne at the Capitol' starts: '"Les femmes doivent penser qu'il est dans cette carrière bien peu de sorte qui puissent valoir la plus obscure vie d'une femme aimée et d'une mère heureuse." – Madame de Staël.' And Hemans's poem 'A Parting Song' also quotes from *Corinne*: '"O mes amis! rapellez-vous quelquefois mes vers! mon âme y est empreinte." – Corinne.'

5   Rossetti's two named poems about Sappho are 'Sappho' which was composed in 1846 and published in the privately printed *Verses: Dedicated to Her Mother* (London, at G. Polidori's, 1847) and 'What Sappho Would have Said had her Leap Cured instead of Killing Her' which was written in 1848 but never published in Christina's lifetime.

6   Because femininity is often associated with imagery in western cultural practice, while masculinity is associated with either the artist-producer of the image or the viewer-consumer of art, then concepts of the production and value of the art-object itself become entangled with the ideological effects of sexual difference. See John Berger (1972) and Teresa de Lauretis (1984). Recent theorists writing on the assumptions of heterosexuality in the conceptualizing of art practice have shown how women artists use themselves as subjects *and* objects in order to undermine these apparent givens. See particularly Lynda Nead, *The Female Nude: Art, Obscenity and Sexuality* (London, 1992). The self-reflexive work of the Victorian women poets pre-figures these twentieth-century strategies.

7   Compare poems such as Christina Rossetti's 'In An Artist's Studio', Lizzie Siddal's 'The Lust of the Eyes', May Probyn's 'The Model' or Constance Naden's 'The Two Artists'; all in Leighton and Reynolds (1995).

8   While the taking of death masks modelled on the corpse was quite a common practice in the eighteenth and nineteenth centuries, the Victorian period also

saw a fashion for portraits painted of the corpse as if to represent the living being. Barrett Browning's sister Arabel saw just such a picture painted of Lady Blanche Georgiana Burlington by John Lucas in 1841 and EBB was much intrigued by her account of it.

9 See Angela Leighton on how the unstoppable flow of the improvising woman poet can be interpreted as unstructured Romantic excess (1992: 58–62).

10 Compare Hélène Cixous: 'Personally, when I write fiction, I write with my body. My body is active, there is no interruption between the work that my body is actually perfoming and what is going to happen on the page. I write very near my body and my pulsions . . .' ('Difficult Joys' 1990: 27). See also Cixous, 'The Laugh of the Medusa' 245–64.

11 It may be, as Camille Paglia tells us it is, that only lesbians (and of course, men) can be great poets. 'Sappho', she says, 'is a great poet *because* she is a lesbian, which gives her erotic access to the Muse. Sappho and the homosexual-tending Emily Dickinson stand alone above women poets because poetry's mystical energies are ruled by a hierarch requiring the sexual subordination of her petitioners . . .' (Paglia, 1991: 672). Applying this conclusion to the work of Victorian women poets would give interesting results in that all of these writers write for and about each other, and certainly have 'erotic access' to their Sappho-muse.

12 It is too easy to assume, from a twentieth-century perspective, that any sexual experience between women happening before modern feminism's permissions, had to be fraught with public anxiety and private self-loathing. Lillian Faderman's argument that only romantic friendship was free of trauma (*Surpassing the Love of Men*, London, 1981; 1985) is not convincing either. Of course, by the time female homosexuality came to be named and derogated by Krafft-Ebing and Ellis and their kind, problems and anxieties were likely to inhibit lesbian sexual practice. But it seems to me that there may have been an historical moment when, in certain contexts, lesbianism was neither invisible, nor condemned. This moment, in my view, runs from about the end of the 1840s to the beginning of the 1890s. Certainly, in the 1850s Barrett Browning, for instance, could quite cheerfully describe the examples of 'female marriage' she saw around her and seems to have been sympathetic to this choice. Certainly also, emancipated women like the Michael Fields knew many homosexual men, including J. A. Symonds, who, whatever public problems they may have encountered, tried in their personal lives to deal honestly and unashamedly with their sexuality. With all the consciousness of disapproval from the outside world, there was, in certain limited liberal circles, a brief time in the nineteenth century when homosexuality seemed to be neither a disease nor a burden.

13 The work of the sexologists Richard von Krafft-Ebing and Havelock Ellis began the disreputable naming of lesbianism, but it was the publicity and prurience surrounding the Oscar Wilde trials in 1895 which put the sexuality of Sappho back into the closet. See Moe Meyer, 'Under the Sign of Wilde: An Archeology of Posing' in Moe Meyer (ed.), *The Politics and Poetics of Camp*, London, Routledge, 1994, 75–109.

List of Contributors

ISOBEL ARMSTRONG is Professor of English at Birkbeck College, London. She is the author of many books and articles on Romantic and Victorian literature, including *Victorian Scrutinies* (1972), *Language as Living Form* (1982) and *Victorian Poetry* (1993).

KATHLEEN BLAKE is the author of *Love and the Woman Question in Victorian Literature* (1983) as well as articles on nineteenth-century poetry.

SUSAN CONLEY teaches English at the Australian National University. She recently completed a PhD thesis on Christina Rossetti at the University of Sydney.

STEVIE DAVIES is Senior Research Fellow at Roehampton Institute, London. She has published four novels, *Boy Blue* (1989), which won the Fawcett Society Prize, *Primavera* (1990), *Arms and the Girl* (1992) and *Closing the Book* (1994). She has published widely on Renaissance poetry, including books on Milton, Donne, Spenser and Shakespeare, as well as three books on Emily Brontë. Her most recent works are *Henry Vaughan: A Critical Biography* (1995), a critical study of *The Taming of the Shrew* (1995) and an edition of Anne Brontë's *The Tenant of Wildfell Hall* (1995).

SANDRA M. GILBERT is Professor of English at the University of California, Davis. She is the author of five collections of poetry, *In the Fourth World*, *The Summer Kitchen*, *Emily's Bread*, *Blood Pressure* and *Ghost Volcano*. She has also published innumerable articles on women's writing, as well as critical works, editions and a memoir. With Susan Gubar, she has co-authored *The Madwoman in the Attic*, *No Man's Land*, vols 1, 2 and 3, and *The War of the Words*, as well as co-edited *Shakespeare's Sisters* and *The Norton Anthology of Literature by Women*. She is the recipient of many literary fellowships and awards.

GILL GREGORY is a lecturer in adult education in London. She is currently completing a PhD on Adelaide Procter at Birkbeck College, London. Her poetry is being published by the Menard Press.

LINDA K. HUGHES is Professor of English and Director of Graduate Studies at Texas Christian University, Fort Worth. She is the author of *The Manyfaced Glass: Tennyson's Dramatic Monologues* and is co-author, with Michael Lund, of *The Victorian Serial*. She was the guest editor of *Victorian Poetry*'s special issue on women poets in 1995. Currently she is completing a critical biography of Rosamund Marriott Watson.

ANGELA LEIGHTON is Reader in English at the University of Hull. She is the author of *Shelley and the Sublime* (1984), *Elizabeth Barrett Browning* (1986) and *Victorian Women Poets* (1992), as well as articles on Romantic and Victorian literature. She is co-editor, with Margaret Reynolds, of *Victorian Women Poets: An Anthology* (1995).

TRICIA LOOTENS teaches at the University of Georgia. Her book, *Lost Saints: Gender, Silence and Victorian Literary Colonization*, is forthcoming from Virginia University Press.

JEROME J. MCGANN is the John Stewart Bryan Professor of English, University of Virginia. He has written extensively on the Romantic period and is the editor of *Byron: The Complete Poetical Works* (1980–93). His new book, *Sentimental Poetics: A Revolution in Literary Style*, will appear shortly from Oxford University Press. His major current project is *The Complete Writings and Pictures of Dante Gabriel Rossetti: A Hypermedia Research Archive*.

KATHARINE MCGOWRAN is a postgraduate student at the University of Hull. She is writing a PhD on late nineteenth-century women poets.

DOROTHY MERMIN is Professor of English at Cornell University. She is the author of *The Audience in the Poem: Five Victorian Poets* (1983), *Elizabeth Barrett Browning* (1989) and *Godiva's Ride: Women of Letters in England 1830–1880* (1993), as well as many articles on nineteenth-century literature.

MARGARET REYNOLDS is lecturer in English at the University of Birmingham. She is the editor of the variorum edition of Barrett Browning's *Aurora Leigh* (1992) and also of the Norton critical edition of the same (1995). With Angela Leighton she has co-edited *Victorian Women Poets: An Anthology* (1995). She has published articles and essays on literature and opera, and broadcasts regularly with the BBC. She is currently writing a book on Sappho and nineteenth-century poetry.

DOLORES ROSENBLUM is currently a social worker, and writes about narrative and medicine. She is the author of *Christina Rossetti: The Poetry of Endurance* (1986) as well as many articles on Victorian women poets.

CHRIS WHITE is a lecturer in literature at Bolton Institute of Higher Education. She is co-editor, with Elaine Hobby, of *What Lesbians Do In Books* (1991) and has published a number of essays, including two on Michael Field, in *Sexual Sameness*, ed. Bristow (1992) and in *Volcanoes and Pearl Divers* ed. Raitt (forthcoming).

JOYCE ZONANA is Associate Professor of English and Director of Women's Studies at the University of New Orleans. She has published articles on Arnold, Swinburne and Mary Shelley. Her article 'The Sultan and the Slave: Feminist Orientalism and the Structure of *Jane Eyre*' won the 1992 Florence Howe Award.

Bibliography

(Editions, letters, diaries are listed under the author's rather than the editor's name.)

Alaya, Flavia (1978) 'The Ring, the Rescue, and the Risorgimento: Reunifying the Brownings' Italy', *Browning Institute Studies*, 6 (1978), 1–41.

Allchin, A. M. (1958) *The Silent Rebellion: Anglican Religious Communities 1845–1900*, London: SCM Press.

Archer, William (1902; rpt. 1970) *Poets of the Younger Generation*, London, New York: AMS Press.

Armstrong, Isobel (1972) (ed.) *Victorian Scrutinies: Reviews of Poetry 1830–70*, London: Athlone Press.

— (1993) *Victorian Poetry: Poetry, Poetics and Politics*, London and New York: Routledge.

Arnold, Matthew (1960–77) *The Complete Prose Works of Matthew Arnold*, 11 vols, ed. R. H. Super, Ann Arbor, Michigan.

— (1965) *The Poems of Matthew Arnold*, ed. Kenneth Allott, London: Longmans.

Auerbach, Nina (1984) 'Robert Browning's Last Word', *Victorian Poetry*, 22 (1984), 161–73.

Bachofen, J. J. (1967) 'The Three Mystery Eggs', in *Myth, Religion, and Mother Right: Selected Writings of J. J. Bachofen*, trans. Ralph Mannheim, Bollingen Series, Princeton: Princeton University Press.

Banier, Antoine (1739–40; rpt. 1976) *The Mythology and Fables of the Ancients Explain'd from History*, New York: Garland.

Baring-Gould, Sabine (1865; rpt. 1973) *The Book of Were-Wolves: Being an Account of a Terrible Superstition*, New York: Causeway Books.

— (1866; rpt. 1914) *Curious Myths of the Middle Ages*, London: Longmans, Green and Co.

Barthes, Roland (1978; 1990) *A Lover's Discourse: Fragments*, Harmondsworth: Penguin.

Battiscombe, Georgina (1981) *Christina Rossetti: A Divided Life*, London: Constable.

Baym, Nina (1978) *Woman's Fiction: A Guide to Novels by and about Women in America, 1820–1870*, Ithaca: Cornell University Press.

— (1992) 'Reinventing Lydia Sigourney', *Feminism and American Literary History*, New Brunswick: Rutgers University Press, 151–66.

Beckson, Karl and John M. Munro (1989) (eds) *Arthur Symons: Selected Letters, 1880–1935*, Iowa: University of Iowa Press.

Beerbohm, Max (1922) *Rossetti and His Circle*, London: Heinemann.

Bell, Mackenzie (1898) *Christina Rossetti: A Biographical and Critical Study*, London.

Berger, John (1977) *Ways of Seeing*, Harmondsworth: Penguin.

Bivona, Daniel (1990) *Desire and Contradiction: Imperial Visions and Domestic Debates in Victorian Literature*, Manchester: Manchester University Press.

Blake, Kathleen (1980) '*Armgart* – George Eliot on the Woman Artist', *Victorian Poetry*, 18 (1980), 75–80.

Blau du Plessis, Rachel (1988) 'Rewriting the Rose: Women, Poetry and the Canon' in *Margin to Mainstream: the Broadening of the American Literary Canon*, ed. Eugene A. Bolt Jr and Constance D. Harsh, Princeton: Princeton University Press.

Blessington, Lady (1969) *Lady Blessington's Conversations of Lord Byron*, ed. Ernest J. Lovell, Princeton N.J.: Princeton University Press.

Bloom, Harold (1973) *The Anxiety of Influence: A Theory of Poetry*, New York: Oxford University Press.

Boone, Joseph (1984) 'Wedlock as Deadlock and Beyond: Closure and the Victorian Marriage Ideal', *Mosaic*, 17 (1984), 65–81.

— (1989) *Tradition Counter Tradition: Love and the Form of Fiction*, Chicago: University of Chicago Press.

Boos, Florence S. (1991) *The Design of William Morris' 'The Earthly Paradise'*, New York: Edward Mellen Press.

Brantlinger, Patrick (1988) *Rule of Darkness*, Ithaca: Cornell University Press.

Bronfen, Elisabeth (1992) *Over Her Dead Body: Death, Femininity and the Aesthetic*, Manchester: Manchester University Press.

Brontë (1932; 1980) *The Shakespeare Head Brontë: Lives and Letters*, 2 vols, Oxford: Blackwell.

Brontë, Anne (1979) *The Poems of Anne Brontë: A New Text and Commentary*, ed. Edward Chitham, Basingstoke and London: Macmillan.

Brontë, Charlotte (1984) *The Poems of Charlotte Brontë*, ed. Tom Winnifrith, Oxford: Blackwell.

Brontë, Emily (1941) *The Complete Poems of Emily Jane Brontë*, ed. C. W. Hatfield, New York: Columbia University Press.

— (1981) *Wuthering Heights*, ed. Ian Jack, Oxford: Oxford University Press.

Brooke, Rupert (1915) *The Collected Poems of Rupert Brooke*, New York: Lane.

Brown, Gillian (1989) 'Nuclear Domesticity: Sequence and Survival', in Cooper et al. 1989, pp. 283–302.

Browning, Elizabeth Barrett (1898; 1899) *Letters of Elizabeth Barrett Browning*, 2 vols, ed. Frederic G. Kenyon, London: Smith; New York: Macmillan.

— (1900; 1973) *Complete Works*, 6 vols, ed. Charlotte Porter and Helen A. Clarke, New York: Crowell, AMS.

— (1900; 1974) *Poetical Works*, ed. Harriet Waters Preston, Cambridge Edition, rpt. with intro. Ruth M. Adams, Boston: Houghton Mifflin.

— (1955) *Elizabeth Barrett to Mr. Boyd*, ed. Barbara McCarthy, New Haven: Yale University Press.

— (1969) *The Letters of Robert Browning and Elizabeth Barrett Browning 1845–1846*, 2 vols, ed. Elvan Kintner, Cambridge, Mass.: Harvard University Press.

— (1974) 'Two Autobiographical Essays by Elizabeth Barrett', ed. William S. Peterson, *Browning Institute Studies*, 2(1974), 119–34.

— (1977) *Casa Guidi Windows*, ed. Julia Markus, New York: Browning Institute.

— (1978) *Aurora Leigh and Other Poems*, intro. Cora Kaplan, London: The Women's Press.

— (1983) *The Letters of Elizabeth Barrett Browning to Mary Russell Mitford: 1836–1854*, 3 vols, ed. Meredith B. Raymond and Mary Rose Sullivan, Winfield, Kans.: Wedgestone Press.

— (1984) *The Brownings' Correspondence*, 10 vols to date, ed. Philip Kelley, Ronald Hudson and Scott Lewis, Winfield, Kans.: Wedgestone Press.

— (1992) *Aurora Leigh*, ed. Margaret Reynolds, Athens, Ohio: Ohio University Press.

Bryans, E. L. (1871) 'Characteristics of Women's Poetry', *Dark Blue* 2(1871), 484.

Bullough, Vern and Bonnie Bullough (1978; 1987) *Women and Prostitution: A Social History*, Buffalo, New York: Prometheus Books.

Burke, Edmund (1958) *A Philosophical Enquiry into the Origin of Our Ideas of the Sublime and the Beautiful*, ed. James T. Boulton, London: Routledge and Kegan Paul.

Byron, George Gordon (1986) *The Complete Poetical Works*, 4 vols, ed. Jerome J. McGann, Oxford: Clarendon-Oxford University Press.

Caird, Mona (1897) *The Morality of Marriage, and Other Essays on the Status and Destiny of Woman*, London.

Cantalupo, Catherine Musello (1987) 'Christina Rossetti: The Devotional Poet and the Rejection of Romantic Nature', in Kent 1987, pp. 274–300.

Case, Alison (1991) 'Gender and Narration in *Aurora Leigh*', *Victorian Poetry*, 19(1991), 17–32.

Castan, C. (1977) 'Structural Problems and the Poetry of *Aurora Leigh*', *Browning Society Notes*, 7(1977), 73–9.

Chevigny, Bell Gale (1976) *The Woman and the Myth: Margaret Fuller's Life and Writings*, Old Westbury, N.Y.: Feminist Press.

Chorley, Henry F. (1836) *Memorials of Mrs Hemans*, 2 vols, London, New York.

Christ, Carol (1977) 'Victorian Masculinity and the Angel in the House', in *A Widening Sphere: Changing Roles of Victorian Women*, ed. Martha Vicinus, Bloomington: Indiana University Press.

Churchill, Kenneth (1980) *Italy and English Literature 1764–1930*, London: Macmillan.

Cixous, Hélène (1976; 1980) 'The Laugh of the Medusa', *Signs*, 1 (1976), 875–93, and in *New French Feminisms: An Anthology*, ed. Elaine Marks and Isabelle de Courtivron, Brighton: Harvester, pp. 245–n64.

— (1990) 'Difficult Joys', in *The Body and the Text: Hélène Cixous, Reading and Teaching*, ed. Helen Wilcox, Keith McWatters, Ann Thompson and Linda R. Williams, Hemel Hempstead: Harvester, pp. 5–30.

Clarke, Norma (1990) *Ambitious Heights: Writing, Friendship, Love – The Jewsbury Sisters, Felicia Hemans, and Jane Welsh Carlyle*, London and New York: Routledge.

Clément, Catherine (1989) *Opera: The Undoing of Women*, London: Virago.

Coleridge, Mary E. (1910) *Gathered Leaves* from the Prose of Mary E. Coleridge, with a Memoir by Edith Sichel, London: Constable.

Coleridge, Mary (1954) *The Collected Poems of Mary Coleridge*, ed. Theresa Whistler, London: Hart Davis.

Coleridge, Samuel Taylor (1964) *Poetical Works*, ed. Ernest Hartley Coleridge, London: Oxford University Press.

Coleridge, Sara (1873) *Memoir and Letters of Sara Coleridge edited by her daughter*, London.

Colley, Linda (1989) 'Radical Patriotism in Eighteenth-Century England', in Samuel 1989, pp. 169–87.

Connor, Steven (1984) '"Speaking Likenesses": Language and Repetition in Christina Rossetti's *Goblin Market*', *Victorian Poetry*, 22(1984), 439–48.

Cooper, Helen (1979) 'Working into Light: Elizabeth Barrett Browning', in *Shakespeare's Sisters: Feminist Essays on Women Poets*, ed. Sandra M. Gilbert and Susan Gubar, Bloomington: Indiana University Press.

— (1988) *Elizabeth Barrett Browning, Woman & Artist*, Chapel Hill and London: University of North Carolina Press.

Cooper, Helen M., Adrienne Auslander Munich, and Susan Merrill Squier (1989) 'Arms and the Woman: The Con[tra]ception of the War Text', in Cooper et al, 1989, pp. 9–24.

Cooper, Helen M., Adrienne Auslander Munich, and Susan Merrill Squier, eds. (1989) *Arms and the Woman: War, Gender, and Literary Representation*, Chapel Hill: University of North Carolina Press.

Culler, Jonathan (1982) *Deconstruction: Theory and Criticism after Structuralism*, Ithaca, N.Y: Cornell University Press.

Cunningham, Hugh (1989) 'The Language of Patriotism', in Samuel 1989, pp. 57–89.

Curtius, Ernst Robert (1953) *European Literature and the Latin Middle Ages*, trans. W. R. Trask, New York: Harper and Row.

Daly, Mary (1984) *Pure Lust: Elemental Feminist Philosophy*, Boston: Beacon Books.

— (1987) *Websters' First New Intergalactic Wickedary of the English Language*, Boston: Beacon Books.

Dangarembga, Tsitsi (1988) *Nervous Conditions*, London: The Women's Press.

Dante (1985) *The Divine Comedy*, trans. Mark Musa, Harmondsworth: Penguin.

David, Deirdre (1985) '"Art's a Service": Social Wound, Sexual Politics, and *Aurora Leigh*', *Browning Institute Studies*, 13(1985), 113–36.

— (1987) *Intellectual Women and Victorian Patriarchy*, London: Macmillan.

Davies, Stevie (1994) *Emily Brontë: Heretic*, London: The Women's Press.

de Beauvoir, Simone (1952; 1972) *The Second Sex*, trans. H. M. Parshley, New York, Harmondsworth: Penguin.

DeJean, Joan (1989) *Fictions of Sappho: 1546–1937*, Chicago and London: University of Chicago Press.

de Lauretis, Teresa (1984) *Alice Doesn't: Feminism, Semiotics, Cinema*, Bloomington, Indiana: Indiana University Press.

— (1987) *Technologies of Gender: Essays on Theory, Film and Fiction*, Bloomington, Indiana: Indiana University Press.

Derrida, Jacques (1976) *Of Grammatology*, trans. Gayatri Chakravorty Spivak, Baltimore and London: Johns Hopkins University Press.

— (1980) 'The Law of Genres', *Glyph*, 7(1980), 202–32.

Deshazer, Mary K. (1986) *Inspiring Women: Reimagining the Muse*, New York: Pergamon Press.

de Staël, Madame (1807; 1833) *Corinne, Or Italy*, trans. Isabel Hill with metrical versions of the odes by L. E. Landon, London.

— (1807; 1979) *Corinne ou l'Italie*, ed. Claudine Herrman, Paris: Des Femmes.

— (1836) *Sapho*, in *Oeuvres de Madame de Staël*, 3 vols, Paris: III, 693–711.

Dickens, Charles (1859) (ed.) *All the Year Round*, London.

Dickinson, Emily (1955) *The Poems of Emily Dickinson*, 3 vols, ed. Thomas H. Johnson, Cambridge, Mass.: Harvard University Press.

— (1960) *Complete Poems of Emily Dickinson*, ed. Thomas Johnson, Boston: Little.

Diehl, Joanne Feit (1978) '"Come Slowly – Eden": An Exploration of Women Poets and Their Muse', *Signs*, 3(1978), 572–87.

Dobbs, Brian and Judy (1977) *Dante Gabriel Rossetti: An Alien Victorian*, London: Macdonald and Jane's.

Dobell, Sydney (1876) *Thoughts on Art, Philosophy, and Religion*, London.

Donne, John (1977) *Poetical Works*, ed. H. J. C. Grierson, Oxford: Oxford University Press.

Douglas, Ann (1977) *The Feminization of American Culture*, New York.

Dubois, Ellen C. and Linda Gordon (1983) 'Seeking Ecstasy on the Battlefield: Danger and Pleasure in Nineteenth-Century Feminist Sexual Thought', *Feminist Studies*, 9(1983), 7–25.

Eliot, George (1857) 'Aurora Leigh', *Westminster Review*, 67(January 1857), 306–10.

— (1874) *Armgart*, in *The Legend of Jubal and Other Poems*, London and Edinburgh.

— (1885) *Works of George Eliot*, 12 vols, Edinburgh and London.

— (1956; 1965) *Middlemarch*, Cambridge, Mass.: Harvard University Press; Harmondsworth: Penguin.

Ellis, Henry Havelock (1897; 1911) *Studies in the Psychology of Sex*, 6 vols, London: Random House.

Engels, Frederick (1972) *The Origin of the Family, Private Property and the State*, intro. Eleanor Burke Leacock, London: Lawrence and Wishart.

Faderman, Lillian (1985) *Surpassing the Love of Men: Romantic Friendship and Love between Women from the Renaissance to the Present*, London: The Women's Press.

Faderman, Lillian and Louise Bernikow, 'Comment on Joanne Feit Diehl's "'Come Slowly – Eden': An Exploration of Women Poets and Their Muse"', *Signs*, 4(1978), 188–95.

Fairchild, Hoxie Neale (1939; 1957) *Religious Trends in English Poetry*, 5 vols, New York: Columbia University Press.

'Felicia Hemans', *Leisure Hour*, 1(1852), 72–6.

Felman, Shoshana (1975) 'Women and Madness: The Critical Phallacy', *Diacritics*, 5 no 4(1975), 2–10.

— (1981) 'Rereading Femininity', *Yale French Studies*, 62(1981), 19–44.

'Female Penitentiaries', (1848) *The Quarterly Review*, 83(1848), 375–6.

Field, Michael (1884) *Callirrhoë: Fair Rosamund*, London.

— (1889) *Long Ago*, London.

— (1892) *Sight and Song Written by Michael Field*, London.

— (1893) *Underneath the Bough: A Book of Verses by Michael Field*, London.

— (1907) *Mystic Trees*, London: Eveleigh Nash.

— (1908) *Wild Honey from Various Thyme*, London: T. Fisher Unwin.

— (1930) *The Wattlefold: Unpublished Poems by Michael Field*, ed. Emily C. Fortey, Oxford: Basil Blackwell.

— (1933) *Works and Days: From the Journal of Michael Field*, ed. T. and D. C. Sturge Moore, London: John Murray.

Fiske, John (1871) 'Werewolves and Swan-Maidens', *Atlantic Monthly* (August 1871), 144.

Foster, Jeannette H. (1958) *Sex Variant Women in Literature*, London: Frederick Muller.

Foucault, Michel (1979) *Discipline and Punish: The Birth of the Prison*, trans. Alan Sheridan, New York.

— (1976; 1979; 1981) *History of Sexuality*, vol. 1, trans. Robert Hurley, Harmondsworth: Penguin.

— (1982) 'The Subject and Power', *Critical Inquiry*, 8(1982), 777–95.

Freeman, Barbara (1989) 'Epitaphs and Epigraphs: The End(s) of Man', in Cooper et al. 1989, pp. 303–22.

Freeman, John (1970) 'George Eliot's Great Poetry', *Critical Quarterly*, 5(1970), 25–40.

Freud, Sigmund (1938) *Totem and Taboo*, in *The Basic Writings of Sigmund Freud*, trans. and ed. A. A. Brill, New York: Modern Library, pp. 807–930.

— (1953–74) *The Standard Edition of the Complete Psychological Works of Sigmund Freud*, 24 vols, ed. James Strachey, London: Hogarth Press.

— (1963) 'Female Sexuality', trans. Joan Riviere, in his *Sexuality and the Psychology of Love*, ed. Philip Rieff, New York: Collier, pp. 194–211.

Friedman, Susan (1986) 'Gender and Genre Anxiety: Elizabeth Barrett Browning and H.D. as Epic Poets', *Tulsa Studies in Women's Literature*, 5(1986), 203–28.

Fulgentius (1971) *Mythologies*, in *Fulgentius the Mythographer*, trans. Leslie George Whitbread, Columbus: Ohio State University Press.

Gallaher, Catherine (1983) 'More about "Medusa's Head"', *Representations*, 4(1983), 55–7.

Gallop, Jane (1985) *Reading Lacan*, Ithaca N.Y.: Cornell University Press.

Gelpi, Barbara (1981) 'Aurora Leigh: The Vocation of the Woman Poet', *Victorian Poetry*, 19(1981), 35–48.

Gilbert, Sandra M. (1984) 'From *Patria* to *Matria*: Elizabeth Barrett Browning's Risorgimento', *PMLA*, 99(1984), 194–209.

Gilbert, Sandra M., and Susan Gubar (1979) *The Madwoman in the Attic: The Woman Writer and the Nineteenth-Century Literary Imagination*, New Haven: Yale University Press.

Gilbert, W. S. and Arthur Sullivan (n.d.) *Iolanthe: or, The Peer and the Peri*, arranged Berthold Tours, London.

Gilman, Charlotte Perkins (1915; rpt. 1979) *Herland*, New York: Pantheon.

Gittings, Robert (1978) *Thomas Hardy's Later Years*, Boston: Little, Brown.

Gladstone, William (1968–86) *The Gladstone Diaries*, 14 vols, ed. M. R. D. Foot and H. C. G. Matthew, Oxford: Clarendon Press.

Goldenberg, Naomi (1976) 'A Feminist Critique of Jung', *Signs*, 2(1976), 443–9.

Golub, Ellen (1975) 'Untying Goblin Apron Strings: A Psychoanalytic Reading of "Goblin Market"', *Literature & Psychoanalysis*, 25(1975), 158–65.

Greenwell, Dora (1861) *Poems*, Edinburgh.

— (1866) *Essays*, London and New York.

Greer, Germaine (1975) Introduction to Christina Rossetti, *Goblin Market*, New York: Stonehill Press.

Greg, W. R. (1850) 'Prostitution', *Westminster Review*, 53(1850), 448–506.

Griffin, Susan (1978) *Woman and Nature: The Roaring Inside Her*, New York: Harper and Row.

Grillparzer, Franz (1876) *Sappho: A Tragedy in Five Acts*, trans. Ellen Frothingham, Boston.

Gubar, Susan (1981) '"The Blank Page" and Issues of Female Creativity', *Critical Inquiry*, 8(1981), 243–63.

— (1983) 'She in Herland: Feminism as Fantasy', in *Coordinates: Placing Science Fiction and Fantasy*, ed. George E. Slusser, Eric S. Rabkin, and Robert Scholes, Carbondale: Southern Illinois University Press, pp. 139–49.

— (1984) 'Sapphistries', *Signs*, 10(1984), 43–62.

Gutwirth, Madelyn (1978) *Madame de Staël, Novelist: The Emergence of the Artist as Woman*, Urbana: University of Illinois Press.

Haight, Gordon (1965) (ed.) *A Century of George Eliot Criticism*, London: Methuen.

— (1968) *George Eliot*, Oxford: Oxford University Press.

Haines, C. R. (1946) *Sappho: The Poems and Fragments*, London: Routledge.

Hair, Donald S. (1981) *Domestic and Heroic in Tennyson's Poetry*, Toronto.

Hallett, Judith P. (1979) 'Sappho and her Social Context: Sense and Sensuality', *Signs*, 4(1979), 447–64.

Hansson, Laura Marholm (1896) *Six Modern Women: Psychological Sketches*, trans. Hermione Ramsden, Boston.

Hardy, Thomas (1925) *Collected Poems of Thomas Hardy*, New York: Macmillan.

— (1978) *The Collected Letters of Thomas Hardy*, 7 vols, ed. Richard Little Purdy and Michael Millgate, Oxford: Clarendon Press.

Harper, Frances E. W. (1988) *Complete Poems*, ed. Maryemma Graham, New York: Oxford University Press.

Harris, Wendell V. (1991) 'Canonicity', *PMLA*, 106(1991), 110–21.

Harrison, Antony (1988) *Christina Rossetti in Context*, Hemel Hempstead: Harvester.

Hatton, Gwynneth (1955) *An Edition of the Unpublished Poems of Christina Rossetti*, PhD dissertation, St Hilda's College, Oxford.

Hawkshaw, Ann (1842) *Dionysius the Areopagite*, London and Manchester.

— (1847) *Poems for My Children*, London and Manchester.

— (1854) *Sonnets on Anglo-Saxon History*, London.

Hayter, Alethea (1962) *Mrs. Browning: A Poet's Work and Its Setting*, London: Faber.

Hazlitt, William (1969) 'On Patriotism: A Fragment', *The Round Table: Characters of Shakespear's Plays*, New York: Dutton. pp. 67–8.

H.D. [Hilda Doolittle] (1975) *Tribute to Freud: Writing on the Wall, Advent*, New York: McGraw-Hill.

Hegel, Georg Wilhelm Friedrich (1977) *Phenomenology of Spirit*, trans. A. V. Miller, Oxford: Oxford University Press.

— (1990) *Phänomenologie des Geistes*, ed. Wolfgang Bonsiepen and Reinhard Heede, Hamburg: Meiner.

Hemans, Felicia (1836) *Poetical Works*, Philadelphia.

— (1839) *The Works of Mrs. Hemans: With a Memoir of Her Life by Her Sister*, 7 vols, Edinburgh.

— (1854) *The Poetical Works of Mrs. Felicia Hemans*, Boston.

— (1873) *The Poetical Works of Felicia Hemans*, ed. William Michael Rossetti, London.

— (1900) *Poetical Works of Mrs. Hemans*, London: Warne.

— (1978) *Poems, England and Spain, Modern Greece*, intro. Donald H. Reiman, New York: Garland.

Herbert, George (1974) *The English Poems of George Herbert*, ed. C. A. Patrides, London: Methuen.

Hesiod (1959) *Theogony*, trans. Richmond Lattimore, Ann Arbor: University of Michigan Press.

Hickok, Kathleen (1984) *Representations of Women: Nineteenth-Century British Women's Poetry*, Westport, Conn.: Greenwood Press.

Hillis Miller, J. 'The Limits of Pluralism, II: "The Critic as Host"', *Critical Inquiry*, 3 439–47

Hind, C. Lewis (1917) Introduction to Stephen Phillips, *Christ in Hades*, London: John Lane.

Hobsbawm, E. J. (1962) *The Age of Revolution*, Cleveland: World.

Holloway, Julia Bolton 'Aurora Leigh *and* Jane Eyre', *Brontë Society Transactions*, 17(1977), 130–3.

Holman, C. Hugh (1972) *A Handbook to Literature*, New York.

Holmes, Richard (1989) *Coleridge: Early Visions*, Harmondsworth: Penguin.

Holt, Terrence (1990) '"Men sell not such in any town": Exchange in *Goblin Market*', *Victorian Poetry*, 28(1990), 51–67.

Homans, Margaret (1980) *Women Writers and Poetic Identity: Dorothy Wordsworth, Emily Brontë, and Emily Dickinson*, Princeton, N.J.: Princeton University Press.

— (1985) '"Syllables of Velvet": Dickinson, Rossetti, and the Rhetorics of Sexuality', *Feminist Studies*, 11(1985), 569–93.

Homer (1951) *The Iliad*, trans. Richmond Lattimore, Chicago: University of Chicago Press.

Horsfield, Louisa (1862) *The Cottage Lyre*, 2nd ed., London and Leeds.

Hughes, Linda (1994) '"Fair Hymen holdeth hid a world of woes": Myth and Marriage in Poems by "Graham R. Tomson" (Rosamund Marriott Watson)', *Victorian Poetry*, 32(1994), 97–120.

Hughes, Mary Vivian (1934) *A London Child of the Seventies*, Oxford: Oxford University Press.

Hutton, R. H. (1858) 'Novels by the Authoress of "John Halifax"', *North British Review*, 29(1858), 467.

Irigaray, Luce (1985) *Speculum of the Other Woman*, trans. Gillian C. Gill, Ithaca, N.Y.: Cornell University Press.

Jacobus, Mary (1986) *Reading Woman: Essays in Feminist Criticism*, New York: Columbia University Press.

Jameson, Anna (1855) *Sisters of Charity: Catholic and Protestant, Abroad and at Home*, London.

[Jeffrey, Francis] (1829) 'Felicia Hemans', *Edinburgh Review*, 50(1829), 32–47.

Jenkyns, Richard (1982) *Three Classical Poets: Sappho, Catullus and Juvenal*, London: Duckworth.

Jiménez, Nilda (1979) *The Bible and the Poetry of Christina Rossetti: A Concordance*, Westport, Conn. and London.

Johnston, Ellen (1862) *Autobiography, Poems and Songs*, Glasgow.

Kaplan, Cora (1975) *Salt and Bitter and Good: Three Centuries of English and American Women Poets*, New York and London: Paddington Press.

Keble, John (1869) *Miscellaneous Poems*, Oxford and London.

— (1912) *Keble's Lectures on Poetry, 1832–1841*, 2 vols, ed. Edward Kershaw Francis, Oxford: Oxford University Press.

Keightley, Thomas (1838) *The Mythology of Ancient Greece and Rome*, 2nd ed., London.

Kent, David (1979) 'Sequence and Meaning in Christina Rossetti's Verses (1893)', *Victorian Poetry*, 17(1979), 259–64.

— (1987) '"By thought, word, and deed": George Herbert and Christina Rossetti', in Kent (ed.) *The Achievement of Christina Rossetti*, Ithaca and London: Cornell University Press, pp. 250–73.

Kipling, Rudyard (1909) *The Writings in Prose and Verse*, 32 vols, New York: Scribner's.

Krafft-Ebing, Richard von (1882; 1965) *Psychopathia Sexualis*, trans. M. E. Wedneck, New York: Putnams.

Krishnamurti, G. (1991) (ed.) *Women Writers of the 1890's*, London: H. Southeran.

Kristeva, Julia (1980) *Desire in Language: A Semiotic Approach to Literature and Art*, ed. Leon S. Roudiez, trans. Thomas Gora, Alice Jardine, and Leon S. Roudiez, New York: Columbia University Press.

— (1982) *Powers of Horror: An Essay on Abjection*, trans. Leon S. Roudiez, New York: Columbia University Press.

— (1984) *Revolution in Poetic Language*, trans. Margaret Waller, London, New York: Columbia University Press.

Lacan, Jacques (1977) *Ecrits: A Selection*, trans. Alan Sheridan, New York: Norton.

— (1981) *The Four Fundamental Concepts of Psycho-Analysis*, trans. Alan Sheridan, New York: Norton.

Landon, Letitia Elizabeth (1835) 'On the Character of Mrs. Hemans' Writings', *Colburn's New Monthly Magazine* (August 1835), 425–33.

— (1838) *The Poetical Works of Letitia Elizabeth Landon*, 4 vols, London.

— (1841) *Life and Literary Remains of L.E.L.* 2 vols, ed. Laman Blanchard, London.

— (1850) *Poetical Works*, 2 vols, London.

— (1855) *Poetical Works*, 2 vols, London.

— (1873) *Poetical Works*, ed. William B. Scott, London.

Landow, George (1980) *Victorian Types, Victorian Shadows: Biblical Typology in Victorian Literature, Art, and Thought*, Boston: Routledge and Kegan Paul.

Langbauer, Laurie (1989) 'Women in White, Men in Feminism', *Yale Journal of Criticism*, 2 no. 2(1989), 219–43.

Lawrence, D. H. (1972) 'The Lemon Gardens', in *D. H. Lawrence and Italy*, New York: Compass-Viking, pp. 32–54.

Lecky, William (1869; 1955) *History of European Morals*, 2 vols in one, New York: George Braziller.

Leigh, Arran [Katherine Bradley] (1875) *The New Minnesinger and Other Poems*, London.

Leighton, Angela (1986) *Elizabeth Barrett Browning*, Brighton: Harvester Press, and Bloomington: Indiana University Press.

— (1989) '"Because men made the laws": The Fallen Woman and the Woman Poet', *Victorian Poetry*, 27(1989), 109–27.

— (1992) *Victorian Women Poets: Writing Against the Heart*, Hemel Hempstead: Harvester; Virginia: Virginia University Press.

Leighton, Angela, and Margaret Reynolds (1995) *Victorian Women Poets: An Anthology*, Oxford: Basil Blackwell.

Levine, Philippa (1990) *Feminist Lives in Victorian England: Private Roles and Public Commitment*, Oxford: Blackwell.

Levy, Amy (1884) *A Minor Poet And other Verse*, London.

— (1889) *A London Plane-Tree, and other Verse*, London.

— (1915) *A Ballad of Religion and Marriage* (12 privately printed), London: British Library Catalogue.

Lipking, Lawrence (1990) 'Donna Abandonata', in *The Don Giovanni Book: Myths of Seduction and Betrayal*, ed. Jonathan Miller, London: Faber, pp. 36–47.

Lochnan, Katherine (1978) 'Images of Confinement', *Victorian Studies Bulletin*, 2(Dec 1978), 1–15.

Lootens, Tricia (1994) 'Hemans and Home: Victorianism, Feminine "Internal Enemies", and the Domestication of National Identity', *PMLA*, 109(1994), 238–53.

Lucas, John (1990) *England and Englishness: Ideas of Nationhood in English Poetry, 1688–1900*, Iowa City: University of Iowa Press.

MacDonald, George (1923) *Phantastes: A Faerie Romance*, London: J. M. Dent and Sons.

Macrobius (1952) *Commentary on the Dream of Scipio*, trans. William Harris Stahl, New York: Columbia University Press.

Mahaffy, J. P. (1874) *Social Life in Greece from Homer to Menander*, London.

Marchand, Leslie (1957) *Byron: A Biography*, New York: Knopf.

Maurice, Rev. F. D. (1863) 'On Sisterhoods', *The Victoria Magazine*, 1(August 1863), 289–301.

May, Caroline (1848) *The American Female Poets*, Philadelphia.

McGann, Jerome J. (1980) 'Christina Rossetti's Poems: A New Edition and a Revaluation', *Victorian Studies*, 23(1980), 237–54.

— (1983) 'The Religious Poetry of Christina Rossetti', *Critical Inquiry*, 10(1983), 133–41.

— (1995) 'Mary Robinson and the Myth of Sappho', *Modern Language Quarterly*, 56(1995), 55–76.

McGregor, O. R. (1957) *Divorce in England: A Centenary Study*, London: Heinemann.

Mermin, Dorothy (1981) 'The Female Poet and the Embarrassed Reader: Elizabeth Barrett Browning's *Sonnets from the Portuguese*', *English Literary History*, 48(1981), 351–67.

— (1985) 'Heroic Sisterhood in *Goblin Market*', *Victorian Poetry*, 21(1985), 107–18.

— (1986) 'The Damsel, The Knight, and the Victorian Woman Poet', *Critical Inquiry*, 13(1986), 64–80.

— (1986b) 'Genre and Gender in *Aurora Leigh*', *Victorian Newsletter*, 69(1986), 7–11.

— (1989) *Elizabeth Barrett Browning: The Origins of a New Poetry*, Chicago and London: University of Chicago Press.

Mew, Charlotte (1981) *Charlotte Mew: Collected Poems and Prose*, ed. Val Warner, Manchester: Carcanet with Virago.

Meynell, Alice (1895) 'Christina Rossetti', *The New Review*, NS 12(1895), 203.

— (1940) *The Poems of Alice Meynell*, London: Oxford University Press.

— (1947) *Alice Meynell: Prose and Poetry*, intro. V. Sackville-West, London: Jonathan Cape.

Miles, Alfred H. (1891; rpt. 1967) *The Poets and the Poetry of the Century*, 10 vols, London, New York.

Millgate, Michael (1971) *Thomas Hardy: His Career as a Novelist*, New York: Random House.

— (1973) 'Thomas Hardy and Rosamund Tomson', *Notes & Queries*, NS 20(1973), 253–55.

Milton, John (1957) *Paradise Lost* in *Complete Poems and Major Prose*, ed. Merritt Y. Hughes, Indianapolis: Odyssey Press.

Mitchell, Sally (1981) *The Fallen Angel: Chastity, Class and Women's Reading 1835–1880*, Bowling Green, Ohio: Bowling Green University Popular Press.

Mix, Katharine Lyon (1960) *A Study in Yellow: The 'Yellow Book' and Its Contributors*, London: Constable; Lawrence: University of Kansas Press.

Moers, Ellen (1976; 1978) *Literary Women*, New York: Doubleday; London: The Women's Press.

Montefiore, Jan (1987) *Feminism and Poetry: Language, Experience, Identity in Women's Writing*, London: Pandora.

Moulton, Charles Wells, ed. (1902) 'Felicia Dorothea Hemans', *The Library of Literary Criticism*, Buffalo: Moulton.

Mulvey, Laura (1975) 'Visual Pleasure and the Narrative Cinema', *Screen*, 16 no. 3(1975), 6–18.

Murdoch, Blaikie (1911; rpt. 1970) *The Renaissance of the Nineties*, London: Folcroft; Pennsylvania: Folcroft Press.

Mure, William (1850) *A Critical History of the Language and Literature of Ancient Greece*, 3 vols, London: III, 272–326.

Nemoianu, Virgil (1991) 'Literary Canons and Social Value Options', in *The Hospitable Canon: Essays on Literary Play, Scholarly Choice, and Popular Pressures*, ed. Virgil Nemoianu and Robert Royal, Philadelphia: Benjamins, pp. 215–47.

Nichol, John (1857) '*Aurora Leigh*', *Westminster Review*, 68(1857), 401.

Nightingale, Florence (1979) *Cassandra*, Old Westbury, N.Y.: Feminist Press.

Norton, Caroline (1830) *The Undying One and Other Poems*, London.

—— (1840) *The Dream and Other Poems*, London.

Ostriker, Alicia (1982) 'Body Language: Imagery of the Body in Women's Poetry', in *The State of the Language*, ed. Leonard Michaels and Christopher Ricks, Berkeley and Los Angeles: University of California Press.

—— 'The Thieves of Language: Women Poets and Revisionist Mythmaking', *Signs*, 8(1982), 68–90.

Ovid (1986) *Metamorphoses*, trans. Mary Innes, Harmondsworth: Penguin.

Packer, Lona Mosk (1963) *Christina Rossetti*, Cambridge: Cambridge University Press; Berkeley and Los Angeles: University of California Press.

Paglia, Camille (1990) *Sexual Personae*, New Haven: Yale University Press.

Patmore, Coventry (1949) *The Poems of Coventry Patmore*, ed. Frederick Page, London: Oxford University Press.

Peacham, Henry (1971) *The Garden of Eloquence*, Menston, England.

Peel, Ellen (1982) 'Both Ends of the Candle: Feminist Narrative Structures in Novels by Staël, Lessing, and Le Guin', PhD dissertation, Yale University.

Pennell, Elizabeth Robins (1916) *Nights: Rome and Venice in the Aesthetic Eighties, London and Paris in the Fighting Nineties*, 2nd edn, Philadelphia: J. B. Lippincott.

—— (1929) *Joseph Pennell*, Boston: Little, Brown and Co.

Pizan, Christine de (1982) *The Book of the City of Ladies*, trans. Earl Jeffrey Richards, New York: Persea.

Plath, Sylvia (1965) *Ariel*, New York: Harper.

Poe, Edgar Allan (1902) *The Complete Works of Edgar Allan Poe*, 17 vols, ed. James A. Harrison, New York: Cornell University Press.

Pontalis, J. B. (1993) 'Dream as an Object', in *The Dream Discourse Today*, ed. Sara Flanders, London: Routledge.

Poovey, Mary (1984) *The Proper Lady and the Woman Writer: Ideology as Style in the Writings of Mary Wollstonecraft, Mary Shelley, and Jane Austen*, Chicago: Chicago University Press.

Probyn, May (1895) *Pansies*, London.

Procter, Adelaide (1906) *Legends and Lyrics and Other Poems*, London and New York.

— (1914) *Legends and Lyrics*, with an introduction by Charles Dickens, Oxford: Oxford University Press.

Rayor, Diane (1991) *Sappho's Lyre: Archaic Lyric and Women Poets of Ancient Greece*, Berkeley, Los Angeles and Oxford: University of California Press.

Redinger, Ruby (1925) *George Eliot: The Emergent Self*, New York: Knopf.

'Religious Character of the Poetry of Mrs Hemans', *Christian Review*, 5(1840), 23–33.

Rich, Adrienne (1963) *Snapshots of a Daughter-in-Law: Poems 1954–1962*, New York: Norton.

Robertson, Eric S. (1883) *English Poetesses: A Series of Critical Biographies, with Illustrative Extracts*, London.

Robinson, Agnes Mary Frances (later Darmesteter, later Duclaux) (1902) *The Collected Poems, Lyrical and Narrative of Mary Robinson*, London: T. Fisher Unwin.

Robinson, David M. (1925) *Sappho and Her Influence*, London: George G. Harrap.

Robinson, Mary (1796) *Sappho and Phaon in a series of legitimate sonnets*, London.

— (1806) *The Poetical Works of the Late Mrs Mary Robinson*, 3 vols, London.

Rogers, Samuel (1854) *The Complete Poetical Works of Samuel Rogers*, ed. Epes Sargent, Boston: Phillips, Sampson.

Rosenblum, Dolores (1979) 'Christina Rossetti: The Inward Pose', in *Shakespeare's Sisters: Feminist Essays on Women Poets*, ed. Sandra M. Gilbert and Susan Gubar, Bloomington: Indiana University Press, pp. 82–98.

— (1982) 'Christina Rossetti's Religious Poetry: Watching, Looking, Keeping Vigil', *Victorian Poetry*, 20(1982), 33–49.

— (1983) 'Face to Face: Elizabeth Barrett Browning's *Aurora Leigh* and Nineteenth-Century Poetry', *Victorian Studies*, 26(1983), 321–38.

— (1986) *Christina Rossetti: The Poetry of Endurance*, with a foreword by Dorothy Mermin, Carbondale: Southern Illinois University Press.

Ross, Marlon B. (1989) *The Contours of Masculine Desire*, New York and Oxford: Oxford University Press.

— (1991) 'Romancing the Nation-State: The Poetics of Romantic Nationalism', in *Macropolitics of Nineteenth-Century Literature*, ed. Jonathan Arac and Harriet Ritvo, Philadelphia: University of Pennsylvania Press, pp. 56–85.

Rossetti, Christina Georgina (1879) *Seek and Find: A Double Series of Short Studies of the Benedicite*, London.

— (1883) *Called to be Saints: The Minor Festivals Devotionally Studied*, London.

— (1885) *Time Flies: A Reading Diary*, London.

— (1892) *The Face of the Deep: A Devotional Commentary on the Apocalypse*, London.

— (1904; 1911; 1928) *The Poetical Works of Christina Georgina Rossetti*, ed. with a 'Memoir' by William Michael Rossetti, London: Macmillan.

— (1908) *The Family Letters of Christina Georgina Rossetti*, ed. William Michael Rossetti, London: Brown, Langham.

— (1963) *The Rossetti-Macmillan Letters*, ed. Lona Mosk Packer, Berkeley and Los Angeles: University of California Press.

— (1979–90) *The Complete Poems of Christina Rossetti: A Variorum Edition*, 3 vols, ed. R. W. Crump, Baton Rouge and London: Louisiana University Press.

— (1994) *Poems and Prose*, ed. Jan Marsh, London: Everyman.

Rossetti, Dante Gabriel (1911) *The Works of Dante Gabriel Rossetti*, rev. and ed. W. M. Rossetti, London: Oxford University Press.

— (1967) *Letters of Dante Gabriel Rossetti*, 4 vols, ed. Oswald Doughty and John Robert Wahl, Oxford: Clarendon Press.

— (1976) *Dante Gabriel Rossetti and Jane Morris: Their Correspondence*, ed. John Bryson and Janet Camp Troxell, Oxford: Oxford University Press.

Ruskin, John (1955) *Ruskin's Letters from Venice 1851–1852*, ed. J. L. Bradley, New Haven: Yale University Press.

— (1956) *The Diaries of John Ruskin*, ed. J. Evans and J. H. Whitehouse, Oxford: Oxford University Press.

Ruthven, K. K. (1984) *Feminist Literary Studies: An Introduction*, Cambridge: Cambridge University Press.

Sagan, Miriam (1980) 'Christina Rossetti's "Goblin Market" and Feminist Literary Criticism', *Pre-Raphaelite Review*, 3(1980), 66–76.

Samuel, Raphael ed. (1989) *Patriotism: The Making and Unmaking of British National Identity*, 3 vols, New York and London: Routledge.

Sappho (1990) *Greek Lyric I: Sappho and Alcaeus*, ed. and trans. David A. Campbell, Loeb edition, Cambridge, Mass. and London: Harvard University Press.

Sarton, May (1984) *Letters from Maine: New Poems*, New York: Norton.

Sassoon, Siegfried (1983) *The War Poems of Siegfried Sassoon*, London: Faber.

Savage, Gail L. (1983) 'The Operation of the 1857 Divorce Act, 1860–1910: A Research Note', *Journal of Social History*, 16(1983), 106.

Schenck, Celeste M. (1986) 'Feminism and Deconstruction: Re-Constructing the Elegy', *Tulsa Studies in Women's Literature*, 5(1986), 13–24.

Shaw, W. David (1980) 'The Optical Metaphor: Victorian Poetics and the Theory of Knowledge', *Victorian Studies*, 23(1980), 293–324.

Shelley, P. B. (1967) *Shelley: Poetical Works*, ed. Thomas Hutchinson, London: Oxford University Press.

Showalter, Elaine (1977) *A Literature of Their Own: British Women Novelists from Brontë to Lessing*, Princeton: Princeton University Press.

Sigerson (Shorter), Dora (1907) *Collected Poems*, intro, George Meredith, London: Hodder and Stoughton.

Solomon, Robert C. (1983) *In the Spirit of Hegel*, New York: Oxford University Press.

Spitzer, Leo (1963) *Classical and Christian Ideas of Cosmic Harmony: Prolegomena to an Interpretation of the Word "Stimmung"*, ed. Anna Granville Hatcher, Baltimore: Johns Hopkins University Press.

Steinmetz, Virginia V. (1981) 'Beyond the Sun: Patriarchal Images in *Aurora Leigh*', *Studies in Browning and His Circle*, 9(1981), 18–41.

— (1983) 'Images of "Mother-Want" in Elizabeth Barrett Browning's *Aurora Leigh*', *Victorian Poetry*, 21(1983), 351–67.

Stevenson, Lionel (1972) *The Pre-Raphaelite Poets*, Chapel Hill: University of North Carolina Press.

Stodart, Mary Ann (1842) *Female Writers: Thoughts on Their Proper Sphere and on Their Powers of Usefulness*, London.

Stone, Marjorie (1985) 'Taste, Totems, and Taboos: The Female Breast in Victorian Poetry', *Dalhousie Review*, 64(1985), 748–70.

— (1987) 'Genre Subversion and Gender Inversion: *The Princess* and *Aurora Leigh*', *Victorian Poetry*, 25(1987), 101–27.

Sturgeon, Mary (1922) *Michael Field*, London: Harrap.

Swinburne, Algernon Charles (1914) *The Living Age*, 280(1914), 817–18.

— *Complete Works*, (1925) 20 vols, ed. Edmund Gosse and Thomas James Wise, London: Bodley Head.

Swindells, Julia (1985) *Victorian Writing and Working Women: The Other Side of Silence*, Cambridge: Polity Press.

Symonds, John Addington (1967–9) *The Letters of John Addington Symonds*, 3 vols, ed. Herbert M. Schueller and Robert L. Peters, Detroit: Wayne State University Press.

Symons, A. J. A. (1928) *An Anthology of 'Nineties Verse*, London: Elkin Matthews and Marrot.

Taplin, Gardner B. (1957) *The Life of Elizabeth Barrett Browning*, New Haven: Yale University Press.

Tennyson, Alfred (1969) *Poems of Tennyson*, ed. Christopher Ricks, London: Longmans.

Tennyson, G. B. (1981) *Victorian Devotional Poetry: The Tractarian Mode*, Cambridge, Mass.: Harvard University Press.

Thackeray, William Makepeace (1855) *The Newcomes*, 2 vols, London.

— (1987) *Vanity Fair*, New York: Oxford University Press.

Timpanaro, Sebastiano (1965) 'Alcune Osservatione Sul Pensiero Del Leopardi', in *Classicismo e Illuminismo nel' Ottocento Italiano*, Pisa: Nistri-Lischi, pp. 133–82.

Tomson, Graham [Rosamund Marriott Watson] (1889) *Selections from the Greek Anthology*, London.

— (1889) *The Bird-Bride: A Volume of Ballads and Sonnets*, London.

— (1891) *A Summer Night and Other Poems*, London.

Tristan, Flora (1982) *The London Journal of Flora Tristan 1842 or The Aristocracy and the Working Class of England*, trans. Jean Hawkes, London: Virago.

Troxell, Janet Camp (1937) (ed.) *Three Rossettis: Unpublished Letters to and from Dante Gabriel, Christina, William*, Cambridge, Mass.: Harvard University Press.

Tynan, Katharine (1913) *Twenty-Five Years: Reminiscences*, London: Constable.

— (1916) *The Middle Years*, London: Constable.

Virgil (1981) *The Aeneid*, trans. Allen Mandelbaum, Berkeley: University of California Press.

Walker, Cheryl (1982) *The Nightingale's Burden: Women Poets and American Culture before 1900*, Bloomington: Indiana University Press.

Waller, Ross D. (1935) (ed.) *Letters Addressed to Mrs Gaskell by Celebrated Contemporaries*, Manchester: Manchester University Press.

Waltman, John L. (1976) 'The Early London Journals of Elizabeth Robins Pennell', PhD dissertation, University of Texas.

Warner, Marina (1994) *From the Beast to the Blonde: On Fairy Tales and Their Tellers*, London: Chatto and Windus.

Watson, Rosamund Marriott [Graham Tomson] (1912) *The Poems of Rosamund Marriott Watson*, London: John Lane.

Weathers, Winston (1968) 'Christina Rossetti: The Sisterhood of Self', *Victorian Poetry*, 3(1968), 81–9.

Webster, Augusta (1866) *Dramatic Studies*, London and Cambridge.

— (1870; 1893) *Portraits*, London.

— (1895) *Mother & Daughter: An Uncompleted Sonnet-Sequence*, intro. W. M. Rossetti, London.

Welsh, Alexander (1971) *The City of Dickens*, Oxford: Oxford University Press.

Wharton, Edith (1905) 'An Alpine Posting Inn', in *Italian Backgrounds*, New York: Scribners, pp. 3–14.

Wharton, Henry Thornton (1885; 1887) *Sappho: Memoir, Text, Selected Renderings and a Literal Translation*, London.

White, Chris (1990) '"Poets and lovers evermore": Interpreting Female Love in the Poetry and Journals of Michael Field', *Textual Practice*, 4(1990), 197–212.

Wilde, Oscar (1908; rpt. 1969) *The Poems of Oscar Wilde*, ed. Robert Ross, London: John Lane.

William, Harold H. (1918) *Modern English Writers: Being a Study of Imaginative Literature 1890–1914*, London: Sidgwick and Jackson.

Wollstonecraft, Mary (1792; 1975) *Vindication of the Rights of Woman*, Harmondsworth: Penguin.

Woodring, Carl (1970) *Politics in English Romantic Poetry*, Cambridge, Mass.: Harvard University Press.

Woolf, Virginia (1929; 1945) *A Room of One's Own*, Harmondsworth: Penguin.

— (1932) 'Aurora Leigh', in *The Second Common Reader*, New York: Harcourt, pp. 182–92.

— (1933) *Flush: A Biography*, New York: Harcourt.

Woolford, John (1979) 'EBB: Woman and Poet', *Browning Society Notes*, 9(1979), 3–5.

Wordsworth, William (1952) *The Poetical Works of William Wordsworth*, 5 vols, ed. E. de Selincourt, Oxford: Oxford University Press.

— (1994) *William Wordsworth*, ed. Stephen Gill and Duncan Wu, Oxford: Oxford University Press.

Zonana, Joyce (1989) 'The Embodied Muse: Elizabeth Barrett Browning's *Aurora Leigh* and Feminist Poetics', *Tulsa Studies in Women's Literature*, 8(1989), 241–62.

Index